Free Markets and Social Regulation: A Reform Agenda of the Global Trading System

FREE MARKETS AND SOCIAL REGULATION: A REFORM AGENDA OF THE GLOBAL TRADING SYSTEM

SUNGJOON CHO

KLUWER LAW INTERNATIONAL
LONDON / THE HAGUE / NEW YORK

Published by:
Kluwer Law International,
P.O. Box 85889, 2508 CN The Hague, The Netherlands
sales@kluwerlaw.com
http://www.kluwerlaw.com

Sold and distributed in North, Central and South America by:
Aspen Publishers, Inc.
7201 McKinney Circle, Frederick, MD 21704, USA

Sold and distributed in all other countries by:
Turpin Distribution Services Limited
Blackhorse Road, Letchworth, Herts.,
SG6 1HN, United Kingdom

A C.I.P. Catalogue record for this book is available from the Library of Congress.

Printed on acid-free paper.

ISBN 90-411-9892-X

Printed and bound in Great Britain by MPG Books Limited, Bodmin, Cornwall

Table of Contents

Preface

This book seeks to diagnose challenges and to prescribe solutions for reconciling the clash between free markets and state regulation in international economic law. Against the backdrop of a transformation in the *telos* of the global trading system, from the narrow 'anti-protectionist' emphasis of GATT 1947 toward the much broader vision of the WTO, with its focus on 'integration,' 'anti-unilateralism' and 'sustainable development,' the book identifies a strong 'pro-trade' bias in the line of GATT jurisprudence and problematizes such bias in terms of a 'dual crisis' involving both regulatory and trade failure. As a solution to this crisis, the book introduces a new line of jurisprudence under the WTO system—principally, the so-called 'chapeau' test highlighting the *manner* in which a domestic regulation is adopted or applied rather than the *substance* of the regulation itself—which offers considerable promise as a means for achieving the dual goals of free trade and regulatory autonomy.

Yet, despite the potential benefits of this new jurisprudence, the book points out that the pro-trade bias still remains due to a structural 'dichotomy' between general obligations such as National Treatment, and exceptions under Article XX, to which the chapeau belongs. To bridge this dichotomy, the book demonstrates that the pursuit of the dual ideal of free trade and autonomous state regulation is treated in a more intellectually sophisticated and balanced fashion under the side agreements (SPS and TBT) than under the GATT. The book then deals with the 'domestic' issue of compliance and implementation under which the detailed behavioral changes must take place in order to execute those prescriptions to the dual crisis that the GATT/WTO jurisprudence and agreements offer.

Finally, the book surveys the phenomenon of convergence between the WTO and other representative polities and institutions, which may be observed to the extent that the management of the interface between free markets and state regulation is sought through treaties, jurisprudence and implementation of rules and regulation. In the context of such convergence, the book proposes a '*jus gentium* of international trade on domestic regulations' as a common legal precept that is capable of guiding, in a coherent and integrative way, the reconciliation of the clash between free markets and state regulations within the far-reaching field of international economic law, a precept that encompasses not only the WTO, but also other polities and institutions, such as the EU, the US and NAFTA.

Acknowledgements

This book is the crystallization of the care and support of many good minds, for which I express my deep gratitude.

Most of all, I am eternally grateful to my father, Joonghyung Cho, and my mother, Bockhi Woo, who gave me life and who raised me with such extraordinary sacrifice and care. I am forever in their debt. I also would like to sincerely thank my father-in-law, Jongeui Song, and my mother-in-law, Jungja Moon, for their special love and support, which has been my privilege ever since I came to know them.

I would like also to extend my gratitude to the wonderful teachers who have guided my education. In particular, I thank Professor Joseph H. H. Weiler from the bottom of my heart for his treasured mentorship, without which this book would never have come to light. Despite many difficulties, he accepted me as his student, and kindly taught me how to learn, how to think and how to teach. I am honored and proud to be his student. I also thank Professors William P. Alford and Anne-Marie Slaughter for their continuous and consistent encouragement and support ever since I came to Harvard. It has been my privilege to know them not just as teachers, but personally as well.

I would also like to thank Professors John H. Jackson and José E. Alvarez for the valuable guidance and support that they provided to me at the University of Michigan Law School. I am also deeply indebted to Professors Oliver Oldman and Sanghyun Song for the exceptional support which has made my life at Harvard possible and so enriching. In the process of formulating the ideas set forth in my book, I benefited greatly from discussions with Professors Robert Howse, Joel Trachtman and William Davey, for which I express my sincere appreciation.

Special thanks are due my fellow colleagues at Harvard Law School, Chaihark, Okrial, Youngjeen, Dongsheng, Matt, John, Nikitas, Petja, George and Annecous. Gail Hupper and Cait Clarke gave me valuable suggestions that enriched and sharpened my thesis. Beth, Wing-Sy and Anne provided me with patient and untiring support of a kind that enabled me to study in a more comfortable environment. I would be ungrateful if I did not acknowledge the extraordinary service that the Library staff kindly provided to me. I also thank Inge and Emile Noël Fellows, Imola, Hyungyoon, Constanze, Sieglinde and Professor Araki for their encouragement and friendly care. I also wish to acknowledge the generous financial support I received from the Graduate Program, Clark Byse Fellowship and East Asian Legal Studies.

I express profound gratitude to my wife, Mehyun, and my three daughters, Hayun, Hari, and Hajin, for their constant love and support. As a doctoral student herself, Mehyun has been a super woman ever since we came to the United States.

She has been a caring mother, a dedicated wife and a good student. Her patience knows no bounds. My little darlings, Hayun, Hari, and Hajin, have grown healthy and lovely, for which I thank them as their father. I would also like to thank my brother, Sungbum, and my sister, Sungeun, for their support and care.

Finally, I dedicate this book to my late brother-in-law, Seokyun, who died young, but who will live long in our memories, for he taught us what life is.

Introduction

In recent years the world has witnessed an unprecedented degree—both in speed and scope—of economic integration geared by the expansion of international trade. Often cited as an icon of globalization, the volume of world trade now measures fourteen times what it did just fifty years ago. Money flowing through the international financial market in a given day amounts to one trillion dollars. As the former WTO[1] Director-General Renato Ruggiero once said, 'the global market is becoming an internal market—and *vice versa*.'[2] Many factors, ranging from technological innovation to the fall of the Berlin wall, help to explain this dramatic phenomenon. Yet of practical significance for the present discussion is the fact that, thanks to this expansion of international trade, many countries including newly industrialized economies (NIEs) such as Korea, have been able to escape from the misery of poverty and dramatically raise their standards of living.[3]

Nevertheless, the effects of trade expansion and consequent economic integration have not been uniformly positive. In many situations they have constrained the free exercise of regulatory power in non-trade matters by sovereign states. For example, orthodox conceptions of free trade are viewed as incompatible with domestic bans on the importation of hormone-treated beef or genetically modified foods because such measures have the potential to hinder or impede global trade in agricultural products. On the other hand, critics of such perspectives would argue that free trade should not necessarily be allowed to force a reluctant citizenry to tolerate a lower level of regulatory protection. That is, if the people of a nation abhor exposure to asbestos and therefore choose a zero tolerance policy, free trade in asbestos-based products must yield under certain conditions. Yet, it is also problematic and undesirable if such regulatory considerations result in an inundation of regulatory unilateralism fatal to international trade. In fact, regulatory heterogeneity itself is a serous trade barrier whether or not it originates from protectionist intent. Global free trade is hard to

1. Marrakech Agreement Establishing the World Trade Organization, April 15, 1994, Final Act Embodying the Results of the Uruguay Round of Multilateral Trade Negotiations [hereinafter WTO Agreement], LEGAL INSTRUMENTS—RESULTS OF THE URUGUAY ROUND [hereinafter RESULTS OF THE URUGUAY ROUND], 6, 6–18; 33 I.L.M. 1140, 1144–1153 (1994).
2. Renato Ruggiero, A Borderless World, Address to the OECD Ministerial Conference (Ottawa, Oct. 7, 1998), *available at* <http://www.wto.org/english/news_e/sprr_e/ott_e.htm> (last visited on Sep. 27, 2001).
3. Regarding the role of trade in the economic development of Korea, *see e.g.*, THE MULTILATERAL TRADING SYSTEM IN A GLOBALIZING WORLD (Lee-Jay Cho & Yoon Hyung Kim eds. 2000); TUN-JEN CHENG ET AL., INSTITUTIONS, ECONOMIC POLICY AND GROWTH IN THE REPUBLIC OF KOREA AND TAIWAN PROVINCE OF CHINA (1996); DAVID C. COLE ET AL., THE KOREAN ECONOMY: ISSUES OF DEVELOPMENT (1980).

imagine under circumstances in which each country seeks to regulate domestic social affairs in its own way, without regard to international norms.

This tension between free markets and state regulation, which is often termed 'interface,' 'linkage,' or 'trade and . . .,' inevitably leads to a dual crisis—trade failure *and* regulatory failure. In other words, the relationship between free trade and state regulations tends to be a zero sum game: if one is pushed too far, a benefit for one is likely to come at a cost to the other. Therefore, an essential mission of the global trading system is to reconcile clashes between these two paramount values. Against this backdrop, this book considers how this mission has been pursued in the field of international economic law, identifies problems with these existing approaches and, finally, attempts to offer a more compelling solution. Importantly, the book addresses the 'legitimacy' of the global trading system. It is suggested herein that a proper reconciliation of the clash will tend to make the system operate more smoothly and thus enhance its acceptability among governments, traders and other stakeholders alike.

The dawn of the modern global trading system dates back to 1947 when the General Agreement on Tariffs and Trade (GATT)[4] was launched as a pillar of the Bretton Woods system, which represented a new postwar international economic order. The framers of GATT realized the vital importance of a global free market after the painful and costly lessons of economic Balkanization, which had been pandemic during the interwar period and which eventually led to the outbreak of the Second World War. What the framers of the system sought to accomplish through GATT was to foster free trade by tariff reduction and to police self-defeating mercantilist protection. This *telos* of anti-protection or anti-mercantilism, which echoed the ideas of Lochnerism, was also backed by an economic philosophy rooted in Ricardian comparative advantage as well as in the economic liberalism of James Madison, who cautioned against heeding the egocentric voices of domestic interest groups. Moreover, as seen in the name 'General Agreement on Tariffs and Trade,' tariffs were at the heart of international trade when GATT was born. One of the main objectives of GATT was to provide contracting parties with a forum for continuous rounds of tariff reduction negotiations. Therefore, even the legal mechanisms of GATT, such as the National Treatment obligation, were originally meant to preserve the balance of tariff concessions, rather than to establish an independent set of norms.

This anti-protectionist *telos* and tariff-oriented structure eventually led to a built-in *pro*-trade bias in GATT itself. Non-trade social concerns, such as human health and environmental protection, have been treated as mere exceptions to general obligations, such as National Treatment or Prohibition of Quantitative Restriction. In other words, non-trade policy objectives have typically been taken into account only *after* general obligations are found to be violated, and not at the initial stage when general obligations are examined. This pro-trade bias, which stems from the textual dichotomy between general obligations and exceptions, was aggravated by another form of pro-trade bias embedded in the interpretive practice of GATT panels. Under the old GATT dispute settlement system, exceptions were interpreted

4. General Agreement on Tariffs and Trade, October 30, 1947, T.I.A.S. No. 1700, 55 U.N.T.S. 187 [hereinafter GATT 1947].

narrowly and underwent stringent tests, such as the 'least trade-restrictive means' test. Therefore, under the old GATT regime, social values tended to receive inferior consideration vis-à-vis the liberal, free market ideology enshrined in general obligations, a phenomenon which John Gerard Ruggie described as 'embedded liberalism.'[5] Surprisingly, not a single domestic regulation was justified under GATT Article XX (General Exception) before the WTO was launched.

In addition, the legacy of tariff negotiation and its item-by-item style led general jurisprudence under the old GATT to what may be termed a *product*-oriented approach, which was symbolized by the 'like product' test. This product-oriented jurisprudence tended to deflect interpretive attention from *measures*, which are nothing but domestic regulations for protecting certain social values. For instance, panels confronting GATT Article III:4 (National Treatment in Domestic Regulation) spent most of their interpretive energy in determining whether two products in question—domestic and imported—were alike. By contrast, interpretation of another important requirement, that is 'less favorable treatment,' was relatively marginalized and thus the scrutiny of measures suffered. Indeed, if GATT panels had consistently developed a jurisprudence anchored by measures, not products, then domestic regulations could potentially have been redeemed as non-discriminatory at the stage of Article III before going to the exception clause for justification.

Nevertheless, this pro-trade bias could not be sustained when the winds of change began to blow in the late eighties and early nineties. First, domestic regulations received greater attention than before. More domestic regulations have been issued in response to the popular demands of the welfare state as well as to novel risks associated with the creation of modern technology. Second, traditional trade policy measures, such as tariffs and quotas, have begun to vanish partly because tariffs were lowered dramatically and partly because governments realized that protection of certain domestic industries tended to be very costly, often harming the economic interests of their own citizens. Under these new circumstances, the original pro-trade bias, coupled with a tariff-oriented approach, if left unchanged, would have failed to properly address the new status quo, thereby de-legitimizing the global trading system.

Notwithstanding the potential value of domestic regulation for addressing certain legitimate social policy objectives, the repudiation of GATT's pro-trade bias need not result in the rejection of free trade as a basic value. In fact the proliferation of non-protectionist and legitimate domestic regulations has resulted in regulatory heterogeneity. This functions as a serious non-tariff barrier to the achievement of free trade. Moreover, the trade-restrictive nature of domestic regulations has only intensified as national economies have become more interdependent.

Consequently, the global trading system has come to require a new *telos*, capable of transcending the narrow purpose of anti-protection while at the same time connoting a much broader ideal of 'integration' that ensures that trade values and social values can be upheld not in a competing, but in a coherent and synergistic fashion. The foremost initiative for accommodating this new *telos* has appeared in the form of a new treaty-making process, namely the launch of the WTO Charter

5. John Gerard Ruggie, *International Regimes, Transactions and Change: Embedded Liberalism in the Postwar Economic Order*, 36 INT. ORG. 379, 415 (1982).

and its side agreements, after several years of the Uruguay Round negotiations. The Preamble of the WTO Charter expresses the ideal of 'integration' and 'sustainable development,' which certainly goes beyond the narrow anti-protectionist motto embedded in the old GATT. Furthermore, a more concrete and positive attempt to address the clash between free trade and state regulation was conducted through independent agreements, such as the Agreement on Sanitary and Phytosanitary Measures (SPS)[6] and the Agreement on Technical Barriers to Trade (TBT).[7] The SPS Agreement, for instance, handles sophisticated regulatory issues such as harmonization and risk assessment in order to preserve the Members' regulatory autonomy while avoiding a negative impact on trade flows.

The new *telos* embedded in the WTO Charter was also reflected in the interpretive attitude of the Appellate Body, created as part of the new WTO dispute settlement mechanism. Facing typical cases concerning discriminatory domestic regulations or import bans, the Appellate Body has tackled the traditional pro-trade bias through a reinterpretation of GATT Article XX (General Exceptions). Under the old GATT, panels focused on the 'content' of a given domestic regulation itself in interpreting Article XX, which often resulted in a presumptive conclusion that such regulation was not 'necessary' or even rationally 'unrelated' to the furtherance of social values of the regulating state. This 'second-guessing' or negation of legitimate policy objectives often infuriated domestic policy-makers and thus diminished the perception of GATT's legitimacy.

However, the Appellate Body directed its interpretive focus to the 'manner' in which a certain domestic regulation is adopted or applied, and not to the regulation itself. In its jurisprudence, the Appellate Body has emphasized the function of the 'chapeau,' or preambular language in Article XX that prohibits arbitrary or unjustifiable discrimination, as well as other disguised restrictions to trade. Through the interpretation of the chapeau, the Appellate Body has decided on a case by case basis whether a given domestic regulation was applied consistently or whether it respected due process, rather than reinvestigating, on its accord, whether the substance of the regulation itself is necessary or related to the furtherance of the regulating states' social policy goals. The result of the chapeau test was to safeguard the Members' regulatory autonomy in that it acknowledged the legitimacy—namely, the necessity or relatedness—of a given domestic regulation to its policy goals. Even if the measure turned out to be a violation, the outcome would not be catastrophic but merely suspensive, demanding only a change of application, rather than a repeal of the regulation itself. In sum, the focus on the manner of application in the Appellate Body's jurisprudence tends to mitigate the pro-trade bias, because it guarantees free movement of goods as long as the Members exercise their regulatory autonomy in good faith, by consistently following their own internal administrative processes.

Importantly, one finds in the chapeau test implications that run much deeper than a mere interpretive change. First, the principle of good faith inherent in the chapeau,

6. Agreement on Sanitary and Phytosanitary Measures, Annex 1 A, the WTO Agreement, *supra* note 1 [hereinafter SPS Agreement].
7. Agreement on Technical Barriers to Trade, Annex 1 A, the WTO Agreement, *supra* note 1 [hereinafter TBT Agreement].

which prevents Members' abuse of regulatory competence, represents 'general principles of law,' which are most often associated with the principles of equity, estoppel or consistency. Accordingly, the chapeau can rely on general principles of law as an interpretive guidepost, which tends to bestow greater legitimacy on the adjudicated outcome. Secondly, the chapeau test enables the Appellate Body to conduct a 'teleological' interpretation, transcending narrow textualism and reflects the emerging *telos* of the global trading system. In its interpretation of the very abstract language of the chapeau, the Appellate Body managed to imbue the new *telos*, such as 'integration' or 'sustainable development,' to its interpretation of the chapeau, leaving such important questions as 'duty to cooperate' or 'due process' to domestic administrative processes. Last, but not least, the chapeau test is linked to trade governance by virtue of its federalistic emphasis on establishing an integrated global marketplace while guaranteeing the regulatory autonomy of each Member.

Despite the foregoing jurisprudential evolution, the pro-trade bias resulting from the dichotomy still remains in the context of GATT 1994 because such dichotomy is textually structured in GATT Articles III:4 (National Treatment) and XX (General Exceptions). No matter how legitimate a domestic regulation may be, it is condemned as a violation of general obligations in the first place before it is eventually justified under the exception clause. This lingering pro-trade bias is addressed fundamentally under the side agreements, such as the SPS and the TBT. In pre-emptive fashion, the Preambles to both the SPS and the TBT emphasize that no country should be prevented from taking measures for the protection of human health or the environment. Moreover, legitimate regulatory concerns are no longer marginalized as mere 'exceptions,' but redefined as 'rights.' For instance, SPS Article 2.1 specifies that 'Members have the right to take sanitary and phytosanitary measures necessary for the protection of human, animal or plant life or health ....' At the same time, such autonomous rights are juxtaposed with various 'obligations,' such as SPS Articles 3.3 (scientific justification requirement) and 5.1 (risk assessment requirement), which mirror the chapeau test in focusing on the *manner* in which a domestic regulation is adopted and applied. Three cases, *Hormones* (1997),[8] *Australian Salmon* (1998)[9] and *Japanese Agricultural Products* (1999)[10] under the WTO dispute settlement mechanism, which concerned human, animal and plant health, respectively, have resulted in the development of a representative jurisprudence involving the SPS Agreement, and contributed to a sophisticated coherence and reconciliation between trade and regulatory values.

So far, we have found that the clash between the free market ideology and state regulation under the WTO system has been addressed through the jurisprudential

8. European Communities—Measures Affecting Meat and Meat Products (Hormones), WT/DS26, Appellate Body and the Panel Report, as modified, adopted on Feb. 13 1998, *available at* <http://www.wto.org/english/tratop_e/dispu_e/distab_e.htm> (last visited on Sep. 27, 2001) [hereinafter *Hormones* (1997)].
9. Australia—Measures Affecting Importation of Salmon, WT/DS18, Appellate Body and Panel Report, as modified, adopted on Nov. 6, 1998, *available at* <http://www.wto.org/english/tratop_e/dispu_e/distab_e.htm> (last visited on Sep. 27, 2001) [hereinafter *Australian Salmon* (1998)].
10. Japan—Measures Affecting Agricultural Products, WT/DS 76, Appellate Body and Panel Report, as modified, adopted on Mar. 19, 1999, *available at* <http://www.wto.org/english/tratop_e/dispu_e/distab_e.htm> (last visited on Sep. 27, 2001) [hereinafter *Japanese Agricultural Products* (1999)].

evolution of GATT, as well as through legislative initiative in a set of new side agreements, followed by a derivative jurisprudence. Nevertheless, even if various efforts in the WTO treaties seek to reconcile the clash between trade and regulatory values, and even if the more mature, intellectually refined GATT/WTO jurisprudence tends to produce decisions that safeguard the coherence of these concerns, such reconciliation cannot be attained without the actual behavioral change on the part of Members. That is to say, Members must meticulously incorporate their international obligations into their respective domestic regimes, in addition to executing the changes prescribed by individual panel and the Appellate Body reports. Without such compliance, WTO treaties and jurisprudence would fail to accomplish the dual objective of fostering both international trade and domestic regulatory sovereignty.

Here compliance has two dimensions. From a broad, long-term perspective, compliance concerns a wide spectrum of state activities devoted to implementing WTO treaties. These implementation activities may need a substantial amount of time and energy, yet, some Members lack the capacity to implement certain rules despite their good faith intentions to do so. For instance, lack of budget and technology discourages developing countries from conducting a comprehensive evaluation of health risks associated with the importation of certain agricultural or fishery products that may carry certain diseases. Accordingly, they tend to narrow down their regulatory options to drastic measures such as an import ban, instead of seeking a reasonable inspection policy, thereby making it hard for them to fully implement the SPS Agreement. Under these circumstances, financial and technical assistance becomes an important instrument to induce compliance with the SPS Agreement in that such assistance helps these countries to establish prudent regulatory policies, and at the same time it avoids trade-restrictive measures like import bans. On the other hand, from a narrow, short-term perspective, compliance means whether a losing party respects and implements a specific adjudicative decision by panels or the Appellate Body. This dimension is accompanied by a retaliatory mechanism for enforcing those adjudicative reports by way of ensuring compliance.

At this juncture, the conceptual distinction of these two modes of compliance bears practical significance. In the foregoing hypothesis, if a Member, which exports those agricultural or fishery products, challenges the import ban by the developing country before a WTO panel, it would be hard for the panel to rule that the importing country *violated* the SPS Agreement since the country adopted and applied the regulatory measure, i.e., the import ban, taking into account 'technical and economic feasibility.' In other words, adjudication alone does not suffice to fully realize a dual goal of free markets and state regulation when a Member has a limited level of capacity. The only way to overcome this predicament is to enhance such 'technical and economic feasibility' through technical and financial assistance by other Members, which involves a broad, long-term dimension of compliance. Furthermore, many regulatory irregularities, which cause trade frictions, are deep-rooted and hidden, and therefore, often slow to develop into formal disputes. Although such trade frictions may not cause more serious trade distortions on an immediate basis, their cumulative effect on free trade is potentially harmful. To address these trade frictions and thus to prevent them from developing into more serious trade distortions, a managerial model seems effective, such as the Trade

Policy Review Mechanism (TPRM),[11] which also fall within the rubric of a broad, long-term dimension of compliance. However, this accentuated importance of a broad, long-term concept of compliance should not unduly shrink the role of a narrow, short-term one involving adjudication; the stability of the global trading system would be seriously damaged if losing parties continuously fail to comply with panel and the Appellate decisions. In sum, through both dimensions of compliance, legal obligations instilled in treaties and jurisprudence to reconcile free markets and state regulation will be eventually transformed into reality.

Finally, in the broader context of international economic law, the clash between free markets and state regulation is not limited to the WTO system. Similar phenomena are occurring in other polities or institutions, such as the European Union (EU),[12] the US and the North American Free Trade Agreement (NAFTA).[13] In the process of reconciling this clash different vectors can be identified according to the particular institutional characteristics of these various polities or institutions, however, such vectors tend to converge thanks to the ever-growing interaction among these entities, as well as to the inherent constitutional nature of the clash itself. Out of such convergence, a common legal precept can be formulated. Not surprisingly, this common legal precept is nothing but an inward-looking imperative crystallizing, on the one hand, general principles of law—namely, good faith or consistency—and reflecting, on the other, the integrative *telos* legitimizing the communitarian duty to cooperate. This common legal precept, which may be termed under the rubric of '*jus gentium* of international trade,' is not a recipe, but a reference for managing the clash between free markets and state regulation in the field of international economic law, no matter where, geographically, such clash takes place.

Importantly, this *jus gentium* of international trade generates legitimacy in this highly integrative global marketplace in that it transcends narrow and overly contextualized legal doctrines which have, up to now, addressed the clash only in a specific institutional setting; as a consequence, this common legal precept serves to enhance the predictability of the global trading system as a whole. With the help of a *jus gentium* of international trade that can be referred to reconcile *any* clash between free markets and state regulation, even a European state acquainted with the EU formula for reconciling the clash will be able to fine-tune its trade and regulatory policies in a manner that is more consistent with the WTO or the NAFTA regime. Furthermore, such *jus gentium* of international trade, if fully developed and utilized, will provide a foreign producer headquartered in the EU with a chance of freer forum shopping between filing its complaint directly with the European Court of Justice to invalidate a discriminatory regulation by a European state, and persuading its home country to champion the complaint before the WTO panel.

11. Trade Policy Review Mechanism, Annex 3, WTO Agreement, *supra* note 1 [hereinafter TPRM].
12. Treaty of Amsterdam Amending the Treaty on European Union, the Treaties Establishing the European Communities and Certain Related Acts, Oct. 2, 1997, O.J. (C340) 1; Treaty Establishing the European Community, Nov. 10, 1997, O.J. (C 340) 3 (1997) [hereinafter EC Treaty]; Treaty Establishing the European Economic Community, Feb. 7, 1992, O.J. (C 224) 1 (1992), *reprinted in* European Union, Consolidated Treaties 35 (1997), *available at* <europa.eu.int/eur-lex/en/treaties/dat/ec-cons-treaty- en.pdf> (last visited on Jan. 19, 2001).
13. North American Free Trade Agreement, Dec. 17, 1992, Can.–Mex.–U.S., 32 I.L.M. 296 [hereinafter NAFTA].

Against this backdrop, this book seeks to diagnose challenges and to prescribe solutions for reconciling the clash between free markets and state regulation in international economic law, taking into account the transformed *telos* of the global trading system described above. Towards these ends, Chapter I sketches the historical background of the global trading system and discusses different ideological attitudes toward the clash. Significantly, Chapter I analyzes the transformation of the *telos* of the global trading system through two paramount constitutional moments: the birth of GATT 1947 and the launch of the WTO.

Chapter II examines the evolution of GATT jurisprudence to reconcile the clash between free markets and state regulation. A handful of key GATT provisions that remain unamended suggest that the jurisprudence has been the only realistic channel by which the necessary changes could be made. Consequently, close scrutiny of this jurisprudential development is critical to understanding how the old GATT and the new WTO have sought to address the clash. First, conventional GATT jurisprudence centering on the Law of National Treatment (Article III:4), the Law of Market Access (Article XI:1) and the Law of Justification (Article XX) are examined as concrete expressions of the Principle of Non-Discrimination. It will be argued that because of its strong pro-trade bias, the conventional GATT jurisprudence provoked widespread discontentment and precipitated a movement toward regulatory unilateralism. This inherited tradition of pro-trade jurisprudence resulting in regulatory unilateralism is criticized for giving rise to the dual crisis mentioned above: regulatory failure and trade failure.

As a solution to this dilemma, Chapter II then introduces the new jurisprudence developed by the Appellate Body under the new WTO dispute settlement mechanism. The gist of this new jurisprudence, the 'chapeau' test, is analyzed through a number of cases including *Gasoline* (1996)[14] and *Turtle* (1998).[15] Certain vital implications of this chapeau test will also be discussed, including its reliance on general principles of law, its teleological nature and its constitutional message. Despite the development of this new jurisprudence, it will be argued that an inherent pro-trade bias remains. These remnants of bias are based primarily on the dichotomy between general obligations (National Treatment) and exceptions (Article XX). They are problematized by reference to the hotly debated *Asbestos* (2001)[16] case. Finally, Chapter II attempts to glean comparative insights from the jurisprudential experiences of the EU and the US.

Chapter III discusses the WTO's harmonization initiative and its derivative jurisprudence. Side agreements, such as the SPS and the TBT Agreement, mend the aforementioned dichotomy, because the legal notion of 'exception' no longer exists

14. United States—Standards for Reformulated and Conventional Gasoline, WT/DS2/9, Appellate Body and Panel Report, as amended, adopted on May 20,1996, *available at* <http://www.wto.org/english/tratop_e/dispu_e/distab_e.htm> (last visited on Sep. 27, 2001) [hereinafter *Gasoline* (1996)].
15. United States–Import Prohibition of Certain Shrimp and Shrimp Products, WT/DS58, Appellate Body and Panel Report, as amended, adopted on Nov. 6, 1998, *available at* <http://www.wto.org/english/tratop_e/dispu_e/distab_e.htm> (last visited on Sep. 27, 2001) [hereinafter *Shrimp-Turtle* (1998)].
16. European Communities—Measures Affecting the Prohibition of Asbestos and Asbestos Products, WT/DS135, Appellate Body and Panel Report, as amended, adopted on Apr. 5, 2001, *available at* <http://www.wto.org/english/tratop_e/dispu_e/distab_e.htm> (last visited on Sep. 27, 2001) [hereinafter *Asbestos* (2001)].

in both the SPS and the TBT Agreement. Rather, the exceptions have been converted to autonomous *rights* of the Members, on the basis of which the latter may pursue legitimate policy objectives, such as the protection of human health or the environment. These rights, however, are not unbridled. They are matched by various obligations, such as scientific justification and risk assessment requirements. As indicated above, these requirements mirror the chapeau test in that they concern the 'manner' in which a certain measure is adopted or applied, rather than the measure itself. Moreover, the side agreements also embody other obligations reflecting trade values, such as the requirement of applying less trade restrictive measures rather than more restrictive ones to achieve the same result. In sum, the pursuit of the dual ideal of free market liberalism and effective, autonomous state regulation is treated in an intellectually more mature, balanced fashion under the side agreements than under the GATT. Chapter III thus explores the jurisprudence derived from the SPS and TBT Agreements, while seeking to supplement the discussion with comparative insights from other institutions that share similar experiences.

Chapter IV is devoted to compliance pull. All that has been addressed thus far in this thesis is limited to the international dimension. Yet it is in the domestic sphere that the detailed behavioral changes take place, changes which are necessary if the dual mission of free markets and state regulation is to be accomplished in a coherent fashion. In other words, each national government is ultimately responsible for ensuring that its domestic regulation is not trade restrictive while still preserving its own regulatory autonomy. Accordingly, Chapter IV deals with, firstly from a broad, long-term perspective, issues concerning implementation and nationalization. It examines how the SPS and TBT Agreements, as well as certain aspects of the GATT jurisprudence, which have been discussed so far in terms of reconciling the clash, should be understood, incorporated and put into practice by Members. From a narrow, short-term perspective, Chapter IV also examines post-adjudicative issues concerning how a losing party must accept, often reluctantly, a specific formula for reconciling a particular clash between free markets and state regulation, as prescribed by panel and the Appellate Body decisions.

Finally, Chapter V surveys the convergence phenomenon among the WTO and other representative polities and institutions, to the extent that the reconciliation of the collision between free markets and state regulation is sought through treaties, jurisprudence and implementation. In the context of such a convergence, the final Chapter explores the possibility of finding a common legal precept capable of guiding, in a coherent and integrative way, the reconciliation of the clash in the field of international economic law, a legal precept which encompasses not only the WTO, but also other polities and institutions, such as the EU, the US and NAFTA.

Chapter I
Background: two constitutional moments and the transformation of the telos

1.1 Overview

Each human life is marked by certain critical moments. In any biography, such foundational and transformative moments form the most important chapters. Likewise, every single polity or institution has its own critical moments of creation, transformation, and evolution. Those moments may be dubbed 'constitutional moments' in that they dictate the very identity of the polity or institution. For the US, such moments may be found in the Revolution, the Civil War and the Great Depression.[1] For the EU, they may be found in the Treaty of Rome, the Single European Act and the Maastricht Treaty.[2] In the case of the global trading community, the creation of the old GATT in 1947 and the Uruguay Round culminating in the birth of the WTO in 1986–95 may be regarded as constitutional moments.

Critically, for the purpose of a thesis that purports to examine the reconciliation of a clash between trade value and regulatory value in the international economic law, these two constitutional moments tend to show the transformation of the *telos* of the global trading community, which explains the changing ideological balance sheets of free markets and state regulation.

1.2 Birth of GATT 1947

The birth of the modern global trading community can be traced back to the late forties when the Western Allies launched a new postwar international economic order in Bretton Woods, a small town in New Hampshire. The resulting 'Bretton Woods system' represented a response to two major tragedies of the twentieth century, World Wars I and II, which had resulted, in part, from a misguided

1. *See* Bruce A. Ackerman, *The Storrs Lectures: Discovering the Constitution*, 93 YALE L. J. 1013, 1071 (1984); Bruce A. Ackerman, *Constitutional Politics/Constitutional Law*, 99 YALE L. J. 453, 489–90 (1989) (regarding 'failed' constitutional moments).
2. *See* JOSEPH H. H. WEILER, THE CONSTITUTION OF EUROPE: 'DO THE NEW CLOTHES HAVE AN EMPEROR?' AND OTHER ESSAYS ON EUROPEAN INTEGRATION 3 (1999).

ideology of trade. The 'beggar-thy-neighbor' spirit of mercantilism, which had been the dominant economic ideology from the eighteenth to the early twentieth centuries, distorted trade flows in a mutually-destructive manner, eventually leading to mismanagement of the affluence accumulated throughout the world thanks to the industrial revolution. In the early twentieth century, mercantilism gave rise to imperialism, which played a critical role in the events leading to World War I.[3] Then, only a decade later, mercantilism helped nurture totalitarianism, which contributed similarly to the outbreak of World War II.[4]

Therefore, for the framers of the Bretton Woods system, the painful and costly lessons of economic balkanization underscored the vital importance of free trade, which they understood in terms of anti-mercantilism and anti-protection. More importantly, the lessons of war spurred the creation of an institution to foster free trade and police mercantilist protection: the 'General Agreement on Tariffs and Trade (GATT).' From this historical background, one can readily identify one original *telos* of the GATT system: 'anti-protection.' Such was the concern with rooting out protection, in fact, that the GATT 1947 system quickly prioritized trade values over other social values, resulting in a distinct 'pro-trade bias'[5] in addressing the interface of free markets and state regulation.

1.3 The Uruguay round and the creation of the WTO

Yet, technological developments based on unprecedented scientific discoveries have recently brought winds of change, forever altering traditional notion of time and space. Thanks to such progress, the depth and breadth of cross-border transactions have expanded on an enormous scale and at a rapid pace. As the volume, frequency and velocity of international commerce have increased in parallel with this unprecedented technological innovation, economic integration has accelerated on a global scale. Adding fuel to this trend, the past decade witnessed the resolution of the long-standing ideological confrontation of the Cold War.[6] The result is a world more interdependent and more integrated than ever before, a world in which international problems can no longer be tackled solely by a few large countries and where domestic problems are no longer confined to a local area.

---

3. *Cf.* KENNETH N. WALTZ, THEORY OF INTERNATIONAL POLITICS 26–7 (1979).
4. *See* Patrica Clavin, *The Triumph of Regionalism over Globalism: Patterns of Trade in the Interwar Period, in* REGIONAL TRADE BLOCS, MULTILATERALISM, AND THE GATT: COMPLEMENTARY PATHS TO FREE TRADE 31–33 (Till Geiger & Dennis Kennedy eds., 1996).
5. Concerning the use of the term 'pro-trade bias,' *see* Hannes L. Schloemann & Stefan Ohlhoff, *'Constitutionalization' and Dispute Settlement in the WTO: National Security as an Issue of Competence*, 93 AM. J. INT'L L. 424, 451 (1999).
6. After the disintegration of the former Soviet Union and the fall of the Berlin Wall, the absence of ideological competition and the consequent spread of the principles of market economics expedited the process of globalization across the former East–West demarcation. This process of accelerated globalization initially started on a regional basis, creating the European Bank for Reconstruction and Development (EBRD) in 1991, the Asia Pacific Economic Cooperation (APEC) in 1989, a single European market (Europe 1992), the North American Free Trade Agreement (NAFTA) in 1993, and finally culminated in the launch of the World Trade Organization (WTO) in 1995.

Greater economic integration and interdependence have altered the concept of the 'international community' in a fundamental way. This community no longer consists of discrete sovereign states symbolized by independence and non-interference. Instead, the international community has become a society based on the 'awareness of increased solidarity and the aspiration to a greater unity over-spanning ideological and economic differences.'[7] It is now structured by the 'will to transcend the traditional international society made up of juxtaposed egoism' as well as by the 'quest for the common goods and common values.'[8] Critically, the global trading community remains an essential feature of the international community, and merits much of the credit for driving the transformation described above. In other words, international trade has been a principal engine powering the economic integration among members of the international community. Many centuries ago, central Asian peoples developed a trade route known as the 'Silk Road,' which changed the physiognomy of human civilization forever. Today, their descendants can buy or download their favorite Finnish song spontaneously via the Internet, which has become a kind of *cyber* Silk Road.

Although these changes may appear on their face to be a total blessing, they have introduced numerous new policy challenges.[9] First, new trade barriers have began to emerge. The use of conventional protectionist measures, such as tariffs and quotas, has recently diminished dramatically in parallel with the general trend of trade liberalization, as governments have come to realize the actual economic and political costs of protection.[10] Instead, domestic regulations that purport to improve social hygiene under the banner of 'welfare state,' such as environmental regulations or those related to human health and safety, have begun to proliferate and have taken the place of conventional trade policy measures, such as tariffs and quotas. Although they are 'non-protectionist' and thus reflect 'legitimate' policy objectives,[11] in the context of heightened economic interdependency, these emerging social regulations tend to severely hinder or impede the stream of global commerce due to their regulatory heterogeneity.[12] These 'Non-Tariff Barriers' (NTBs) are often portrayed

---

7. Prosper Weil, *Towards Relative Normativity in International Law?*, 77 AM. J. INT'L L. 413, 422 (1983).
8. *Id.* One interesting feature of this transformation of international community is that the concept of state sovereignty is *disaggregated* into a meaningful set of social actors, such as government agencies, specific departments, pressure groups and/or individuals. *See* Anne-Marie Slaughter, *International Law in a World of Liberal States*, 6 EUR. J. INT'L L. 503, 535 (1995). This disaggregation tends to enable states' functional parts, *e.g.*, agencies or departments, to constitute a *network* among themselves by which to accomplish a specific regulatory object. *Id.* This disaggregation phenomenon tends to engage more experts in certain regulatory fields, facilitating the depoliticization and bottom-up decision-making process.
9. *See* John H. Jackson, *Global Economics and International Economic Law*, 1 J. INT'L ECON. L. 1, 1–4 (1998).
10. *See* GLOBAL TRANSFORMATION: POLITICS, ECONOMICS AND CULTURE 187 (David Held et al. eds., 1999) [hereinafter GLOBAL TRANSFORMATION].
11. Sometimes, governments disguise their protectionist intent by using these seemingly legitimate regulatory objectives. Such disguised protection is called 'protectionism,' in contrast with direct 'protection.' *See* OECD, FOOD SAFETY AND QUALITY: TRADE CONSIDERATION 53 (1999) [hereinafter FOOD SAFETY].
12. A number of scholars have already paid attention to this phenomenon. For instance, Sol Picciotto observed that: 'Regulatory regimes have been brought into greater interaction as the removal of direct barriers to the flows of goods and money between states (tariffs, quotas and exchange controls) has shifted attention towards regulatory difference as a barrier to entry of commodities or capital.' Sol

as 'invisible' or 'behind-the-border' measures. More importantly, the old *telos* of anti-protection cannot effectively deal with these NTBs since they are non-protectionist in nature.

Secondly, new trade areas have begun to emerge. Traditionally, the field of international trade was concerned mostly with trade in *goods* and with *goods*-related trade measures, such as tariffs and quotas. However, as trade relationships deepened among trading partners and technological innovations blossomed, trade in 'services,' which had once been regarded as non-tradable, have been spotlighted as a promising new area.[13] Moreover, certain areas that were previously treated as trade-neutral, such as investment and intellectual property rights, have begun to influence trade more regularly and to a greater extent than before.

Thirdly, anxieties about developmental disparity have accompanied the acceleration of economic integration. Similar questions regarding distributional justice have been raised in response to the widening income gap among trading partners that persists despite overall economic growth. The disturbingly persistent dyad of North and South remained unresolved under the GATT 1947, threatening the integrity of the global trading community.

These daunting challenges could not be properly addressed by a GATT system with a *telos* limited to policing 'protection,' rather than one more audaciously promoting 'economic integration.'[14] This frustrating reality eventually led trading nations to gather their collective political capital and to launch a bold and comprehensive negotiation round in Punta del Este, Uruguay, in September 1986, dubbed the 'Uruguay Round.' This initiative culminated in the monumental and historic creation of the World Trade Organization (WTO) in January 1995. As a formal international institution, the WTO has overcome many of the old GATT's defects in responding more effectively to the new challenges described above.[15] For

---

contd

Picciotto, The Regulatory Criss-Cross: Interaction between Jurisdictions and the Construction of Global Regulatory Networks, in International Regulatory Competition and Coordination: Perspectives on Economic Regulation in Europe and the United States 89 (William Bratton et al eds. 1996) [hereinafter Regulatory Competition and Coordination]. Likewise, some economists have also noted that:

> As globalization proceeds, however, it has become increasingly evident that one nation's economic policies can affect other countries. When nations were separated by high trade barriers and trade flows were limited, one country could ignore another nation's domestic economic policies. As barriers have come down, other countries' domestic policies have become much more important.

Globaphobia: Confronting Fears About Open Trade 89 (Gary Burtless et al eds. 1998). *See also* Aaditya Mattoo, *Discriminatory Consequences of Non-Discriminatory Standards*, WTO, WTO Staff Working Papers, TISD-96-01, Dec. 1997, *available at* <http://www.wto.org/english/res_e/reser_e/wpaps_e.htm> (last visited on April 19, 2001).

13. *See* WTO, *GATS: Facts and Fiction, Why is the Liberalization of Services Important?*, *available at* <http://www.wto.org/english/tratop_e/serv_e/gats_factfiction2_e.htm> (last visited on Apr. 3, 2001).
14. Of course, even under the old GATT system some dynamics oriented to interdependence and integration, albeit limited, could be found. *See* Jock A. Finlayson & Mark W. Zacher, *The GATT and the Regulation of Trade Barriers: Regime Dynamics and Functions*, 35 Int'l Org. 273, 306–8 (1981) (distinguishing between 'sovereignty norms' and 'interdependence norms' in the GATT and maintaining that the latter is key to the strength of the GATT regime).
15. *Cf.* Ernst-Ulrich Petersmann, *The Transformation of the World Trading System through the 1994 Agreement Establishing the World Trade Organization*, 6 Eur. J. Int'l L 161, 189 (1995) (arguing that the 1994 WTO Agreement 'completes the original design of the Bretton Woods system' and

instance, new trade and regulatory concerns in association with NTBs, were addressed through side agreements, including the Agreement on Sanitary and Phytosanitary Measures (SPS), the Agreement on Trade Barriers to Trade (TBT), the General Agreement on Trade in Services (GATS) and the Agreement on Trade-Related Intellectual Property Rights (TRIPs).

A systematic description of the novelty of the new WTO system vis-à-vis the old GATT regime could occupy many volumes of text. What is most important for present purposes, however, is to note that the *telos* of the WTO extends well beyond the narrow and conventional anti-protectionist purpose of GATT 1947 to cover a much broader range of matters relating to 'integration' and 'sustainable development.'[16] Under this integrationist *telos*, a pro-trade bias in addressing the interface of free markets and state regulation cannot be sustained, but must yield to a more mature and nuanced approach aimed at achieving the dual objectives of free trade and regulatory autonomy, which will be explored in the following chapters.

---

contd

'reduces the existing fragmentation of international economic law, by a 'global integration law' for international movements of goods, services, persons, investments and payments').

16. WTO Agreement, *supra* note 1, Introduction, pmbl. Professor Cottier also notes 'while the GATT was an agreement the purpose of which was almost exclusively the reduction of trade barriers, the WTO increasingly assumes *constitutional* functions in a globalizing economy' (emphasis added). Thomas Cottier, *The WTO and Environmental Law: Some Issues and Ideas*, Trade & Development Center Essay Series, *available at* <http://www.itd.org/issues/essay1.htm> (last visited on Mar. 29, 2001). *Cf.* Brian F. Fitzgerald, *Trade-Based Constitutionalisms: The Framework for Universalizing Substantive International Law?*, 5 U. MIAMI Y. B. INT'L L. 111, 129 (1996–97) (arguing that 'the Uruguay Round of the GATT has presented us with a trade structure that no longer seeks only to deregulate or regulate in the names of some narrow universal principle of free trade, but that seeks to regulate sovereignties for the purpose of finding universality').

Chapter II
Evolution of GATT jurisprudence

2.1 GATT jurisprudence: the past and the present

Under the GATT system, two key provisions, Articles III:4 and XI:1, conceptualize 'free market' ideology[1] in contrasting ways. Article III:4 represents the National Treatment or Non-Discrimination principle that prevents protectionist or discriminatory treatment for imported products vis-à-vis domestic products in competition. In contrast, Article XI:1 stands for the Free Market Access principle that prohibits quantitative restrictions or any other measure equivalent to quantitative restrictions. As the latter obligation does not necessarily involve 'comparison' between imported and domestic *products* in competition, or *measures* imposed on these imported and domestic products, any trade barrier or obstacle can potentially fall under Article XI:1.

On the other hand, Article XX (General Exceptions) represents 'state regulations,' though in a limited dimension. Ten exhausted items in Article XX reflect legitimate policy objectives that take precedence over the foregoing general obligations protecting free trade values, such as Articles III:4 and XI:1. Therefore, GATT can be said to permit a certain degree of 'justifiable discrimination' with respect to certain regulatory concerns of contracting parties (Members).

From the creation of the old GATT through the launch of the new WTO system, panels and the Appellate Body (AB) have interpreted these three provisions in various ways to address the interface between the two frequently conflicting goals of free markets and state regulation. Deeply embedded in textual structure, this conflict reflects a rather fundamental 'dichotomy' between material obligations representing free trade values and exceptions representing regulatory values. The jurisprudential evolution of GATT panels and the WTO AB has resulted in a shifting ideological balance sheet with respect to the paramount values of free trade and state regulation. Specifically, this jurisprudential evolution tracks, fairly closely, the transformation of the *telos* of the global trading system from 'anti-protection' to 'integration' or 'anti-unilateralism.'

1. The discussion that follows addresses only so-called 'vertical' non-discrimination: that is, non-discrimination between imported and domestic products. By contrast, 'horizontal' non-discrimination, which refers to non-discrimination among products imported from different countries and which is best illustrated by the Most-Favored Nation (MFN) principle, is not addressed herein.

2.1.1 MATERIAL OBLIGATIONS AND EXCEPTIONS: CONVENTIONAL JURISPRUDENCE

2.1.1.1 The Law of National Treatment (Article III: 4)

Provision

Article III: 4 provides that:

> The products of the territory of any contracting party *imported into the territory of any other contracting* party shall be accorded treatment *no less favourable* than that accorded to *like products of national origin* in respect of *all laws, regulations and requirements affecting* their internal sale, offering for sale, purchase, transportation, distribution or use.[2]

Overview: from a diplomatic tool to a legal obligation

As a crucial pillar of the Bretton Woods system, GATT 1947 was originally meant to support the goal of free trade through tariff reduction.[3] Since the US took a leading role in creating the GATT system, it is only natural that basic modalities of GATT 1947 have their roots in pre-war US bilateral trade agreements, and particularly in the body of US trade agreements negotiated after 1935.[4] Such agreements concerned mainly bilateral tariff reductions as well as the bargained-for exchange of 'reciprocity.'[5]

Once tariff reduction negotiations were concluded, the next logical step was to preserve the results and prevent any backsliding. For this purpose, the framers of GATT 1947 *bound* schedules of tariff concessions under Article II,[6] and tried to secure the values reflected in those tariff concessions through general obligations, such as the National Treatment principle (Article III). Thus, legal obligations were originally just one option among various kinds of 'diplomatic' instruments, intended to maintain the value of tariff concessions.[7] In other words, what GATT framers were trying to achieve through Article III was the preservation of the balance of

2. General Agreement on Tariffs and Trade 1994, Annex 1 A, *supra* note 1, Introduction, art. III, ¶ 4 [hereinafter GATT 1994] (emphasis added).
3. Regarding the historical background of post-war global economic developments and the birth of GATT, *see generally* GILBERT R. WINHAM, THE EVOLUTION OF INTERNATIONAL TRADE AGREEMENTS (1992); A. G. KENWOOD & A. L. LOUGHEED, THE GROWTH OF THE INTERNATIONAL ECONOMY 1820–1970 (3d ed. 1992); ROBERT E. HUDEC, THE GATT LEGAL SYSTEM AND WORLD TRADE DIPLOMACY (2d ed. 1990); KENNETH W. DAM, THE GATT: LAW AND INTERNATIONAL ECONOMIC ORGANIZATION (1970).
4. Robert E. Hudec, *The GATT Legal System: A Diplomat's Jurisprudence*, 4 J. WORLD TRADE L. 615, 616–36 (1970) [hereinafter Hudec, *A Diplomat's Jurisprudence*].
5. *Id.*; Ernst-Ulrich Petersmann, *The Dispute Settlement System of the World Trade Organization and the Evolution of the GATT Dispute Settlement System since 1948*, 31 COMMON MKT. L. REV. 1157, 1171 (1994); ERNST H. PREEG, TRADERS AND DIPLOMATS: AN ANALYSIS OF THE KENNEDY ROUND OF NEGOTIATIONS UNDER THE GENERAL AGREEMENT ON TARIFFS AND TRADE 23–24 (1970); Edwin Vermulst & Bart Driessen, *An Overview of the WTO Dispute Settlement System and its Relationship with the Uruguay Round Agreements*, 29 J. WORLD TRADE 131, 136 (1995).
6. *See* GATT 1994, *supra* note 2, art. II.
7. Hudec, *A Diplomat's Jurisprudence*, *supra* note 4, at 624.

tariff concessions bound by Article II, rather than the establishment of a unified and integrated set of norms and structures.[8]

Over time, however, the initially supplementary role of Article III was gradually transformed to a central one through rich jurisprudential development. Specifically, Article III (National Treatment) began to establish the concept of an autonomous obligation, beyond merely protecting the value of tariff binding. As a general legal obligation, Article III was interpreted to apply even to products that are not bound by Article II.[9]

Two contrasting views: protection v. discrimination

The rationale of Article III:4 (National Treatment in Domestic Regulation) may be found in the objective and purpose (*telos*) of the GATT 1947 system itself. As discussed above, based on the belated realization that World War II had resulted from a mutually destructive economic balkanization among key trading partners during the

---

8. The supplementary role of Article III vis-à-vis Article II (tariff binding) has been confirmed by panels in various cases. *See, e.g.*, Japan—Taxes on Alcoholic Beverages, WT/DS8, WT/DS10, WT/DS11, Appellate Body and Panel Report, as modified, adopted on November 1 1996, *available at* <http://www.wto.org/english/tratop_e/dispu_e/distab_e.htm> (last visited on Sep. 27, 2001) [hereinafter *Japanese Shochu II* (1996)]. The Panel noted the following:

   > 6.13 The Panel then turned to other contextual elements that have to be taken into account, as required by Article 31 VCLT. The Panel noted in this respect the relationship between Articles II and III of GATT 1994. The Panel concluded, as had previous panels that dealt with the same issue, that one of the main purposes of Article III is to guarantee that WTO Members will not undermine through internal measures their commitments under Article II. The Panel noted in this respect that an adopted panel report that had dealt with this issue had stated that: '... one of the basic purposes of Article III was to ensure that the contracting parties' internal charges and regulations were not such as to frustrate the effect of tariff concessions granted under Article II ...' (*citing the panel report on 'Canada—Import, Distribution and Sale of Certain Alcoholic Drinks by Provincial Marketing Agencies,' adopted on 18 February 1992, BISD 39S/27, ¶¶ 5.30–5.31*).
   >
   > The Panel further noted that another adopted panel report had concluded with respect to the same issue that: '... The most-favoured-nation requirement in Article I, and also tariff binding under Article II, would become ineffective without the complementary prohibition in Article III on the use of internal taxation and regulation as a discriminatory non-tariff trade barrier.' (*citing the panel report on 'United States—Measures Affecting Alcoholic and Malt Beverage,' adopted on 19 June 1992, BISD 39S/206, ¶ 5.9*).

   Professor Hudec also observed that, until the sixties, contracting parties had not used legal instruments very extensively in the operation of the GATT; rather, they had relied mainly upon diplomatic channels. *See* Robert E. Hudec, *The Expedition to Darkest Geneva*, 20 MICH. J. INT'L L. 121, 121–22 (1999).

9. GENERAL AGREEMENT ON TARIFFS AND TRADE, ANALYTICAL INDEX—GUIDE TO GATT LAW AND PRACTICE 127 (1994) [hereinafter ANALYTICAL INDEX]. *See also* The First Working Party Report on Brazilian Internal Taxes, GATT/CP.3/42, adopted on 30 June 1949, II/181, 182, ¶ 4; Panel Report on EEC—Regulation on Imports of Parts and Components, L/6657, adopted on 16 May 1990, 37S/132, 191–192, ¶ 5.4; *Japanese Shochu II, supra* note 8, pt. F (Interpretation of Article III). The Appellate Body held that:

   > The sheltering scope of Article III is not limited to products that are the subject of tariff concessions under Article II. The Article III national treatment obligation is a general prohibition on the use of internal taxes and other internal regulatory measures so as to afford protection to domestic production. This obligation clearly extends also to products not bound under Article II. This is confirmed by the negotiating history of Article III.

   Regarding a comprehensive analysis of this case, *see* Serena B. Wille, *Recapturing a Lost Opportunity: Article III:2 GATT 1994 Japan—Taxes on Alcoholic Beverages 1996*, 9 EUR. J. INT'L L, *available at* <http://www.ejil.org/journal/Vol9/No1/sr1b.html> (last visited on August 29, 2001).

interwar period, the framers of GATT placed top priority on the elimination of domestic protection. Therefore, what the framers envisioned was the goal of free, or liberal, trade worldwide without any governmental intervention for patronizing or protecting particular domestic industries or producers. The existence of Article III:1 (the requirement of 'not being applied so as to afford protection') tends to support this observation. In sum, the term 'discrimination,' which is used frequently in Article III, is equated with 'protection.' This view could also be translated alternatively as the permission of any governmental intervention without such protectionist intent.

Yet it is possible to distinguish between these two terms, 'discrimination' and 'protection,' based on the observation that the former is a broader concept than the latter. According to this view, Article III:4 should be applied not only to protectionist measures, but also to measures that are technically 'non-protectionist' yet still discriminatory or trade-restrictive. In other words, any domestic regulation must be prohibited if it results in a disparate impact on trade, even if the relevant government had no protectionist intent in launching or maintaining such measure. This line of interpretation appears to take free trade concerns more seriously than the first view, by tending to restrict the regulatory space of governments within the meaning of Article III:4.

These two views regarding the scope of Article III:4 have alternated continuously throughout the GATT/WTO jurisprudential history, influencing interpretations of important parameters of Article III:4, such as 'like products' and 'no less favorable treatment.'

Like products

Neither GATT panels nor the Contracting Parties (the General Council of Members) ever worked out a general definition of 'like products.' Nevertheless, the 'Report of the Working Party on Border Tax Adjustments' contains a widely accepted statement regarding the interpretation of 'like products.' The Report noted that:

> ... the interpretation of the term should be examined on a case-by-case basis. This would allow a fair assessment in each case of the different elements that constitute a 'similar' product. Some criteria were suggested for determining, on a case-by-case basis, whether a product is 'similar": the product's end-uses in a given market; consumers' tastes and habits, which change from country to country; the product's properties, nature and quality.[10]

Considering that the foregoing Report has been frequently quoted and cited by other panels, it would appear that a general consensus has been established, at least as to the *flexibility* of this concept. Consistent with this assessment, one panel report was not adopted because the panel had interpreted like products too narrowly, namely as 'more or less the same' products.[11] In sum, it would be fair to say that the concept of

10. Report of the Working Party on Border Tax Adjustments, B.I.S.D. 18S/97, ¶ 18 [hereinafter Border Tax Adjustments].
11. ANALYTICAL INDEX, *supra* note 9, at 171.

like products mirrors an accordion,[12] existing in a broad spectrum and waiting to be defined in a specific case.

As discussed above, one or the other of two contrasting views on the rationale of Article III: 4—namely, whether it disciplines 'protection' only or whether it also covers the much broader concept of 'discrimination'—tends to determine the degree of such flexibility in a given case, thereby influencing directly the interpretation of 'like products.' According to the 'protection' view, Members' regulatory intentions, whether protectionist or non-protectionist, should be taken into account even when determining like products. This view considers Article III: 1, which provides the requirement of 'not being applied so as to afford protection,' as a general, basic obligation that should also apply to Article III: 4.

Under GATT 1947 panel practice, this line of interpretation prevailed in a couple of panel decisions. Dubbed the 'aim and effect' test, this jurisprudence employed two yardsticks in smoking out protectionist intents: a regulatory goal that each measure pursues (*aim*), and a trade effect that such measure is expected to bring (*effect*). Although the appellation of this test indicates that it comprises two parallel criteria, 'aim' and 'effect,' the 'effect' part of the test was marginalized in practice by the 'aim' part of the test. In other words, the requirement in paragraph 1 ('not applied so as to afford protection'), which basically stands for the 'aim' test, was allowed to play such a crucial interpretive role that any possible disparate impact related to the 'effect' test would be rationalized in practice as merely incidental or fortuitous, as long as the questioned measure was determined to carry no protectionist motivation.

The aim and effect test was a conspicuous feature of the *Malt Beverages* (1992) case. In this case, certain US states differentiated between beers with an alcohol content of 3.2% or lower, and those with a higher alcohol content. Based on this differentiation, a number of states have imposed various restrictions in terms of license, points of sale, labeling requirement, etc., on beers with a higher alcohol content.[13] Canada, one of the largest exporters of beers having a higher alcohol content, argued that less favorable treatment was offered to imported (Canadian) products as compared to domestic (US) products, with the result that Canada's competitive position in the US beer markets was harmed.[14]

Following the so-called 'aim and effect' test, the Panel first noted that the determination of 'like products' between low alcohol beer and high alcohol beer should be made based on 'physical characteristics,' but also with a view to the 'purpose of Article III,' namely, the 'not as to afford protection' requirement.[15] The Panel also emphasized that:

> the like product determination in the context of Article III be made in such a way that it *not unnecessarily infringe upon the regulatory authority* and domestic policy options of contracting parties.[16]

12. *Japanses Shochu II*, *supra* note 8, pt. H (art. III:2).
13. United States—Measures Affecting Alcoholic and Malt Beverage, Panel Report adopted on 19 June 1992, B.I.S.D. 39S/206, Panel Report, ¶ 2.32 [hereinafter *Malt Beverages* (1992)].
14. *Id.*, ¶ 3.9.
15. *Id.*, ¶ 5.71.
16. *Id.*, ¶ 5.72 (emphasis added).

Against this background, the Panel essentially conducted an abbreviated mode of Article XX examination by considering the 'policy goals and legislative background of the laws regulating the alcohol content of beer' in terms of 'protecting human life and health' and 'upholding public morals.'[17] Finally, the Panel concluded that 'the alcohol content of beer has not been singled out as a means of favoring domestic producers over foreign producers.'[18] In the same vein, an unadopted panel report in *Luxury Tax* (1994) also held that a measure is deemed to have a protectionist purpose if more competitive opportunities on domestic products are a *desired* outcome, rather than a merely incidental consequence of the pursuit of a legitimate policy goal.[19]

The aim and effect test certainly tends to guarantee Members' regulatory autonomy within the meaning of Article III:4. Once a domestic product is determined to be 'unlike' an imported one on account of the non-protectionist intentions of a measure applied to the domestic product, such measure is redeemed as consistent with Article III:4, once and for all. The redeemed measure does not need to undergo another test ('disparate impact' test) under Article III:4—i.e., 'no less favorable treatment'—nor a justification stage under Article XX. In fact, the 'disparate impact' test is marginalized in the aim and effect test because any negative trade effect tends to be regarded as incidental and thus negligible as long as the measure in question carries no protectionist intentions.

Under the competing view, which adopts a much boarder concept of 'discrimination,' the determination of 'like products' tends not to be as flexible as the aim and effect test, because this view does not take into account regulatory intentions in the Article III:4 stage. Rather, the 'like products' test is considered just one parameter within Article III:4, and a conventional test focusing on product-related properties, represented by the Working Party Report on Border Tax Adjustment, is used. The real interpretive focus of this view, however, lies in another parameter. Specifically, the emphasis rests on the 'disparate impact' test ('no less favorable treatment between imported and domestic products'), which decides whether a questioned measure distorts the conditions of competition in the marketplace, without respect to regulatory intentions.

---

17. The Panel implicitly relied on historical background ranging from the Temperance Movement to the repeal of the 18th Amendment (the Prohibition) for its finding against protectionist discrimination in regulating the alcohol content of beer. *Id.*, ¶ 5.74.
18. *Id.*
19. US—Taxes on Automobiles, panel report unadopted, circulated on 11 October 1994, DS31/R [hereinafter *Luxury Tax* (1994)]. The Panel held that:

    5.10 The Panel then proceeded to examine more closely the meaning of the phrase 'so as to afford protection.' The Panel noted that the term 'so as to' suggested both aim and effect. Thus the phrase 'so as to afford protection' called for an analysis of elements including the aim of the measure and the resulting effects. A measure could be said to have the *aim* of affording protection if an analysis of the circumstances in which it was adopted, in particular an analysis of the instruments available to the contracting party to achieve the declared domestic policy goal, demonstrated that a change in competitive opportunities in favour of domestic products was a desired outcome and not merely an incidental consequence of the pursuit of a legitimate policy goal. A measure could be said to have the *effect* of affording protection to domestic production if it accorded greater competitive opportunities to domestic products than to imported products. The effect of a measure in terms of trade flows was not relevant for the purposes of Article III, since a change in the volume or proportion of imports could be due to many factors other than government measures.

Although the aim and effect test may contribute to the preservation of Members' regulatory autonomy, certain textual contradictions militate against its application to domestic regulations. Although various paragraphs of Article III, including paragraphs 2 and 5, explicitly refer to paragraph 1, namely the requirement of 'not being applied so as to afford protection,' paragraph 4 omits such reference.[20] This is no trivial omission: unlike the cases of 'taxation' (paragraph 2) and 'internal quantitative regulation' (paragraph 5), 'domestic regulations' (paragraph 4) may be inconsistent with Article III without this requirement. Against this backdrop, the aim and effect test met its official demise in the new WTO jurisprudence. After referencing its holding in *Japanese Shochu II* (1996), the Appellate Body in *Bananas III* (1997) ruled that the same reasoning must be applied to the interpretation of Article III:4.[21] It concluded that an interpretation of Article III:4 does not require a separate consideration of whether a measure 'afford[s] protection to domestic production' because Article III: 4 does not specifically refer to Article III:1.[22]

No less favorable treatment

As discussed above, the 'no less favorable treatment' parameter directs scrutiny toward any disparate trade impact that may be caused by the questioned measure. Free from the Article III: 1 requirement, as seen in *Bananas III* (1997), this parameter does not take regulatory intention into account in its scrutiny. Instead, it focuses on whether equal opportunities of competition involving domestic and imported products may be undermined by the questioned measure. For instance, the *Section 337* (1989) Panel ruled that this parameter 'calls for *effective equality of opportunities* for imported products in respect of the application of laws, regulations and requirements affecting the internal sale, offering for sale, purchase, transportation, distribution or use of products.'[23] Therefore, it could be said that this parameter stands for a strong pro-trade position with respect to 'market access' concerns.

Reflecting such market access considerations, the scope of measures that the 'no less favorable treatment' parameter covers has been broadly interpreted. Even in the early days of the old GATT, the *Italian Tractor* (1958) Panel, highlighting the implications of the selection of the word 'affecting,' opined that the drafters of the Article intended to cover in paragraph 4 'not only the laws and regulations which directly governed the conditions of sale or purchase but also any laws or

20. GATT 1994, *supra* note 2, art. III, ¶¶ 1, 2, 4, 5.
21. EC—Regime for the Importation, Sale and Distribution of Bananas, Appellate Body Report adopted on September 25 1997, WT/DS27/AB/R, ¶ 216 [hereinafter *Banana III* (1997)].
22. *Id.*
23. United States—Section 337 of the Tariff Act of 1930, Panel Report adopted on Nov. 7, 1989, B.I.S.D.36S/386, ¶ 5.11 (emphasis added) [hereinafter *Section 337* (1989)]. *See also* Canada—Administration of the Foreign Investment Review Act, Panel Report adopted 7 February 1984, B.I.S.D. 30S/140, 159–161, ¶¶ 5.7–5.11 [hereinafter *FIRA* (1984)]; Canada—Import, Distribution and Sale of Certain Alcoholic Drinks by Provincial Marketing Agencies, DS17/R, Panel Report adopted on 18 February 1992, B.I.S.D. 39S/27, 75–76, ¶ 5.5 [hereinafter *Canadian Alcoholic Drinks* (1992)]; *Malt Beverages*, *supra* note 13, ¶¶ 5.30–5.33.

regulations which might adversely modify the conditions of competition between the domestic and imported products on the internal market.'[24] The Panel also noted that if the scope of Article III:4 were limited to certain types of laws and regulations, the general value of non-discrimination could be easily diluted.[25] The *Italian Tractor* Panel has been cited frequently in subsequent cases as a means of subjecting any domestic trade-related measures to the discipline of the national treatment obligation. Later, in *Banana III* (1997), the AB reaffirmed this point. At issue in this appeal was the question of whether the EC rules for 'the *distribution* of import licenses for imported bananas among eligible operators *within* the European countries' fell within the scope of Article III:4.[26] The EC argued that Article III:4 could not be applied to the EC licensing system because it was not an internal measure, but one that operated *before* bananas had cleared through customs.[27] However, the AB observed that the 'operator category rules,' under which '30% of import licenses for third-country and non-traditional ACP bananas are allocated to operators that market EC or traditional ACP bananas,' as well as 'activity function rules,' under which 'Category A and B licenses are distributed among operators on the basis of their economic activities as importers, custom clearers or ripeners,' do *affect* 'the internal sale, offering for sale, purchase ...' beyond the allocation of import licenses to the actual administration of the tariff quota.[28]

In addition to this broad scope of measures viewed as covered by the term 'affecting,' the 'no less favorable treatment' parameter also extends to '*de facto* discrimination' or 'disguised discrimination,'[29] which imposes a disparate impact to foreign products vis-à-vis domestic ones despite an explicitly origin-neutral treatment, let alone to '*de jure* discrimination' which flatly discriminates against foreign products in favor of domestic ones.

Importantly, the market access considerations embedded in this parameter also made it unnecessary to demonstrate actual 'trade effects' to establish inconsistency with Article III:4. For instance, the *US Tobacco* (1994) Panel confirmed that the *magnitude* of the negative trade effects of a particular measure was not relevant to its consistency

24. Italy—Discrimination against Imported Agricultural Machinery, Panel Report adopted on Oct. 23, 1958, B.I.S.D. 7S/60, ¶ 12 [hereinafter *Italian Tractor* (1958)]. Such an expansive interpretation of *affecting* mirrors the similarly broad jurisprudence of the U.S. Commerce Clause.
25. *Id.*, ¶ 15.
26. *Banana III*, AB Report, *supra* note 21, ¶ 211.
27. *Id.*, ¶ 33.
28. *Id.*, ¶ 211.
29. *See* John H. Jackson, *National Treatment Obligations and Non-Tariff Barriers*, 10 MICH. J. INT'L L. 207, 212–14 (1989); Robert E. Hudec, *GATT/WTO Constraints on National Regulation: Requiem for an 'Aim and Effects' Test*, 32 INT'L LAW. 619, 623–24 (1998) [hereinafter *Aim and Effects*]. '*De facto* discrimination' is tantamount to 'indistinctively applicable' measures in the ECJ jurisprudence. *Aim and Effects*, *supra*, at 620. McGinnis and Movsesian portrayed this disguised pattern of discrimination as 'covert protectionism,' which is expressly aimed at legitimate objectives, such as the protection of the environment or human health, but actually imposes burdens on competing importers. John O. McGinnis & Mark L. Movsesian, *The World Trade Constitution*, 114 HARV. L. REV. 511, 549–50 (2000) [hereinafter *World Trade Constitution*]. In addressing such covert protectionism, McGinnis and Movsesian rejected the 'regulatory model,' which attempts to harmonize or universalize regulatory standards within the WTO on the ground that this model is vulnerable to lobbying by concentrated interest groups, and instead advocated the 'anti-discrimination model,' which is based on an adjudicative system. *Id.*, at 549–72.

with Article III, which protected 'expectations on the competitive relationship' between imported and domestic products, instead of 'export volumes.'[30] The Panel in *Oilseeds* (1990) also noted that 'the exposure of a particular imported product to a *risk* of discrimination constitutes, *by itself*, a form of discrimination.'[31] In the similar context, the concept of offsetting or 'balancing' *less* favorable treatment in one case against *more* favorable treatment in another case was not allowed. As the *Section 337* (1989) Panel noted, to allow such balancing would lead to great uncertainty about the competitive conditions between imported and domestic products, thereby undermining the rationale of Article III.[32]

More recently, under the WTO dispute settlement system, two cases confronted the task of interpreting 'no less favorable treatment.' In *Korean Beef* (2001),[33] Australia and the US challenged the Korean 'dual retails system' under which 'separate distribution channels' exist for certain imported and domestic beef products.[34] The Panel highlighted the 'effective equality of opportunities' when interpreting the 'no less favorable treatment' element in Article III: 4, and concluded that any regulatory difference based *exclusively* on the origin of the products is inconsistent with Article III, even in the absence of any demonstrable trade effects.[35] This Panel's interpretation seems to be motivated by the 'market access' concerns embedded in Article III: 4.[36] However, the AB rejected the Panel's *general* interpretation, referring to the *Section 337* (1989) case stating that explicitly different treatment of imported products is not in itself deterministic in establishing a violation of Article III: 4.[37] Instead, the AB stressed that further analysis is needed regarding whether a measure modifies the 'conditions of competition' to the detriment of imported products.[38] After observing that the dual retail system resulted in 'a drastic reduction of commercial opportunities to reach, and hence to generate sales to, the same consumers served by the traditional retail channels for domestic beef,' the AB finally concluded that the dual retail system did violate Article III: 4.[39]

The AB's interpretation seems more sophisticated than the Panel's. The AB actually broadened the regulatory space in which Members can exercise their regulatory authority by acknowledging the possibility of explicitly different, yet nonetheless, acceptable treatment between domestic and imported products. For the

30. United States—Measures Affecting the Importation, Internal Sale and Use of Tobacco, DS44/R, Panel Report adopted on 4 October 1994, B.I.S.D. 41S/131, ¶¶ 99–100. *See also* The 1949 Working Party Report on 'Brazilian Internal Taxes' GATT/CP.3/42, adopted 30 June 1949, II/181, 185, ¶ 16; United States—Taxes on Petroleum and Certain Imported Substances (*Superfund*), adopted on Jun. 17, 1987, B.I.S.D. 34S/136, ¶ 5.1.9 [hereinafter *Superfund* (1987)]; *Malt Beverages*, *supra* note 13, ¶ 5.6.
31. EEC—Payments and Subsidies Paid to Processors and Producers of Oilseeds and Related Animal-Feed Proteins, Panel Report adopted on 25 January 1990, B.I.S.D. 37S/86, ¶ 141 (emphasis added).
32. *Section 337*, *supra* note 23, ¶ 5.14.
33. Korea—Measures Affecting Imports of Fresh, Chilled and Frozen Beef, WT/DS 161, Appellate Body and Panel Report, as modified, adopted on Jan. 10, 2001, *available at* <http://www.wto.org/english/tratop_e/dispu_e/distab_e.htm> (last visited on Sep. 27, 2001) [hereinafter *Korean Beef* (2001)].
34. *Id.*, AB Report, ¶ 1.
35. *Id.*, Panel Report, ¶ 627.
36. *Id.*
37. *Id.*, AB Report, ¶ 134.
38. *Id.*, ¶¶ 137, 144.
39. *Id.*, ¶ 148.

AB, a more central element in establishing the consistency with Article III: 4 than facial discrimination itself is the test for 'disparate impact' to trade, which can be translated into scrutiny of the 'effective equality of opportunities.' Although the Panel also took this test seriously, it failed to carry out the test in practice. From the AB's 'disparate impact' analysis, one could easily conclude that the dual retail system had, in fact, resulted from an attempt to protect domestic beef producers against the imported beef. Nevertheless, although a finding of protection could be inferred from the AB's ruling, the AB itself never relied explicitly upon the identification of protectionist intent for its analysis. This ruling demonstrates that Article III: 4 can be interpreted in a less confrontational way, for the purpose of regulating Members, than the 'aim and effect' test, which highlights protectionist intent in establishing inconsistency with Article III:4.[40]

In a frustrating development, however, a divergent view adopted in a recent ruling by the AB was allowed to eclipse the coherent jurisprudence described in the preceding paragraph. Following the traditional jurisprudence, the Panel in *Asbestos* (2001) concluded that the EC had *de jure* treated imported chrysolite fibers and chrysolite-cement products in a less favorable manner than domestic substitute fibers (PVA, cellulose or glass fiber) and fibro-cement products, because the Decree did not impose the same ban on the latter group of products.[41] Although this issue was not appealed, the AB nonetheless left an *obiter dictum*, which was deeply problematic for its astounding departure from established jurisprudence. The AB found that:

> The term 'less favorable treatment' expresses the general principle, in Article III:1, that internal regulations 'should not be applied ... so as to afford protection to domestic production.' If there is 'less favorable treatment' of the group of 'like' imported products, there is, conversely, 'protection' of the group of 'like' domestic products.[42]

This *dictum* is unacceptable from the 'discrimination' perspective. As discussed above, the anti-protection requirement ('not so as to afford protection') under Article III: 1 does not directly inform Article III:4 in textual terms, unlike an opposing case under the second sentence of Article III:2 involving taxation aiming to protect domestic products against 'directly competitive or substitutable' foreign products.[43] In the same vein, the jurisprudence developed and established in *Banana III* (1997) clearly maintains that in the case of domestic regulations the anti-protection requirement is not necessary to show that those regulations violate Article III:4.[44]

---

40. Interestingly, the AB's 'disparate impact' test tends to blur the doctrinal distinction between *de jure* and *de facto* discrimination because both types of discrimination are equally subject to the test. Yet, in the case of *de jure* discrimination, it would be easier for a challenging party to establish a *prima facie* case of a violation of Article III: 4, while a defending party tends to be subject to a heavier burden in refuting it than is the case with *de facto* discrimination. Nonetheless, in view of the contemporary trend away from flat discrimination, the necessity of distinguishing between these two forms of discrimination is diminished somewhat.
41. *Asbestos*, Panel Report, *supra* note 16, Introduction, ¶ 8.115.
42. *Id.*, AB Report, ¶ 100.
43. *Compare* GATT 1994, *supra* note 2, art. III, ¶ 4 *with* ¶ 2.
44. *See supra* note 21.

In sum, as far as domestic regulations are concerned, 'discrimination' means something more than mere 'protection.' This is the very threshold that both text and jurisprudence of Article III: 4 obviously set for the purpose of interpreting 'less favorable treatment.' If we were to follow the line of argument presented by the AB in the foregoing *Asbestos* case, the goal of free trade would be seriously jeopardized since any discriminatory, yet non-protectionist measure, could easily escape the reach of Article III: 4, which would result in an inundation of *unilateral* regulatory measures. This is why the AB's dictum in paragraph 100 of the *Asbestos* Report is so problematic.

2.1.1.2 The Law of Market Access (Article XI: 1)

Provision

Article XI: 1 provides that:

> *No prohibitions or restrictions* other than duties, taxes or other charges, whether made effective through quotas, import or export licences or *other measures*, shall be instituted or maintained by any contracting party *on the importation* of any product of the territory of any other contracting party or on the exportation or sale for export of any product destined for the territory of any other contracting party.[45]

Draconian rule on market access

Article XI:1 is clear and unambiguous in prohibiting quantitative restrictions such as quotas. What is more, after stating unequivocally that 'no prohibitions or restrictions ... shall be instituted or maintained,' Article XI:1 goes on to extend the prohibition to 'other measures' that amount to quantitative restrictions. Domestic regulations fall within the purview of 'other measures,' within the meaning of Article XI:1.

This inflexible quality of the Article has naturally resulted in jurisprudential treatment in which the mere existence of a trade restriction itself would suffice to find a violation of the Article. In this context, the Panel in *Japanese Leather* (1984) observed that:

> [T]he existence of a quantitative restriction should be presumed to cause nullification or impairment not only because of any effect it had had on the volume of trade but also for other reasons e.g., it would lead to increased transaction costs and would create uncertainties which could affect investment plans.[46]

As for the scope of application, 'other measures' have been interpreted broadly by

45. GATT 1994, *supra* note 2, art. XI, ¶ 1 (emphasis added).
46. Japanese Measures on Imports of Leather, Panel Report adopted on 15/16 May 1984, B.I.S.D. 31S/94, 113, ¶ 55 [hereinafter *Japanese Leather* (1984)].

the GATT/WTO Panels and the AB, echoing the market access consideration. Accordingly, the modality of 'other measures' varies, ranging from non-mandatory 'administrative guideline'[47] to the 'minimum price system.'[48] The most frequently detected type of measure falling under 'other measures' within the meaning of Article XI:1 is the 'import ban,'[49] which is the unadorned prohibition of importation. Yet, this import ban differs little in its effects from 'domestic regulation,' other than the fact that it is enforced at the border. Under these circumstances, it has been disputed whether a given import ban should fall under Article III: 4 (National Treatment in Domestic Regulation) or Article XI:1 (Prohibition of Quantitative Restriction and Measures Equivalent to Quantitative Restriction).[50]

Infrequent invocation

Despite the abovementioned definite nature, Article XI:1 has not been applied very frequently. The first reason for this infrequent invocation is found in the 'historical' context of the old GATT. The possibility of invoking Article XI:1 was to a large extent reduced from the outset due to the fact that various exceptions and derogations overshadowed Article XI:1. Although there was widespread interest in restructuring the world economy through freer trade after World War II, political realities among contracting parties were not so accommodating. First, the proliferation of exceptions can be attributed to the decision of GATT framers to abort the establishment of the International Trade Organization (ITO) in favor of the Protocol of Provisional Application (PPA), which immediately proved its regulatory impotence by blatantly grandfathering in a great deal of existing legislation that could be viewed as inconsistent with general obligations like Article XI.[51]

On top of this, post-war macroeconomic conditions were devastating in most countries, compelling them to devise the so-called balance of payment (BOP) exception (Article XII), which was made generally applicable to all provisions including Article XI:1. In addition to traditional greenhouse industries like agriculture, many economically non-viable industries were also given special treatment vis-à-vis Article XI:1 through the waiver in Article XI:2 and XXV:5.[52] Moreover, as a general assistance to economic development, developing countries often controlled imports in order to safeguard their external financial positions

---

47. Japan—Trade in Semi-Conductors, Panel Report adopted on 4 May 1988, B.I.S.D. 35S/157–158, ¶ 117.
48. EEC—Programme of Minimum Import Prices, Licences and Surety Deposits for Certain Processed Fruits and Vegetables, Panel Report adopted on 18 October 1978, B.I.S.D. 25S/68, 99, ¶ 4.9.
49. Thailand—Restrictions on Importation of and Internal Taxes on Cigarettes, adopted on Nov. 7, 1990, B.I.S.D. 37S/200, ¶ 67 [hereinafter *Thai Cigarette* (1990)]; *Shrimp-Turtle* (1998), Panel Report, *supra* note 15, Introduction, ¶ 7. 13.
50. *See infra* § 2.1.1.3.
51. JOHN H. JACKSON ET AL., LEGAL PROBLEMS OF INTERNATIONAL ECONOMIC RELATIONS—CASES, MATERIALS AND TEXT ON THE NATIONAL AND INTERNATIONAL REGULATION OF TRANSNATIONAL ECONOMIC RELATIONS 296–300 (3d ed. 1995) [hereinafter JACKSON ET AL., INTERNATIONAL ECONOMIC RELATIONS].
52. *See id.*, at 421–422; The Quantitative Restrictions in the Major Trading Countries, Executive Branch GATT Studies, No. 6, 90–93 (1973), Subcomm. on International Trade of the Senate Comm. on Finance, 93d Cong., 2d Sess. 90–93 (compilation of 1973 Studies Prepared by the Executive Branch: Comm. Print. March, 1974).

(Article XVIII:B). In sum, all of these exceptions and derogations tended to shrink the use of Article XI:1. Although the aforementioned exceptions and derogations began to disappear in the eighties and nineties in response to changes in the underlying economic situations of these countries, this positive development cannot erase a half century of regulatory atrophy for Article XI:1.[53]

Another reason for such infrequent use of the Article is found in its textual structure, that is, an included interpretive note (Note *Ad* Article III) converts border measures under Article XI:1 to domestic regulations under Article III:4. The relationship between these provisions will be discussed below.

2.1.1.3 *The relationship between Article III:4 and Article XI:1*

Internal measure v. border measure

The conventional view of the relationship between these two provisions has been that Articles III: 4 and XI: 1 are mutually exclusive in scope of application, applying to *internal* measures and *border* measures, respectively. This distinction is based on the *stage* at which an imported product crosses a border and is subsequently marketed within a foreign territory.

Against this backdrop, the Panel in *Italian Tractor* (1958) took the view that the framers' intent was for Article III to treat domestic and imported products alike, once the latter had been *cleared through customs*.[54] The Panel in *FIRA* (1984) also observed that 'the General Agreement distinguishes between measures affecting the "importation" of products, which are regulated in Article XI:1, and those affecting "imported products," which are dealt with in Article III.'[55] Likewise, the panel in *Malt Beverages* (1992) ruled that the relevant determination with respect to the listing and delisting practices at issue was not whether they affected the *importation as such*, but whether they accorded less favorable treatment to *imported* wine vis-à-vis domestic wine.[56]

However, this seemingly logical distinction between Articles III:4 and XI:1 is undermined by the interpretive note (Note *Ad* Article III), as discussed below.

Interpretive note (Note Ad Article III)

Note *Ad* Article III in the Notes and Supplementary Provisions in Annex I to GATT 1994 states that:

---

53. This imperfection was to a large degree addressed at the launch of the new WTO system through the abrogation of such waivers and grandfathered rights. GATT 1994, ¶ 1 (emphasis added):
 1. The General Agreement on Tariffs and Trade 1994 ('GATT 1994') shall consist of:
  (a) the provisions in the General Agreement on Tariffs and Trade, dated 30 October 1947, annexed to the Final Act Adopted at the Conclusion of the Second Session of the Preparatory Committee of the United Nations Conference on Trade and Employment (*excluding the Protocol of Provisional Application*), as rectified, amended or modified by the terms of legal instruments which have entered into force before the date of entry into force of the WTO Agreement.
54. *Italian Tractor* (1958), *supra* note 24, ¶ 11.
55. *FIRA*, supra note 23, ¶ 5. 14.
56. *Malt Beverages*, *supra* note 13, ¶ 5.63.

> Any internal tax or other internal charge, or *any law, regulation or requirement* of the kind referred to in paragraph 1 *which applies to an imported product and to the like domestic product and is collected or enforced in the case of the imported product at the time or point of importation*, is nevertheless to be regarded as an internal tax or other internal charge, or a law, regulation or requirement of the kind referred to in paragraph 1, and is accordingly *subject to the provisions of Article III*.[57]

According to its legislative history, this interpretive note purports to cover internal taxations and regulations, which would normally fall under Article III, but which are collected or enforced at the border at the time of importation for 'administrative reasons.'[58] In parallel with this legislative history, the Panel in *Canadian Alcoholic Drinks* (1992) ruled that:

> ... according to the Note Ad Article III, a regulation is subject to the provisions of Article III if it 'applies to an imported product and to the like domestic product' *even if* it is 'enforced in case of the imported product *at the time or point of importation*'. The Panel found that, as the minimum prices were applied to both imported and domestic beer, they fell, according to this Note under Article III.[59]

Noticeably, the *Tuna I* (1991) Panel observed that even an 'equally, indistinctively applicable measure,' which applies both to imported and like domestic *products* in an origin-neutral way, should be '*product*-related' in order to be subject to the interpretive note and thus Article III: 4.[60] The Panel, accordingly, refused to apply the interpretive note to the US import ban on certain yellow fin tuna and their products on the grounds that such a ban was not borne by *products* as such, but by their *process and production methods*, namely the harvesting method relating to the incidental killing of dolphins.

Yet, it would be hard to consider the *Tuna I* ruling as the established jurisprudence, not only because the report was unadopted, but also because a subsequent WTO Panel report in *Shrimp-Turtle* (1998), confronted a similar fact pattern but elected not to adopt the '*product*-relatedness' test devised by the *Tuna I* Panel in order to determine whether the interpretive note should apply to the case. In the face of an import ban (embargo) on the shrimps, which had been harvested with a conventional fishing technology by non-certified countries, the Panel in *Shrimp-Turtle* (1998) found the embargo to be inconsistent with Article XI: 1, based simply on the plain texts of the Article and US Section 609(b)(1).[61]

As a matter of fact, the US embargo in *Shrimp-Turtle* (1998) could have been subject to the interpretive note, hence Article III:4, because the embargo was another

57. Annex 1, GATT 1994, *supra* note 2 (Ad *Article III*) (emphasis added).
58. Analytical Index, *supra* note 9, at 136.
59. *Canadian Alcoholic Drinks* (1992), *supra* note 23, ¶ 5.28 (emphasis added).
60. United States—Restrictions on Imports of Tuna, DS21/R, unadopted, 3 September 1991, B.I.S.D. 39S/155, 193–194, ¶¶ 5.9, 5.11–5.12 [hereinafter *Tuna I* (1991)].
61. *Shrimp-Turtle*, Panel Report, *supra* note 15, Introduction, ¶ 7. 16.

manifestation of US Section 609, which applied to imported and domestic shrimps alike. The particular modality of application, namely enforcement at the border at the time of importation, could have been justified by 'administrative reasons,' which would have represented the very rationale of the interpretive note. Therefore, it is fair to say that no crystal clear criteria have been developed so far for determining whether an import ban should fall within Article III:4 or Article XI:1 under the GATT/WTO jurisprudence.

From a comparative perspective, it may be worth noting a case under the US—Canada Free Trade Agreement (CUSFTA)[62] involving the same issue. Facing a US law ('an amendment to the Magnuson Act') prohibiting the sale or transport in or from the US of 'sub-sized lobsters,' the *Lobster* (1989)[63] Panel was split on the issue whether this US measure would fall under Article III:4 or XI:1. The majority view concluded that GATT Article III:4 should be applicable to this measure based on the interpretive note,[64] while the minority view observed that GATT Article XI:1 should be applicable to the measure since it constituted the import restriction (embargo) in the first place.[65]

No need to distinguish?

The interpretive note tends to *convert* equally, indistinctively applicable measures, which would have fallen under Article XI:1 because they are enforced at the border, to internal measures subject to Article III. If these equally applicable measures fell under Article XI:1, they would be subject to its strict discipline. Yet such measures are subject to a relatively less rigorous obligation under Article III:4. This aspect would provide a strong incentive for defendants to rely on the interpretive note in order to avoid the more burdensome legal obligations of Article XI.

Nonetheless, considering the 'market access' and 'predictability' concerns embedded in the 'trade impact test' under the parameter of 'no less favorable treatment' in Article III:4, it would be hard to say that the legal burden under Article III:4 is necessarily lighter than that imposed by Article XI. In other words, just as a complaint brought under Article XI:1 need only establish the existence of an import ban in order to challenge the ban, it is sufficient for a complaint brought under Article III:4 to establish the mere existence of a disparate impact resulting from an internal regulation. There is, in fact, no need to demonstrate actual trade effects or protectionist intentions under the latter provision.

In a number of decisions, the GATT jurisprudence also affirmed the doctrinal parallelism existing between Articles XI:1 and III:4. For instance, the *Superfund* (1987) Panel observed that:

62. United States—Canada Free Trade Agreement, Jan. 2, 1988, 27 I.L.M. 281 (1988) [hereinafter CUSFTA].
63. In the Matter of Lobsters from Canada, USA 89-1807-01, *available at* <http://www.sice.oas.org/DISPUTE/uscanfta/Uc89010e.asp> (last visited on Mar. 23, 2001) [hereinafter *Lobster*].
64. *Id.*, pt. 7.
65. *Id.*, pt. 8.

> The general prohibition of quantitative restrictions under Article XI . . . and the national treatment obligation of Article III ... have essentially the same rationale, namely to protect expectations of the contracting parties as to the *competitive relationship* between their products and those of the other contracting parties. Both articles are not only to protect current trade but also to create the *predictability* needed to plan future trade.[66]

Another factor that tends to diminish the necessity of distinguishing between Articles III:4 and XI:1 with respect to this issue, is the existence of Article XX (General Exceptions). Once an import ban is found to violate *either* provision, the defendants are most likely to rely on Article XX, the exception clause, in arguing that the measure in question is a justified exception under *either* provision. For instance, in the *Shrimp-Turtle* (1998) Panel Report, the US did not dispute that its embargo constituted an import restriction within the meaning of Article XI:1.[67] Rather, the US argument seemed to focus directly on Article XX for justification of its embargo as an exception.[68]

Recent jurisprudence: Asbestos (2001)

In *Asbestos* (2001) case, when examining the application of GATT 1994 to the French measure at issue, the question of which provision(s) should be applied to the measure was adjudicated in a preliminary sense. The import ban in the French Decree would fall under Article III:4 (National Treatment in Domestic Regulations) *or* Article XI:1 (Prohibition of Quantitative Restrictions and Measures Equivalent to Quantitative Restrictions) *or* both.

Canada argued that the Interpretive Note did not apply to the French measure since an 'explicit' import ban was only a *border* measure, not an *internal* measure.[69] Canada emphasized that 'France neither produces nor mines asbestos fibers on its territory.'[70] In contrast, the EC argued that the import ban is just the 'logical corollary' of the general prohibition on the use of asbestos and asbestos-containing products.[71] Therefore, the position of the EC was that Article III must apply since its measure applies to both domestic and imported products.[72]

The conflicting views of Canada and the EC can be understood from a strategic standpoint. For Canada, which was attacking the French measure, it would be preferable for the measure to fall under Article XI:1 because of its draconian format stressing 'market access.' The Canadian position, in other words, was that no prohibition whatsoever should be allowed in the first analysis, but that such prohibitions should only be justified *ex post* through the exceptions in Article XX. For the EC, however, which was defending its own measure, it would be more

---

66. *Superfund, supra* note 30, at ¶ 5.2.2 (emphasis added).
67. *Shrimp-Turtle*, Panel Report, *supra* note 15, Introduction, ¶ 7. 15.
68. *Id.*, ¶ 7. 13.
69. *Asbestos*, Panel Report, *supra* note 16, Introduction, ¶ 8.89.
70. *Id.*
71. *Id.*, ¶ 8.90.
72. *Id.*

advantageous for the measure to fall under Article III:4 so that it could be *redeemed* at that initial stage without the necessity of relying on Article XX for a finding that the measure in question was not 'discriminatory.'

Employing case law developed in *Section 337* (1989),[73] the Panel sided with the EC:

> The Panel notes in this connection that the fact that France no longer produces asbestos or asbestos-containing products does not suffice to make the Decree a measure falling under Article XI:1. It is in fact because the Decree prohibits the manufacture and processing of asbestos fibres that there is no longer any French production. The cessation of French production is the consequence of the Decree and not the reverse. Consequently, the Decree is a measure which 'applies to an imported product and to the like domestic product' within the meaning of Note *Ad Article III*.[74]

As the Panel's ruling was not appealed, it can be said that the decision in *Asbestos* constitutes the authoritative case law on this point. Accordingly, to a considerable degree, the *Asbestos* case seems to have settled this controversial issue of whether an import ban falls under Article III:4 or XI:1, though, as observed above, the issue may be not of great significance in practice.

2.1.1.4 The Law of Justification (Article XX)

Provision

> Subject to the requirement that such measures are not applied in a manner which would constitute a means of arbitrary or unjustifiable discrimination between countries where the same conditions prevail, or a disguised restriction on international trade, nothing in this Agreement shall be construed to prevent the adoption or enforcement by any contracting party of measures:
> (a) necessary to protect public morals;
> (*b*) necessary to protect human, animal or plant life or health;
> (*c*) relating to the importations or exportations of gold or silver;
> (*d*) necessary to secure compliance with laws or regulations which are not inconsistent with the provisions of this Agreement, including those relating to customs enforcement, the enforcement of monopolies operated under paragraph 4 of Article II and Article XVII, the protection of patents, trade marks and copyrights, and the prevention of deceptive practices;
> (*e*) relating to the products of prison labour;
> (*f*) imposed for the protection of national treasures of artistic, historic or archaeological value;
> (*g*) relating to the conservation of exhaustible natural resources if such measures are made effective in conjunction with restrictions on domestic production or consumption;

73. *See supra* note 23.
74. *Id.*, ¶ 8.91

(*h*) undertaken in pursuance of obligations under any intergovernmental commodity agreement which conforms to criteria submitted to the CONTRACTING PARTIES and not disapproved by them or which is itself so submitted and not so disapproved;
(*i*) involving restrictions on exports of domestic materials necessary to ensure essential quantities of such materials to a domestic processing industry during periods when the domestic price of such materials is held below the world price as part of a governmental stabilization plan; *Provided* that such restrictions shall not operate to increase the exports of or the protection afforded to such domestic industry, and shall not depart from the provisions of this Agreement relating to nondiscrimination;
(*j*) essential to the acquisition or distribution of products in general or local short supply; *Provided* that any such measures shall be consistent with the principle that all contracting parties are entitled to an equitable share of the international supply of such products, and that any such measures, which are inconsistent with the other provisions of the Agreement shall be discontinued as soon as the conditions giving rise to them have ceased to exist. The CONTRACTING PARTIES shall review the need for this subparagraph not later than 30 June 1960.

Overview

Article XX is structured as a 'general' exception. Therefore, any material obligation under the GATT can be made subject to Article XX. Yet, in most cases Articles III:4 and XI:1 are the two representative obligations whose violations are to be justified under Article XX. This 'dichotomy' between *trade*-related *obligations* and *regulation*-related *exceptions* reflects fundamental characteristics of the GATT.[75] This dichotomy, in itself, voices a pro-trade bias, as under the dichotomy, legitimate regulatory objectives are subordinated as exceptions, which are examined only *after* violations of trade-related obligations are found. Yet, the dichotomy is insurmountable within the GATT because it is inherent and embedded in the black letter law.

Article XX consists of preambular language (chapeau), and a rather anachronistic list of ten specific exceptions. Although this purports to be an exhaustive list, most of the items are in fact fossils, reflecting not contemporary realities but pressing concerns from the time of the Article's adoption in the forties. In fact, only three items (paragraphs (b), (d) and (g)) out of ten ever figured significantly in GATT jurisprudence. Moreover, the list is closed to the addition of any new regulatory objectives, such as consumer protection. On top of these inherent weaknesses, actual interpretations of this exception under the old GATT were very strict, allowing no single case of justification.

75. Professor Donald McRae described this pro-trade dichotomy as a 'hierarchy' between substantive obligations and exceptions to those obligations. *See* Donald M. McRae, *GATT Article XX and the Appellate Body*, *in* NEW DIRECTIONS IN INTERNATIONAL ECONOMIC LAW: ESSAYS IN HONOR OF JOHN H. JACKSON 232 (Marco Bronckers & Reinhard Quick eds. 2000).

Chapeau

According to the *traveau préparatoire*, the chapeau was originally inserted into the exception clause in order to prevent any abuse or misuse of the exception for the purpose of 'indirect protection.'[76] As a reflection of this rather modest role, invocations of the chapeau under the old GATT regime were rare. In addition, panel interpretations of the chapeau adhered closely to the text in an effort to remain faithful to its ordinary meaning.

In terms of 'arbitrary or unjustifiable discrimination,' it seems that GATT panels interpreted the phrase to mean 'targeted' discrimination that singled out particular countries for discrimination. For instance, the *Canadian Tuna* (1982) Panel ruled that the US measure against imports of tuna and tuna products from Canada was not necessarily arbitrary or unjustifiable discrimination, because similar measures had been applied against imports from *other* countries for similar reasons.[77] Likewise, the *Automotive Spring Assemblies* (1983) Panel viewed that the US exclusion order was not applied in a manner that would constitute a means of arbitrary or unjustifiable discrimination because the measure was launched against imports of certain automotive spring assemblies manufactured in violation of a valid US patent 'from *all* foreign sources, and not just from Canada.'[78]

In terms of 'disguised restriction[s] on international trade,' GATT panels seem to have equated this element with the 'publication' requirement. For instance, the *Canadian Tuna* (1982) Panel observed that the US import ban should not be considered a disguised restriction on international trade because the ban was published as a trade measure.[79] In the same vein, the *Automotive Spring Assemblies* (1983) Panel concluded that the US exclusion order was not applied in a manner that constituted a disguised restriction on international trade, taking into account various considerations including the fact that the exclusion order was published in the Federal Register.[80]

Necessary

As a general rule, the necessary test has had draconian effects in practice. Its derivative test—the 'least-trade-restrictive' test—has often provoked somewhat emotional reactions from parties engaged in sensitive sectors, such as the environment or human health. This is no trivial issue, considering that most cases involving Article XX exceptions emerge from precisely these sectors. The dogmatic tendency of trade tribunals to prioritize free trade principles and subordinate other social concerns has often frustrated, and sometimes even infuriated domestic governments, regulatory agencies and various NGOs. An interpretive process,

76. ANALYTICAL INDEX, *supra* note 9, at 563–64; McRae, *supra* note 75, at 227.
77. United States—Prohibition of Imports of Tuna and Tuna Products from Canada, Panel Report adopted on 22 February 1982, B.I.S.D. 29S/91, 108, ¶ 4.8 [hereinafter *Canadian Tuna* (1982)].
78. United States—Imports of Certain Automotive Spring Assemblies, adopted on 26 May 1983, B.I.S.D. 30S/107, 125, ¶¶ 54–55 [hereinafter *Automotive Spring Assemblies* (1983)].
79. *Canadian Tuna*, *supra* note 77, ¶ 4.8.
80. *Automotive Spring Assemblies*, *supra* note 78, ¶ 56.

seeking the least trade restrictive measure or the most proportionate measure, was often criticized for being a kind of judicial legislation that exceeded that traditional judicial function.[81] As a consequence, numerous activists, including some NGOs, have questioned the legitimacy and *raison d'être* of the multilateral trading system as a whole, while certain domestic constituencies have lamented their loss of sovereignty.

For instance, in the *Thai Cigarette* (1990) case, the old GATT panel rejected a local need to restrict the importation of tobacco as flatly unnecessary to protect human health on the grounds that this measure was not the least trade restrictive.[82] The *Thai Cigarette* Panel concluded that the import restrictions could be considered necessary '*only if* there were *no* alternative measure consistent with the General Agreement or less inconsistent with it, which Thailand could reasonably be expected to employ to achieve its health policy objectives.'[83] The Panel's decision left a serious question regarding whether a measure should be always the *least* trade-restrictive to be justified as necessary, and, even if so, *who* would be the more relevant (or legitimate) arbiter for the purpose of determining what is the least trade restrictive regulatory measure under a specific local situation.

More problematically, the Panel, in the course of its ruling, emphasized that *other* countries had introduced 'strict, non-discriminatory labeling and ingredient disclosure regulations' in similar situations to protect people from the harm of cigarettes.[84] The reference to regulatory practices of other countries, including *developed* countries, strongly implied that Thailand should also adopt the same or equivalent measures to attain its regulatory goal, namely the protection of human health. This attitude is very troubling because it is almost tantamount to the Panel's imposition of a certain type of measure that it deems desirable when it *interprets* Article XX (b). Such behavior would truly be excessive, a significant step beyond the traditional judicial function.

Moreover, judicial activism in such cases is not only problematic in theory, but also dangerous in practice, as it fails to take into account the special concerns that arise in a particular regulatory environment—issues such as the degree of economic development, patterns of culture, or the nature and strength of local demand. In the unpleasant, yet irrefutable, North and South context, the foregoing hermeneutics centering on the least trade restrictive measure may tend to dilute the comparative advantage of developing countries by unfairly leveling the playing fields.[85] In the

81. Regarding the reaction to this criticism, *see infra* sub-sec. 2.1.3.6.
82. 81. In sum, the Panel considered that there were various measures consistent with the General Agreement which were reasonably available to Thailand to control the quality and quantity of cigarettes smoked and which, taken together, could achieve the health policy goals that the Thai government pursues by restricting the importation of cigarettes inconsistently with Article XI:1. The Panel found therefore that Thailand's practice of permitting the sale of domestic cigarettes, while not permitting the importation of foreign cigarettes was an inconsistency with the General Agreement not 'necessary' within the meaning of Article XX(b).

    Thai Cigarette, *supra* note 49, ¶ 81.
83. *Id.*, ¶ 75 (emphasis added).
84. *Id.*, ¶ 77.
85. *See* JAGDISH BHAGWATI, A STREAM OF WINDOWS: UNSETTLING REFLECTIONS ON TRADE, IMMIGRATION AND DEMOCRACY 247–68 (1998) [hereinafter A STREAM OF WINDOWS].

same vein, many pundits[86] have criticized the Panel's sheer dismissal of the World Health Organization's (WHO) requested opinion, strongly suggesting that in a developing country like Thailand, a ban on the advertisement and even the importation of tobacco could be an effective measure to protect human health.[87]

Relating

The 'relating' test under the old GATT resulted in scrutiny of domestic legislation that was not only intrusive, but also *regressive*, despite the Panel's acknowledgement that the relating test covered a wider range of measures than did the necessary test.[88] In *Herring and Salmon* (1988), the Panel stated that even if a trade measure is not essential, i.e., unnecessary for the conservation of an exhaustible natural resource, the measure should still be 'primarily aimed at' conservation in order to be regarded as 'relating' to

---

86. *See e.g.*, Salman Bal, *International Free Trade Agreements and Human Rights: Reinterpreting Article XX of the GATT*, 10 MINN. J. GLOBAL TRADE 62, 85 (2001); Bruce Neuling, *The Shrimp-Turtle Case: Implications for Article XX of the GATT and the Trade and Environment Debate*, 22 LOY. L.A. INT'L & COMP. L. REV. 1, 18–9 (1999); David P. Fidler, *Neither Science Nor Shamans: Globalization of Markets and Health in the Developing World*, 7 IND. J. GLOBAL LEGAL STUD. 191, 200–1 (1999) (criticizing the Thai Cigarette Panel's interpretation of 'necessary to protect human health') [hereinafter *Neither Science Nor Shamans*].

87. 52. According to the representatives of the WHO, ... Locally-produced cigarettes were unlike those manufactured in western countries in that sophisticated manufacturing techniques such as the use of additives and flavourings, or the downward adjustment of tar and nicotine were not generally available, or were primitive in comparison to the techniques used by the multinational tobacco companies. These differences were of public health concern because they made smoking western cigarettes very easy for groups who might not otherwise smoke, such as women and adolescents, and create the false illusion among many smokers that these brands were safer than the native ones which consumers were quitting. ... If the multinational tobacco companies entered the market, the poorly-financed public health programmes would be unable to compete with the marketing budgets of these companies, as had been the case in other Asian countries whose markets had been opened. As a result, cigarette consumption and, in turn, death and disease attributable to smoking would increase.

    53. ... The health effects of cigarette additives were being analyzed by the U.S. Department of Health and Human Services which considered this task to be 'enormously complex and expensive.' Serious concerns about the presence in cigarettes of certain additives had been raised by the American Health Foundation which acted as a consultant to the Department of Health and Human Services on this issue. However, there was no scientific evidence that one type of cigarette was more harmful to health than another. ...

    55. ... Multinational tobacco companies had routinely circumvented national restrictions on advertising through indirect advertising and a variety of other techniques. ...

    56. The representatives of the WHO stated that their organization had convened in 1982 an Expert Committee on 'Smoking Control Strategies in Developing Countries' which had made a number of recommendations designed to reduce smoking. In particular, this Committee, many of whose recommendations had already been adopted in Thailand, had recommended to developing countries that all advertising and promotion of tobacco products be prohibited, including through the sponsorship of sporting events, that where tobacco is a commercial crop, its role be reduced in the economy through alternative use of land and labor for which the assistance of organizations within the UN system, such as FAO and the World Bank, would be sought. The same Committee had recommended to developed countries, *inter alia*, that any action possible be taken to curb activities aimed at promoting and selling tobacco products and that any exported tobacco products conform to standards obtaining in the exporting country in terms of health warnings, emissions and product information.

    Thai Cigarette, supra note 49.

88. *See* Canada—Measures Affecting Exports of Unprocessed Herring and Salmon, adopted on Mar. 22, 1988, B.I.S.D. 35S/98, 113–115, ¶¶ 4.4–4.7 [hereinafter *Herring and Salmon* (1988)].

conservation for the purpose of Article XX (g).[89] The Panel then concluded that the imposition by Canada of a limitation in purchasing unprocessed herring and salmon only with respect to foreign processors and consumers, could not be deemed primarily aimed at the conservation of salmon and herring stocks.[90]

This interpretation is a form of unacceptable regressivism that transforms a justification stage (exception) to an initial violation stage (general obligation), with the exception clause practically nullified in the process. Ultimately, such regressivism has the effect of ignoring the legitimate concern for domestic environmental protection falling within the ambit of Article XX (g)—i.e., conservation of exhaustible natural resources—because justification through Article XX(g) is nearly impossible under such an interpretation.[91] Consequently, a discriminatory measure, if it is distinctively applicable, would never benefit from Article XX(g), but would only result in confirmation of the initial finding of violation.

2.1.1.5 Summary and prospect

Under GATT, two different doctrines exist to prevent trade-restrictive or trade-prohibitive effects caused by domestic regulations: the Law of National Treatment (Article III:4) and the Law of Market Access (Article XI:1). Although one might expect greater reliance upon the draconian text of Article XI:1, Article III:4 has been more frequently invoked because of the existence of the interpretive note and the waivers and other derogations to Article XI:1. Nevertheless, it is significant that a rigorous jurisprudence motivated by 'market access' concerns has prevailed even under Article III:4, with such issues as 'no actual trade effects,' 'equal opportunities for competition' and 'predictability' given priority. This market access consideration tends to result in convergence of the doctrinal function of Articles III:4 and XI:1 under GATT.

Yet, this prevalent market access consideration represents, on the obverse side, a strong 'pro-trade bias' that has tended to restrict the regulatory autonomy of contracting parties (Members). Legitimate policy objectives are structurally subordinated as 'exceptions' under Article XX to general pro-trade obligations such as those set forth in Articles III:4 and XI:1. Moreover, this exception clause is an 'exhaustive' list, most of which has been obsolete since its inception a half century ago. More importantly, even these imperfect exceptions were never really embraced due to strict interpretative postures such as the one reflected in the 'least trade-

89. *Id.*

90. *Id.*

91. In the same vein, the Appellate Body in *Gasoline* noted that:

> One problem with the reasoning in that paragraph is that the Panel asked itself whether the 'less favourable treatment' of imported gasoline was 'primarily aimed at' the conservation of natural resources, rather than whether the 'measure,' i.e. the baseline establishment rules, were 'primarily aimed at' conservation of clean air. In our view, the Panel here was in error in referring to its legal conclusion on Article III:4 instead of the measure in issue. The result of this analysis is to turn Article XX on its head. Obviously, there had to be a finding that the measure provided 'less favourable treatment' under Article III:4 before the Panel examined the 'General Exceptions' contained in Article XX. That, however, is a conclusion of law. The chapeau of Article XX makes it clear that it is the 'measures' which are to be examined under Article XX(g), and not the legal finding of 'less favourable treatment.

Gasoline, AB Report, *supra* note 14, Introduction, at 16.

restrictive means' test. Of course, this pro-trade bias is to some extent understandable, considering the high spirit of the old GATT regime that aimed at preventing another destructive economic balkanization and reconstructing the world economy through the promotion of free trade. In fact, what GATT sought to accomplish during its half-century history extends beyond the narrow scope of 'anti-protection' to something more closely approximating 'market integration.'

Although it cannot be denied that this strong pro-trade bias contributed greatly to global economic growth, one might still question whether the current GATT/WTO system could sustain such a high level of free market ideology in the face of the Members' anxieties over regulatory self-determinism. Most of all, the breadth and depth of social regulations was less dramatic in the old GATT era than it is today. The degree of state intervention into the everyday lives of ordinary citizens was limited in comparison with what is common today. Accordingly, actual trade disputes growing out of domestic regulations did not proliferate under the old GATT regime, notwithstanding its strongly pro-trade jurisprudence. More recently, however, these situations have changed. Under the banner of 'welfare states,' modern governments have begun to respond actively to the regulatory demands of citizens in such areas as the environment and human health. Moreover, new scientific discoveries and technological development have led to an increase in the number and complexity of regulations.

Under these changed circumstances, the pattern of pro-trade bias witnessed under the old GATT regime is certainly problematic and may lead to 'regulatory failure.' Yet, if the traditional goal of free trade were to be unduly compromised by these new regulatory demands, that would constitute another type of failure, namely 'trade failure.' This *dual* crisis of regulatory and trade failure has emerged as the single greatest challenge to the contemporary global trading system.

2.1.2 A DILEMMA OF DUAL CRISIS

2.1.2.1 Regulatory failure

The pro-trade bias is structured and embedded in the GATT. In the first place, the term 'affecting' under Article III:4 tends to preordain the 'interface' between trade and other non-trade social values. To wit, all domestic measures (laws, regulations and requirements), which aim to attain those social values and yet affect trade activities, fall under Article III:4. However, Article III:4 governs this interface in the sense that it regulates domestic regulations affecting trade activities, not trade activities affecting domestic regulations. On account of this structural pro-trade bias, the interface is expressed, for instance, as 'trade and the environment,' not as 'the environment and trade.'

Of course, the GATT contains the 'exception' clause[92] through which essential trade canons (general obligations), such as the national treatment principle, can be compromised by certain non-trade (social) policy objectives, such as the protection

92. GATT 1994, *supra* note 2, art. XX (a)–(j).

of human health listed in Article XX. Ironically, however, the very existence of these exceptions and resultant 'dichotomy'[93] (general obligations and their exceptions) tends to nurture the *pro*-trade bias as exceptions are taken into account only *after* general obligations are found to be violated, never the other way around or even simultaneously.[94] This dichotomy tends in the first place to take a very suspicious stance toward any measure in question. It is also likely to produce a situation in which a given measure may be too hastily determined to be a violation, due to the existence of a second defense (exceptions). Furthermore, overwhelmed by this bias, GATT panels have interpreted exceptions narrowly,[95] an approach necessary to enshrine canons, which are general obligations like national treatment, without becoming unduly diluted by those exceptions.[96] All these problematic features resulting from the dichotomy might have been mitigated if the exception clause had been frequently accepted so that non-trade social values would be adequately upheld and respected. Unfortunately, however, throughout the old GATT panel history, not a single Article XX justification ever succeeded.[97]

On top of this, the list of general exceptions in GATT Article XX is both exhaustive and obsolete. Its limited range of non-trade regulatory objectives is troubling in itself. Indeed, it is quite difficult to imagine that contemporary social concerns could be fully addressed by a mere ten exceptions. Moreover, only two or three items[98] of the ten have ever really been used in practice, the rest being fossils.[99] In fact, this limited list, which was designed about a half century ago, has never been amended. Thus, the old list reflects the regulatory sensitivities of the 1940s[100] and

93. *See* Daniel A. Farber & Robert E. Hudec, *Free Trade and the Regulatory State: A GATT's-Eye View of the Dormant Commerce Clause*, 47 VAND. L. REV. 1401, 1427 (1994) [hereinafter *A GATT's-Eye View*] (noting that Article III:4-*cum*-Article XX separates the question of violation of general obligation from that of regulatory justification).

94. *Cf.* Hannes L. Schloemann & Stefan Ohlhoff, *'Constitutionalization' and Dispute Settlement in the WTO: National Security as an Issue of Competence*, 93 AM. J. INT'L L. 424, 451 (1999) (arguing that the WTO dispute settlement system's ability to incorporate the necessary elements of policy consideration to avoid a 'protrade bias' will be the barometer of the constitutionalization of global order); Daniel K. Tarullo, *Norms and Institutions in Global Competition Policy*, 94 AM. J. INT'L L. 478, 504 (2000) (arguing that rules on diverse policy issues such as food safety and the environment *within* the trading system tend to develop into trade policy instruments rather than regulatory harmonization).

95. *See e.g.*, United States-Restrictions on Imports of Cotton and Man-Made Fiber Underwear, WT/DS24/R, Panel Report, adopted as modified by the Appellate Body on Feb. 25, 1997, ¶ 7. 21, *available at* <http://www.wto.org/english/tratop_e/dispu_e/distab_e.htm> (last visited on Sep. 27, 2001); Canada–Import Restrictions on Ice Cream and Yogurt, Panel Report adopted on Dec. 5, 1989, B.I.S.D. 36S/68, 84, ¶ 59. *See also* Joel P. Trachtman, *The Domain of WTO Dispute Resolution*, 40 HARV. INT'L L. J. 333, 341 (1999).

96. This tendency—a narrow interpretation of exceptions—was even welcomed as a general principle of law. G. Richard Shell, *Trade Legalism and International Relations Theory: An Analysis of the World Trade Organization*, 44 DUKE L.J. 829, 907 n.349 (1995).

97. *See* Robert Howse, *Managing the Interface between International Trade Law and the Regulatory State: What Lessons Should (and Should Not) Be Drawn from the Jurisprudence of the United States Dormant Commerce Clause*, *in* REGULATORY BARRIERS AND THE PRINCIPLE OF NON-DISCRIMINATION IN WORLD TRADE LAW 142 (Thomas Cottier & Petros C. Mavroidis eds. 2000) [hereinafter Howse, *Interface*].

98. GATT 1947, *supra* note 2, art. XX, ¶¶ (b), (d) and (g).

99. *Id.*, ¶¶ (a), (c), (e), (f), (h), (i) and (j).

100. I owe this insight to Professor Joseph Weiler. *See also* Mike Meier, *GATT, WTO, and the Environment: To What Extent Do GATT/WTO Rules Permit Member Nations to Protect the Environment When*

fails to echo contemporary regulatory concerns such as consumer protection. This *lacuna* weakens the effectiveness of the WTO and at times leads interested parties to question its legitimacy, thereby undermining its *raison d'etre*.

Moreover, as discussed above, an interpretive tool for justification, *e.g.*, the 'necessary test,' which was paraphrased as the 'least trade-restrictive test' in the old GATT jurisprudence, has proven difficult for contracting parties to satisfy. Still, the necessary test tends to be overly influential in that GATT panels, not domestic regulators, determine whether a certain measure is necessary or unnecessary to attain a certain regulatory objective based on hypothetical policy alternatives.[101] In addition, this test is likely to focus mainly on a portion of a statute (or regulation) itself in terms of its language and structure. Nevertheless, unless a statute in question is dispositive as such or else grants no discretion for implementation, a panel cannot rightly assume any general or specific impact on trade before its actual application; nor can a panel strike down the statute as a whole simply because it happened to be applied once in an inconsistent way with the provisions of GATT.

In sum, the conventional jurisprudence on justification is both superficial and imposing in that it tends only to condemn, rather than respect, legitimate policy objectives as trade restrictive, eventually dismissing them. Consequently, this approach is likely to lead a sovereign state to lose or to sacrifice its own regulatory autonomy in various areas of social policy, solely, for the collective aim of efficiently allocating resources or increasing the general level of welfare. In the same vein, a sovereign state could fail to achieve its own optimal level of regulation relating to certain fields of social concern, such as environment or human health, because the draconian free trade discipline will not tolerate the trade-restrictive impact of a given regulation.[102]

Lastly, but not least, a pro-trade *ethos* is likely to lead states to establish competitive strategies and practices based solely on an efficiency-driven philosophy, which is 'dysfunctional and at best disruptive.'[103] In other words, a free-trade-only philosophy may result in the so-called 'regulatory race-to-the-bottom' or 'regulatory arbitrage.'[104] Likewise, in the absence of a sufficient degree of global harmonization, which is extremely difficult to attain, different judicial responses in different jurisdictions to the same regulatory challenge may in themselves complicate the attainment of certain regulatory goals. This complication is particularly likely when such goals are global rather than local. All these circumstances can be characterized

contd

Doing So Adversely Affects Trade?, 8 COLO. J. INT'L ENVTL. L. & POL'Y 241, 281 (1997) (observing that the old GATT is a 'relic of 1947, when economic development was the priority').

101. *See supra* sub-sec. 2.1.1.4.

102. *See e.g.*, Corinne Sam, *World Trade Organization Caught in the Middle: Are TEDs the Only Way Out?*, 29 ENVTL. L. 185, 189 (1999); Sean T. Fox, *Responding to Climate Change: The Case for Unilateral Trade Measures to Protect the Global Atmosphere*, 84 GEO. L.J. 2499, 2532 (1996); Stanley M. Spracker & David C. Lundsgaard, *Dolphins and Tuna: Renewed Attention on the Future of Free Trade and Protection of the Environment*, 18 COLUM. J. ENVTL. L. 385, 399–401 (1993).

103. William W. Bratton et al., *Introduction: Regulatory Competition and Institutional Evolution*, *in* REGULATORY COMPETITION AND COORDINATION, *supra* note 13, at 3.

104. *See generally* Amir Licht, *Regulatory Arbitrage for Real: International Securities Regulation in a World of Interacting Securities Markets*, 38 VA. J. INT'L L. 563 (1998). *But see* ADRIENNE HÉRITIER ET AL., RINGING THE CHANGE IN EUROPE: REGULATORY COMPETITION AND THE TRANSFORMATION OF THE STATE 1 (1996) (finding that 'European clean-air policy is the product of regulative contest between leading Member States').

as situations of 'regulatory failure,'[105] which so often infuriates many governments as well as domestic constituencies in general.[106]

2.1.2.2 Trade failure

Confronting the aforementioned regulatory failure under the GATT system, one might simply suggest that panels and the AB should reduce their interpretive rigor in such a way that Members are able to secure adequate breathing room to freely exercise their regulatory rights, thereby safeguarding certain legitimate policy values. However, any unbridled regulatory libertarianism employed by Members could also be disastrous. In other words, if Members were allowed to enforce their own regulatory policies unilaterally and without restraint against their trading partners,

---

105. Some scholars have highlighted various aspects of such regulatory failure. Though their concerns may be completely relevant and legitimate, their solutions remain largely deficient. In other words, such scholars are good at issue-spotting, but fail to render workable prescriptions, especially in terms of hermeneutics. *See, e.g.*, Philip M. Nichols, *GATT Doctrine*, VA. J. INT'L L. 379, 464 (1996) (observing that 'to the extent the World Trade Organization translates GATT doctrine into a rigidity that consistently exalts trade above all other social values, it could seriously undermine the free trade regime's popular acceptance'); Philip M. Nichols, *Trade without Values*, 90 NW. U. L. REV. 625 (1996). The author warns that the current WTO system's failure to reflect the 'fundamental nature of societal values' may make it hard for Member states to support the system. He argues, therefore, that the WTO must create new exceptions, in addition to pre-existing ones, that would permit Member states to conduct certain domestic regulatory policies to enshrine legitimate societal values such as 'environment,' 'labor' and 'cultural identity' either through amendment of the treaty or doctrinal innovation, as long as their trade effect is incidental. However, the amendment solution seems nearly impossible at present; few people would favor such idea. Doctrinal innovation similar to that observed in the European Court of Justice may be a good candidate, but the problem is *how* to do it. Nichols fails to suggest a clear and applicable hermeneutics. *See also* Jeffrey L. Dunoff, *The Death of the Trade Regime*, 10 EUR. J. INT'L L. (1999). The author argues that the panels could delegitimize the whole WTO system if they continue to deal with 'trade and ...' issues. He is basically concerned about the 'pro-trade' bias embedded in the GATT/WTO system which may overlook or bypass important social values. As a strategy for overcoming this problem, he suggests that the WTO panels avoid addressing the merits of 'trade and ...' which is analogous to the practice of judicial caution (*e.g.*, political question doctrine) in U.S. constitutional jurisprudence. However, considering the ever-increasing interface between trade and non-trade (societal or social) values, which is inevitably geared by ever-increasing interdependency, such an extremely deferential approach cannot but be overly evasive. The whole point lies in the solemn fact that people want the WTO to take on hard cases. Avoidance of such complicated issues, in fact, not only imperils the legitimacy of the WTO, but also undermines its *raison d'etre*.
106. Some scholars argue that the WTO is not the best forum in which to address non-trade social regulations because it lacks relevant institutional and technical expertise. *See e.g.*, David A. Wirth, *International Trade Agreements: Vehicles for Regulatory Reform?*, 1997 U. CHI. LEGAL F. 331 (1997); David A. Wirth, *The Role of Science in the Uruguay Round and NAFTA Trade Disciplines*, 27 CORNELL INT'L L. J. 817,859 (1994) (maintaining that the WTO panels should be 'highly deferential' to the scientific determinations of national regulatory agencies). This proposition may be true in terms of the 'rule-making' dimension. When it comes to judicial scrutiny on domestic regulations, however, panels or the Appellate Body cannot declare '*non-liquet*' simply because the WTO has no substantive regulatory agreements directly addressing the issues in question, in which case panels can be assisted by various outside experts, just like domestic courts. Understanding on Rules and Procedures Governing the Settlement of Disputes, Annex 2 of the WTO Agreement, *supra* note 1, Introduction, art. 13 [hereinafter DSU]. *But cf.* Michael J, Trebilcock & Robert Howse, *Trade Liberalization and Regulatory Diversity: Reconciling Competitive Markets with Competitive Politics*, 6 EUR. J. L. & ECON. 5, 28 (1998) (arguing the case for 'substantial national political autonomy in formulating domestic regulatory and related policies, even though such policies will often have significant impacts on resulting trade flows').

exporters would face serious trade barriers, with free trade becoming sacrificed enormously in the process. Even in the absence of a disguised form of protection, regulatory unilateralism and the resultant phenomenon of regulatory heterogeneity tend to hinder and impede international trade in various ways.

First, if Member States issue regulatory standards that are irreconcilable with each other, any producer who wishes to export products to foreign countries would be forced to maintain multiple production lines matching multiple regulatory jurisdictions. Considering the ever-growing state of economic interdependence and integration, to say nothing of the new and highly efficient phenomenon of 'electronic commerce,' regulatory multiplicity threatens to prevent huge potential gains from trade for producers who wish to expand their markets. Moreover, while large multinational enterprises (MNEs) may survive the proliferation of different regulatory jurisdictions due to economies of scale resulting from their huge market shares, small and medium-sized enterprises (MSEs) lacking such economies of scale would suffer most. These consequences would undoubtedly undermine the prosperity of international commerce.

More seriously, if some Member States were to adopt 'trade sanctions' as a bulwark for their own domestic regulations, and then unilaterally imposed such sanctions in response to a violation by another Member State, fatal trade wars would likely follow. This could possibly lead to a state of economic balkanization reminiscent of interwar history. To complicate things further, most developing countries, and particularly the least-developed countries, cannot possibly afford the luxury of costly compliance with demanding and sophisticated regulations enacted by developed countries. Under these circumstances, forced compliance would offset any comparative advantages because of the associated higher costs. Nor do many developing countries possess the technical capacity to comply with such regulations.[107] Nonetheless, some domestic constituencies of developed countries argue for a 'level playing field' in order to realize their own version of 'fair trade.'[108] Yet, leveling the playing field may seem 'unfair' to developing countries, as it would result in the loss of their comparative advantages. Indeed, developing countries often suspect that such arguments represent camouflaged forms of protection,[109]

---

107. In this specific context, as the SPS Article IV (Equivalence) provides, the importing developed countries should not ban or restrict the exporting developing countries' health and safety measures simply because they are different, if the health and safety result is 'equivalent' to that of the importing countries' own measures. *See* WTO, *WTO News: 2000 News Items (WTO Highlights January–August 2000), available at* <www.wto.org/english/news_e/news00_e.htm> (last visited on Jan. 19, 2001).

108. Regarding the 'fair trade' and 'free trade' debate, *see e.g.*, B.A. Langille, *General Reflections on the Relationship of Trade and Labor (Or Fair Trade is Free Trade's Destiny), in* FAIR TRADE AND HARMONIZATION: PREREQUISITES FOR FREE TRADE? (vol. 2, Legal Analysis) 231 (Jagdish Bhagwati & Robert E. Hudec eds., 1996); E. de Wet, *Labor Standards in the Globalized Economy: The Inclusion of a Social Clause in the General Agreement on Tariffs and Trade/World Trade Organization*, 17 HUM. RTS. Q. 443 (1995).

109. If the momentum for international trade is lost, then the specter of protectionism and interventionism will emerge. In this vein, Alan Greenspan once warned that when positive trends in economic growth subside, the support for market-oriented resource allocation will diminish and the latent forces of protectionism and state interventionism will start to surface in many countries, including the U.S. *See Greenspan Defends Globalization*, WTOWatch, August 25 2000, *available at* <www.wtowatch.org/news/index.cfm?ID=2166>(last visited on Jan. 19, 2001). Often, strict domestic regulations are in consideration of powerful domestic industries, which David Vogel coined 'Baptist-bootlegger alliance.' *See* Howse, *Interface*, *supra* note 97, at 147 (quoting David Vogel, TRADING UP: CONSUMER AND ENVIRONMENTAL PROTECTION IN A GLOBAL ECONOMY 20–22 (1995)).

such as 'green protectionism'[110] or 'blue protectionism.'[111]

Furthermore, the existing developmental tension tends to be exacerbated by the spread of global poverty[112] and the consequent yawning income gap among trading partners, despite the ambitions of the WTO system. It cannot be denied that the global marketplace will collapse if a critical mass of the human population is too poor to consume the goods and services supplied in the market, a state of affairs that is likely to lead to a severe global recession.[113] In addition, the cost of assisting the world's poor in such situations could create a great strain upon the budgets of rich countries.[114] As the recent Asian financial crisis demonstrates, this scenario is becoming increasingly plausible in view of the growing interdependency of the global economy.[115] It is increasingly apparent that no single economy will be able to insulate itself completely from such global disaster.

In sum, the proliferation of trade unilateralism[116] resulting from unrestrained or extraterritorial regulatory sovereignty, would drag the nascent 'rule of law' in international trade down to the level of a Hobbesean 'rule of the jungle.'[117] A global marketplace fragmented along the lines of exclusive regulatory jurisdictions would be disastrous: the streams of international commerce would be choked off until the multilateral trading system resembled nothing so much as a dry desert. Thus, the second crisis in the international trade system is the crisis of 'trade failure.'

2.1.2.3 A dilemma

The foregoing dual crisis of 'regulatory failure' and 'trade failure' results in a profound dilemma. Emphasis on the remedy of one aspect tends to undermine the remedy of the other. In other words, if trade liberalization and market access are

---

110. *See* WTO, *Environment: History 1, Early Years: Emerging Environment Debate in GATT/WTO*, available at <http://www.wto.org/english/tratop_e/envir_e/hist1_e.htm> (last visited on Mar. 19, 2001).

111. *But see* Michael J, Trebilcock & Robert Howse, *The Fair Trade—Free Trade Debate: Trade, Labor, and the Environment*, 16 INT'L REV. L. & ECON. 61, 78–9 (1996) (arguing that 'fair trade claims related to environmental and labor standards are not necessarily groundless, nor self-serving of protectionist interests, nor as threatening to the liberal world trading order as free traders often make out').

112. A Malthusian concern tends to aggravate global poverty problems. *See* Mike Moore, Director General, World Trade Organization, Prospects for the Developing Countries in the Next Round, Address to the Development Committee of the European Parliament, Feb. 21 2000, *available at* <www.wto.org/wto/speeches/mm25.htm> (last visited on Jan. 19, 2001) ('Two billion extra souls will share our crowded planet within the next 30 years. We will have to double food production within 20 years.'

113. *Cf.* JOHN BENINGTON, LOCAL DEMOCRACY AND THE EUROPEAN UNION: THE IMPACT OF EUROPEANIZATION ON LOCAL GOVERNANCE 20 (1994).

114. *Id.*

115. *See* John H. Jackson, *International Economic Law: Reflections on the 'Boilerroom' of International Relations*, 10 AM. U. J. INT'L L. & POL'Y 595 (1995).

116. *Cf.* Jens Ladefoged Mortensen, *The Institutional Requirements of the WTO in an Era of Globalization: Imperfections in the Global Economic Polity*, 6 EUR. L. J. 176, 193–96, 203 (2000) (arguing that the privatization of dispute resolution in trade conflict, as seen in the U.S. trade policy tools in terms of 'fair trade,' is especially problematic). *But cf.* Yong K. Kim, *The Beginnings of the Rule of Law in the International Trade System despite U.S. Constitutional Constraints*, 17 MICH. J. INT'L L. 967, 1013 (1996) (observing that the US is 'slowly developing a respect for the Rule of Law').

117. *But cf.* H. F. Chang, *An Economic Analysis of Trade Measures to Protect the Global Environment*, 83 GEO. L. J. 2131 (1995) (defending 'unilateral sticks' to protect the global environment).

pushed too strongly, anxious voices from domestic regulators and even NGOs will immediately follow. Yet, if all the unilateral regulatory concerns from various sources are accommodated too promiscuously at the expense of the trade agenda, the international trade system will lose its momentum and even its *raison d'etre*. This is the dilemma that currently challenges the global trading system, which can be transposed to its 'legitimacy crisis' in that both trade and regulatory failure undermine the acceptability of the system to its users, governments as well as traders.

2.1.3 A NEW JURISPRUDENCE: CHAPEAU TEST

2.1.3.1 Overview

It is imperative that the foregoing 'dual crisis' be addressed through a non-confrontational and harmonious approach, taking into account both trade and non-trade (social) values.[118] Yet, the question that quickly arises is *how* can this be done? Most importantly, the spirit of free trade should no longer be conceptualized as conflicting directly with non-trade (social) values. By the same token, social values should not merely be exceptionalized by or subordinated to free trade dogma. More radically, this perspective can be viewed as restoring authority over professional regulatory decisions, which had been usurped by trade tribunals, to the relevant domestic regulatory agencies.[119] Nevertheless, this restoration must not deprive the trade tribunal of its basic adjudicative role. Rather, it should transform only the *manner* in which the trade tribunal adjudicates. This daunting task requires a well-defined hermeneutics as well as a more nuanced approach from the trade tribunal.[120]

In sum, at its inception the new WTO dispute settlement system faced the challenge of considering Members' regulatory autonomy even while it continuously upheld the conventional goal of free trade. This stance reflected the new *telos* of the WTO system represented by an *integrated* multilateral trade system through *sustainable* development.[121] Therefore, under the WTO system, a novel jurisprudence had to be found which could respond and appeal simultaneously to concerns of free trade and regulatory autonomy. The origin of this novel jurisprudence turned out to

118. *See e.g.*, Joel P. Trachtman, *Unilateralism, Bilateralism, Regionalism, Multilateralism, and Functionalism: A Comparison with Reference to Securities Regulation*, 4 TRANSNAT'L L. & CONTEMP. PROBS. 69, 116 (1994) (arguing that 'at every level, but especially at the multilateral level, it seems necessary to combine the trade perspective with the regulatory perspective'); Daniel C. Esty & Damien Geradin, *Market Access, Competitiveness, and Harmonization: Environmental Protection in Regional Trade Agreements*, 21 HARV. ENVTL. L. REV. 265, 336 (1997) (arguing that 'trade liberalization and environmental protection are ineluctably connected' and that 'trade agreements that address this linkage expressly will ultimately be more durable because they incorporate environmental thinking and are positioned to maximize the social welfare gains that flow from freer trade').

119. A similar view can be found in the jurisprudence of the European Court of Human Rights through the doctrine of 'margin of appreciation.' *See* Rolv Ryssdall, *Opinion: The Coming Age of the European Convention on Human Rights*, 1 EUR. HUM. RTS. L. REV. 18, 25 (1996); R. St. J. MacDonald, *The Margin of Appreciation*, *in* THE EUROPEAN SYSTEM FOR THE PROTECTION OF HUMAN RIGHTS 83–5 (R. St. J. MacDonald et al. eds, 1993).

120. Steven P. Croley & John H. Jackson, *WTO Dispute Procedures, Standard of Review, and Deference to National Governments*, 90 AM. J. INT'L L. 193, 212–13 (1996).

121. WTO Agreement, *supra* note 1, Introduction, pmbl.

be the 'chapeau,' the preambular language of GATT Article XX. Unlike in the old GATT regime, the chapeau has begun to play a more positive, teleological role beyond its textual meaning under the new WTO system.

2.1.3.2 From 'necessary/relating' to the 'chapeau'

The aforementioned strong pro-trade bias, evidenced by the necessary and relating tests, underwent a dramatic shift after the WTO and its innovative Appellate Body were officially launched. Originally, the first WTO panel report in *Gasoline* (1996) followed conventional interpretive practice by conducting a draconian scrutiny of a US domestic environmental measure. In this environmental case, the US sought to establish a baseline for a non-degradation requirement by applying 'individual baselines,' created using past performance, on domestic refiners, while applying 'statutory baselines,' which tended to be more burdensome than the individual baselines, on foreign refiners.[122] The US tried to justify this differential treatment between domestic and foreign refiners mainly on the basis of administrative difficulties that it faced when collecting relevant data for establishing individual baselines from foreign countries.[123] In response to the US argument, the *Gasoline* Panel held that there was no 'direct connection' between less favorable treatment of imported gasoline that was chemically identical to domestic gasoline, and the US objective of improving air quality.[124] Therefore, following *Herring & Salmon* (1988), the Panel concluded that those baseline establishment rules were not 'primarily aimed at' the conservation of exhaustible natural resources, and thus not 'relating to' the conservation of natural resources, as required by Article XX (g).[125]

However, the first Appellate Body in the new WTO dispute settlement system overcame the conventional regressivism by rightly avoiding a re-examination of 'less favorable treatment,' which had already been addressed in the previous stage of Article III:4. In reversing the Panel's decision, it recognized a 'substantial relationship'[126] between the US measure in question (the baseline establishment rules) and the US environmental regulatory objective enshrined in the Gasoline Rule ('non-degradation' requirements). Accordingly, the Appellate Body concluded that the measure was appropriately 'primarily aimed at' and thus 'relating to' the conservation of natural resources for the purpose of Article XX (g).[127] In so ruling, the Appellate Body restored the legitimacy and autonomy of the US environmental regulatory policy, which the Panel had previously denied solely because of inconsistency with the National Treatment obligation regarding different treatment between foreign and domestic gasoline.

The Appellate Body then made a revolutionary move by shifting its interpretive focus to the 'chapeau'—the Preamble of Article XX. First, the Appellate Body underscored that the chapeau addresses the *manner* in which a questioned measure is

---

122. *Gasoline*, Panel Report, *supra* note 14, Introduction, ¶¶ 2.5–2.11.
123. *Id.*, ¶ 3.19.
124. *Id.*, ¶ 6.40.
125. *Id.*
126. *Gasoline*, AB Report, *supra* note 14, Introduction, at 19.
127. *Id.*, at 20.

applied, rather than the measure itself or its specific *content*.[128] Secondly, the Appellate Body upheld the Panel's view in emphasizing that the US argument regarding the inevitability of discrimination due to administrative difficulties that individual baselines for foreign refiners would have generated (e.g., the impracticability of verification and enforcement of foreign refiner baselines), was insufficient to justify allowing individual baselines for domestic, but not for foreign refiners. In responding to the US argument, the Appellate body highlighted the US practice in other contexts, such as anti-dumping laws, in which the accepted practice is to resort to other information only when the information sought is not supplied or is regarded as unverifiable.[129] In the same vein, the Appellate Body stressed that the US should have explored the possibility of entering into 'cooperative arrangements' with both foreign refiners and foreign governments, which would have allowed the US to overcome the alleged administrative problems.[130] In reaching this conclusion, the Appellate Body very persuasively highlighted 'a number of precedents that the US have considered it [international cooperation] prudent to use to help overcome problems confronting enforcement agencies' in other US regulatory laws of this kind, e.g., in the fields of anti-trust law, securities exchange law, and tax law.[131]

This shift of interpretive focus to the chapeau[132] was epochal and revolutionary. It encouraged a form of 'regulatory cooperation' among governments that would enable them to retain some discretion in formulating domestic regulations even while enjoying the benefits of free trade. In this context, it is very significant that the Appellate Body based its ruling regarding the chapeau, namely an interpretation of 'unjustifiable discrimination' and 'disguised restriction on international trade,' on the failure of the US government to explore the possibility of entering into cooperative arrangements with the governments of Venezuela and Brazil.[133] This interpretive revolution has continued and has been further concretized in subsequent cases, such as *Shrimp-Turtle* (1998). In that case, the Appellate Body, once again focusing on the chapeau, ruled that the application of the US turtle-conservatory measure was 'arbitrary discrimination' in that the US certification process was not 'transparent' or 'predictable,' and did not provide any 'formal opportunity for an

128. *Id.*, at 22.
129. *Id.*, at 26–7.
130. The Appellate Body emphasized that:

> The U.S. must have been aware that for these established techniques and procedures to work, cooperative arrangements with both foreign refiners and the foreign governments concerned would have been necessary and appropriate. ... [I]t appears to the Appellate Body, that the United States had not pursued the possibility of entering into cooperative arrangements with the governments of Venezuela and Brazil or, if it had, not to the point where it encountered governments that were unwilling to cooperate. ... But it does not reveal what, if any, efforts had been taken by the United States to enter into appropriate procedures in cooperation with the governments of Venezuela and Brazil so as to mitigate the administrative problems pleaded by the United States.

Id., at 27.
131. *Id.*, n.52.
132. Over the course of GATT panel history, there have been very few cases that have directly involved the interpretation of the chapeau. *See* ANALYTICAL INDEX, *supra* note 9, at 563–65.
133. *Gasoline*, AB Report, *supra* note 14, Introduction, at 27.

applicant country to be heard, or to respond to any arguments that may be made against it.'[134]

More recently, however, a wrinkle has been found in the integrity of this chapeau jurisprudence. In *Argentinean Leather* (2001),[135] the Panel examined an Argentinean tax measure—'pre-payment of part of value-added tax and income tax upon importation of goods'—under the chapeau. The Panel, viewing that that the nature of the inquiry under the chapeau is to find whether a measure in question is *justifiable* discrimination,[136] focused on whether 'the extra tax burden imposed on importers in the form of interest lost or paid' due to the pre-payment system was *unavoidable*.[137] The Panel finally observed that such extra burden on importers was avoidable and therefore, unjustifiable, since Argentina could and should have worked out one alternative, namely 'to reimburse importers for the additional interest foregone or paid.'[138]

This Panel's ruling on a policy 'alternative' reveals some serious problems. First, from a doctrinal standpoint, such an approach is regressive in the sense that the Panel *de facto* conducted the 'least trade-restrictive' test, which falls under the 'necessary' test, at the chapeau stage. Secondly, the Panel repeated a mistake committed earlier by the *Thai Cigarette* Panel.[139] That is, the Panel nearly imposed a hypothetical policy alternative upon Argentina without sufficient consideration of the economic and technical feasibility of such an alternative from the perspective of Argentina. Rather, the Panel merely *assumed* the availability of such an alternative.[140] Furthermore, the Panel rejected Argentina's argument regarding technical infeasibility in implementing the suggested alternative, i.e., the difficulties associated with quantifying the loss or the amount of reimbursement, by raising another alternative such as the use of 'average market rates' to serve for the quantification. Yet, the Panel should have raised such additional questions as to whether an alternative would be available to a developing country like Argentina or whether artificial quantification would be compatible with Argentina's policy objective of preventing tax evasion—a policy with which the Panel sympathized. One might reasonably speculate that if the Panel report had been appealed, this part of the ruling would probably have been modified by the AB.

Another point merits attention regarding the chapeau in the recent jurisprudence. As the chapeau has become spotlighted in connection with Article XX scrutiny, the historically strict 'least trade-restrictive' test has been softened somewhat in a series

---

134. *Shrimp-Turtle*, AB Report, *supra* note 15, Introduction, para 180; Gregory Shaffer, *International Decision: United States—Import Prohibition of Certain Shrimp and Shrimp Products*, 93 AM. J. INT'L L. 507, 512 (1999). In the chapeau test, 'discrimination' does not mean 'violations of substantial obligation' such as Article III (National Treatment), but 'procedural deficiencies.' Gráinne de Búrca & Joanne Scott, *The Impact of the WTO on EU Decision-Making*, JEAN MONNET WORKING PAPER 26 (No.6/00) (2000) [hereinafter *The Impact*].

135. Argentina—Measures Affecting the Export of Bovine Hides and the Import of Finished Leather, WT/DS155, Panel Report adopted on Feb. 16, 2001, *available at* <http://www.wto.org/english/tratop_e/dispu_e/distab_e.htm> (last visited on Sep. 27, 2001) [hereinafter *Argentinean Leather* (2001)].

136. *Id.*

137. *Id.*, ¶ 11.324.

138. *Id.*, ¶ 11.325.

139. *See supra* text accompanying notes 82–83.

140. *Argentinean Leather*, Panel Report, *supra* note 135, ¶ 11.325.

of cases represented by *Argentinean Leather* (2001) and *Asbestos* (2001). This trend contributed eventually to affirmative rulings on, 'necessary', under Article XX for the first time in GATT/WTO history. In *Argentinean Leather* (2001), the Panel conducted a *de facto* 'rational relationship' test when interpreting 'necessary.' This seems to mark an implicit reduction in the level of scrutiny, which may be analogous to a shift from 'strict' scrutiny to 'rational' scrutiny under the US constitutional jurisprudence. The Panel first focused on the relationship of Argentina's policy goals of ensuring compliance with its domestic laws on value-added tax and income tax, and the general 'design and structure' of the measure in question.[141] Then, showing great sympathy with Argentina's policy objectives, including the prevention of tax evasion, the Panel concluded in a rather effortless way that the Argentinean measure was necessary within the meaning of Article XX (d).[142]

In the same vein, the *Asbestos* Panel quoted the paradigmatic case, i.e., *Sec. 337* (1989), in light of the 'necessary' test, but departed from past practice in highlighting the 'reasonableness' language, instead of the 'least degree of inconsistency' language.[143] The Panel considered that 'the existence of a reasonably available measure must be assessed in the light of the economic and administrative realities facing the Member concerned.'[144] Accordingly, the Panel concluded that France might reasonably consider that an alleged alternative, namely 'controlled use,' did not provide protection that paralleled the level contemplated by the policy objectives, due to difficulties associated with the application of the alternative.[145]

While the AB upheld the Panel's findings,[146] it left interesting traces that mirrored the SPS jurisprudence in its interpretation of 'necessary.' First, the AB concluded that 'there is no requirement under Article XX(b) of the GATT 1994 to *quantify*, as such, the risk to human life or health.'[147] Secondly, the AB affirmed that 'WTO Members have the right to determine the level of protection of health that they consider appropriate in a given situation.'[148] Thirdly, the AB conducted a test similar to 'risk assessment' taking into account 'scientific evidence' as well as 'residual risk.'[149] The decision by the *Asbestos* AB to employ the SPS jurisprudence in interpreting Article XX was an important development in the sense that the latter may have the potential to enrich and complement an existing body of Article XX jurisprudence that has been based on rather vague language. Indeed, it was especially helpful in this particular case, where the AB declined to address the TBT Agreement, which shares many critical features with the SPS Agreement, but relied instead solely on Article XX.

In sum, two recent jurisprudential developments can be interpreted as signs of a major trend against the conventional pro-trade bias and towards enhanced protection of Members' regulatory autonomy. These are, first, the easing of interpretive rigor when construing 'necessary,' away from 'least trade-restrictive'

141. *Id.*, ¶ 11.303.
142. *Id.*, ¶ 11.305.
143. *Asbestos*, Panel Report, *supra* note 16, Introduction, ¶ 8.207.
144. *Id.*
145. *Id.*
146. *Id.*, AB Report, ¶ 175.
147. *Id.*, ¶ 167.
148. *Id.*, ¶ 168.
149. *Id.*, ¶ 174.

toward a search for a 'reasonably available' measure, and secondly, the employment of the SPS jurisprudence. Critically, these developments regarding the 'necessary' test, parallel the shift of an interpretive focus from 'necessary' to the 'chapeau.'

However, despite these propitious jurisprudential developments, a divergent, and even regressive, ruling was recently issued in *Korean Beef* (2001) regarding the same issue of the interpretation of 'necessary.' In the first place, the AB in *Korean Beef* seemed to soften the term 'necessary' by declaring that a 'necessary' measure falls along a continuum ranging from 'indispensable' to 'making contribution to,' albeit closer to the former pole. In a troubling next step, however, the AB delivered a highly objectionable ruling. The AB observed that:

> In sum, determination of whether a measure, which is not 'indispensable,' may nevertheless be 'necessary' within the contemplation of Article XX (d), involves in every case a process of *weighing* and *balancing* a series of factors which prominently include the *contribution* made by the compliance measure to the enforcement of the law or regulation at issue, the *importance* of the common interests or values protected by that law or regulation, and the accompanying impact of the law or regulation on imports or exports.[150]

This ruling represents a departure from the established Article XX jurisprudence, and is even regressive in that it actually denies the regulatory autonomy of Members and second-guesses their legitimate policy objectives. First of all, the ruling is certainly divergent from the AB's ruling in *Hormones* (1997), which emphasized that WTO Members have the *right* to establish the level of protection that they consider appropriate in a given situation.[151] The *Hormones* AB acknowledged that even a 'zero-tolerance' level that a regulating Member may establish for the purpose of achieving its own appropriate level of protection could, in some cases, be justified.[152] In the same vein, the AB in *Argentinean Leather* (2001) and *Asbestos* (2001) was very *deferential* in determining whether there was a reasonably available alternative to the measure in question.[153] In contrast, the AB in *Korean Beef* (2001) rejected the higher level of protection from fraud that Korea had attempted to achieve through an *ex ante* measure like the 'dual retail system' in favor of the lower level of protection achieved through *ex post* investigations.[154] Accordingly, the AB in *Korean Beef* (2001) seemed to impose a higher threshold with respect to 'reasonable alternatives' than it had in the earlier two cases.

Conclusively, the AB should not be allowed to determine by itself the question of to what extent a specific compliance measure contributes to law enforcement, nor should it evaluate by itself the importance of the policy objectives that such measure seeks to achieve. That is, the AB must not itself *weigh* and *balance* these factors, for these responsibilities should more appropriately be handled under the rubric of

150. *Korean Beef*, AB Report, *supra* note 33, ¶ 164 (emphasis added).
151. *Asbestos*, AB Report, *supra* note 16, Introduction, ¶ 168.
152. *Hormones*, AB Report, *supra* note 8, Introduction, ¶ 172.
153. *Argentinean Leather*, Panel Report, *supra* note 135, ¶¶ 11.304, 11.305; *Asbestos*, AB Report, *supra* note 16, Introduction, ¶ 174.
154. *Korean Beef*, AB Report, *supra* note 33, ¶ 175.

Members' regulatory prerogatives. The AB should have respected the regulatory autonomy of Korea by acknowledging that the dual retail system was necessary to secure compliance with the Korean Unfair Competition Act. Indeed, the AB could have achieved the same result as in the decision rendered by finding that the measure amounted to 'arbitrary discrimination' under the chapeau, taking into account 'like situations' where different instruments such as fines, record-keeping and policing are used. Such an approach would have responded better to the regulatory as well as the trade concerns of Members.

2.1.3.3 From 'on its face' to 'as applied'

When dealing with the necessary (relating) test, panels under the old GATT tended to focus on the general architecture of a ground measure or a domestic statute as such instead of its application. For example, the *Thai Cigarette* (1990) Panel focused on the very content of the Thai Tobacco Act of 1966, conducting its analysis premised on the strong assumption that an import ban under the Act could be deemed necessary within the meaning of Article XX(b) only if there was no alternative measure consistent with the General Agreement.[155] The Panel then condemned the import ban as 'unnecessary' by asserting that Thai regulatory concerns embedded in the Act could and should have been addressed by other less trade restrictive measures available in other (developed) countries.[156] Undoubtedly, this blatant and authoritative attitude by the Panel undermined the regulatory autonomy of the Thai government.[157]

Since the past panels' interpretations were conducted in a top-down or macro style, they also disregarded the fact that even a measure found to be a *prima facie* violation could still be consistent with the GATT in terms of its *actual* application under certain circumstances. Under this approach, moreover, there would be little guarantee that panels' decisions will actually be accommodated and implemented due to the political embarrassment that a losing party would be forced to endure as a result of being forced by an external authority to amend or repeal an internal measure in order to comply with the decisions. One likely scenario is that changes made by a losing party to its domestic law in response to a panel report, will prove to be simple window dressing, rather than genuine reform.

Therefore, judicial scrutiny should center on the actual application of a measure, fully taking into account the specificity of each case, rather than bluntly reviewing a ground statute or regulation itself.[158] As discussed above, the chapeau could form

155. *Thai Cigarette*, *supra* note 49, ¶ 75.
156. *Id.*, ¶¶ 77–78.
157. *See e.g.*, *Neither Science Nor Shamans*, *supra* note 86, at 200–1.
158. The recent *Canadian Aircraft* (1999) Panel reemphasized this point by citing the *U.S. Tobacco* (1994) panel reports holding that '... legislation which merely gave the discretion to the executive authority ... to act inconsistently with the General Agreement could not be challenged as such; only the actual application of such legislation inconsistent with the General Agreement could be subject to challenge.' Canada—Measures Affecting the Export of Civilian Aircraft, WT/DS70/R, Appellate Body and Panel Report adopted on Aug. 20, 1999, ¶ 9. 124 [hereinafter *Canadian Aircraft*] (citing Panel Report on United States—Measures Affecting the Importation, Internal Sale and Use of Tobacco, adopted on 4 October 1994, B.I.S.D. 41S/131, 174–75, ¶ 118 [hereinafter *U.S. Tobacco*]).

the basis for such an inquiry into the actual application because it is not designed to address the contents of a questioned measure, but rather the manner in which it is *applied*.[159] Put differently, this characteristic of the chapeau tends to provide a litmus test for an appropriate implementation of, or compliance with, the trade treaty obligations in 'good faith.'[160]

Consequently, even if it fails to meet the chapeau test on a specific occasion, a regulating state need not repeal or amend its legislation or regulation because this legislation or regulation would not be struck down on its face; rather, the regulating authority only has to change its way of implementing the legislation or regulation in practice, so as to remain coherent and consistent with GATT/WTO rules. In this regard, the new hermeneutics accentuating the actual application is more persuasive than the old one, which tends to have a condemning and stigmatizing effect on losing parties. Accordingly, this application-oriented hermeneutics is likely to minimize inconsistency of domestic regulations with trade treaty obligations, as well as avoiding unnecessary interference with domestic regulatory control. Concomitantly, this hermeneutics also fits well with a basic doctrine of public international law, according to which a national law should always be interpreted so as to avoid conflict with international law, if possible.[161]

In the same vein, the recent AB report in the *Shrimp-Turtle* case eloquently manifested the application-oriented chapeau test. First, the Appellate Body overruled the Panel's approach, which had bypassed the interpretation of Article XX (g) to deal directly with the chapeau instead. The AB reproached the Panel for having been obsessed with the 'design of the measure itself,' and thus having failed to inquire specifically into how the *application* of Section 609 constitutes 'a means of arbitrary or unjustifiable discrimination' in addressing the chapeau.[162] The AB then highlighted a flaw in the actual application by the US of its own Section 609. Specifically, it highlighted that the US had never seriously attempted to negotiate a cooperative agreement with the four complainants while 'multilateral procedures' such as the Inter-American Convention for the Protection and Conservation of Sea Turtles were 'available and feasible.'[163] However, despite losing its case, the US was not compelled to amend Section 609 itself, but only its application of, and practice with respect to, the Section 609.[164]

Of course, a separate jurisprudential approach did exist for those situations in which the scrutiny of a measure (legislation or regulation) *itself* might be warranted. Under this jurisprudence, when a complaining party challenges a statute *as such*, it should prove that it is violative in itself, based on its terms (*expressis verbis*), design

---

159. *See* GATT 1994, *supra* note 2, art. XX.
160. *See* I. C. MacGibbon, *Estoppel in International Law*, 7 INT'L & COMP. L. Q. 468, 472 (1958).
161. *See* L. OPPENHEIMER, OPPENHEIMER'S INTERNATIONAL LAW 81–2 (Robert Jennings & Arthur Watts eds., 9th ed. 1992). *Cf.* Murray v. The Charming Betsy, 6 U.S. (2 Cranch) 64, 118 (1804). Chief Justice Marshall ruled that 'an act of congress ought never to be construed to violate the law of nations, if any other possible construction remains ....' *Id.*
162. *Shrimp-Turtle*, AB Report, *supra* note 15, Introduction, ¶ 115.
163. *Id.*, ¶¶ 166–170; Shaffer, *supra* note 134, at 512.
164. Reacting to the Appellate Body Report in *Shrimp-Turtle*, the USTR emphasized that the U.S. law (Section 609) had been left intact by the Report. USTR, *Press Release: WTO Appellate Body Found US Sea Turtle Law Meets WTO Criteria But Faults US Implementation*, on Oct. 12, 1998, *available at* <http://www.ustr.gov/releases/1998/10/98-92.pdf> (last visited on Mar. 21, 2001).

and architecture.[165] In other words, in order to prevail, the complaining party needs to show that the law is so dispositive that a violation occurs without executive intervention beyond mere mechanical application.[166] However, in many cases this mode of challenge would be difficult to establish and maintain since challenges of this type often tend to be hypothetical and subjective as there is no recourse to real practices and applications. Furthermore, recent jurisprudence compellingly demonstrates that even the scrutiny of a measure *as such*, should eventually take into account *application*-related aspects of the measure. In fact, this novel jurisprudence eloquently shows that this application-oriented scrutiny could be employed even without reference to the chapeau.

In this parallel, *Section 301* (1999) initially held that one of the measures in question, Section 304, constituted a *prima facie* violation of Article 23.2 (a) of the DSU because the 'statutory' language of the Section 304, *on its face*, tended to result in unilateral determinations on WTO-illegal measures by other Members without a recourse to the WTO dispute settlement system.[167] However, after examining certain 'non-statutory' elements of Section 304 such as the 'US Statement of Administrative Action (SAA),' the 'US statements before the panel' and the 'USTR practice under Section 304,' the Panel finally concluded that Section 304 was not inconsistent with US obligations under Article 23.2 (a) of the DSU.[168] This ruling is especially significant in that it affirmed that even when a panel must address the consistency of a challenged measure with the WTO *as such*, an initial presumption of violation based on the general architecture of the legislation (statutory language) can nonetheless be rebutted by the regulating Member's subsequent commitments or other practices concerning its actual application of the legislation. In other words, the hermeneutical focus has already been shifted from the legislation itself to its application. In this connection, one critical *obiter dicta* by the Panel is likely to be echoed in future cases:

> Should the undertakings articulated in the SAA and confirmed and amplified by the U.S. to this Panel be repudiated or in any other way removed by the U.S. Administration or another branch of the U.S. Government (legislature, executive and judiciary), this finding of conformity would no longer be warranted.[169]

---

165. In this situation, a statute may be challenged even without an actual enforcement. *See Superfund*, *supra* note 30, ¶ 5.2.2.
166. For instance, the *Apples and Pears* (1989) Panel held that a statute is mandatory in character by its terms or expressed intent. Norway—Restrictions on Imports of Apples and Pears, adopted on 22 June 1989, B.I.S.D. 36S/306, ¶ 5.7 [hereinafter *Apples and Pears*]. Likewise, the *Non-Rubber Footwear* (1992) Panel held that the automatic backdating provisions of Sec. 331 of the U.S. Trade Act of 1974 and Sec. 104 (b) of the 1979 Trade Agreements Act are mandatory legislation that cannot be modified by the executive. United States—Denial of Most-Favoured Nation Treatment as to Non-Rubber Footwear from Brazil, adopted on June 19, 1992, B.I.S.D. 39S/128, ¶ 6.13 [hereinafter *Non-Rubber Footwear*].
167. *See* United States—Sections 301–310 of the Trade Act of 1974, WT/DS152/R, Panel Report adopted 27 January 2000, ¶ 7.97, *available at* <http://www.wto.org/english/tratop_e/disput_e/distab_e.htm> (last visited on Sep. 27, 2001) [hereinafter *Section 301*].
168. *Id.*, ¶ 7.135.
169. *Id.*, ¶ 7.136.

Following the same hermeneutics employed in *Section 301*, the Panel in *1916 Anti-Dumping Act* (2000)[170] paid full attention to the various aspects of the application of the US Anti-Dumping Act of 1916 beyond its text, though the EC contested the consistency of the Act with the WTO *on its face*. The Panel held that:

> 6.48. The understanding of a law the WTO-compatibility of which has to be assessed begins with an analysis of the terms of that law. However, we consider that we should not limit ourselves to an analysis of the text of the 1916 Act in isolation from its interpretation by U.S. courts or other U.S. authorities, even if we were to find *that text to be clear on its face*. If we were to do so, we might develop an understanding of that law *different from the way it is actually understood and applied* by the U.S. authorities. This would be contrary to our obligation to make an objective assessment of the facts of the case, pursuant to Article 11 of the DSU. Therefore, we must look at all the aspects of the domestic legislation of the United States that are relevant for our understanding of the 1916 Act . . .[171]

Critically, this application-oriented approach would retain its prescriptive impact on everyday administrative behaviors since the audience of such scrutiny is more likely to be the 'executive,' rather than 'politicians.' In particular, nowadays, new generation trade issues such as 'trade facilitation,'[172] 'behind-the-border measures' or 'invisible obstacles' are drawing increasing attention. In these kinds of cases, it would be irrelevant and useless to make illegal such sophisticated and complicated measures, on their face based on a general scheme, because those measures tend to have completely different impacts on the market, depending on how they are implemented. Therefore, microscopic scrutiny of the actual application of such measures would be more effective under such circumstances than a direct challenge to a statute itself, the full effects of which remained unclear. Finally, since actual application is conducted by the executive in most cases, the more plausible that such scrutiny appears to the executive, the more positive would be the effect on future domestic policies, thereby eventuating in-depth compliance.[173]

---

170. United States—Anti-Dumping Act of 1916, WT/DS136, the AB and Panel Report, *upheld* by the AB, adopted on Sep. 26, 2000, *available at* <http://www.wto.org/english/tratop_e/dispu_e/distab_e.htm> (last visited on Sep. 27, 2001) [hereinafter *1916 Anti-Dumping Act* (2000)].

171. *Id.*, Panel Report, ¶ 6.48 (emphasis added).

172. Trade facilitation is often defined as 'the simplification and harmonization of international trade procedures or cutting the red tape that still exists in moving goods across borders.' WTO, *Trade Facilitation on the WTO Website, available at* <http://www.wto.org/english/tratop_e/tradfa_e/tradfa_e.htm> (last visited on Mar. 21, 2001). *See also* United Nation Economic and Social Council, International Trade Procedures Working Group (ITPWG), *National Trade Facilitation Bodies (Draft Revision of Recommendation No. 4)*, 3–5, TRADE/CEFACT/1999/11, Jan. 27, 1999 (defining trade facilitation as the 'formalities, procedures, documents and operations related to international trade transactions' and arguing that 'its goals are simplification, harmonization and standardization so that transactions become easier, quicker and more economical than before').

173. *See* Ronald D. Mitchell, *Compliance Theory: An Overview, in* IMPROVING COMPLIANCE WITH INTERNATIONAL ENVIRONMENTAL LAW 3–4 (James Cameron et al. eds., 1993) (distinguishing between 'compliance with a treaty's *explicit* obligations' and 'treaty-induced compliance').

2.1.3.4 Reincarnation of general principles of law

The emergence of the chapeau test after the launch of the new WTO dispute settlement system led to a renewed emphasis on general principles of law.[174] What the AB in *Gasoline* (1996) tried to echo in interpreting the chapeau was nothing more than the general legal principles of law, such as 'good faith,' 'estoppel' (consistency) and 'fairness.'[175] For instance, the AB in *Gasoline* noted that the US measure in question was contrary to its practice in other comparable contexts, which would constitute a breach of estoppel, and that the US had ignored the possibility of entering into cooperative arrangements with foreign counterparts to ease its administrative problems, which signaled a lack of good faith.[176] As another example, the AB in *Shrimp-Turtle* (1998) noted that the US certification process seemed to be 'singularly informal and casual,' hence, that exporting countries applying for certification were denied basic 'fairness' and 'due process.'[177]

This reincarnation of general principles of law in the sphere of international trade law[178] is significant in that it alters the conventional perspective of the aforementioned dogmatic dichotomy between trade and non-trade (social) values, which are manifested by general obligations and exceptions, respectively. Specifically,

---

174. *Shrimp-Turtle*, AB Report, *supra* note 15, Introduction, ¶ 158 (underlining added):
    158. The chapeau of Article XX is, in fact, but one expression of the principle of good faith. This principle, at once a general principle of law and a general principle of international law, controls the exercise of rights by states. One application of this general principle, the application widely known as the doctrine of abus de droit, prohibits the abusive exercise of a state's rights and enjoins that whenever the assertion of a right 'impinges on the field covered by [a] treaty obligation, it must be exercised bona fide, that is to say, reasonably.'
175. *But cf.* Phillip R. Trimble, *Globalization, International Institutions, and the Erosion of National Sovereignty and Democracy*, 95 MICH. L. REV. 1944, 1957 (1997) (reviewing THOMAS M. FRANCK, FAIRNESS IN INTERNATIONAL LAW AND INSTITUTIONS (1995)) (arguing that 'a Western process-like approach to determining what is fair will seem to some people as another version of western cultural imperialism').
176. The reverse side of this hermeneutics may be that even an apparently unilateral regulation should be accepted if it has exhausted reasonable efforts for regulatory cooperation. For instance, the EU Cosmetics Directive (Council Directive 76/768) banning the marketing of cosmetics containing ingredients tested on animals may be consistent with the new hermeneutics (chapeau test) considering the EU's explicit efforts to develop internationally acceptable alternatives to testing on animals. *The Impact*, *supra* note 134, at 12. In this regard, De Búrca and Scott expanded this manner-oriented hermeneutics found in the chapeau test to include a Habermasian 'deliberative' ideal. *Id.*, at 34.
177. *Shrimp-Turtle*, AB Report, *supra* note 15, Introduction, ¶ 181 (underlining added):
    181. The certification processes followed by the United States thus appear to be *singularly informal and casual*, and to be conducted in a manner such that these processes could result in the negation of rights of Members. There appears to be no way that exporting Members can be certain whether the terms of Section 609, in particular, the 1996 Guidelines, are being applied in a fair and just manner by the appropriate governmental agencies of the United States. It appears to us that, effectively, exporting Members applying for certification whose applications are rejected are denied basic fairness and due process, and are discriminated against, vis-à-vis those Members which are granted certification.
    See John H. Jackson, *Comments on Shrimp/Turtle and the Product/Process Distinction*, 11 EUR. J. INT'L L. 303, 305 (2000) (assessing the Appellate Body's reliance on 'a series of procedural prerequisites' as 'very healthy').
178. *See The Impact*, *supra* note 134, at 1, 28.

general principles of law such as 'estoppel'[179] or the 'rule of consistency'[180] enable each trade tribunal to engage in a more coherent and constructive interpretation since the tribunal focuses on the *manner* (good faith or due process) in which each regulatory jurisdiction exercises its authority or competence, rather than on the *content* of a regulation,[181] the scrutiny of which is better left to regional or domestic regulators.[182]

Notably, this permeation of general principles of law into the realm of

179. The original notion of estoppel, which finds deep roots in the common law tradition (i.e., '*He who seeks equity must do equity*') and which may be traced to Roman law ('*venire contra factum proprium*'), also supports this interpretive approach highlighting the *manner* in which a regulatory jurisdiction (a regional trade regime or a individual state) exercises its authority in a much broader regulatory field such as a supranational or international trade regime. According to the original concept of estoppel, a person exercising a right, such as ownership of land or use of water, must not abuse the right in the sense of using it 'in such a manner that its anti-social effects outweigh the legitimate interests of the owner of the right.' Wolfgang Friedmann, *The Uses of 'General Principles' in the Development of International Law*, *in* INTERNATIONAL LAW IN THE TWENTIETH CENTURY 254 (Leo Gross ed. 1969). According to Bin Cheng, estoppel is the general principle of law 'which courts of law have in modern times most usefully adopted.' BIN CHENG, GENERAL PRINCIPLES OF LAW AS APPLIED BY INTERNATIONAL COURTS AND TRIBUNALS 141–42 (1987) [hereinafter GENERAL PRINCIPLES OF LAW] (explaining the principle of '*allegans contraria non est audiendus*').

180. The law of consistency can be found in many legal texts. *See e.g.*, GATT 1994, *supra* note 2, art. XX (chapeau); SPS Agreement, *supra* note 6, Introduction, pmbl., art. 2.3. In a much broader sense, consistency, which is the 'treatment of like cases alike through the consistent application of the law' increases the legitimacy of the legal system as a whole, as seen in both common law ('stare decisis') and civil law systems ('la jurisprudence constante'). *See* Jonathan I. Charney, *Third Party Dispute Settlement and International Law*, 36 COLUM. J. TRANSNAT'L L. 65, 84 (1997) [hereinafter *Third Party Dispute Settlement*].

181. *Cf.* Martin Shapiro, CODIFICATION OF ADMINISTRATIVE LAW: THE US AND THE UNION, 2 EUR. L. J. 26, 37 (1996) (emphasis added) (observing that 'judges would generally prefer to fault the actions of their fellow governors on *procedural* rather than substantial grounds').

182. This manner- or process-oriented approach that I claim here finds its analogy in recent anti-dumping rulings under the auspices of various international trade tribunals, such as panels of the Canada–U.S. Free Trade Agreement (CUSFTA), the North American Free Trade Agreement (NAFTA) and the WTO. Traditionally, anti-dumping decisions have been considered to fall within the rubric of sovereign determination thanks to their legal complexity and political significance. Each state applies its own anti-dumping laws to cases filed by its domestic industries and these domestic rulings are closely guarded from international (or supranational) review vis-à-vis other domestic measures. *See* Agreement on Implementation of Article VI of the General Agreement on Tariffs and Trade 1994, art. 17.6, Annex 1 A of the WTO Agreement, *supra* note 1, Introduction [hereinafter Anti-Dumping Code]; NAFTA, *supra* note 13, Introduction, arts. 1902, 1904. Nonetheless, this seemingly self-serving standard of review does not guarantee that domestic tribunals or courts are free to issue unilateral and final determinations regarding anti-dumping measures entirely free from outside review. What appears on the surface to be a lax standard of review does not, in fact, prevent international (supranational) tribunals from conducting substantial scrutiny over domestic anti-dumping determinations. The scrutiny conducted in this field is focused on the *manner* in which each state applies its own anti-dumping law, rather than on *substance* (fact-finding issues or the domestic anti-dumping legislation itself), which enjoys a high degree of deference. *See* Anti-Dumping Code, *supra*, art. 17.6. Therefore, a panel tends to highlight whether any administrative tribunal or domestic court failed to apply its own anti-dumping law in good faith and in a principled, justifiable and reasonable way. *See e.g.*, In the Matter of Certain Corrosion-Resistant Steel Sheet Products Originating in or Exported from the United States of America, CDA-94-1904-03, Nov. 2, 1995, *available at* <http://www.sice.oas.org/DISPUTE/nafta/english/ca940403.asp> (last visited on Mar. 20, 2001). More recently, McGinnis and Movsesian argued for the use of 'procedure-oriented' jurisprudence highlighting 'transparency,' 'performance-orientation' and 'consistency' in striking down covertly protectionist measures. *World Trade Constitution*, *supra* note 29, at 573–83. However, the major focus of these authors is on overcoming the influence of interest groups in order to realize a Madisonian vision of democracy. *Id.*

international trade law provides fairly compelling evidence of the 'legalization' of the international trade order. In fact, under the old GATT 1947 system, very few cases referred to or cited general principles of law when interpreting GATT provisions. The central reason for this is that trade under the old GATT was less legalized and thoroughly adjudicated than under the WTO,[183] in part because the origins of the old GATT system were merely instrumental, rather than purposive in themselves. Core GATT 1947 provisions, such as national treatment, were basically aimed at maintaining the subtle balance of tariff bargaining, not at establishing a unified legal regime.[184] Although the dispute settlement system later evolved along more legalized lines,[185] so much emphasis continued to be placed on finding a friendly 'settlement' satisfactory to both parties concerned, and losing parties essentially found themselves with what amounted to veto power over the panel decision.[186] Within such a framework, the practical use of general principles of law could not but be marginalized.[187] The interpretative practices of panels were limited to fleshing out the meaning of somewhat technical terms such as 'like product.'[188]

However, enarmored of a more legalized dispute settlement mechanism,[189] the new WTO system has dramatically changed the foregoing situation. Two important reforms, *inter alia*, facilitated this transformation: the appellate review system, and the automatic adoption of panel and the AB reports. The new opportunity for appeal on issues of *law* has tended to elucidate the legal rights and obligations of the disputing parties. At the same time, the elimination of the veto possibility has tended to sustain this flourishing of legal interpretation. Consequently, decisions of the WTO tribunals—especially the AB reports—have begun to resemble ordinary court rulings in referring more frequently, whether explicitly or implicitly, to general principles of law.[190] These general principles, in turn, are invoked through the medium of the chapeau.

---

183. Regarding the comparison of the old GATT 1947 and the new WTO system in terms of the rule-orientedness, *see generally* Michael K. Young, *Dispute Resolution in the Uruguay Round: Lawyers' Triumph over Diplomats*, 29 INT'L LAW. 389 (1995).
184. *A Diplomat's Jurisprudence*, *supra* note 4, at 624.
185. *See e.g.*, Understanding Regarding Notification, Consultation, Dispute Settlement and Surveillance, B.I.S.D. 26S/216 (1979).
186. *See* Robert E. Hudec, *The New WTO Dispute Settlement Procedure: An Overview of the First Three Years*, 8 MINN. J. GLOBAL TRADE 1, 9 (1999).
187. This situation is analogous to the rare use of general principles of law by the International Court of Justice in that traditional international law also focused on the diplomatic relations between states rather than on the legal rights and obligations existing between them, and the acceptability of the Court's decision was dependent upon the consent of the parties concerned. Friedmann, *supra* note 179, at 247.
188. *See e.g.* Japan—Customs Duties, Taxes and Labeling Practices on Imported Wines and Alcoholic Beverages, adopted on 10 November 1987, B.I.S.D. 34S/83 [hereinafter *Japanese Shochu I*]; *Malt Beverage*, *supra* note 13.
189. *See* Young, *supra* note 183.
190. Robert Howse found the 'adjudicative legitimacy' in the Panel and the AB's reliance on these general principles of law for their decision. Robert Howse, *Adjudicative Legitimacy and Treaty Interpretation in International Trade Law: The Early Years of WTO Jurisprudence*, *in* THE EU, THE WTO, AND THE NAFTA: TOWARDS A COMMON LAW OF INTERNATIONAL TRADE? 41–42 (Joseph H. H. Weiler ed. 2000) [hereinafter *Adjudicative Legitimacy*].

2.1.3.5 Teleological interpretation

The chapeau test is 'teleological' in that it tends to signal the future *direction* in which our multilateral trading system should develop in the midst of expanding global interdependency and integration.[191] Specifically, the new hermeneutics suggests that each Member state should be able to trade more freely than ever while also enjoying regulatory autonomy, but should also be required to 'foster a process of taking foreign interests into account,'[192] which represents the 'integrationist' and at the same time 'anti-unilateralist' new *telos* under the WTO, in contrast to the narrow anti-protectionist *telos* of GATT 1947.[193] Moreover, it implies a due consideration for 'development' issues in trade, in that 'taking foreign or developing countries' interests into account'[194] inevitably involves 'technical and financial assistance,' instead of a 'unilateral trade sanction.' In other words, this new *telos* mandates that developed countries should endeavor to cooperate with and assist developing countries to achieve global—or even internal—regulatory objectives, rather than relying upon unilateral and sometimes extraterritorial enforcement of their own domestic regulations.

As a potential source of useful comparative perspectives, a similar teleology can be found in the European Community context. In *De Peijper* (1976),[195] the Court rejected a Dutch regulation requiring parallel importers of pharmaceutical products to submit to the national health authorities certain documents obtainable only from the manufacturers of the products or their appointed distributor on the grounds that 'collaboration' between the Dutch government and the manufacturer's Member State would have been less trade restrictive. This precedent is significant in that the Court implied that a 'positive duty to collaborate between Member States' existed under certain circumstances for the purpose of attaining the goals of free movement of goods and protection of public health in a *coherent* way.[196]

---

191. Though the chapeau provides a textual basis for the new hermeneutics, the new hermeneutics tends to surpass or transcend the chapeau's original or lexicographical meaning, toward articulation of a certain *telos*. *Cf.* K.N. Llewellyn, *The Constitution as an Institution*, 34 COLUM. L. REV. 1, 31 (1934) (emphasis original) (maintaining that 'a sane theory would utterly disregard a Documentary text *if any relevant practices existed* to offer a firmer, more living basis for the ideal picture.')
192. *See* McRae, *supra* note 75, at 231, 235; Shaffer, *supra* note 134, at 513. *Cf.* Takis Tridmas, *The Court of Justice and Judicial Activism*, 21 EUR. L. REV. 199, 204–6 (1996) (discussing teleological integration in the EC context).
193. International trade lawyers have recently devoted serious discussion to this new telos. *See generally Symposium: Unilateralism in International Trade: What Place Can it Have in Light of the Emerging Multilateral Regime?*, 11 EUR. J. INT'L L. (2000).
194. Shaffer, *supra* note 134, at 513.
195. Case 104/75 [1976] ECR 613.
196. Donald P. Kommers & Michel Waelbroeck, *Legal Integration and the Free Movement of Goods: The American and European Experience*, *in* FORCES AND POTENTIAL FOR A EUROPEAN IDENTITY (BOOK 3), METHODS, TOOLS AND INSTITUTIONS (VOLUME 1), INTEGRATION THROUGH LAW: EUROPEAN AND THE AMERICAN FEDERAL EXPERIENCE 204–5 (Mauro Cappelletti et al eds. 1985). Such teleology can also be found in ex Article 5 TEC, which mandates the duty of cooperation to safeguard the 'fiduciary duty' of Member States. Laurence W. Gormley, PROHIBITING RESTRICTIONS ON TRADE WITHIN THE EEC: THE THEORY AND APPLICATION OF ARTICLES 30–36 OF THE EEC TREATY 257 (1985) [hereinafter PROHIBITING RESTRICTIONS].

2.1.3.6 Evaluation

It has been argued thus far that a new jurisprudence focusing on the *manner* or *application*, rather than the *content* of a specific measure itself, is the only way in which the dual crisis of trade and regulatory failure can realistically be overcome. Yet in spite of the theoretical superiority of this new jurisprudence, its 'political' implications demand sober evaluation. The sensitive political issues worthy of careful consideration can be stated in the form of the following questions: first, does a trade tribunal exceed its political capacity in conducting the type of manner-oriented or application-oriented scrutiny described above? Or, does such scrutiny remain excessively intrusive in the sense that it undermines sovereignty? Secondly, does such scrutiny constitute a politically tolerable form of judicial activism?

Sovereignty

The first of these politically sensitive issues is a familiar one and may be restated in terms of a concern that highly detailed manner- or application-oriented scrutiny of legislation could result in an undesirable degree of interference in domestic affairs. The question itself reflects a certain bias in favor of 'sovereignty' of the kind that some countries advocated in reaction to the recent *Shrimp-Turtle* (1998) case in which the WTO AB ruled that the US had violated the WTO treaty by acting unilaterally on its own domestic regulation relating to the preservation of natural resources. This ruling contributed in large part to the anti-WTO protests that culminated at the Seattle WTO Ministerial Meeting in December 1999.[197] Yet criticism related to the loss of sovereignty is not limited to the WTO. Similar misgivings have also been expressed in the EU[198] as well as the U.S. context.[199]

Nevertheless, such accusations are easily repudiated through an analytical comparison of the new jurisprudence with conventional tests, such as the 'necessary' test ('least trade-restrictive' test), the 'proportionality' test, and the 'balancing' test. As a matter of fact, these traditional tests are themselves intrusive. The embedded pro-trade bias of the tests often leads panels to 'second-guess' legitimate regulatory objectives established by Member States through their domestic democratic procedures, and sometimes to 'impose' a specific legislative alternative in the name of the 'least trade-restrictive' measure. In other words, the traditional tests tend to result in prescription of whatever specific *recipe* a trade tribunal believes to be the most suitable for a regulating state in a given case. Moreover, under the traditional tests, a regulating state is generally required to amend or repeal its own domestic legislation or regulation in order to comply with the tribunal's ruling.

By contrast, the new jurisprudence—symbolized by the chapeau test—is not concerned with specific regulatory *recipes*, but rather the *manner* in which a regulation is applied. This approach is more consistent with the normative aims and processes of a multilateral trading system. In essence, the new hermeneutics does

197. *See e.g.,* The Voice of the Turtle, *The Turtle Salutes ...*, Dec. 7, 1999, *available at* <www.voiceoftheturtle.org/salutes/wto.htm> (last visited on Nov. 1, 2001).
198. *See infra* sub-sec. 2.2.2.1.
199. *See infra* sub-sec. 2.2.3.1.

render sufficient breathing space for Member States to regulate certain subject-matters that they think are important. This pluralistic and federalistic perspective on trade governance mirrors the *Keck* jurisprudence, as well as the principles of subsidiarity and 'margin of appreciation,'[200] which pertain to the regulatory competence of Member States vis-à-vis the European Union.

Moreover, the concept of sovereignty itself needs to be modified in this era of ever-growing interdependency.[201] That is, to the extent that the concept of sovereignty retains its traditional narrow-minded obsession with the peremptory exercise of unbridled power, it must be transformed into a more mature concept that is constructive and participatory.[202] In this connection, the pre-eminent international trade law scholar, John H. Jackson has incisively observed that sovereignty has an 'emotional appeal' and is often used 'in a blunt and undifferentiated way as a surrogate argument by opponents of some government proposal.'[203] Jackson recommends that all international norms be scrutinized in a 'decomposed' or 'disaggregated' way in order to assess the relative advantages and disadvantages of reinforcing particular norms.[204] Such an approach would eventually assist governments to identify those important 'policy' issues that confront the entire international community.[205] From a slightly different yet similar angle, John G. Ruggie has criticized the 'territorial' implication embedded in modern sovereignty. Ruggie prefers to highlight the concept of the non-territorial 'region' within the world economy; that is, 'a decentered yet integrated space-of-flows, operating in real time, which exists alongside the spaces-of-places that we call national economies.'[206]

---

200. *See generally* HOWARD CHARLES YOUROW, THE MARGIN OF APPRECIATION DOCTRINE IN THE DYNAMICS OF EUROPEAN HUMAN RIGHTS JURISPRUDENCE (1996).

201. *Cf.* Jack Goldsmith, *Sovereignty, International Relations Theory, and International Law*, 52 STAN. L. REV. 959, 966 (2000) (reviewing STEPHEN D. KRASNER, ORGANIZED HYPOCRISY (1999)) (introducing the 'contingent and plastic' view of constructivists on sovereignty) [hereinafter *International Relations Theory*].

202. *See* ABRAM CHAYES & ANTONIA HANDLER CHAYES, THE NEW SOVEREIGNTY: COMPLIANCE WITH INTERNATIONAL REGULATORY AGREEMENTS 27 (1995); *cf.* John H. Jackson, *International Economic Law in Times That Are Interesting*, 3 J. INT. ECON. L. 3, 13–14 (2000). The author, after noting that in this highly interdependent world that we live in virtually all international solutions involve 'a degree of intrusiveness into domestic governance,' stresses the necessity of a cooperative mechanism, including 'appropriate allocation of power,' between international institutions and diverse national legal systems. *Id.*, at 10–12.

203. John H. Jackson, *The Great 1994 Sovereignty Debate: The United States Acceptance and Implementation of the Uruguay Round Results*, 36 COLUM. J. TRANSNAT'L L. 157, 187–88 (1997) [hereinafter *The Great 1994 Sovereignty Debate*]. *See also* Ronald A. Brand, *Semantic Distinctions in an Age of Legal Convergence*, 17 U. PA. J. INT'L ECON. L. 3, 6 (1996) (arguing that 'theories of sovereignty borrowed from prior centuries can no longer accommodate economic and political reality at the end of the twentieth century').

204. *The Great 1994 Sovereignty Debate*, *supra* note 203, at 187–88.

205. *Id. Cf.* Arie Reich, *From Diplomacy to Law: The Juridicization of International Trade Relations*, 17 NW. J. INT'L L. & BUS. 775, 776 (1996–97) (asserting that nowadays more States wish to regulate trade relations by using norms, rather than through sovereignty and flexibility).

206. John Gerard Ruggie, *Territoriality and Beyond: Problematizing Modernity in International Relations*, 47 INT. ORG. 139, 172 (1993). *But cf.* Philip R. Trimble, *International Trade and the 'Rule of Law,'* 83 MICH. L. REV. 1016, 1027 (1985) (reviewing JOHN H. JACKSON ET AL., IMPLEMENTING THE TOKYO ROUND: NATIONAL CONSTITUTIONS AND INTERNATIONAL ECONOMIC RULES (1984)) (arguing that 'the kind of international law-making envisioned by the authors cannot be easily reconciled with the American political tradition').

Judicial activism

The essence of this question is the extent to which judicial scrutiny could overshadow the role of the relevant legislative branch, namely the General Council of the WTO.[207] From this perspective, an overzealous trade tribunal could be criticized for exercising 'judicial legislation,' thereby overstepping the competence of the legislative branch and jeopardizing the institutional balance.[208] As a matter of fact, under the WTO system, the judicial function of the dispute settlement system is defined rather narrowly. The official mission of the panels and the AB is to 'assist' the Dispute Settlement Body (i.e., the General Council) to 'settle' disputes between Member States by delivering 'recommendations.'[209] Any interpretation of a specific provision of covered agreements under the WTO can be overruled by an 'authoritative interpretation' issued by the General Council.[210] Furthermore, recommendations delivered by judicial bodies are not permitted to *add to* or *diminish* the rights and obligations of Member States.[211] Therefore, if a panel or the AB adopts a 'teleological' approach in its ruling, such a proactive stance may appear to constitute another form of judicial legislation. For instance, some would criticize the AB for exceeding its mandate by urging 'regulatory cooperation' among countries having different regulatory backgrounds and stages of economic development when it applied the chapeau test in *Gasoline* (1996) and *Shrimp-Turtle* (1998). Indeed, the same critics might also argue that such regulatory cooperation should not be the concern of the AB but of the Members or their representative organs such as the General Council.

Yet, in view of the myriad of problems that the WTO is expected to address, not to mention the reality of a rigid legislative mechanism,[212] the teleological approach

---

207. *Cf.* Louis Fisher, Book Review, 16 J. LEGAL EDUC. 135, 138 (1996) (reviewing MARTIN H. REDISH, THE CONSTITUTION AS POLITICAL STRUCTURE (1995)) (observing that 'how much activism we should want from the judiciary has been debated ever since 1789, with no resolution to date and no resolution expected for the future').
208. However, as Stone Sweet and Shapiro highlight, adjudication has a 'rule-making' function beyond mere dispute settlement in terms of jurisprudence and case law. *See* Alec Stone Sweet, *The New GATT: Dispute Resolution and the Judicialization of the Trade Regime in* LAW ABOVE NATIONS: SUPRANATIONAL COURTS AND THE LEGALIZATION OF POLITICS 139 (Mary L. Volcansek ed., 1997). *Cf.* David A. Strauss, *Common Law Constitutional Interpretation*, 63 UNIV. CHI. L. REV. 877, 884 (1996) (discussing the 'prevalence and importance of non-textual amendments'); HERSCH LAUTERPACHT, THE DEVELOPMENT OF INTERNATIONAL LAW BY THE INTERNATIONAL COURT 155–266 (1982) (addressing 'judicial legislation'); EDWARD MCWHINNEY, SUPREME COURTS AND JUDICIAL LAW-MAKING: CONSTITUTIONAL TRIBUNALS AND CONSTITUTIONAL REVIEW 168 (1988) (discussing the 'imperative principles' of a novel *jus gentium*); RENE DAVID, ARBITRATION IN INTERNATIONAL TRADE 3 (1985) (arguing that 'independent judges' in international trade tribunals can develop a *jus gentium* free from the contingencies of the various States).
209. DSU, *supra* note 106, art.19.1.
210. WTO Agreement, *supra* note 1, Introduction, art. 9.2.
211. DSU, *supra* note 106, arts. 3.2, 19.2
212. *See* Donald M. McRae, *The WTO in International Law: Traditional Continued or New Frontier?*, 3 J. INT'L ECON. L. 27, 40 (2000) (arguing that the WTO dispute settlement system fosters the 'development of principles of international law through judicial decisions at a much faster pace than has occurred under existing international legal institutions'). *See* Philippe Sands, '*Unilateralism,' Values, and International Law*, 11 EUR. J. INT'L L. 291, 301 (2000) (advocating the Appellate Body's 'enhanced role for a self-confident judiciary, filling in the gaps which states in their legislative capacity have been unwilling—or unable—to fill'). *Cf.* Shimon Shetreet, *Judging in Society: The Changing Role of Courts, in* THE ROLE OF COURTS IN SOCIETY 469 (Shimon Shetreet ed., 1988)

reflected in the AB's application of the chapeau test may be more realistically interpreted as a useful manifestation of 'judicial prudentialism,'[213] rather than as rash judicial activism. In other words, the real mission of the WTO dispute settlement system must be understood from the standpoint of *functional* institutional balance, not from the perspective of lofty Montesquiean notions of separation of powers that are better suited to the domestic context.

2.1.3.7 Summary and prospect

Confronting a dual crisis of trade and regulatory failure, the newly launched WTO dispute settlement system came to devise a novel jurisprudence, dubbed the 'chapeau test.' Under this test, the AB directed its interpretive focus toward the 'manner' in which a certain domestic regulation is adopted or applied, and away from the substance of the regulation itself. This jurisprudence tends to promote both goals of free trade and regulatory autonomy because material free trade obligations, such as those contained in Articles III:4 and XI:1, are respected while Members are still free to regulate *what* they want. In a doctrinal sense, the chapeau test is rooted in 'general principles of law' such as estoppel, equity, consistency and fairness. This tends to bestow greater legitimacy on the adjudicated outcome.

Importantly, use of the chapeau test represents an implicit argument for rejecting the narrow 'anti-protectionist' *telos* of the old GATT regime in favor of the broad 'integrationist' and 'anti-unilateralist' *telos* of the WTO system as the best future course for the multilateral trading system amid ever-growing economic interdependency and integration. The recommended course is toward symbiotic co-existence for the purpose of enhancing mutual prosperity; in other words, toward a situation in which Member States are permitted to maintain their own regulatory diversity even as, collectively, they pursue the common goal of creating a free(r) market.

2.1.4 AN UNSOLVED PROBLEM: DICHOTOMY

Despite the jurisprudential evolution described above, the pro-trade bias symbolized by the 'dichotomy' is preserved in the current GATT, principally in the form of Articles III:4 and XX. In other words, no matter how legitimate a domestic regulation may be, it will be justified under the exception clause of Article XX only after it is first condemned as a violation of general obligations, such as the National Treatment under Article III:4. This is a lingering problem that even the chapeau test cannot address. The recent *Asbestos* (2001) case spotlighted this problem in a dramatic way. In this case, the EC was dissatisfied with its victory in the Panel Report since the French ban had to be condemned as a *violation* of Article III:4 before it was eventually saved by Article XX(b).

---

contd

(observing that 'legislatures are generally slow to introduce law reforms to ensure that the law adapts to changing times and changing social and moral norms').

213. *Cf.* Russell Gabriel & Louis B. Sohn, *Equity in International Law*, 82 AM. SOC'Y INT'L L. PROC. 277, 283–84 (1988) [hereinafter *Equity*].

2.1.4.1 Asbestos (2001) saga

Asbestos, a 'fibrous mineral of hydrated silicates,' has been widely used in the manufacture of industrial and consumer products and in the building industry due to favorable qualities such as resistance to high temperatures and to chemical reactions.[214] However, in response to the discovery that asbestos may be carcinogenic, the French government moved to protect workers and consumers from the associated health risks by adopting a measure banning asbestos from all stages of manufacture, processing, sale, and import.[215] Decree No. 96-1133 entered into force on 1 January 1997.[216] Canada, one of the largest producers and exporters of asbestos, challenged this Decree before the WTO, arguing that it violated the TBT Agreement and GATT 1994.

The Panel followed the traditional track on this issue, as represented by the 'Working Party Report on Border Tax Adjustment.'[217] The Panel noted three criteria—'the products' properties, nature and quality,' 'the products' end-uses in a given market,' and 'consumers' tastes and habits'—by which to examine 'like products,' and added 'tariff classification' to the list.[218] The Panel stressed that this examination of like products would 'inevitably involve a degree of discretionary judgment.'[219]

In examining the likeness between asbestos fibers and substitute fibers, the Panel concentrated its interpretive focus on the 'properties' criterion. In the context of 'market access,' it observed that 'for a given utilization, the properties are the same to the extent that one product can replace the other.'[220] As for the other criteria of 'likeness,' the Panel paid little attention. The Panel observed that a difference in 'chemical and physical characteristics' (nature and quality) between asbestos fibers and substitute fibers is not decisive when examining likeness, since an emphasis on such characteristics would deprive panels or the AB of the *flexibility* given to them, eventually narrowing down the scope of like products.[221] As for the end-use, the Panel concluded that the respective properties of asbestos (chrysotile fibers) and other substitute fibers (e.g., PVA, cellulose or glass fibers) *allowed* certain 'identical or at least similar' end-uses.[222] The Panel rejected as unnecessary the two other criteria, consumers' tastes and habits, and tariff classification.[223] The Panel took the same approach in examining likeness between products containing asbestos and certain other products before concluding that chrysotile-fiber products and fibro-cement products are like products.[224]

The most fundamental question in examining likeness was raised in association

---

214. *Asbestos*, Panel Report, *supra* note 16, Introduction, ¶¶ 2.1, 2.2.
215. *Id.*, ¶ 2.3.
216. *Id.*
217. Border Tax Adjustments, *supra* note 10, ¶ 18.
218. *Asbestos*, Panel Report, *supra* note 16, Introduction, ¶¶ 8. 112, 113.
219. *Id.*, ¶ 8. 114.
220. *Id.*, ¶ 8. 124.
221. *Id.*, ¶ 8. 123.
222. *Id.*, ¶ 8. 136.
223. *Id.*, ¶¶ 8. 139, 8. 143.
224. *Id.*, ¶ 8. 150.

with the application of the properties criterion: whether the 'risk' of the product could fall under the rubric of 'properties.' The EC argued that chrysolite fibers possess the unique property of fragmenting into extremely fine particles that can penetrate the lung and cause various lung diseases, including lung cancer.[225] The EC therefore argued that chrysolite fibers (asbestos) are not like other substitute fibers.[226] Nevertheless, the Panel rejected the EC's argument based on the 'economy' of GATT 1994.[227] The Panel reasoned that GATT 1994 is structured in such a way that certain disciplines, including Article III:4, are initially applied to domestic regulations, but that certain policy objectives may nonetheless take precedence over those disciplines later under Article XX.[228] The Panel added that the introduction of 'risk' factors into the analysis of likeness would 'largely nullify' the effect of Article XX(b).[229]

The AB, however, flatly rejected the Panel' ruling. Put simply, the AB opined that the health *risk* factor associated with asbestos and asbestos-containing products should be incorporated in the determination of their *properties* and eventually of *likeness*. In upholding the EC's position, the AB found that:

> Panels must examine *fully* the physical properties of products. In particular, panels must examine those physical properties of products that are likely to *influence* the competitive relationship between products in the marketplace. In the case of chrysolite asbestos fibers, their molecular structure, chemical compositions, and fibrillation capacity are important because the microscopic particles and filaments of chrystolite asbestos fibers are carcinogenic in humans, following inhalation.[230]
>
> This carcinogenicity, or toxicity, constitutes, as we see it, a defining aspect of the physical properties of chrysotile asbestos fibers. The evidence indicates that PCG fibers, in contrast, do not share these properties, at least to the same extent. We do not see how this highly significant physical difference *cannot* be a consideration in examining the physical properties of a product as part of a determination of 'likeness' under Article III:4 of the GATT 1994.[231]

The AB's ruling seems to be in sync with the so-called 'aim and effect' test. This test assumes that a product associated with a non-protectionist, and thus legitimate, aim and effect should be regarded as 'unlike' other products within the meaning of GATT Article III, even if their properties are similar. In the actual operation of the test, the 'aim' is highlighted since the 'trade effect' tends to be easily determined as coincidental or fortuitous once the aim has been found to be non-protectionist.[232] This test finds its rationale in the 'not so as to afford protection' language of Paragraph 1 of GATT Article III.

---

225. *Id.*, ¶ 8. 128.
226. *Id.*
227. *Id.*, ¶ 8. 130.
228. *Id.*
229. *Id.*
230. *Asbestos*, AB Report, *supra* note 16, Introduction, ¶ 114 (emphasis added).
231. *Id.* (underlining added).
232. *See e.g.*, *Luxury Tax*, *supra* note 19, ¶¶ 5.10, 5.13, 5.15.

Although this test was explicitly rejected by the AB in *Japanese Shochu II* (1996) and *Banana III* (1997),[233] the AB in *Asbestos* (2001) nonetheless seemed intent on reviving it, at least implicitly, when it stressed that the term 'like product' in Article III:4 must be interpreted to give 'proper scope and meaning' to the 'general principle' in Article III:1 ('not so as to afford protection').[234] Yet, the AB failed to respond clearly to the criticism that its position might nullify the effect of Article XX(b). It merely asserted that 'Article III:4 and Article XX(b) are distinct and independent provisions of the GATT 1994 each to be interpreted on its own.'[235] Notwithstanding this assertion, the AB was ultimately forced to incorporate the Article XX(b) element of 'health risks,' into its Article III:4 consideration of 'competitive relationship in the marketplace.'[236]

Obviously, the most serious problem with this kind of ruling is that too many domestic regulations may be *redeemed* as non-discriminatory without relevant *justifications*. The legal threshold in the aim and effect test is typically so low that a mere finding of non-protectionist intent can save a disputed measure. If adopted as the authoritative paradigm, the *Asbestos* ruling could eventually have the effect of nullifying Article XX(b). Yet it remains to be seen how the AB will try to overcome this jurisprudential pitfall in future cases.

2.1.4.2 Aim and effect test revisited

Admittedly, the aim and effect test tends to challenge the 'dichotomy' between the general obligation of Article III:4 and the exceptions of Article XX. Due to this dichotomy, a defendant in a case brought under GATT normally bears the burden of justifying that the challenged measure is necessary or the least trade restrictive. Absent such a dichotomy, the burden of proof would be reversed. For example, under the US Dormant Commerce Clause jurisprudence, the plaintiff (e.g., the federal government) bears the burden of proving that a state measure is protectionist or not even-handed.[237] This is because the US system treats trade and non-trade values in the same dimension under the Dormant Commerce Clause. There is no dichotomy.

This way of thinking may apply to the aim and effect test in the same manner, and thus the burden of proof may be reversed vis-à-vis the dichotomy approach.[238] This is why the proponents of the test highlight 'sovereign' regulatory autonomy. This is also why France was not wholly satisfied with the *Asbestos* Panel Report despite its victory.[239] France might not bear the idea of being condemned as a violator in the

233. *See supra* sub-sec. 2.1.1.1.
234. *Asbestos*, AB Report, *supra* note 16, Introduction, ¶ 98.
235. *Id.*, ¶ 115
236. *Id.* From a more radical standpoint, a *concurring* opinion expressed its dissatisfaction with the majority's 'economic approach' that followed a conventional 'like product' test focusing on 'end-uses' as well as 'consumers' tastes and habits.' *Id.*, ¶ 152. The concurring opinion seemed to view that the apparent 'health risk' in asbestos should be the most crucial criterion of the AB's interpretation.
237. *See infra* sub-sec. 2.2.4.1.
238. *But see Asbestos*, Panel Report, *supra* note 16, Introduction, ¶ 8. 130 ('The burden of proof would not of course be greatly modified because the EC would still have to prove the risk of the product, applying the principle of *probatio incumbit ejus que dixit*.') (emphasis original).
239. *Asbestos*, AB Report, *supra* note 16, Introduction, ¶¶ 30–35.

first place, even if its measure was later saved (justified) under the exception clause. France almost certainly did not appreciate having to adduce all of the detailed evidence necessary for its 'legitimate' measure to be justified. Indeed, there can be little doubt that France would have preferred Canada to bear the initial burden of proving that its ban was illegitimate or protectionist.

Nevertheless, the weak standard of review embedded in the aim and effect test still remains problematic and even dangerous. Considering past applications of the test, it would seem that any unilateral regulation could be redeemed at the stage of Article III, and thus freed from the discipline of GATT, provided that its non-protectionist architecture could be shown. This is a result of the test's tendency to overlook any disparate impact to trade, which such regulation may cause, as incidental. In the past, such a loose test might have been tolerated as long as a domestic regulation was indistinctively applicable—in other words, *de jure* non-discriminatory—because the potential harm of equally applicable and non-protectionist measures to the global trading community seemed to be relatively contained and manageable due to the comparatively limited range of economic interdependence. However, in a highly integrated global marketplace, greater effort must be exerted to prevent the disintegrationist impact that even a legitimate measure can bring.

To address this lack of interpretive rigor in the test, one might recommend using a stronger standard of review, which is tantamount to the 'chapeau' test under Article XX, when operating the aim and effect test. In that way, various administrative procedure-related considerations such as 'due process' and 'duty to cooperate' could be effectively scrutinized even at the initial stage of Article III. If a legitimate regulation were found to meet this improved test and thus deemed a non-arbitrary or justifiable measure, it could be redeemed *ex ante* without the necessity of *ex post* justification. This improved test would help to overcome the foregoing dichotomy by treating trade and regulatory values within the same dimension—that is, at the same stage in the analysis.

2.1.4.3 PPM debate

A similar argument to the aim and effect test has been raised under the GATT/WTO in the name of the 'PPM debate' to defy the dichotomy. The term PPM, 'Processes and Production Method,' is defined as 'the way in which products are manufactured or processed and natural resources extracted or harvested.'[240] A PPM can directly affect the characteristics of a product ('Product Related PPM'), but in some cases, it may not alter them ('Non-Product Related PPM').[241] Under the old GATT, it was widely accepted that a non-product related PPM would be *prima facie* inconsistent with GATT Article III:4 since it had no impact on the characteristics of the product

240. *See generally* OECD, PROCESSES AND PRODUCTION METHODS (PPMS): CONCEPTUAL FRAMEWORK AND CONSIDERATIONS ON USE OF PPM-BASED TRADE MEASURES, *available at* <http://www.olis.oecd.org/olis/1997doc.nsf/linkto/ocde-gd(97)137> (last visited on September 1, 2000).
241. *Id.*

itself.[242] For instance, a domestic regulation prohibiting the use or sale of imported meat or meat products harvested by a cruel trap, which applied equally to like domestic products, would constitute a violation of Article III:4 in the first place, even though such regulation could be justified later by Article XX (General Exceptions). In fact, this doctrine originates from the very structure of the GATT, which concerned trade in *goods*. Therefore, contracting parties mainly conceived regulations associated with *products*, viewing 'process-based conditions as extra conditions that were never part of the bargain.'[243]

Yet, critics of this PPM doctrine argue that this doctrine imposed an 'unwarranted legal burden' on all regulations which purport to protect legitimate values, such as the environmental protection, since they must be justified by regulating Members.[244] The European Parliament even urged the European Commission to advocate that:

> the WTO should draw up a Statement of Understanding concerning the application of the principle of 'like products,' which enables otherwise identical products to be differentiated where the production or processing of such products have different impacts on the environment.[245]

Therefore, those critics contend that regulatory distinctions grounded on legitimate policy objectives should be regarded as consistent with Article III:4, 'whether product- or process-based,' in the first place without any further need to be saved by Article XX (General Exceptions).[246] In other words, those legitimate, non-protectionist regulations should be redeemed, not justified.

In a doctrinal sense, those critics' position parallels that of the advocates of the 'aim and effect' doctrine. Both contend regulatory distinctions should be instilled to the 'like product' test, interpreting foreign products violating certain legitimate internal regulations as unlike vis-à-vis domestic products complying with these regulations. Although it is true that those critics of the PPM doctrine defy the problematic pro-trade dichotomy, the same counterargument against the aim and effect test is still applicable to the argument maintained by those critics, which renders their position also hard to accept.[247]

242. Robert E. Hudec, *The Product-Process Doctrine in GATT/WTO Jurisprudence*, *in* New Directions in International Economic Law: Essays in Honor of John H. Jackson 187 (Marco Bronckers & Reinhard Quick eds. 2000) [hereinafter, Hudec, *The Product-Process Doctrine*].

243. *Id.*, at 192.

244. *Id.*, at 188.

245. *Id.*, at 189, n.5; European Parliament Resolution A-40125/98 (adopted April 30, 1998), quoted in Marco Bronckers & Natalie McNelis, *Rethinking the 'Like Product' Definition in WTO Law: Anti-Dumping and Environmental Protection*, *in* Regulatory Barriers and the Principle of Non-discrimination in World Trade Law 345–85 (Thomas Cottier & Petros Mavroidis eds. 2000).

246. *See generally* Robert Howse & Donald Regan, *The Product/Process Distinction—An Illusory Basis for Disciplining 'Unilateralism' in Trade Policy*, 11 Eur. J. Int'l L. 249 (2000).

247. *See supra* sub-sec. 2.1.4.2.

2.1.4.4 *Summary and prospect*

The *Asbestos* saga eloquently demonstrated the dilemma associated with a pro-trade 'dichotomy' between general obligations, which represent the free trade ideology, and exceptions, which symbolize legitimate regulatory concerns. Considering the ferocity of France's reaction to the original Panel Report, despite its victory, it would seem that the unavoidable legal consequences of the dichotomy represent a profound annoyance to Members whose regulations turn out to be legitimate and non-protectionist. Indeed, there are negative political consequences associated with condemning a sovereign country as a violator at the Article III stage, despite the absence of any demonstrated protectionist intent, even where it is assumed that the measure in question will ultimately be justified at a later stage under Article XX.

Naturally, this problematic feature of the dichotomy led to the revival of a jurisprudence that tends to *redeem* a non-protectionist, yet still discriminatory, measure at the Article III:4 stage, instead of waiting to justify the measure as an Article XX exception. The *Asbestos* (2001) AB initiated this revival by invoking *de facto* the aim and effect test that had been declared dead by the AB itself in an earlier case. In addition, some scholars followed this tendency through the PPM debate. They argued that Article III:4 should be interpreted in such a way as to create a legal distinction between products having different regulatory distinctions.

Yet, the Achille's heel of this line of argument is that it tends to invite an influx of 'regulatory unilateralism' contributing to market disintegration. Although each Member might be able to enjoy its own exclusive regulatory scheme under such situation, international commerce would contract enormously in the face of massive regulatory heterogeneity. Therefore, the approach embodied in the aim and effect test remains *an* option, though not a very desirable one.

As I argue in the following Chapter, it would be more prudent to search for a solution to the dichotomy among a different set of legal instruments that lie outside the relatively narrow confines of GATT provisions.

2.2 Comparative insight

2.2.1 POINT OF COMPARISON: DUAL CRISIS

International *Lochnerism*—freedom to trade without any local interference[248]—was among the influences forming the rationale that begot the old GATT system. This liberal, deregulatory philosophy underlying the old GATT *telos* of 'anti-protection'

248. Shell, *supra* note 96, at 906–7. Regarding the birth and the demise of *Lochnerism*, *see generally* LAURENCE H. TRIBE, AMERICAN CONSTITUTIONAL LAW 1342–71 (3d ed. 2000); *but see* Cass Sunstein, *Lochner's Legacy*, 87 COLUM. L. REV. 873 (1987) (suggesting that 'the case should be taken to symbolize not merely an aggressive judicial role, but an approach that imposes a constitutional requirement of neutrality, and understands the term to refer to preservation of the existing distribution of wealth and entitlements under the baseline of the common law').

was in fact ascribed to the fear of world-wide economic balkanization precipitated by the state-led competitive protectionist interventions that contributed to the outbreak of the World War II.[249] Likewise, the *telos* of the European Community's internal trade regime—the *telos* of a common market radiating the *mega-telos* of European integration—and its early obsession with the *Dassonville* formula, may also be understandable against the backdrop of the desperate need to reconstruct and rehabilitate Europe after two tragic wars. It is quite undeniable that both the GATT/WTO system and the EU have been unprecedented successes in terms of the growth of trade volume and its colossal contribution to global economic welfare in general. Also, the US interstate commerce regime has undergone a notably similar process, yet in a different setting of time and space. The development of the Commerce Clause and Dormant Commerce Clause jurisprudence reveals the spirit of federalization and nation-building in which market integration is an indispensable element.

However, new challenges have been emerging. Over the past two decades, non-trade social values such as the protection of the environment, as well as human health and safety, have been highlighted thanks to a worldwide demand for a better quality of life. These regulatory demands can be attributed in various ways to the enhanced welfare, as well as to the new risks associated with scientific development and technological innovation.[250] Governments have responded to concern and anxiety over social values by creating a tremendous amount of new legislation and new institutions, including special statutes and special agencies. Non-governmental organizations (NGOs) and civil society in general have voiced strong support for these non-trade social values. Obviously, this mounting regulatory concern tends to result in centrifugal reactions within each polity or institution. Each regulatory jurisdiction or state struggles to defy homogenization of non-trade (social) values driven by a pro-trade rationale, desiring to maintain a form of regulatory uniqueness that remains deeply imbued with its own peculiar socio-cultural characteristics.[251] This reaction reflects a common anxiety surrounding 'regulatory failure,' i.e., that it may eventually deprive each independent jurisdiction of regulatory autonomy or self-determination. On the other hand, this centrifugal reaction, if allowed to proceed unchecked, is likely to exert a serious disintegrationist impact upon the regional and global market, decreasing by turns the scale and volume of regional and global trade and darkening the prospects of future prosperity. This is what is meant by 'trade failure' and its regressive impact would fall disproportionately upon poor members.

In sum, the dual crisis of regulatory and trade failure[252] is not confined to the

249. *See* Dennis Kennedy, *Regional Trading Blocs, Multilateralism and the New GATT Agreement: An Introduction* [hereinafter *Introduction*], *in* REGIONAL TRADE BLOCS, MULTILATERALISM, AND THE GATT: COMPLEMENTARY PATHS TO FREE TRADE 1 (Till Geiger & Dennis Kennedy eds., 1996) [hereinafter COMPLEMENTARY PATHS]; Patrica Clavin, *The Triumph of Regionalism over Globalism: Patterns of Trade in the Interwar Period, in* COMPLEMENTARY PATHS, at 31–33.

250. FOOD SAFETY, *supra* note 11, Chapter I, at 10–2.

251. For an argument that globalization has diminished the effectiveness of local regulations, *see, e.g.*, Alfred C. Aman, Jr., *A Global Perspective on Current Regulatory Reforms: Rejection, Relocation, or Reinvention?*, 2 IND. J. GLOBAL LEGAL STUD. 429 (1995).

252. *Cf.* Martin Shapiro, *The Globalization of Law*, 1 IND. J. GLOBAL LEGAL STUD. 37, 51 (1993) (discussing an identifiable conflict between the 'globalization of markets' and the 'globalization of law').

GATT/WTO context, but also afflicts the EU and US systems. The following subsections will explore the parameters of the dual crisis as encountered in the EU and US contexts, as well as trace the development within these polities of jurisprudential approaches for reconciling the clash between free markets and state regulation.

2.2.2 EUROPEAN UNION

2.2.2.1 Conventional jurisprudence on the interface of free markets and state regulation: Dassonville, Cassis de Dijon and Keck

The same anti-protectionist *telos* that animated the old GATT could also be said to characterize the European Union's internal trade regime in general, but with a slightly different spin. Unlike GATT 1947, the European Community aimed from inception at the establishment of a customs union and subsequently a common market.[253] In comparison to GATT 1947, the early stage of European Community-building had more radical effects within the internal market in that it drastically eliminated tariffs and other quantitative barriers, and only allowed a relatively short transition period.[254] The urgent need for an integrated internal common market can be easily understood by reference to the motivations of the framers of the Community. As is evident from the Schuman Declaration,[255] the framers' motivation in initiating such an audacious enterprise among states that had so recently waged a deadly war against each other was to integrate Europe to such an extent that any future war would be inconceivable.[256]

To a large degree, this *telos* mirrors the *telos* of GATT 1947, which aimed to reconstruct the international economic order over the ruins of the World War II. However, the Community's *telos* was much more ambitious and received comparatively greater institutional support.[257] Consisting of a rather homogeneous group of founding members, the Community could realistically aim for a common market—a level of economic integration that would go well beyond the merely anti-protectionist aims of the old GATT.[258] Among other advantages, the Community

---

253. *See* Jo Shaw, Law of the European Union 9–11 (2d ed. 1996).

254. *See* Paul Craig & Gráinne De Búrca, EU Law: Text, Cases, and Materials 11–2 (2d ed. 1998) [hereinafter EU Law].

255. *See* Fascal Fontaine, A New Idea for Europe: The Schuman Declaration—1950–2000, *available at* <http://europa.eu.int/comm/dg10/publications/brochures/docu/50ans/txt01_en.html> (last visited on Mar. 19, 2001).

256. *See id* ('The solidarity in production thus established will make it plain that any war between France and Germany becomes *not merely unthinkable, but materially impossible.*') (emphasis added).

257. This weak *telos* in the old GATT 1947 is also evidenced by the incomplete and transient structure illustrated by the 'Protocol of Provisional Application,' which inundated the agreement with grandfathering rights and waivers. In this system, integration was limited because *past* barriers could not be lifted. By contrast, the EC system was able to eliminate many of the old disintegrative barriers in Member States and thus proceeded with integration either in a negative or judicial way (*i.e.*, mutual recognition), or in a positive or legislative way (*i.e.*, harmonization). Interestingly, the new WTO system has an intermediate status. It permits no grandfathering rights and very few waivers; it expressly aims for global economic integration through a solid multilateral trading system; and it is also equipped with side agreements such as the SPS and the TBT serving for (quasi-) harmonization.

258. The integrated common market system that necessitated the prohibition of any unjustified obstacles to trade was a superior 'legal commitment to free trade' than the mere elimination of discrimination and protection that was envisaged in GATT 1947. *See* Joseph H. H. Weiler, *The Constitution of the*

began with a workable legislative mechanism for harmonization,[259] as well as a full-blown adjudicative system represented by the European Court of Justice (ECJ).

Silhouetted against the transformation of its decision-making (harmonization) mechanism, the development of the ECJ jurisprudence, with respect to the interface of free markets and state regulation, has oscillated as it pursues an appropriate balance between deeper integration and domestic regulatory autonomy.[260] The ex Article 30 of the Treaty Establishing the European Economic Community (EEC),[261] which amounts to a combination of GATT Article III:4 (National Treatment) and XI:1 (Prohibition of Quantitative Restrictions and Measures Equivalent to Quantitative Restrictions), reads as follows:

> Quantitative restrictions on imports and all measures having an equivalent effect shall, without prejudice to the following provisions, be prohibited between Member States.

Before the seventies, there was a spectrum of views on the interpretation of the Article, ranging from narrow (the 'protection' test) to wide (the 'obstacle' test).[262] The narrow view focused on 'formal' discrimination, maintaining that measures indistinctively applied to domestic and foreign products would not constitute measures having an effect equivalent to quantitative restrictions.[263] The wide view, by contrast, highlighted the 'impact' of measures on trade between Member States, concluding that even indistinctively applicable measures should fall within the Article so long as they constitute an 'obstacle' to trade between Member States, and that those measures could only be saved later by derogations within ex Article 36 EEC.[264]

---

cont.

Common Market Place: Text and Context in THE EVOLUTION OF THE FREE MOVEMENT OF GOODS IN THE EVOLUTION OF EU LAW 352 (Paul Craig & Gráinne de Búrca eds. 1999) [hereinafter *Text and Context*].

259. Of course, the nature and pattern of the decision-making process within the EC has undergone critical changes as the Community (Union) evolves. *See* EU LAW, *supra* note 254, at 13–48.

260. In this context, Joel Paul noted that 'the classical view of national regulation threatened by the stream of free movement is fundamental to the jurisprudence in this area.' Joel R. Paul, *Free Trade, Regulatory Competition and the Autonomous Market Fallacy*, 1 COLUM. J. EUR. L. 29 (1995). Interestingly, however, harmonization could also mitigate national politicians' burden resulting from lobbies of domestic constituencies, thus creating a certain political incentive for further integration. *See* Jacques Pelkmans, *Removing Regulatory Access Barriers—The Case of 'Deep' Integration* 10, OECD, TD/TC(96)9, Feb. 15, 1996 (observing that 'national politicians could free themselves from excessive 'capture' at the national level by turning the EC 1992 project into a drive for pro-market dynamism').

261. This provision is now Article 28 of the Treaty Establishing the European Community after the Amsterdam amendments. *See supra* note 12, Introduction.

262. PROHIBITING RESTRICTIONS, *supra* note 196, at 10.

263. *Id.*, at 13–14.

264. The old version of Article 36 of the Treaty Establishing the European Economic Community (EEC) (now Article 30 of the Treaty Establishing the European Community after the Amsterdam amendments) reads as follows:

> The provisions of Articles 30 to 34 shall not preclude prohibitions or restrictions on imports, exports or goods in transit justified on grounds of public morality, public policy or public security; the protection of health and life of humans, animals or plants; the protection of national treasures possessing artistic, historic or archaeological value; or the protection of industrial and commercial property. Such prohibitions or restrictions shall not, however, constitute a means of arbitrary discrimination or a disguised restriction on trade between Member States.

See also id., at 14–15.

Meanwhile, the intermediate view adopted by the Commission was that indistinctively applicable measures would fall within the prohibition of ex Article 30 EEC only if they are 'disproportionate.'[265] Interestingly, all of these three different hermeneutics were later resurrected at various stages of the ECJ jurisprudential development: the wide view in *Dassonville* (1974),[266] the intermediate view in *Cassis de Dijon* (1979),[267] and the narrow view in *Keck* (1993).[268]

The first of these cases, *Dassonville* (1974), which essentially embraced the wide view's obstacle test, silenced previous debates and extended the analysis of the free movement of goods well beyond the narrow concept of 'protection' or 'formal discrimination' by establishing a canonical 'anti-obstacle' principle. The Dassonville Court famously stated:

> All trading rules enacted by Member States which are *capable* of hindering, directly or *indirectly*, actually or *potentially*, intra-Community trade are to be considered as measures having an effect equivalent to quantitative restrictions.[269]

This strong *pro*-trade bias against the domestic regulations of Member States negated any challenge to the principle of free movement of goods at least at the initial stage of scrutiny prior to the derogation through ex Article 36 EEC. Nonetheless, the *Dassonville* Court did not forget to leave an outlet for escape from an overly draconian application of the rule as long as the questioned measure was found to be 'reasonable' and 'indistinctively applicable' to all Community nationals. This outlet was available even for purposes that lay beyond the gamut of the exhaustive list in ex Article 36 EEC, such as the prevention of unfair practices. Subsequently, *Cassis de Dijon* (1979) elaborated upon this prototype of the 'rule of reason,' by tempering further the interpretive rigors of *Dassonville*.[270] The Court ruled that:

> Obstacles to movement within the Community resulting from disparities between the national laws relating to the marketing of the products in question must be accepted in so far as those provisions may be recognized as being *necessary* in order to satisfy *mandatory requirements* relating *in particular* to the effectiveness of fiscal supervision, the protection of public health, the fairness of commercial transactions and the defense of the consumer.[271]

Two significant hermeneutical innovations for overcoming the pro-trade bias embedded in the *Dassonville* line of case law emerged from *Cassis de Dijon*. First, the

---

265. *Id.*, at 16–18.
266. Procureur du Roi v Benoit and Gustave Dassonville, Case 8/74, Jul. 11 1974, [1974] ECR. 837, [1974] 2 C.M.L.R. 436 [hereinafter *Dassonville*].
267. Rewe-Zentral AG v. Bundesmonopolverwaltung für Branntwein, Case 120/78, Feb. 20, 1979, [1979] E.C.R. 649, [1979] 3 C.M.L.R. 494 [hereinafter *Cassis de Dijon*].
268. Criminal Proceedings against Keck & Mithouard, Joined Cases C-267 and268/91, Nov. 23, 1993, [1993] ECR I-6097 [hereinafter *Keck*].
269. *Dassonville*, *supra* note 266, ¶ 5 (emphasis added).
270. PROHIBITING RESTRICTIONS, *supra* note 196, at 15.
271. *Cassis de Dijon*, *supra* note 267, ¶ 8 (emphasis added).

formerly closed or exhaustive list in ex Article 36 EEC came to enjoy new additions through the 'mandatory requirements.' Under *Cassis de Dijon*, any policy objective other than the protection of certain domestic industries would fall within the rubric of the mandatory requirements. Secondly, the problem of dichotomy between general obligations (e.g., ex Article 30 EEC) and derogations (e.g., ex Article 36 EEC) was addressed by considering both at the same stage. Therefore, if any measure could be justified by the rule of reason, ex Article 36 EEC would not need to be applied.

Despite the *Cassis de Dijon* Court's attitude granting considerable regulatory leeway to Member States, the shadow of *Dassonville* remained an overwhelming presence for a significantly long time. In particular, even indistinctively or equally applicable measures still needed to be 'justified' by the proportionality test in order to escape the reach of ex Article 30 EEC. This vestigial rigor, which continuously interfered with domestic regulatory autonomy and often contradicted local socio-political sensibility, turned out to be more severe and burdensome as integrative (centripetal) market forces embraced Member States to an ever-increasing degree. Angst over diminishing regulatory sovereignty was also reflected and fueled by the *ethos* of 'subsidiarity,'[272] which influenced the Social Charter movement (1989)[273] and the Maastricht Treaty (1991-1993). Collectively, these developments signaled an important jurisprudential change that was soon to overtake the ex Article 30 EEC hermeneutics. Against this backdrop, the *Keck* decision, issued in 1993, excluded certain regulatory areas (concerning 'certain selling arrangements') from the domain of ex Article 30 EEC interpretation and, therefore, from the rigorous 'justification' (proportionality test) process required by the *Cassis de Dijon* line of cases.[274] Therefore, Member States came to secure more ample regulatory leeway in *certain* subject matters than they did in the pre-*Keck* era.

Overall, the jurisprudence governing intra-Community trade can be considered more advanced or mature in comparison with the GATT/WTO jurisprudence in that the EC trade jurisprudence, pertaining to indistinctively or equally applicable measures, does not 'exceptionalize' legitimate regulatory objectives vis-à-vis the principle of free movement of goods. Moreover, it has overcome the *lacuna* embedded in the first sentence of ex Article 36 EEC. According to the 'rule of reason' developed through *Dassonville* (1974) and *Cassis de Dijon* (1979), any legitimate regulatory objective can be scrutinized solely at the stage of ex Article 30 EEC.[275] In other words, a legitimate policy objective need not be confirmed as a violation at first only to be justified later by separately provided exceptions like ex Article 36 EEC. Therefore, domestic regulatory concerns, and by extension the non-trade social values they embody, can be reviewed at the same level as the principle of free movement of goods rather than being exceptionalized, provided that they are applied equally, without distinction as among domestic and foreign commerce. This 'non-exceptionalizing' or 'unifying' interpretation of ex Article 30 EEC was made more salient by *Keck*, wherein measures falling under certain selling arrangements came to

---

272. *See* SHAW, *supra* note 253, at 86.
273. *Id.*, at 46.
274. *See Keck*, *supra* note 268, ¶ 16.
275. *See Text and Context*, *supra* note 258, at 366.

be 'redeemed' without the burden of being subject to the rigors of the traditional *Dassonville* justification.[276]

Nevertheless, it would be hard to say that the traditional intra-Community trade jurisprudence is fully immune to the dual crisis that the GATT/WTO trade regime is now facing. First of all, according to the conventional reading of *Keck*, the criteria for '*certain* selling arrangements' are still nebulous. It is likely that many domestic regulations with considerable trade-distorting effects can survive ex Article 30 EEC scrutiny thanks to the *Keck* case law. Moreover, the *Keck* jurisprudence seems to have returned to the early narrow view (protection test) with regard to the interpretation of ex Article 30 EEC mirroring the early *telos* of the GATT (non-discrimination or anti-protection).[277] Though this hermeneutical shift may be understandable in light of the aforementioned political landscape of subsidiarity, it may also prove to be a regressive and disintegrationist move in that many regulations falling within the rubric of 'certain selling arrangements' would bypass the justification process and easily escape the discipline of free movement of goods.[278] As Paul Craig and Gráinne De Búrca trenchantly observed, thanks to the *Keck* jurisprudence, it would no longer be necessary to examine whether regulatory objectives pursued by contested national legislation was legitimate from a Community perspective.[279] This tendency amounts to 'trade failure'.

On the other hand, in the cases that have followed *Dassonville* and *Cassis de Dijon*, any equally applicable measure must be subject to a 'proportionality test,' which tends to be just as problematic as the necessary test from the GATT/WTO jurisprudence. The hermeneutic similarity between the necessary test and the proportionality test is easily detected in many cases.[280] Yet, on account of this similarity, certain criticisms commonly leveled against the necessary test also tend to apply to the proportionality test; foremost among these are complaints about judicial legislation, about the commandeering nature of the test, and about its lack of consideration toward local regulatory sensitivities. Simply put, the ECJ may not necessarily be in the best position to decide what is and what is not proportionate to a particular policy objective that a Member State aims at within its own context.

For instance, in *Cassis de Dijon* (1979), the ECJ ruled that obstacles to free movement of goods within the Community could be justified only if the German

---

276. *See* Laurence W. Gormley, *Two Years After Keck*, 19 FORDHAM INT'L L.J. 866, 870 (1996) [hereinafter *After Keck*].

277. *See e.g.*, *Infant Milk*, *infra* note 287, ¶ 16 ('Moreover, the legislation objected to by the Commission, *which applies, without distinction according to the origin of the products in question, to all of the traders operating within the national territory, does not affect the sale of products originating in other Member States any differently from that of domestic products.*') (emphasis added).

278. *See After Keck*, *supra* note 276, at 885–86.

279. EU LAW, *supra* note 254, at 619.

280. For instance, in *Cinéthèque*, the Court held that a prohibition is not compatible with the principle of free movement of goods unless any obstacle to intra-Community trade thereby created does not exceed what is *necessary* to attain the objective. Cases 60 and 61/84, Cinéthèque SA v. Fédération Nationale des Cinémas Francais [1985] ECR 2605, [1986] 1 CMLR 365, ¶ 22 [hereinafter *Cinéthèque*]; EU LAW, *supra* note 254, at 612–14. Likewise, in *Danish Bottle*, the ECJ responded to the Commission's argument that the Danish laws were *disproportionate* by holding that it should be examined whether all the restrictions which the contested rules impose on the free movements of goods are *necessary* to achieve the objectives pursued by those rules. Case 302/86, Commission v. Denmark [1988] ECR 4607, [1989] 1 CMLR 619, ¶ 12 [hereinafter *Danish Bottle*]; *id.*, at 643.

provision (Article 100 of the Branntweinmonopolgesetz) aiming to fix the minimum alcohol content of certain drinks might be recognized as being *necessary* to satisfy mandatory requirements such as the 'fairness of commercial transactions.'[281] The *Cassis de Dijon* Court then blatantly held that the German measure could not be accepted as being an 'essential' or 'necessary' guarantee of the fairness of commercial transactions because a 'less trade restrictive' alternative such as 'labeling' was available.[282] In other words, the *Cassis de Dijon* Court subtly *imposed* a legislative alternative (labeling) against the pre-existing German regulation (the mandatory fixing of minimum alcohol content) purportedly to improve the fairness of commercial transactions.[283] Likewise, the *Danish Bottle* (1988) Court *imposed* its own evaluation regarding the policy value of Denmark's 3000-hectoliter restriction, and concluded effortlessly that the restriction was disproportionate to Denmark's environmental policy objective.[284] Under such limited regulatory space, as defined by the Court, 'regulatory failure' can easily result.[285]

2.2.2.2 New approach through new interpretations: Keck, Graffione and Familiapress

A jurisprudential response to the aforementioned dual crisis (trade *and* regulatory failure) within the EU context can be analyzed in two ways: by rediscovering the

281. *Cassis de Dijon*, *supra* note 267, ¶ 8.
282. *Id.*, ¶ 13.
283. *Cassis de Dijon*, *supra* note 267, ¶ 13.
284. *See Danish Bottle*, *supra* note 280, ¶¶ 20–22. *See* Lisa Crosby, Note, *Green Beer: When is an Environmental Measure a Disguised Restriction on International Trade?*, 7 GEO. INT'L ENVTL. L. REV. 537, 548 (1995).
285. Of course, the Court had nonetheless been circumspect enough to employ a measure of judicial restraint with respect to certain sensitive areas involving 'national socio-cultural characteristics' as seen in *Torfaen* (1990). Torfaen Borough, Case 145/88 [1990], 1 CMLR 337, 23 November 1989 [hereinafter *Torfaen*]. In *Torfaen*, the Court admitted that a certain political and economic choice whose purpose is to ensure that 'working and non-working hours are so arranged as to accord with national or regional socio-cultural characteristics' is, in the *present* state of Community law, a matter for the Member states. *Id.*, ¶ 14. In the same vein, the Court also deferred to the national court the 'balancing' test of whether the restrictive effects on Community trade resulting from the prohibition of Sunday trading exceeded the effects intrinsic to rules of that kind. *Id.*, ¶¶ 15–6. Generally speaking, in pre-Keck jurisprudence, the ECJ explicitly gave more deference to national courts in cases relating to sensitive regulatory areas such as 'public health and safety' and 'public morality' reflecting 'socio-cultural characteristics' vis-à-vis other less sensitive fields such as 'economic policies.' In Case 53/80, Officier van Justitie v. Koninklijke Kaasfabriek Eyssen BV, [1981] ECR 409 (*Nisin*), the Court ruled that due to the lack of precise information on health risks that nisin (a natural antibiotic from cheese) might cause and in particular, the 'different eating habits in the various Member States,' the Dutch prohibition on the addition of nisin to cheese could have been justified as an alternative to labeling on grounds of public health. Furthermore, in Case 34/79, Regina v. Henn and Darby, [1979] ECR 3795 (*Henn and Darby*), the Court validated the English application of its legislation on pornography to imports of publications of Danish origin despite its flatly discriminatory treatment between domestic (English) and foreign (Danish) pornography. The Court stressed that 'in principle, it is for each member State to determine in accordance with its own scale of values and in the form selected by it the requirements of public morality in its territory.' In stark contrast, in cases involving economic policies such as minimum or maximum prices, the Court disciplined the application of domestic price controls to imports in the name of free movement of goods facing even equally applicable measures. *See e.g.*, Joined Cases 16 to 20/79, Openbaar Ministerie v. Danis and Others, [1979] ECR 3327; Joined Cases 88 to 90/75, Societa SDAM v. Comitato Interministeriale dei Prezzi, [1976] ECR 323; Kommers & Waelbroeck, *supra* note 196, at 203–17.

Keck case (1993), as well as by exploring new case law in the non-*Keck* line. First, with regard to measures falling under the rubric of 'certain selling arrangements,' one could observe the shift in the Court's interpretive focus from the traditional 'rule of reason' test to a combination of the 'applied evenhandedness' test and the 'manner' test. This shift can be illustrated by the following text respectively: 'so long as those provisions *apply* to *all* relevant traders operating within their national territory' and 'so long as they affect in the same *manner*, in law and in fact, the marketing of domestic products and of those from other Member States.'[286] The essence of hermeneutical change under the *Keck* test is that in the case of certain selling arrangements, the legal rigor embedded in the conventional rule of reason, including the 'proportionality' test, gave way to an 'application-and manner-oriented' test. This shift has also been noticeable in post-*Keck* case law.[287] As a result, the way in which the Court addressed highly sensitive and political issues, such as the regulation of shops' closing times, also changed dramatically from sheer deference to the national court, as seen in *Torfaen*, to the *Keck* test which scrutinizes the evenhanded application of the regulation in question as well as the manner in which a regulation affects marketing in law and in fact.[288]

On the other hand, with respect to those measures that fall outside the rubric of certain selling arrangements and thus outside the scope of the *Keck* jurisprudence, the Court has envisaged an even more bold and general departure from its past authoritative examination of the proportionality of Member States' measures. In stark contrast with the Court's own scrutiny of the issues of mandatory requirements and proportionality that continued through *Dassonville* and *Cassis de Dijon*, the recent jurisprudence surrounding the free movement of goods indicates the Court's willingness to respect national judges for determination of legal issues of that kind. Yet, along with this deference came critical interpretive guidelines concerning various checkpoints relating to the circumstances influencing the *manner* in which a questioned measure is actually *applied*.[289] This deference to national courts with

---

286. *Keck*, *supra* note 268, ¶ 16
287. In *Huenermund*, the Court held that:

> [T]hat rule (the German prohibition of the advertisement of quasi-pharmaceutical products outside the pharmacy), which applied without distinction as to the origin of the products in question to all pharmacists regulated by the professional association, does not affect the marketing of goods from other member States differently from that of domestic products.

Huenermund, Case C-292/92 1993 [ECR] I-6787, December 15, 1993. ¶ 23. Likewise, in *Infant Milk*, the Court also held that:

> [T]he legislation (the Greek law providing that processed milk for infants may be sold only in pharmacists' shops except in municipalities possessing no pharmacists' shop) objected to by the Commission, which applies 'in fact,' without distinction according to the origin of the products in question, to all of the traders operating within the national territory, does not affect the sale of products originating in other Member States any differently from that of domestic products.

Commission v. Greece, Case C-391/92 [1995] ECR I-1621, April 04, 1995, ¶ 16 [hereinafter *Infant Milk*].

288. *See* Tankstation 't Heukske, Joined Cases C-401/92 and C-402/92 [1994] ECR I-2199, June 2, 1994, ¶¶ 14–5; Punto Casa and PVV, Joined Cases C-69/93 and C-258/93 [1994] ECR I-2363, June 2, 1994; Semeraro Casa Uno Srl and Others v. Sindaco Del Comune Di Erbusco and Others, Joined Cases C 418–421, 460–462 & 464/93, C 9–11, 14–15, 23–24 and 332/94 [1996] 3 CMLR 648, 20 June, 1996.
289. Such deference is reminiscent of the kind that was envisaged in the *Torfaen* case law involving 'national socio-cultural characteristics.' However, unlike the *Torfaen* case law allowing for a 'flat' deference, the pattern of deference observed here in very recent post-*Keck* cases can be characterized as a form of deference that includes the provision of 'interpretive guidelines,' which amount to 'formulae' that the Court wishes national courts to follow.

concrete checkpoints tends to lead national judges to focus on *how* Member States administer the questioned measures in response to those fact-sensitive circumstances reflected in the checkpoints, and on whether such response is proportionate to the attainment of given policy objectives. As a result, national courts eventually conduct a manner- and/or application-oriented scrutiny on the questioned measures on behalf of the Court.

For instance, in *Graffione* (1996), the question referred to the Court was whether ex Articles 30 and 36 EEC granted an exception to a national measure for protecting consumers against unfair competition in the marketing of products coming from a Member State in which they are lawfully marketed, on the grounds that those products carried an illegal trademark in the importing state because it was misleading to consumers.[290] Reiterating the settled case law on ex Articles 30 and 36, the Court held that the principle of free movement of goods cannot be overridden, and that barriers to trade are thus unjustified even if there is a risk of misleading consumers—unless such risk is sufficiently serious.[291] The Court then *deferred* to an Italian court for a final assessment after charging it with reviewing several concrete issues such as 'the circumstances in which the products are sold, the information set out on the packaging of the products, and the clarity with which it is displayed, the presentation and content of advertising material, and the risk of error in relation to the group of consumers concerned.'[292] This deference undoubtedly stems from the Court's recent realization that national courts are in a better position to consider the various circumstances under which such legislation is *applied* and implemented.

Similarly, in *Familiapress* (1997), which dealt with the subtle issue of whether a prohibition on 'games with prizes on newspapers' is proportionate to the maintenance of pluralism in the press and whether this objective might be attained by measures less restrictive of both intra-Community trade and freedom of expression, the Court once again *deferred* to the national court for a final determination. In this case, the national court was guided to review 'whether a probability of winning constitutes an incentive to purchase which can cause demand shift.'[293]

In sum, *Keck* case law can be read as highlighting the evenhanded application of a regulation in question and the manner in which the regulation affects the marketing in law and in fact, while the non-*Keck* case law emphasizes deference to national courts, but with interpretive guidelines leading national courts to scrutinize the manner in which a measure is actually applied.[294] Notably, this two-tiered ECJ jurisprudence,

---

290. Case C-313/94, F.lli Graffione SNC v. Ditta Fransa, 26 November 1996, *available at* <http://europa/eu.int/cj/en/act/act 96/9632en.htm#C-313/94> (last visited on February 20, 2000) [hereinafter *Graffione*].

291. *Id.*

292. *Id.* A similar type of judicial deference may be found in the WTO context. *Cf.* United States—Restrictions on Imports of Cotton and Man-Made Fibre Underwear, Panel Report adopted as modified by the Appellate Body on Feb. 25, 1997, WT/DS24/R, ¶ 7. 12 (rejecting a *de novo* review).

293. Case C-368/95, Vereinigte Familiapress Zeitungsverlags- und vertriebs GmbH v. Heinrich Bauer Verlag, 26 June 1997, *available at* <http://europa/eu.int/cj/en/act97/9719en.htm#C-368/95> (last visited on February 20, 2000) [hereinafter *Familiapress*].

294. However, the deference here would not be 'absolute.' Even 'inaction' by a Member state under some circumstances may be violative of ex Article 30 EEC. For instance, in *French Vandalism*, the ECJ declared that 'by failing to adopt all necessary and proportionate measures in order to prevent the free movement of fruit and vegetables from being obstructed by actions by private individuals, the

recently developed regarding free movement of goods, mirrors the aforementioned hermeneutical transformation in the GATT/WTO jurisprudence.[295] As is the case in the chapeau test, the new jurisprudence tends to provide more regulatory leeway to Member States in that the Court does not need to second-guess whether the questioned measures are necessary—that is, proportionate *per se*—to attain whatever legitimate objectives that those measures intend to pursue. Rather, Member States are required to prove that their measures are implemented and enforced in an evenhanded manner consistent with the Treaty. This should be the jurisprudential response to the 'regulatory failure' within the context of the European Union.

At the same time, the abovementioned tendency in the judicial scrutiny highlighting the regulatory *process* is likely to lead to more methodical exercise of the Member States' regulatory discretion and thus regulatory disciplines, which by turns contribute to reducing actual and potential trade-restricting effects of domestic regulations. In fact, the judicial emphasis on regulatory process tends to converge the regulatory processes of the Member States, centering on essential procedural precepts, such as due process. This procedural convergence or 'quasi-harmonization,' fosters further market integration among Member States through facilitating free movement of goods. This should be the jurisprudential response to the 'trade failure' within the context of the European Union.

2.2.3 United States

2.2.3.1 Conventional jurisprudence on the interface of free markets and state regulation: the Dormant Commerce Clause and the federal balance

Insofar as 'trade' or 'foreign/interstate commerce' is concerned, the experience of the United States parallels that of the GATT/WTO and the EU. After coming into existence, the US also had to establish a free trade system at the federal level among different states, while those states continued their attempts to meet their own local regulatory demands. Historically, a desire for market integration in the US was much more intense than was seen in the EU because the *telos* of the US system was 'nation-building' through federalization. Yet the federalization process was no smoothly paved road. To begin with, the initial heterogeneity among colonial states was quite profound.[296] In addition, the pre-Constitution 'Articles of Confederation' failed in the end mainly because the states waged devastating trade wars against each

cont.
French Republic had failed to fulfill its obligations under Article 30 of the EC Treaty.' Commission of the European Communities v. French Republic, Case C-265/95, December 9, 1997, *available at* <http://europa.eu.int/cj/act/act97/9734en.htm#C-265/95> (last visited on March 20, 2000).

295. *See supra* sub-sec. 2.1.3.

296. *See* Mauro Cappelletti, *Forward to the Florence Integration Project Series in* A Political, Legal and Economic Overview (Book 1), Methods, Tools and Institutions (Volume 1), Integration Through Law: European and the American Federal Experience v–xix (Mauro Cappelletti et al eds. 1985) (quoting John Adams deploring on September 25, 1777 that: 'Tedious, indeed, is our Business. Slow, as Snails. Fifty Gentlemen meeting together, all Strangers, are not acquainted with Each other's Language, Ideas, Views, Designs. They are . . . jealous of each other—fearful, timid, skittish.').

other,[297] a process that was to be repeated among countries prior to World War II. Such trade wars influenced the Supreme Court's teleological interpretation[298] of the Dormant Commerce Clause, which was intended to prevent a return to economic balkanization as well as to create a single 'federal common market.'[299]

The US internal (inter-state) trade regime has been driven by two main engines: the 'Commerce Clause' and the 'Dormant Commerce Clause.' The Commerce Clause, which is in fact very vague in its text,[300] has been frequently and extensively[301] invoked by the Supreme Court to strike down conflicting state legislation or even to declare state constitutional provisions unconstitutional in light of the Federal Constitution. This single clause has resulted in an amazing expansion of the operational competence of the federal government and has thus contributed dramatically to regulatory harmonization at the federal level. On the other hand, the so-called Dormant Commerce Clause,[302] which refers to an interpretive doctrine developed by the Supreme Court, is a negative reading of the Commerce Clause. According to this

---

297. *See* THE FEDERALIST No. 7, at 30–34 (Alexander Hamilton) (Clinton Rossiter ed., Mentor 1999) (1961) (arguing that the separate commercial policies and resultant exclusion could drive war among states). This common diagnosis—a diagnosis that the 'biased accountability' of states' politicians to their constituencies urged them to pursue their narrow and self-protective local economic interests at the expense of those of other states and the nation as a whole—forms the basis of the far-reaching Madisonian interpretation of the Commerce Clause, which was later supported and elaborated by Chief Justice Marshall. LAURENCE H. TRIBE, AMERICAN CONSTITUTIONAL LAW 1044–46 (3d ed., Vol. I., 2000). This broad interpretation was challenged by Marshall's successor as Chief Justice, Roger Taney, who opposed such severe limitations on state power and instead supported the view that the Commerce Clause left states free to regulate interstate commerce as long as states' regulations (legislations) did not conflict with federal legislations. *Id.*, at 1045. More recently, Justices Thomas and Scalia have a similar view. *See Id.*,1043–4; n.2.
298. It can be said that the US' uniqueness in constitutional practice, *i.e.* strong 'judicial review' by the Supreme Court, which had been nurtured since *Marbury v. Madison* 1 Cranch 137 (1803), enabled the federal government to proceed with an integration process. *See* Lawrence Lessig, *Translating Federalism: United States v. Lopez*, 1995 SUP. CT. REV. 125 (1995). Lessig argues that the U.S. Supreme Court has been responding to ever-deepening integration through an interpretive *cycle* between 'originalism' respecting the Framers' intention (interpretive fidelity) and 'textualism' focusing more on the current context (case), thereby reassuring and sometimes fine-tuning the federal balance. He also suggests that this practice, which he terms 'translation,' is constrained by certain fundamental requirements such as the political question doctrine.
299. In this context, Justice Cardozo included a famous sentence in his opinion in *Baldwin*: '[The Constitution] was framed upon the theory that the peoples of the several states must *sink or swim together*' (emphasis added). *Baldwin v. G.A.F. Seeling, Inc.*, 294 U.S. 511 (1935) [hereinafter *Baldwin*].
300. U.S. CONST. art I, § 8, cl. 3 ('The Congress shall have Power ... To regulate Commerce with foreign Nations, and among the several States, and with the Indian Tribes.').
301. For instance, in an early, but classic case concerning the Commerce Clause, *Gibbons v. Ogden*, Chief Justice Marshall opined that: 'The Congressional power to regulate interstate commerce included the ability to *affect* matters occurring within a state, so long as the activity had some commercial connection with another state. ... No area of interstate commerce is reserved for state control.' (emphasis added). *Gibbons v. Ogden*, 9 Wheat. I (1824). In this opinion, the word 'affect' functioned as a *hook* to trigger the Commerce Clause. Since the word 'affect' was very expansive (nearly catching-all) the broad use of the Commerce Clause had been guaranteed.
302. The Dormant (negative) Commerce Clause is not an independent clause in the U.S. Constitution, but a doctrine derived from the Commerce Clause. Although it is still controversial, as Tribe has noted, whether the 'affirmative grant of commerce power to Congress should be construed to circumscribe state action in some or all cases,' the Supreme Court has continued to uphold this doctrine thus far. *See* TRIBE, *supra* note 297, at 1030. For instance, recent Supreme Court decisions have expressly endorsed the dormant Commerce Clause by holding that '[T]he Commerce Clause does more than confer power on the Federal Government; it is also a substantive restriction on possible state regulation of interstate commerce.' *Id.*; *see also* Dennis v. Higgins, 498 U.S. 439, 446 (1991).

reading, states have limited regulatory autonomy even in the face of legislative acquiescence by Congress. The doctrine is analogous to both the principle of National Treatment under the GATT/WTO trade system and the doctrine of Free Movement of Goods under the intra-EU trade regime.[303] Under this doctrine, states regulations which clearly 'discriminate against' or 'burden' interstate commerce are invalidated, which has contributed greatly to the formation of an integrated federal marketplace.

The long-standing and prevailing concern of the US with managing a federal marketplace while maintaining harmony among fifty states is not unique; both the EU and the WTO have faced similar federalistic or constitutional challenges.[304] The US also faces the same dual crisis as the WTO and the EU. First, the states have recently been vocal about reinstating their regulatory independence from the federal government.[305] This may also be interpreted as a political campaign for more state sovereignty as embedded in the Tenth Amendment.[306] In parallel with this move, during the 1990s, the Supreme Court ruled several times against Congress for having exceeded its authority under the Commerce Clause, or under the Tenth Amendment constraints on exercise of the commerce power.[307] This line of rulings, including *New York* (1992), [308] *Lopez* (1995), [309] *Printz* (1997),[310] and *Morrison* (2000),[311] was understood by some to be a readjustment of the power balance in the

---

303. In this context, Tribe noted that '[I]nternational comparison illustrates that the U.S. approach to these issues of federalism is not the only possible way to accommodate the conflicting interests at stake.' TRIBE, *supra* note 297, at 1027, n.27.
304. McGinnis and Movsesian observed that 'in promoting both free trade and accountable democratic government, the WTO reflects many of the principles that inform federalism.' *World Trade Constitution*, *supra* note 29, at 514.
305. *See* CASS SUNSTEIN, FREE MARKETS AND SOCIAL JUSTICE 336 (1997) (arguing that the 'New Federalism' in the seventies and eighties reinvigorated the states' regulatory autonomy).
306. U.S. CONST. amend. X ('The powers not delegated to the United States by the Constitution, nor prohibited by it to the States, are reserved to the States respectively, or to the people.').
307. Robert Meltz, '*The Commerce Clause as a Limit on Congressional Power to Protect the Environment*,' The Congressional Research Service Issue Brief (March 12, 1999), *available at* <http://www.cnie.org/nle/leg-35.html>, (last visited on January 6, 2000).
308. 505 U.S. 144 (1992). The *New York* court voided a federal law requiring that any state failing to provide for permanent disposal of waste generated within its borders must take title to the waste, holding that Congress may not 'commandeer the legislative processes of the States by directly compelling them to enact and enforce a federal regulatory program.' *See* Meltz, *supra* note 307.
309. 514 U.S. 549 (1995). The Supreme Court struck down a criminal conviction under the Gun-Free School Zones Act of 1990 as beyond Congress' authority under the Commerce Clause. See *Id.*
310. 117 S. Ct. 2365 (1997). In this case, the Supreme Court invalidated a provision of the Brady Handgun Violence Protection Act requiring that the chief law enforcement officer of a local jurisdiction should conduct a background check on would-be purchasers of handguns. The Brady Act thus commanded such officers to participate in administering a federal regulatory scheme. *See* Meltz, *supra* note 307.
311. In *Morrison* (2000), a very recent case concerning federalism (the Dormant Commerce Clause), the Court struck down a federal legislation (42 U.S.C. § 13981), which provides a federal civil remedy for the victims of gender-motivated violence, on the ground that the Congress lacked authority to enact § 13981 under either § 8 of the Commerce Clause or §5 of the Fourteenth Amendment. In so doing, the Court cited *Lopez* (514 U.S. 549) in which it ruled that the Congress lacked authority, based on the Commerce Clause, to enact a federal law prohibiting the possession of a firearm in a school zone due to its 'non-economic' (criminal) nature, and emphasized on similar non-economic nature of 'gender-motivated crimes of violence' found in *Morrison*. The Court concluded that:

    > The Constitution requires a distinction between what is truly national and what is truly local, and there is no better example of the police power, which the Founders undeniably left reposed in the States and denied the central government, than the suppression of violent crime and vindication of its victims.

    United States v. Morrison et al., 000 U.S. 99–5 (2000).

states' favor, as well as a reflection of the historically oscillating line between the proper spheres of federal and state power.[312] Others viewed this line of cases nostalgically, as a welcome return to the framers' intention of federalism.[313] Regardless, this recent trend is reminiscent of 'dual federalism' and the '*Cooley* doctrine,' which separated 'local' issues from 'national' ones.[314] These developments reflect recent anxieties about 'regulatory failure' in the federal level as well as about regulatory autonomy in the local context.

Moreover, a core interpretive parameter of modern Dormant Commerce Clause jurisprudence, i.e., the 'balancing test,'[315] which mirrors the 'necessary test' of GATT/WTO jurisprudence[316] and the 'proportionality test' of EU trade jurisprudence, [317] has been criticized from a perspective similar to that encountered in the WTO and the EU contexts.[318] In particular, the very notion of 'balancing' by the Court as a judicial branch has been most controversial.[319] For instance, in *Bendix,*[320]

312. *See* Meltz, *supra* note 307. *Cf.* Alfred C. Aman, Jr., *The Globalizing State: A Future-Oriented Perspective on the Public/Private Distinction, Federalism, and Democracy*, 31 VAND. J. TRANSNAT'L L. 769, 849 (1998) (maintaining that the 'shift in emphasis from federal power to state autonomy and power coincides with economic and political shifts in the global economy that also encourage decentralization of power').

313. Charles Fried, *Opponents of Federalism Are Mired in a Time Warp*, WALL ST. J., May 16, 2000, at A 26.

314. Tribe views the Cooley doctrine as the 'bridge to the modern cases' in the Dormant Commerce Clause jurisprudence. TRIBE, *supra* note 297, at 1046–9.

315. In *Pike*, the Court held that: 'Where the statute regulates even-handedly to effectuate a legitimate local public interest, and its effects on interstate commerce are only incidental, it will be held unless the burden imposed on such commerce is *clearly excessive* in relation to the putative local benefits' (emphasis added). Pike v. Bruce Church, Inc., 397 U.S. 137 (1970) [hereinafter *Pike*]. *Cf.* Richard H. Fallon, Jr., *Forward: Implementing the Constitution*, 111 HARV. L. REV. 56, 77–79 (1997) (distinguishing between 'balancing in the shaping of doctrinal tests' and 'balancing within constitutional doctrine as shaped by the Supreme Court').

316. Another tier of the modern balancing test holds that a state regulation that discriminates against interstate or out-of-state commerce will be invalid unless those regulations serve a legitimate local purpose and that such purpose cannot be met by 'available nondiscriminatory means.' *See* TRIBE, *supra* note 297, at 1059; *see also* Maine v. Taylor, 477 U.S. 131, 138 (1986) [hereinafter *Taylor*] ; Hughes v. Oklahoma, 441 U.S. 322, 336 (1979). This 'available nondiscriminatory means' can be in parallel with 'least trade-restrictive measures' in the GATT/WTO context, which represents the 'necessary test.'

317. The proportionality test also resembles the necessary test and thus the balancing test. For instance, in *Cinéthèque*, in which a French law prohibited the distribution of films (movies) during the first year of their release for the purpose of encouraging people to go to the cinema (theatre) and thereby protect the cinema industry, the ECJ ruled that:

> [A]rticle 30 of the EEC Treaty must be interpreted as meaning that it does not apply to national legislation which regulates the distribution of cinematographic works by imposing an interval between one mode of distributing such works and another form for a limited period, provided that the prohibition applies to domestically produced and imported cassettes alike and any barriers to intra-Community trade to which its implementation may give rise *do not exceed what is necessary* for ensuring that the exploitation in cinemas of cinematographic works of all origins retains priority over other means of distribution.

Cinéthèque, *supra* note 280, ¶ 12 (emphasis added).

318. *See e.g.*, *Neither Science Nor Shamans*, *supra* note 86, at 200–1 (criticizing the *Thai Cigarette* Panel's interpretation of 'necessary to protect human health').

319. A common criticism of 'balancing,' that this standard is not 'judicially manageable,' can be epitomized as follows:

> (i) It requires courts to collect and appraise 'legislative' facts that they lack practical competence to find and to weigh; (ii) it calls for policy judgments that courts have neither the expertise nor the democratic legitimacy to make; and (iii) it invites results that are too ad hoc to establish meaningful guidance to legislatures and other decision-makers.

WILLIAM B. LOCKHART ET AL., CONSTITUTIONAL LAW 231 (8th ed., 1996).

320. Bendix Autolite Corp. v. Midwesco Enterprises, 486 U.S. 888 (1988) [hereinafter *Bendix*].

one of the most vehement critics of the balancing test, Justice Scalia, criticized the scale analogy associated with *balancing* as inappropriate since the interests on both sides, the states and the federation as a whole, are 'incommensurate.'[321] Scalia argued further that:

> ... weighing the governmental interests of a State against the needs of interstate commerce is, by contrast, a task squarely within the responsibility of Congress, and 'ill-suited to the judicial function'.[322]

In the same context, Donald Regan has argued that:

> ... it is especially inappropriate for any body other than Congress to attempt to evaluate from a national point of view effects that we have specifically chosen, by having a federal system, to leave to varying state evaluations in the normal course.[323]

The natural corollary of this criticism is that the Court should focus solely on 'purposeful protectionism'[324] or discriminatory measures.[325] In other words, as seen in the dissenting opinion in *Dean Milk*,[326] a 'good faith' or non-protectionist state regulation designed to address a local concern such as health and safety should not be invalidated simply because the Court believes that a certain less-burdensome alternative could produce the same result. This stance is consistent with the anxiety of states regarding 'regulatory failure.'[327]

Although this centrifugal tendency does not seem to have engendered an immediate disintegrationist impact within the federal marketplace, certain unilateral local regulations may potentially hinder inter-state commerce. This potential is amplified by the Supreme Court's ruling in *New York* (1992), urging the Congress to *encourage* states to regulate in their own way.[328] Moreover, as the relative shrinkage of federal power backed by the Commerce Clause possibly reduces the degree of

---

321. Scalia opined that: 'This process is ordinarily called 'balancing', but the scale analogy is not really appropriate, since the interests on both sides are incommensurate. It is more like judging whether a particular line is longer than a particular rock is heavy.' *Id.*; TRIBE, *supra* note 297, at 1062.
322. *See Bendix*, *supra* note 320. Moreover, Justice Scalia metaphorically but sarcastically described the Dormant Commerce Clause as the product of 'intellectual adverse possession,' which should be given a restricted standard of review. *See A GATT's-Eye View*, *supra* note 93, at 1408, n.17.
323. Donald H. Regan, '*The Supreme Court and State Protectionism: Making Sense of the Dormant Commerce Clause*,' 84 Mich. L. Rev. 1091, 1153 (1986).
324. *Id.*, at 1093.
325. As a matter of fact, the Supreme Court has been strict regarding plainly discriminatory state regulations. TRIBE, *supra* note 297, at 1063. *See e.g.*, Oregon Waste Sys., Inc. v. Department of Envtl. Quality, 511 U.S. 93, 99 (1994) [hereinafter *Oregon Waste*]. Interestingly, Justice Scalia, who is hostile toward the dormant Commerce Clause balancing test, has been more active in striking down discriminatory state regulations. TRIBE, *supra* note 297, at 1063, n.24. *See also Bendix*, *supra* note 320.
326. Dean Milk Co. v. City of Madison, Wis., 340 U.S. 349 (1951). [hereinafter *Dean Milk*].
327. *Cf. Aim and Effects*, *supra* note 29 at 623. Hudec argues that the 'aim and effects' test is to relax the rigor of GATT Article III and XX regarding 'origin-neutral' regulatory measures. However, the most serious problem of this test is that it bypasses other tests for justification, such as the necessary test and the chapeau test, and validates 'regulatory distinctions' too easily. *See id.*, at 627.
328. *See supra* note 308.

harmonization at the federal level, the proliferation of unilateral regulations issued by individual states threatens to inundate the Dormant Commerce Clause with violations. As the national economy becomes more integrated, such regulations are likely to subject the federal marketplace to negative externalities, the effects of which could be as serious as discriminatory regulations, even if the regulations themselves are neither protectionist nor discriminatory *per se*.[329] Naturally, this concern seems much like the 'trade failure' discussed earlier.

2.2.3.2 New approach through new interpretations: evenhandedness and manner-oriented scrutiny

Close examination of the contemporary jurisprudence of the US Dormant Commerce Clause reveals that the Supreme Court conducts a two-tiered test.[330] First, any state regulation that aims to protect local economic interests against interstate commerce will be invalid unless the state demonstrates both that it serves a legitimate regulatory goal, and that it is the least restrictive alternative.[331] However, if a state regulation is *not* protectionist, it falls under the scrutiny of the *Pike* test, namely the balancing test. According to this test, an evenhanded state regulation serving a legitimate policy objective will be upheld despite an incidental impact on interstate commerce, unless that burden clearly outweighs the benefits achieved at the state or local level.[332] It seems that practical usage of the first tier test seems to be rather limited since flat protections have recently become increasingly costly and unpopular.[333] Therefore, the gravity of scrutiny naturally tends to shift from the first tier (protection) to the second tier (evenhandedness and balancing). Yet, unlike the first-tier test that is applied to protectionist measures in a relatively strict manner, the second-tier test reveals that the court tends to be more generous, in practice, in upholding state regulations without conducting serious balancing, if they are regulated in an evenhanded manner.[334] Therefore, at least as a practical matter, the 'evenhandedness' test can be said to be the determinative element in the US Dormant Commerce Clause jurisprudence.[335]

In a doctrinal sense, evenhandedness suggests fair, consistent and equitable treatment between in-state and out-of-state industries (or products) in like situations.

---

329. TRIBE, *supra* note 297, at 1042, n.52.
330. In the same vein, Farber and Hudec described the U.S. Court's tendency toward a priori characterizations of the measures as 'discriminatory' or merely 'incidentally' burdensome as 'preliminary sorting operation.' *A GATT's-Eye View*, *supra* note 93, at 1426.
331. *Taylor*, *supra* note 316. More recently, the Court seems to have reinforced the latter test. A discriminatory local statute against interstate commerce in favor of local business is '*per se* invalid' unless, in a narrow class of cases, the state shows that it is the least restrictive alternative available to achieve a legitimate state objective. *See* C & A Carbone, Inc. v. Town of Clarkstown, 511 U.S. 383, 392 (1994); TRIBE, *supra* note 297, at 1059, n.2, 1063.
332. *Pike, see supra* note 315.
333. *Cf.* GLOBAL TRANSFORMATION, *supra* note 10, Chapter I, at 187.
334. TRIBE, *supra* note 297, at 1063 n.23. This interpretive leniency or sympathy toward evenhanded state regulations might be influenced by the vulnerability of the balancing test to the criticism of judicial legislation.
335. Strictly speaking, the concepts of 'protection' and 'discrimination' should be distinguished. While the former represents any discriminatory measure motivated by local protection, the latter connotes a non-protectionist, thus legitimate measure which is not, however, evenhanded in application. Therefore, evenhandedness means non-protectionist *and* non-discriminatory.

In this context, Donald Kommers and Michel Waelbroeck observed the recent jurisprudential trend on the Dormant Commerce Clause as follows:

> In the newer cases *what* is regulated is less important than *how* it is regulated. The practical operation of a regulatory scheme is more important than whether it affects intrastate or interstate commerce directly or incidentally.[336]

Notably, this evenhandedness test mirrors the chapeau test under the GATT/WTO framework. In particular, the courts' interpretive practice of emphasizing the 'manner' in which a contested measure is designed and applied, strongly conveys the same doctrinal parameter embedded in the chapeau test: the requirement that no measure should be applied in a 'manner' which would constitute a means of arbitrary or unjustifiable discrimination between countries where the same conditions prevail.[337]

Interestingly, the Supreme Court's jurisprudence on the evenhandedness test underwent a similar hermeneutical dynamic as was seen in the GATT/WTO jurisprudence. The earlier discussion of *Thai Cigarette* (1990) revealed that the decision was intrusive and dismissive of local regulatory sensitivities. One can reasonably detect a surprisingly similar and thus problematic interpretive attitude in *Dean Milk* (1951). In this case, the Court failed to pay due attention to the City of Madison's legitimate concerns about the quality of milk consumed by its residents when it struck down a municipal ordinance requiring the milk to be pasteurized and bottled at nearby approved plants, on the sole grounds that 'reasonable and adequate alternatives' *could have been found.*[338] Here, the Court, just like the *Thai Cigarette* Panel, imposed a regulatory alternative from its own imagination. In fact, three dissenting Justices (Justices Black, Douglas and Minton) in *Dean Milk* stressed that:

> this health regulation should not be invalidated merely because the Court believes that alternative milk-inspection methods might insure the cleanliness and healthfulness of Dean's Illinois milk.[339]

However, departing from its previous position in *Dean Milk* (1951), the Court in *Taylor* (1986) upheld a total ban on the importation of 'live bait fish' even though the defendant, Maine, had apparently used less trade restrictive measures such as sampling and inspection techniques in similar situations involving 'fresh water fish.' The departure rested on the ground that:

> the abstract possibility of developing acceptable procedures, particularly when there is no assurance as to their effectiveness, does not make those procedures

---

336. *See* Kommers & Waelbroeck, *supra* note 196, at 174. The authors observed that in recent Dormant Commerce Clause jurisprudence, the Supreme Court has highlighted *how* something is regulated more than *what* is regulated.
337. GATT 1994, *supra* note 2, art. XX (chapeau).
338. Tribe, *supra* note 297, at 1083; *Dean Milk, supra* note 326, at 354–55.
339. *Dean Milk, supra* note 326, at 357–61.

as 'available non-discriminatory alternative' for the purpose of the Commerce Clause.[340]

This changed jurisprudence is inspiringly compatible with the chapeau test under the GATT/WTO system in that the Court came to pay more attention to a local regulatory concern accompanied by a 'good faith' effort, instead of second-guessing the local regulatory determination and forcing the acceptance of its own prescription. In other words, the Supreme Court accepted Maine's ban on the importation of 'live bait fish,' though an inspection in the *Dean Milk* style would have been the most ideal policy, because the 'uncertain cost' associated with actualizing such an 'abstract possibility' should not be imposed on states, especially when their 'reasonable efforts' in the policy-making and implementation process could be observed.[341]

A further example of such 'manner-oriented' scrutiny enshrined in the evenhandedness test can be seen in a lower court case. In *Bill Kettlewell Excavating, Inc. v. Michigan Department of Natural Resources*, plaintiff Bill Kettlewell Excavating, Inc. challenged the 'Michigan Solid Waste Management Act' (MSWMA), which required explicit county approval for in-county disposal of waste generated outside the county. The plaintiff further challenged the application of the MSWMA by St. Clair County, which banned all out-of-county waste from county landfills, as unconstitutional on the grounds that it violated due process and the Dormant Commerce Clause.[342] The US District Court, however, held that the MSWMA did not discriminate against interstate commerce, either on its face or in its effect. The court concluded that the MSWMA had not, through its *means*, imposed an authoritative preclusion against the importation of all out-of-state waste, which would have been a discrimination against interstate commerce.[343] The court stressed that the MSWMA did not authorize state officials to issue a 'blanket preclusion' against the importation of all out-of-state waste.[344] Instead, the court ruled that the MSWMA did grant each county 'discretion in accepting or denying' importation of waste from any outside source, including other counties within the State. In the same vein, the district court also held that St. Clair County's application

340. *Taylor*, *supra* note 316, at 148.

341. *See* Howse, *Interface*, *supra* note 97, at 144–48. Despite a similar factual setting, in the WTO *Australian Salmon* (1998) case, Australia, unlike the State of Maine, was found to have violated Article 5.5 of the SPS Agreement since Australia committed 'arbitrary or unjustifiable' distinction in levels of protection in the importation of 'fresh, chilled or frozen salmon' in question vis-à-vis other comparable situations (*e.g.*, the importation of live bait or ornamental fish), in particular considering the substantial, but unexplained change in conclusion between the 1995 Draft Report (which recommended allowing the importation of ocean-caught Pacific salmon under certain conditions) and the 1996 Final Report (which recommended continuing the import prohibition). Australian Salmon, *supra* note 9, Introduction. Australian policy inconsistency between comparable situations seemed to be a main factor that could distinguish this case from *Taylor*. Nonetheless, it might be argued that 'heat treatment' which led to the ban would have been a rational policy choice by Australia considering comprehensive empirical work that might have justified or unjustified it.

342. Bill Kettlewell Excavating, Inc. v. Michigan Department of Natural Resources, 732 F. Supp. 761 (1990) [hereinafter *Kettlewell*].

343. *Id.*, at 764.

344. *Id.*, at 765.

of the MSWMA treated in-state solid waste in the same *manner* as out-of-state solid waste by prohibiting the importation of either into the county.[345]

In conclusion, the current jurisprudence on the Dormant Commerce Clause, which is characterized by the 'evenhandedness' and 'manner-oriented' test, overcomes the dual crisis of trade and regulatory failure within the US context. First, by practically replacing the highly controversial balancing test, the current jurisprudence can provide states with relatively broader regulatory leeway in the absence of such balancing of federal and local interests. Under this situation, states can enjoy a wider spectrum of regulatory autonomy or diversity. On the other hand, if a state regulation is adopted or applied in an evenhanded way, that is a state administers its local regulations in good faith, the possibility that it impedes the interstate commerce decreases dramatically, thereby contributing to further market integration. Tellingly, this modern jurisprudential prescription to the dual crisis under the US system parallels the one that is provided by the chapeau test under the GATT/WTO system.

2.2.4 Observation: Divergence and Convergence

2.2.4.1 Divergent structure: dichotomy v. unity

As discussed above, under the GATT/WTO system the dogmatic dichotomy between 'general obligations,' such as national treatment, and 'exceptions,' such as protection of human health, reveals a critical pro-trade bias and tendency to subordinate legitimate regulatory concerns. However, this dichotomy is not necessarily shared by the US or the EU internal trade system. Under the US Dormant Commerce Clause jurisprudence, which governs the interface of free trade principles and regulatory concerns, there is no textual[346] or interpretive dichotomy between any general obligation and its derogation. In other words, a state regulation would not be considered a violation of US Constitutional Law in the first place, and then justified subsequently by certain established exceptions or derogations. Instead, an interpretive *unity* exists in which a state regulation is found to be constitutional if it meets certain tests and unconstitutional if it fails to do so.

Under intra-Community trade jurisprudence, the situation is more complex. Briefly speaking, in terms of 'distinctively or unequally applicable' measures, jurisprudence on the free movement of goods still upholds the foregoing dichotomy between general obligations (ex Article 30 EEC) and exceptions (ex Article 36 EEC). This dichotomy has a clear textual ground. Nonetheless, regarding 'indistinctively or equally applicable' measures, a doctrinal innovation, which was formulated through *Dassonville* (1974) and *Cassis de Dijon* (1979), and dubbed the 'rule of reason,' has come to replace the old dichotomy. Significantly, the rule of reason established a

345. *Id.*
346. As a matter of fact, the Dormant Commerce Clause itself has no textual basis. It is based on the negative connotation of the Commerce Clause. *See* U.S. Const. art I, § 8, cl. 3 ('The Congress shall have Power .... To regulate Commerce with foreign Nations, and among the several States, and with the Indian Tribes.').

unitary interpretive system analogous to that reflected in the US Dormant Commerce Clause jurisprudence. Under the rule of reason, if an 'indistinctively applicable' domestic measure of a Member State succeeds in satisfying certain requirements (e.g., the proportionality test), the Member State would be deemed, once and for all, not to have breached ex Article 30 EEC, thus eliminating the need for the two separate steps that remain applicable in the case of 'distinctively or unequally applicable' measures.

Most tellingly, such contrasting structural stances regarding the textual and interpretive dichotomy (or unity) tend to reveal inherent differences in *telos* or in institutional evolution among the three systems of the WTO, the EU and the US The WTO system is basically a *trade* system, though it has come to cover many other trade-related areas in its course of evolution. It seems natural that such a trade system would have a pro-trade bias, and enshrine non-trade or social values only in the form of narrowly interpreted exceptions.[347] By contrast, the US has been engaged in a continuous process of 'nation-building' through federalization, with interstate commerce forming only one aspect, albeit a critical one, of this grand enterprise.[348] In other words, the establishment of a common market itself is not the final destination of the federation. Rather, it is only a bridge to a much more extensive *telos* of 'one nation.' In this context, when deciding upon an optimal level of market integration or free trade, consideration simply must be given to the various non-trade social values that the 50 states seek to protect in their individual ways. In other words, consideration of these various trade- and non-trade values must be conducted simultaneously in the same dimension because the principle of federalization does not permit either set of values to take precedence over the other.

It can be broadly stated that the EU falls somewhere in between the GATT/WTO and the US, even though its integration is often regarded as *sui generis*.[349] Obviously, the EU project of forming an 'ever closer Union among peoples of Europe' is much more comprehensive than that of the GATT/WTO.[350] A common market is not a static pedestal, but a building block within that huge project. Although the EU is not as highly federalized as the US, its *telos* toward an 'ever closer union' certainly mirrors that of the US, particularly in its early era of federalization.[351] This unique developmental trajectory may explain the EU's intermediate position regarding its interpretive approach between dichotomy and unity.

Importantly, the tension between unity and dichotomy also suggests a practical implication for the 'burden of proof' issue. Under the GATT/WTO jurisprudence, it is well established that a defendant Member State invoking an exception such as

347. *See* David Palmeter & Petros Mavroidis, *The WTO Legal System: Sources of Law*, 92 AM. J. INT'L L. 398, 408 (1998).

348. Created by the Constitution, the U.S. federal system was a 'more perfect union' even at its birth than the European Union, and has since recognized a subtle balance between federal integrative force backed by the Commerce Clause and 'other equally valid values of decentralization' supported by the Tenth Amendment. Kommers & Waelbroeck, *supra* note 196, at 223.

349. *See* PETER HAY, FEDERALISM AND SUPRANATIONAL ORGANIZATION: PATTERNS FOR NEW LEGAL STRUCTURES 43–44 (1966).

350. EC TREATY, *supra* note 12, Introduction, pmbl.

351. *See The Impact*, *supra* note 134, at 2.

GATT Article XX paragraphs (a)–(j) for its own benefit must assume the burden of proof regarding the requirements of the exception.[352] Accordingly, the burden of demonstrating that a measure falling under one of the exceptions does not, as applied, constitute an abuse of the exception under the chapeau also rests with the party invoking the exception.[353] In addition, this burden of proof regarding the chapeau represents a 'heavier task' than that confronted when demonstrating that a certain exception (e.g., Article XX (b)) covers the measure at issue.[354] This stricter rule on the burden of proof regarding the chapeau may be another example of the pro-trade bias inherently embedded in the GATT/WTO system, which manifests itself through the interpretive dichotomy between a general obligation and its exception.[355] More problematically, such strictness surrounding the burden of proof tends to discourage the use of exceptions, thus shrinking the regulatory autonomy of regulating states.

By contrast, under the US Dormant Commerce Clause it is the complaining party, not the defending state, that shoulders the burden of proving that the defending state has no legitimate regulatory purpose other than a discriminatory and protectionist motive, and that the measure at issue is not applied in an evenhanded way.[356] In this situation, a state's regulatory autonomy is presumed *de facto* in the first place before a challenger attempts to rebut this presumption later. Therefore, regulating states in the US enjoy a relatively higher degree of regulatory discretion than is typically achieved under the GATT/WTO system.

In the case of ECJ jurisprudence, a middle-ground rule between the GATT/WTO and the US governs the burden of proof. Initially, the draconian rigor of the *Dassonville* decision[357] required a defendant regulating state to prove that its measure is proportionate and pursues a legitimate policy objective.[358] Likewise, the principle of 'functional parallelism' ('mutual recognition') established in *Cassis de Dijon* reinforced this rule and eventually placed the burden of proof on the regulating state.[359] Under the principle of functional parallelism, a legal prohibition on the

352. Farber and Hudec noted that, unlike in the Dormant Commerce Clause, the explicit terms of GATT Article XX requires defendant governments to raise justification, which is a demanding task to them because they bear the burden of demonstrating each element of the excuse. *See A GATT's-Eye View*, *supra* note 93, at 1420–21; *Aim and Effect*, *supra* note 29, at 622.

353. *See A GATT's-Eye View*, *supra* note 93, at 1420–21.

354. *Id.*

355. *See* McRae, *supra* note 75, at 223–24.

356. *See* Michael E. Smith, *State Discriminations against Interstate Commerce*, 74 CALIF. L. REV. 1203, 1213 (1986) (arguing that regarding on all requirements concerning whether the regulation is discriminatory, including 'what kinds of economic burdens are sufficient to constitute a disfavored discrimination,' and 'what is a sufficiently unequal distribution of burdens and advantages,' the plaintiff challenging the regulation, not the state, has the burden of proof, citing Hughes v. Oklahoma, 441 U.S. 322, 336 (1979)); *see also* R. Randall Kelso, *Considerations of Legislative Fit under Equal Protection, Substantive Due Process, and Free Speech Doctrine: Separating Questions of Advancement, Relationship and Burden*, 28 U. RICH. L. REV. 1279, 1284, n.22 (1994) (explaining that in cases of indirect discrimination on interstate commerce the challenger still has the burden of proof, citing Pike v. Bruce Church, 397 U.S. 137, 138–39 (1970)).

357. 'All trading rules enacted by Member States which are capable of hindering, directly or indirectly, actually or potentially, intra-Community trade are to be considered as measures having an effect equivalent to quantitative restrictions.' *Dassonville*, *supra* note 266, ¶ 5.

358. *Id.*, ¶ 6.

359. *See Text and Context*, *supra* note 258, 364–68.

marketing of goods in an importing state is illegal if the goods have been 'lawfully produced and marketed' in one of the Member States.[360] Therefore, a defendant regulating state needs to prove that its measure is *not* functionally parallel with that of another (exporting) state in which a product in question is lawfully produced and marketed.[361]

Nevertheless, the *Keck* case seems to have resulted in a softening of the burden of proof on regulating states. Under the *Keck* jurisprudence, a regulating state that seeks refuge in the 'certain selling arrangements' language must prove that the measure falls under that rubric, and that it is applied in an evenhanded way. Yet, in current practice, once a measure has been proven to fall within one of those selling arrangements, corresponding proof of evenhanded application is likely to be accepted without much trouble. Indeed, the evenhanded application requirement seems to have considerably less bite vis-à-vis requirements such as the proportionality test that apply to cases not falling under the 'certain selling arrangements' language. On the other hand, a plaintiff is likely to counter vehemently that the measure in question is not applied in an evenhanded manner as a matter of *fact*. This development amounts to a *de facto* transposition of burden of proof from the regulating state to the challenger.

2.2.4.2 Converging jurisprudence

Despite this divergence of trade rules resulting mainly from different depths of integration or federalization, one thing common to all trade regimes is that those trade rules (e.g., National Treatment in the GATT/WTO, Free Movement of Goods in the EU, and Dormant Commerce Clause in the US) are so abstract that they are prone to multiple interpretations. Accordingly, this abstractness tends to develop evolutionary trade jurisprudence reflecting changing circumstances. In this evolutionary process, the role of the judicial organs is critical because their interpretations and hermeneutics retain controlling power in defining and refining actual obligations governing the behaviors of trading nations. Moreover, practical difficulties in amending or revising provisions in trade charters or treaties have tended to highlight the role of the judicial organs. This fluid nature of trade rules and the essential role of judicial organs, which together facilitate jurisprudential evolution, provides a fertile ground for the hermeneutical convergence of different trade regimes.

Against this backdrop, the foregoing structural divergence notwithstanding, one could reasonably identify a notable degree of convergence in the aforementioned recent jurisprudence of the WTO,[362] the EU[363] and the US,[364] respectively, concerning how to address a dual crisis of trade and regulatory failure, as well as the corresponding clash between free markets and state regulation that underlies

360. *Cassis de Dijon*, *supra* note 267, ¶ 14. Regarding potential concern for 'regulatory race-to-the-bottom,' *see id.*, ¶ 12 (3); EU LAW, *supra* note 254, at 608.
361. *See* Case 188/84, Commission of the European Communities v France, 28 January 1986 [1986] ECR 419 [hereinafter *Woodworking*].
362. *See supra* sub-sec. 2.1.3.2, 2.1.3.3.
363. *See supra* sub-sec. 2.2.2.2.
364. *See supra* sub-sec. 2.2.3.2.

it.[365] First, the interpretive focus of trade tribunals tended in the past to emphasize such questions as whether certain exceptions like the protection of human health or environment were 'necessary' or sufficiently 'relating' as to take precedence over free trade principles including national treatment. By contrast, trade tribunals now tend to focus scrutiny on whether each country has in good faith attempted to comply with and implement its legal obligations, while deferring to the local tribunals of Member Countries on the question of necessity or relatedness. Secondly, trade tribunals of the past tended to condemn a piece of domestic legislation itself when they found it to be unnecessary to attain a certain regulatory objective and therefore undeserving of an exception. However, trade tribunals now tend to leave such legislation intact, choosing instead to concentrate on narrowing the scope of its *application*.

In conclusion, the gist of this converging jurisprudence can be described as a shift in the focus of judicial scrutiny from considerations of 'substance' or 'content,' such as whether a piece of US environmental legislation is itself necessary for protecting the environment, to considerations of 'process' or 'manner,' such as whether the US actually applies its domestic law in a consistent way or enforces its own law as it is written.

365. *See notably*, Joseph H. H. Weiler, *Epilogue: Towards a Common Law of International Trade*, *in* THE EU, THE WTO AND THE NAFTA: TOWARDS A COMMON LAW OF INTERNATIONAL TRADE 201 (Joseph H. H. Weiler ed. 2000) (discussing the convergence phenomenon of the WTO and the EU jurisprudence); Howse, *Interface*, *supra* note 97, at 159 (observing that 'the jurisprudence of the dormant Commerce Clause can provide a useful reference point for critical reflection on the way the WTO panels have managed the interface between free trade rules and the regulatory state.'). Similarly, Professor Sykes also identifies the striking 'regularity' among the WTO, the NAFTA, the EU and the U.S. trade system in prohibiting 'regulatory protectionism.' *See* Alan O. Sykes, *Regulatory Protectionism and the Law of International Trade*, 66 U. CHI. L. REV. 1 (1999).

Chapter III
Harmonization initiatives and derivative jurisprudence

3.1 Harmonization treaties

3.1.1 Historical background

The harmonization initiative, which aims to protect both trade and regulatory values through approximating domestic regulations within the field of international trade, dates back to an early phase in the creation of the International Trade Organization (ITO).[1] In fact, the draft of the Havana Charter of the ITO included a reference to the revision of 'internationally agreed standards' under Article 20:2(b), which was the original version of the current GATT Article XI:1.[2] Nevertheless, the framers of the GATT excluded this reference based on the belief that standards should be reviewed and concluded by a 'staff of experts' within the ITO rather than by the Contracting Parties themselves.[3] This incipient harmonization initiative was eventually aborted due to the demise of the ITO.

It was not until conventional protectionist measures began to fade away in response to the intensification of international trade around the late seventies and the early eighties that a harmonization initiative re-emerged.[4] Tariffs became comprehensively lower across all tradable products,[5] and quotas (quantitative restrictions) began to be lifted. It would be safe to say that one of many reasons for this change originated from the ever-increasing cost of protection in the face of globalization. That is, it became increasingly more difficult for any government to continue pinpointing certain industries and protecting them from external competition as the belief became more widespread that such measures tend over the long run to hurt not only foreign competitors, but also other domestic industries

1. The GATT, initially designed as a chapter of the International Trade Organization (ITO), had to assume also an institutional function because of the demise of the ITO, which was brought about mainly by the domestic political situation in the US. However, in a *legal* sense, it was not an international organization *per se*, nor a formal treaty. Regarding the 'birth defect' of the GATT, *see* John H. Jackson, The World Trade Organization: Constitution and Jurisprudence 15–22 (1998) [hereinafter Jackson, Constitution and Jurisprudence].
2. Analytical Index, *supra* note 9, Chapter II, at 353.
3. *Id.*
4. *See* Global Transformation, *supra* note 10, Chapter I, at 187.
5. *But see* Sam Laird, *Multilateral Approaches to Market Access Negotiations*, WTO Staff Working Paper (TPRD-98-02) 3–4 (1998), *available at* <http://www.wto.org/english/res_e/reser_e?ptpr9802.-doc> (last visited on Mar. 19, 2001) (discussing 'tariff peak' and 'tariff escalation' in some sectors).

and consumers who want to access to foreign products that are sometimes relatively cheaper and of better quality than domestic ones.

Although such direct and blatant protectionist measures have generally failed, old and new domestic regulations has become problematic. Regulatory heterogeneity,[6] resulting from even 'legitimate' or non-protectionist regulatory objectives, such as the protection of human health or the environment, has begun to constrain the flow of international trade to a greater extent, causing a disintegrative impact on the global trading community.[7] This tendency was reflected in the agenda of trade rounds even under the old GATT. For example, unlike previous GATT Rounds that mainly focused on 'tariff' reduction, the Tokyo Round (1979) introduced a forum for eliminating or mitigating the so-called 'Non-Tariff Barriers' (NTBs).[8]

Yet the Tokyo Round agreements (codes), which attempted to address NTBs, were not a very effective response to the problem. This is because codes, such as the Standard Code,[9] were promulgated in the form of separate and optional 'plurilateral' agreements—rather than mandatory 'multilateral' agreements—that were basically detached from the GATT system as a whole.[10] A more comprehensive and holistic breakthrough in addressing NTBs took place only under the auspices of the new WTO system. The WTO Agreement was aimed at tackling new challenges such as NTBs by 'developing an *integrated*, more viable and durable multilateral trading system,'[11] in addition to the old *telos* of 'eliminating *discriminatory* treatment in international commerce.'[12] In this regard, the WTO system encompassed new sectors, e.g., services, investment and intellectual property vis-à-vis traditional trade

---

6. *See* Robert Howse, *Democracy, Science, and Free Trade: Risk Regulation on Trial at the World Trade Organization*, 98 MICH. L. REV. 2329, 2331 (2000) [hereinafter Howse, *Democracy*]; Frieder Roessler, *Increasing Market Access Under Regulatory Heterogeneity: The Strategies of the World Trade Organization, in* ORGANIZATION FOR ECONOMIC CO-OPERATION AND DEVELOPMENT (OECD), REGULATORY REFORM AND INTERNATIONAL MARKET OPENNESS 117–30 (1996); Jeffrey L. Dunoff, '*Trade And': Recent Developments in Trade Policy and Scholarship—And Their Surprising Political Implications*, 17 NW. J. INT'L L. & BUS. 759, 760 (1996–7); Alan O. Sykes, *Strategies for Increasing Market Access under Regulatory Heterogeneity* 2–4, OECD, TD/TC(96)8, Feb. 15, 1996.
7. Moreover, thanks to technological innovation as well as increased regulatory complexity, it is becoming increasingly difficult to distinguish between legitimate regulatory objectives and protectionist motivation (*protectionism*) lurking behind those new regulations. *See* Food Safety, *supra* note 10, Chapter I, at 53.
8. Regarding the negotiation on NTBs in the Tokyo Round, *see notably* JOHN H. JACKSON ET AL, IMPLEMENTING THE TOKYO ROUND: NATIONAL CONSTITUTIONS AND INTERNATIONAL ECONOMIC RULES 12–3 (1984) [hereinafter IMPLEMENTING THE TOKYO ROUND].
9. *Id.*, at 15.
10. Belatedly, after three decades had passed since the launch of the GATT, non-tariff measures (NTBs) were beginning to be discussed in the Tokyo Round, and some side agreements such as the Standard Code were created. However, the legal nature of these side agreements was controversial in some situations since the hierarchy of legal obligations both in the GATT and in these side agreements was not clear-cut. Moreover, these side agreements entered into force only among the states that accepted them. This optional situation led to criticism of what was termed 'GATT a la carte.' Finally, there was no unified dispute settlement system across the GATT and these side agreements provided the possibility of 'forum shopping.' JACKSON ET AL., INTERNATIONAL ECONOMIC RELATIONS, *supra* note 51, Chapter II, at 296–97.
11. WTO Agreement, *supra* note 1, Chapter I, pmbl.
12. *Id.*, GATT 1947, *supra* note 4, Chapter I, pmbl.

in goods by incorporating a number of side agreements with the aim of accomplishing rudimentary harmonization in these new areas.[13]

Most remarkably, the WTO system established two important harmonization treaties—namely, the Agreement on Sanitary and Phytosanitary Measures (SPS) and the Agreement on Technical Barriers to Trade (TBT)—for dealing with the important regulatory subjects of sanitary and phytosanitary measures and technical regulation/standards, respectively.

3.1.2 THE AGREEMENT ON SANITARY AND PHYTOSANITARY MEASURES (SPS)

3.1.2.1 Basic structure: no dichotomy

With respect to addressing the clash of free markets and state regulation, the most outstanding difference found in the SPS Agreement vis-à-vis that observed in GATT is that no dichotomy exists between the two values. In other words, legitimate policy objectives concerning the protection of human, animal or plant life or health, are not relegated to an inferior status as 'exceptions' to a general obligation. Rather, SPS overcomes this pro-trade bias by elevating such exceptionalized social values to the status of 'rights' of Members. Nonetheless, these autonomous regulatory rights are not unbridled: Members are obliged to respect certain requirements in exercising such rights. Also, certain portions of the Agreement are devoted to re-emphasizing free trade values.

At the very beginning of the Preamble, Members affirm that:

> *no* Member should be *prevented* from adopting or enforcing measures necessary to protect human, animal or plant life or health, ...[14]

More explicitly, SPS Article 2.1 provides that:

> Members have the *right* to take sanitary and phytosanitary measures necessary for the protection of human, animal or plant life or health, ...[15]

Importantly, most operative provisions of the SPS Agreement are related to obligations stipulating various requirements that Members shall meet when exercising their regulatory rights. In other words, the exercise of these rights is conditioned upon compliance with certain obligations, such as those set forth in the following language: 'subject to the requirement that these measures are not applied in a manner which would constitute a means of arbitrary or unjustifiable

---

13. *See e.g.,* General Agreement on Trade in Services, Annex 1 B of the WTO Agreement, *supra* note 1, Chapter I [hereinafter GATS]; Agreement on Trade-Related Aspects of Intellectual Property Rights, Annex 1C of the WTO Agreement, *supra* note 1, Chapter I [hereinafter TRIPs]; Agreement on Trade-Related Investment Measures, Annex 1 A of the WTO Agreement, *supra* note 1,Chapter I [hereinafter TRIMs].
14. SPS Agreement, *supra* note 6, Introduction, pmbl (emphasis added).
15. *Id.*, art. 2.1 (emphasis added).

discrimination between Members where the same conditions prevail or a disguised restriction on international trade' or 'provided that such measures are not inconsistent with the provisions of this Agreement.' It is worth noting that most of these obligations, including 'scientific justification,' 'risk assessment,' and 'prohibition of arbitrary or unjustifiable discrimination,' mirror the chapeau test in that they concern administrative discipline governing *how* a regulation is adopted or enforced, rather than the substance of such a regulation. Therefore, as David Victor observed, the SPS obligations, such as the risk assessment requirement, focus on 'a convergence in procedures that countries follow when setting SPS policies but not necessarily convergence in particular regulatory outcomes.'[16] In other words, the procedures that Members abide by in adopting or applying SPS measures may converge, while their levels of protection may diverge.[17]

Finally, in the midst of this regulation-oriented structure, the SPS Agreement maintains the balance between regulatory and trade values by emphasizing trade-oriented considerations in various provisions.

3.1.2.2 Harmonization

Nature of harmonization

One of the main functions of the SPS Agreement is to standardize divergent national sanitary or phytosanitary regulations, and thereby to attain, simultaneously, the regulatory goal of enhancing the quality of sanitary or phytosanitary protection in the international dimension, as well as the trade goal of realizing freer trade by avoiding the potential barriers resulting from divergent national regulations. In this context, Annex A of the SPS Agreement defines harmonization as 'the establishment, recognition and application of common sanitary and phytosanitary measures by different Members.'

However, harmonization in the context of the SPS Agreement is different from conventional harmonization as typically encountered in the context of EU directives or regulations, which are basically 'hard law.' In the absence of a decision-making mechanism which is operable at the micro level, the SPS Agreement has no option but to co-opt 'soft law,' such as 'international standards,' for harmonization.[18] Of course, these international standards are developed outside the WTO organizational structure by international organizations such as the Codex Alimentarius Commission, the International Office of Epizootics, or the relevant international and regional organizations operating within the framework of the International Plant Protection Convention.[19]

Due to its non-binding nature, harmonization through these international standards is not enforceable but merely persuasive and hortatory. In the preamble, the SPS Agreement clarifies that Members are not required to *change* their

---

16. David G. Victor, *The Sanitary and Phytosanitary Agreement of the World Trade Organization: An Assessment After Five Years*, 32 N.Y.U.J. INT'L L. & POL. 865, 925 (2000).
17. *Id.*, at 926.
18. SPS Agreement, *supra* note 6, Introduction, pmbl.
19. *Id.*

appropriate level of protection of human, animal or plant life or health.[20] In the same vein, while Article 3.1 obliges Members to base their measures on international standards where they exist,[21] Article 3.3 nonetheless allows Members to depart from international standards subject to certain requirements.[22] This non-binding character is also evidenced by the incentive system by which the SPS Agreement attempts to motivate Members actively to use international standards. Article 3.2 provides that sanitary and phytosanitary measures which 'conform to'—not merely those which are 'based on'—international standards shall be 'deemed'—not merely 'presumed'—to be necessary to protect human, animal or plant life or health.[23] In addition, such measures are presumed to be consistent with other relevant provisions of the SPS Agreement and of GATT 1994.[24]

Finally, in order to promote the process of international harmonization, Articles 3.4 and 3.5 oblige Members to participate fully in the activities of relevant international organizations.[25] In addition, Article 12 establishes the Committee on Sanitary and Phytosanitary Measures to 'provide a regular forum for consultations,' facilitating the implementation of the SPS Agreement, in particular with respect to harmonization.[26]

Effectiveness of international standards

Despite the pervasive textual appearance of international standards in the SPS Agreement, their effectiveness as a contributor to actual harmonization is still controversial for a number of reasons.

First, the SPS Agreement does not reveal much about the relevant international standards, apart from offering vague definitions. Annex A merely refers to 'standards, guidelines and recommendations' established or developed under the auspices of three representative international organizations, that is the Codex Alimentarius Commission (in the case of human health), the International Office of Epizootics (in the case of animal health) and the relevant international and regional organizations operating within the framework of the International Plant Protection Convention (in the case of plant health). Although it may be unrealistic to demand a substantial compilation, a simple illustrative list of these international standards would help Members to understand what they really are.

Secondly, the named international organizations and their standards have not in the past drawn much attention from the outside. Their activities have been conducted by a handful of epistemic professionals and the standards they decided upon were non-binding, advisory and even experimental. Few people cared about such activities and thus little political controversy was involved.[27] Moreover, members could easily walk

---

20. *Id.*
21. *Id.*, art. 3.1.
22. *Id.*, art. 3.3, n.2
23. *Id.*, art. 3.2.
24. *Id.*
25. *Id.*, art. 3.4, 3.5.
26. *Id.*, art. 12.1.
27. *See* Terence P. Stewart & David S. Johanson, *The SPS Agreement of the World Trade Organization and International Organizations: The Roles of the Codex Alimentarius Commission, the International Plant Protection Convention, and the International Office of Epizootics*, 26 SYRACUSE J. INT'L L. & COM. 27, 28 (1998); Victor, *supra* note 16, at 886.

away from such *non-binding* standards if they became reluctant to comply with them later. Under these circumstances, those standards would serve a certain functional or pragmatic purpose to a limited extent. But more recently, as concerns for human health and the environment have become more salient, those standards have begun to receive more attention than ever before. In addition, their appearance in the SPS Agreement as a vehicle for harmonization has added fuel to this phenomenon. At first glance, the idea of powerful harmonization through international standards may seem a blessed opportunity, but in reality it is not. To draw public attention means to become politicized. Those standards are no longer someone's business: they are now everybody's business. Accordingly, it has become harder for members of those international organizations to reach a consensus regarding the adoption of this or that international standard.[28] Under these circumstances, if an international standard were adopted not by a consensus but by a simple majority, voluntary compliance with such standard would be much harder to achieve.

In conclusion, the effectiveness of international standards in the SPS context is still controversial at this stage chiefly because the standards themselves present many problems yet to be addressed. Actually, the impact of international standards in three SPS cases, *Hormones* (1997), *Australian Salmon* (1998) and *Japanese Agricultural Products* (1999), was considered to be minimal.[29] Therefore, for these standards to become powerful and effective in the SPS context, their aura of legitimacy must be broadened in advance. For this purpose, Members should conduct a more comprehensive deliberation before putting forward those standards, involving various actors like the NGOs and developing countries, and subject proposed standards to sufficient testing processes while they are still in draft form and before they appear on the table for approval. Finally, new standards should be approved preferably by consensus or, at the very least, super-majority in order to enhance their legitimacy.

Equivalence: negative harmonization

Definition

Article 4.1 requires Members to accept other Members' sanitary and phytosanitary measures, which may differ from their own, as 'equivalent,' provided that the exporting Member objectively demonstrates to the importing Member that its measures achieve the latter's appropriate level of protection. This rather bold obligation may be termed 'negative harmonization' in that it takes place not through a positive legislative effort among parties concerned, but through negative acceptance by Members of other Members' regulations. In other words, negative harmonization does not offer any 'common' sanitary and phytosanitary measures among different Members.[30]

28. Stewart & Johanson, *supra* note 27, at 52.
29. Victor, *supra* note 16, at 927–29.
30. SPS Agreement, *supra* note 6, Introduction, Annex A (regarding the definition of harmonization, which is 'the establishment, recognition and application of *common* sanitary and phytosanitary measures by different Members') (emphasis added).

Equivalence versus Mutual Recognition

Interestingly, this principle of 'equivalence' or 'negative harmonization' is reminiscent of the well-known doctrine of 'mutual recognition' encountered in the *Cassis de Dijon* (1979) case. In this case, Germany prohibited the marketing of Cassis de Dijon originating from France based on a domestic statute providing that fruit liqueurs, such as Cassis de Dijon, should contain a minimum alcohol content of 25% in order to be marketed in Germany. However, the alcohol content of Cassis de Dijon, which is freely marketed as such in France, is between 15 and 20%. Based on a strong ethos of market integration, the European Court of Justice ruled that alcoholic products, which have been 'lawfully produced and marketed' in one of the Member States (in this case, France) according to its regulation, should be introduced freely to any other Member State (in this case, Germany), even though the latter's regulations may be different from those of the former.[31] The impact of this ruling upon European market integration was tremendous. Influenced by this seminal decision, similar trade-restrictive regulations, which were deep-rooted in the unique legislative traditions of Member States in the absence of harmonization, were also struck down by the ECJ under the principle of mutual recognition.[32]

In sum, what can be found both in the doctrine of mutual recognition and in the principle of equivalence is a negative integration method, which can be summarized as the acceptance or tolerance of foreign regulations at the expense of corresponding domestic regulations.

Yet, despite their apparent similarity, closer scrutiny reveals that these two principles reflect more difference than commonality. First, in the background of the development of *Cassis de Dijon* lay a rather homogeneous socio-cultural atmosphere among Member States of the European Community during the late seventies, which enabled such bold jurisprudence. It is quite doubtful that a WTO membership that currently numbers more than 140 will enjoy the same homogeneity.

Secondly, the burden of proof on the equivalence is reversed under the doctrine of mutual recognition. In that case, an importing Member State is required to demonstrate that its own regulation is functionally non-parallel with the corresponding regulation of the exporting Member State and, in addition, that it is uniquely necessary to pursue the former's own policy objectives. This is in fact another expression of the 'proportionality' test.[33] For instance, in the *Cassis de Dijon* (1979) case, Germany attempted to justify its position by arguing that its mandatory fixing of minimum alcohol content was necessary to guarantee the fairness of commercial transactions, i.e., to ensure that cheap liquors with a lower alcohol content would not

31. *Cassis de Dijon*, *supra* note 267, Chapter II, ¶ 14.
32. *See* EU Law, *supra* note 254, Chapter II, at 608–9 (discussing, *inter alia*, Case 286/86, *Ministère Public v. Déserbais* [1998] ECR 4907 (striking down a French regulation restricting the use of the term 'Edam' to cheese with a fat content of 40 per cent); Case 788/79, *Italian State v. Gilli and Andres* [1980] ECR 2071, [1981] 1 CMLR 146 (striking down an Italian regulation illegalizing the marketing of vinegar that was not made from the fermentation of wine); Case 261/81, *Walter Rau Lebensmittelwerke v. de Smedt Pvba* [1982] ECR 3961, [1983] 2 CMLR 496 (striking down a Belgian regulation requiring all margarine to be marketed in cube-shaped packages)).
33. *See* Joseph H. H. Weiler, *Epilogue: Towards a Common Law of International Trade*, *in* The EU, the WTO, and the NAFTA: Towards a Common Law of International Trade? 231 (Joseph H. H. Weiler ed. 2000) (observing that the mutual recognition doctrine is nothing but a 'banal doctrinal manifestation of the principle of necessity which is also a pillar of GATT jurisprudence').

mislead consumers seeking expensive liquors with a higher alcohol content.[34] However, the Court summarily rejected this argument by demonstrating a less trade restrictive alternative, namely the mandatory labeling of alcohol content.[35] In the *Woodworking* (1986) case, the Court reaffirmed the proportionality test embedded in the doctrine of mutual recognition by ruling that:

> [I]t is not entitled to prevent the marketing of a product originating in another Member State which provides a level of protection of the health and life of humans equivalent to that which the national rules are intended to ensure or establish. It is therefore contrary to the principle of proportionality for national rules to require such imported products to comply strictly and exactly with the provisions or technical requirements laid down for products manufactured in the Member State in question when those imported products afford users the same level of protection.[36]

On the other hand, in the case of the principle of equivalence under the SPS Agreement, the burden of proof is borne by an exporting Member, not an importing one. Article 4.1 expressly provides that 'the exporting Member objectively demonstrates to the importing Member that its measures achieve the importing Member's appropriate level of sanitary or phytosanitary protection.'[37]

This stark contrast in the *locus* of burden of proof between two similar doctrines may be attributable more to structural reasons than to textual considerations. That is to say, in the case of the EU, a strong market integration ethos among rather homogeneous Member States may have required Member States initially to accept foreign products that have been legally produced and marketed in other Member States, unless the former succeed in proving that their own regulations are functionally unique and non-equivalent with the latter's and thus serve a policy objective justifying the resulting trade restriction. However, in case of the WTO, the degree of homogeneity among Members, not to mention the general level of integrationist ethos, is not as high as within the EU. The WTO is still an inter-governmental, as opposed to supranational, organization in which the regulatory sovereignty of Members is strongly upheld. Therefore, it is the exporting Member that should demonstrate that a given regulation is equivalent to the corresponding regulation of an importing Member.

Criticism of equivalence

Although the principle of equivalence is an effective tool for achieving a higher degree of market integration through negative harmonization, it nonetheless remains vulnerable to the criticism that it results in a 'regulatory race-to-the-bottom.' The fact that two different regulations are 'equivalent' does not necessarily mean that they are the 'same,' even though both of them are considered necessary to achieve the appropriate level of regulatory protection. In other words, some countries may still

34. *Cassis de Dijon*, *supra* note 267, Chapter II, ¶ 13.
35. *Id.*
36. *Woodworking* (1986), *supra* note 361, Chapter II, ¶ 16.
37. SPS Agreement, *supra* note 6, Introduction, art. 4.1.

want sophisticated and refined regulations, rather than functionally equivalent yet clumsy ones. These countries basically fear the 'Gresham's Law'[38] which, in the context of regulation, would suggest that good regulations will be driven out by bad regulations due mainly to the economic reason that the latter are cheaper to implement.

In this context, Alexander Donahue warns that equivalence encourages the circumvention by foreign producers of domestic regulations and thus undermines national regulatory autonomy.[39] He views that

> [I]f a foreign standard is treated as equivalent to its domestic counterpart, then a 'back door' is created through which a product can gain approval without meeting the domestic standard.[40]

This criticism demonstrates an inherent weakness of equivalence as a harmonization tool. Due to its 'negative' nature, namely, unilateral acceptance of foreign regulation without any positive change, equivalence seems to play a limited harmonization role. Thus, it should be complemented and supplemented by further harmonization using 'positive' measures that create 'common' regulations.

Mutual Recognition Agreement (MRA)

Article 4.2 encourages Members to achieve another harmonization initiative: 'Mutual Recognition Agreements' (MRA). An MRA is a legislative initiative similar to the doctrine of mutual recognition. It purports to recognize, on a sector-by-sector basis, the specific standards or related procedural requirements, such as conformity assessment and accreditation requirement, of foreign countries. In most cases, the establishment of MRAs is incremental and cumulative. Parties to the MRA tend to agree on the recognition of procedural requirements at the initial stage because the full recognition of others' regulations themselves is very difficult. In addition, the pattern of establishing MRAs usually follows a building block model. That is to say, they are concluded for one sector after another. Due to this incremental and cumulative nature, many MRAs are bilateral or regional, rather than global.

3.1.2.3 Administrative obligations

Internal obligations

Parts of the SPS obligations may be termed 'internal' in that they address a variety of disciplines which a Member is required to respect in the regulatory decision-making process *within* its own government. These obligations are 'inward-looking' in nature.

---

38. The Columbia Electronic Encyclopedia (6th ed., 2000), *available at* <www.encyclopedia.com/articles05419.html> (last visited on Nov. 1, 2001).
39. Alexander M. Donahue, *Equivalence: Not Quite Close Enough for the International Harmonization of Environmental Standards*, 30 ENVTL. L. 363, 363 (2000).
40. *Id.*, at 371.

Risk assessment

Annex A of the SPS Agreement provides a fairly detailed definition of risk assessment. The definition is two-fold according to the nature of risk. In the case of risk associated with 'pest or disease,' a risk assessment is defined as:

> the evaluation of the likelihood of entry, establishment or spread of a pest or disease within the territory of an importing Member according to the sanitary or phytosanitary measures which might be applied, and of the associated potential biological and economic consequences.

On the other hand, in the case of 'food-borne' risk, a risk assessment is defined as:

> the evaluation of the potential for adverse effects on human or animal health arising from the presence of additives, contaminants, toxins or disease-causing organisms in food, beverages or feedstuffs.

It can be logically inferred that the 'existence' of such risk assessment is required when adopting, applying or enforcing any sanitary or phytosanitary measures, in addition to the basic requirement that these measures be 'based on' the risk assessment. In conducting the risk assessment, the SPS Agreement requires Members to take into account a variety of factors to guarantee a better outcome. For example, Article 5.2 requires Members to consider available 'scientific' factors, such as 'available scientific evidence; relevant processes and production methods; relevant inspection, sampling and testing methods; prevalence of specific diseases or pests; existence of pest- or disease-free areas; relevant ecological and environmental conditions; and quarantine or other treatment.'

Moreover, Article 5.3 requires Members to take into account relevant 'economic' factors, such as 'the potential damage in terms of loss of production or sales in the event of the entry, establishment or spread of a pest or disease; the costs of control or eradication in the territory of the importing Member; and the relative cost-effectiveness of alternative approaches to limiting risks.' This provision seems to require use of the so-called 'Regulatory Impact Analysis' (RIA) which the OECD has developed and encouraged Members to conduct when adopting and applying social regulations.[41] RIA is an instrument for regulatory decision-making that results in 'systematically and consistently examining selected potential impacts arising from government action.' It is an empirical type of decision-making process, which is 'based on fact-finding and analysis that defines the parameters of action according to established criteria.'[42]

Interestingly, the SPS Agreement conceptually distinguishes 'determination of the appropriate level of protection' from risk assessment itself. The process of determination of the appropriate level of protection appears to be a next step after risk assessment, which actually shapes specific sanitary and phytosanitary measures.

---

41. OECD, An Overview of Regulatory Impact Analysis in OECD Countries, *available at* http://www.oecd.org//puma/regref/whatria.htm#what> (last visited on Aug. 28, 2001).
42. *Id.*

If risk assessment mainly involves scientific justification, determination of the appropriate level of protection is associated with a political decision-making process that often connotes value judgment. In parallel, the *Hormones* panel described this determination process as 'risk management' vis-à-vis risk assessment, which the AB rejected for the reason that no textual grounds for such distinction exists under the SPS Agreement.[43]

Consistency

Article 5.5 provides that:

> With the objective of achieving *consistency* in the application of the concept of appropriate level of sanitary or phytosanitary protection against risks to human life or health, or to animal and plant life or health, each Member shall avoid *arbitrary or unjustifiable distinctions* in the levels it considers to be appropriate in *different situations*, if such distinctions result in *discrimination or a disguised restriction* on international trade. (emphasis added)

This provision is rooted in general principles of law, such as 'estoppel' and 'good faith.' In an inward-looking dimension, consistency serves as a criterion with which to judge the legality as well as the legitimacy of a regulation, while in an outward-looking dimension, it is a safety valve by which foreign countries can predict a regulating state's course of action.

Article 5.5 almost copies the whole text from the chapeau of GATT Article XX, which provides that:

> Subject to the requirement that such measures are not applied in a manner which would constitute a means of *arbitrary or unjustifiable discrimination* between countries where the *same conditions* prevail, or a *disguised restriction* on international trade, ... (emphasis added)

As discussed above, the chapeau opened a new jurisprudence under the GATT/WTO. Through the interpretation of the chapeau, the AB has decided on a case by case basis whether a given domestic regulation was applied *consistently* or whether it respected due process, rather than reinvestigating, of its own accord, whether the substance of the regulation itself is necessary or related to the furtherance of the regulating states' social policy goals. Therefore, SPS Article 5.5 and the chapeau in GATT Article XX can be said to share not only the same text but also the same spirit, which is traced back to general principles of law.

Nonetheless, one can sensibly detect a critical textual difference between these two similar provisions, which may potentially result in divergent jurisprudence. Under both SPS Article 5.5 and the chapeau in GATT Article XX, two critical phrases are 'arbitrary or unjustifiable discrimination' and 'a disguised restriction on international trade.' Despite the abstract quality of both phrases, the former mainly concerns administrative *processes* that may yield arbitrariness or unjustifiability,

43. *Hormones*, AB Report, *supra* note 8, Introduction, ¶ 181.

while the latter seems to focus on a protectionist intent or a disparate impact to trade. Critically, under the chapeau, these two phrases are linked by 'or,' which makes their relationship alternative. Therefore, a unilateral application of measure can be struck down by the chapeau only for reasons regarding the manner or process through which it is applied, regardless of its protectionist intent or any other trade restrictive impact.

In contrast, under SPS Article 5.5, these two phrases are linked by 'if,' which makes their relationship cumulative, not separate; that is, both elements are required to meet Article 5.5. Therefore, even if a sanitary or phytosanitary measure is unilateral and inconsistent, and thus arbitrary or unjustifiable, it remains free from the grip of Article 5.5, unless it 'results in a disguised restriction to international trade.' This cumulative structure of Article 5.5 seems problematic. Of course, this structure may be understandable considering the dual objective of the SPS Agreement, enshrining both trade and regulatory values. Yet, it would be hard to place this provision into actual operation because it is no easy task to demonstrate that a measure is 'resulting in' a disguised restriction to international trade. In sum, by incorporating another element involving trade effect other than the process-oriented requirement, Article 5.5 would become porous, failing to discipline many unilateral and inconsistent sanitary or phytosanitary measures.

Less trade-restrictive means

SPS Article 5.6 provides that:

> Without prejudice to paragraph 2 of Article 3, when establishing or maintaining sanitary or phytosanitary measures to achieve the appropriate level of sanitary or phytosanitary protection, Members shall ensure that such measures are *not more trade-restrictive* than required to achieve their appropriate level of sanitary or phytosanitary protection, *taking into account technical and economic feasibility*. (emphasis added)

Article 5.6 is also accompanied by an explanatory footnote which states that:

> For purposes of paragraph 6 of Article 5, a measure is not more trade-restrictive than required unless there is another measure, *reasonably available* taking into account *technical and economic feasibility*, that achieves the appropriate level of sanitary or phytosanitary protection and is *significantly* less restrictive to trade. (emphasis added)

Article 5.6 implies, at the outset, that it is within the discretion of Members whether to rely on certain international standards or to determine the appropriate level of protection on their own accord when establishing or maintaining sanitary or phytosanitary measures. Then, for the latter situation, Article 5.6 imposes the so-called 'less trade-restrictive means' test. This test, originally the 'least trade-restrictive means' test, came from the GATT 1947 jurisprudence regarding GATT Article XX, in particular from the interpretation of the term 'necessary.' The Panel in the *Section 337* (1989) case ruled that:

> a contracting party cannot justify a measure inconsistent with other GATT provisions as 'necessary' in terms of Article XX(d) *if an alternative measure which it could reasonably be expected to employ and which is not inconsistent with other GATT provisions is available to it*. By the same token, in cases where a measure consistent with other GATT provisions is not reasonably available, a contracting party is bound to use, among the measures reasonably available to it, that which entails *the least degree of inconsistency* with other GATT provisions.[44]

In a subsequent case, *Thai Cigarette* (1990), the Panel affirmed this approach and struck down an import ban of foreign cigarettes by the Thai Government on the grounds that it failed to adopt a better policy alternative, such as 'strict, non-discriminatory labeling and ingredient disclosure regulations,' rather than an import ban.[45] However, this decision, as well as the 'least trade-restrictive means' test, was harshly criticized for depriving Members (then contracting parties) of their regulatory autonomy because the Panel had, in fact, second-guessed the policy rationale, unduly assumed a hypothetical alternative and imposed such an alternative. This criticism sounded even more plausible considering that Thailand was a developing country that could not afford the necessary funds and relevant technology required to accept the suggested alternative that developed countries had adopted. Even the World Health Organization (WHO) issued an advisory opinion supporting the Thai position.[46]

This lack of 'institutional sensitivity,'[47] as Robert Howse puts it, might have survived under the old GATT system due to its pro-trade bias, but can no longer sustain itself under a new WTO system that features a *telos* of 'integration' or 'sustainable development,' and that takes seriously Members' regulatory autonomy, thereby going well beyond a narrower concept of anti-cheating or anti-protection. Against this background, when SPS Article 5.6 codifies the 'least trade-restrictive means' test, it provides a couple of safety valves for preventing such pro-trade bias and for ensuring a measure of institutional sensitivity.

First, a measure that achieves the appropriate level of sanitary or phytosanitary protection need not be the 'least' but only 'significantly less' trade restrictive in order to satisfy SPS Article 5.6. In other words, a measure can be accepted under Article 5.6 if it is less trade restrictive to a considerable degree than other reasonably available options, even though a better solution could theoretically exist. In practical terms, it is much easier for a Member to demonstrate that its measure is significantly less trade restrictive than to prove that it is the least trade restrictive. Secondly, Article 5.6 emphasizes twice, once in the main text and again in its footnote, that Members take into account 'technical and economical feasibility' to ensure that a given measure is less trade restrictive when achieving the appropriate level of sanitary or phytosanitary protection. This element would have saved the Thai import ban on foreign cigarettes in the *Thai Cigarette* (1990) case, considering that Thailand

---

44. *Section 337*, *supra* note 23, Chapter II, ¶ 5. 26 (emphasis added).
45. *Thai Cigarette*, *supra* note 49, Chapter II, ¶ 77.
46. *Id.*, ¶¶ 52–57.
47. Howse, *Adjudicative Legitimacy*, *supra* note 190, Chapter II, at 62–68.

was a developing country short of funds and technology, a position with which the WHO also agreed.

Precautionary principle
Article 5.7 provides that:

> In cases *where relevant scientific evidence is insufficient*, a Member may *provisionally* adopt sanitary or phytosanitary measures on the basis of available pertinent information, including that from the relevant international organizations as well as from sanitary or phytosanitary measures applied by other Members. In such circumstances, Members shall *seek to obtain the additional information* necessary for a more objective assessment of risk and review the sanitary or phytosanitary measure accordingly *within a reasonable period of time*. (emphasis added)

This provision is an expression of the so-called 'precautionary principle' in the SPS context. Despite its widespread use, particularly in areas related to the environment and human health, no established, official definition of the principle exists.[48] Although many versions have been circulated among trade officials, including a reputed formulation in the Rio Declaration of 1992,[49] their texts are still ambiguous, leaving much room for interpretation, and too contextualized to be referred to as a universal principle. Therefore, it seems doubtful that the SPS Agreement can find any legitimate source for referential reliance in the interpretation of Article 5.7 because of the lack of a coherent precautionary principle. After all, future jurisprudential development will determine the interpretation of Article 5.7, focusing on four critical elements, namely, 'where relevant scientific evidence is insufficient,' 'provisionally,' 'seek to obtain the additional information,' and 'within a reasonable period of time.'

Sound jurisprudential development on Article 5.7 is particularly important to address potential abuse or misuse of this ambiguous principle in the international trade field. On the one hand, it is totally legitimate for a country to have recourse to this principle in order to respond to various new health or environmental risks that cannot be substantially assessed due to the lack of scientific knowledge or information. On the other hand, it should also be noted that this principle could be abused or misused and thus unduly restrict international trade. Current controversies on 'Genetically Modified' (GM) foods shed additional light on this concern.[50]

---

48. *See* Steve Charnovitz, *The Supervision of Health and Biosafety Regulation by World Trade Rules*, 13 TUL. ENVTL. L. J. 271, 294 (2000).
49. It states, under the title of 'Precautionary Approach,' that '[w]here there are threats of serious or irreversible damage, lack of full scientific certainty shall not be used as a reason for postponing cost-effective measures to prevent environmental degradation.' *Id.*, at 293; Rio Declaration on Environment and Development, June 14, 1992, U.N. Conference on Environment and Development, U.N. GAOR, 47th Sess., Agenda Item 9, at 3, princ. 15, U.N. Doc. A/CONF. 151/5/Rev. 1, 31 I.L.M. 874, 879 (1992).
50. Regarding a comprehensive legal analysis on the consistency of GM food regulations with the WTO jurisprudence, *see* Robert Howse & Petros C. Mavroidis, *Europe's Evolving Regulatory Strategy for GMOs—The Issue of Consistency with WTO Law: Of Kine and Brine*, 24 FORDHAM INT'L L. J. 317 (2000).

External obligations

Some portions of obligations in the SPS Agreement may be termed 'external' in that these obligations mainly require Members to inform *other* Members of the new establishment or revision of sanitary or phytosanitary measures so that these measures' trade restrictive effects are minimized, and at the same time, other Members can be provided opportunities to question the validity of these measures. In sum, those obligations are 'outward-looking' in nature.

Transparency

Under the title of 'Transparency,' Article 7 obliges Members to notify changes in their sanitary or phytosanitary measures and provide information on them.[51] Article 7 provides detailed procedures regarding the notification and disclosure of the relevant information in Annex B, which consists of three parts: 'publication of regulations,' 'enquiry points' and 'notification procedures.'[52]

First, Members are obliged to publish all sanitary and phytosanitary regulations that have been adopted in such a manner as to enable interested Members to become acquainted with them.[53] In addition, except for in cases of emergency, Members shall allow a reasonable interval between this publication and its effectuation so that exporting Members' producers can adapt their products and production methods to the requirements of the importing Member.[54] Secondly, Members shall establish one enquiry point to respond to all reasonable answers from interested Members as well as to provide relevant documents, including any sanitary or phytosanitary regulations, any control and inspection procedures, and risk assessment procedures.[55] Thirdly, in situations where no relevant international standard exists or where the content of a proposed regulation is substantially divergent from an existing international standard, Members shall publish a notice at an early stage to acquaint such proposed regulation with interested Members[56] and notify the Secretariat of the objective, rationale and coverage of such regulation with a reasonable interval for any comment to be reflected in a final regulation.[57]

In addition to Article 7 and Annex B, Annex C also requires Members to publish relevant information and to provide documents with respect to control, inspection and approval procedures, such as 'sampling, testing and certification,'[58] which are required to 'check and ensure the fulfillment of sanitary or phytosanitary measures.'[59]

Reason-giving requirement

In addition to the aforementioned publication and notification requirements, the SPS Agreement imposes, under certain conditions, a more active obligation to the

51. SPS Agreement, *supra* note 6, Introduction, art. 7.
52. *Id.*, Annex B.
53. *Id.*, ¶ 1.
54. *Id.*, ¶ 2.
55. *Id.*, ¶ 3.
56. *Id.*, ¶ 5.
57. *Id.*
58. *Id.*, Annex C, n.7.
59. *Id.*, ¶ 1.

Members whose sanitary or phytosanitary regulations do not follow international standards. In other words, Members shall, when requested, explain to the interested Members the 'reasons' for such sanitary or phytosanitary measures.[60]

3.1.2.4 *Free market considerations: balancing the free exercise of autonomous regulatory rights*

We have thus far discussed how the SPS Agreement overcomes a pro-trade bias and the resultant dichotomy between trade and regulatory values that was embedded in the old GATT 1947. The SPS Agreement reinstates an inferior status of regulatory values vis-à-vis trade values to the level of 'rights.' At the same time, however, in order to prevent an abuse of such regulatory rights, various process-oriented obligations, such as the consistency and risk assessment requirement, serve to ensure that the exercise of those rights should not unduly block the free flow of international commerce. In the same context, additional free market considerations scattered in the SPS Agreement serve to avoid the operation of the Agreement from being tilted toward state regulations.

First of all, the preamble juxtaposes language calling for the 'development, adoption and enforcement of sanitary and phytosanitary measures' with a requirement 'to minimize their negative effects on trade.' In other words, the free exercise of autonomous regulatory rights is balanced by trade concerns, eventually contributing to an integrative *telos*, often dubbed 'sustainable development.' In the same line, Article 5.4 provides that 'Members should, when determining the appropriate level of sanitary or phytosanitary protection, take into account the objective of minimizing negative trade effects.'

Yet, it is Annex C that most highlights free market considerations in the exercise of regulatory rights. Annex C deals in particular with 'control, inspection and approval procedures,' that 'check and ensure the fulfillment of sanitary or phytosanitary measures.'[61] These 'conformity assessment' procedures, which include 'sampling, testing and certification,'[62] purport to implement, in the real fields, those sanitary or phytosanitary measures once they are established and adopted. For example, most customs offices at the seaport or airport demand that importers submit various quarantine documents certifying the inspection and control of specimens of imported products. As these procedures directly concern actual transactions that are taking place every day, their trade impact is significant. In particular, various invisible and disguised protectionist elements could lie hidden in these procedures because such inspection and testing are conducted in the domestic territory against imported foreign products that are competitive with domestic products.

Against this background, Annex C stipulates certain non-discriminatory requirements. First, conformity assessment procedures should be conducted no less favorably for imported products than for like domestic products.[63] Secondly, any

60. *Id.*, Annex B, ¶ 5.
61. *Id.*, Annex C, ¶ 1.
62. *Id.*, n.7.
63. *Id.*, ¶ 1(a).

fees charged on imported products should be equitable vis-à-vis those fees imposed on like domestic products or products originating in any other Member.[64] Thirdly, the same criteria should be used for both domestic and imported products in the sample selection as well as in the location of facilities.[65] In addition, Annex C provides that various procedural requirements should be limited to what is 'reasonable and necessary.'[66] Although such trade considerations can be understandable, these obligations seem to be of limited use in practice because it would be hard for outsiders to second-guess what is really 'reasonable and necessary' to achieve the appropriate level of sanitary or phytosanitary protection in the importing (regulating) state. Rather, these procedural requirements might be better addressed by the 'trade facilitation' initiative that purports to simplify and harmonize international trade procedures, including customs procedures.[67] Such an initiative would help to ameliorate complicated and unnecessary documentation requirements.

In sum, Annex C attempts to balance the SPS Agreement with free trade considerations to avoid over-concentration on the exercise of autonomous regulatory rights. Yet, such an attempt may tip the balance once again toward trade values and thus revive the pro-trade bias. For this reason, Annex C fine-tunes the balance between trade and regulatory values at the very end by providing that: 'Nothing in this Agreement shall prevent Members from carrying out reasonable inspection within their own territories.'[68]

3.1.2.5 SPS as a rational deliberation model?

There are a number of reasons for highlighting the relevance of the SPS to the current global situation. First, in many countries, a better quality of life has been placed as a top agenda item as a result of improved economic conditions. It is a natural phenomenon that people pay more attention to social hygiene when they become wealthier. Secondly, modern technology has brought about unprecedented conveniences to people. Yet, every brightness has its own dark side. It has also created new risks and hazards. For instance, technology used for molding plastics and PVCs are often associated with toxic chemicals. Thirdly, new technology has begun to discover new health risks that used to be unknown. Although asbestos has been widely used in construction sites for many years, it was only relatively recently that researchers discovered its carcinogenic nature. Fourthly, the telecommunications revolution has enabled more people to be informed of various kinds of knowledge and information concerning health risks. One cannot worry about a certain risk unless one is informed. Last, but not least, the SPS Agreement, as a side agreement of the WTO Charter, is under the halo of the WTO, thereby easily drawing attention even from ordinary people.

---

64. *Id.*, ¶ 1(f).
65. *Id.*, ¶ 1(g).
66. *Id.*, ¶ 1(c), (e).
67. WTO, Trade Facilitation, *available at* <http://www.wto.org/english/thewto_e/whatis_e/eol/e/wto02/wto2_69.htm#note2> (last visited on Aug. 27, 2001).
68. SPS Agreement, *supra* note 6, Introduction, Annex C, ¶ 3.

Despite this ever-growing attention to the subject, i.e., human health, which the SPS Agreement addresses, the SPS Agreement itself is still distanced from citizens and consumers. In particular, the Agreement's reliance on international standards for harmonization tends to widen the distance because these standards are very technical and are not easily understood without precise and detailed explanation. Therefore, people tend to be curious, anxious and even furious about these esoteric codes as well as the Agreement itself. By the same token, those sanitary regulations, which are based on the Agreement and international standards, are often considered 'undemocratic' since faceless professionals or elites, and not citizens, administer the Agreement and the associated standards. This is the so-called 'democratic deficit.'

Robert Howse attempts to tackle this democratic deficit by reading the Agreement into a 'rational democratic deliberation' model.[69] Howse views provisions of the Agreement not as appropriating legitimate democratic regulatory choices, but as enhancing the quality of democratic decision-making about risks and their control.[70] According to his democratic perspective, the Agreement is used for transferring relevant regulatory information and knowledge to citizens and receiving their feedback in the regulatory decision-making process. In this way, Howse seems to place relatively less priority upon the role of scientific expertise and regulators than the actual voices of citizens, and even cautions against closed and arbitrary scientific conclusions by those expertise and regulators. In this context, he quoted Richard Pildes and Cass Sunstein who have written that:

> the appropriate role of scientific expertise in the regulatory process is not to trump citizens' *intuitive* judgments about which risks are acceptable and which not, but rather to help ensure that citizens' judgments result from an appropriately structured deliberative process.[71]

Howse's perspective appears quite helpful in understanding both provisions of the SPS Agreement and its jurisprudence. By placing transparency and openness at the core of the deliberative process, he suggests a manner-oriented approach as a practical way of achieving a 'win-win for democracy and free trade.'[72] Nonetheless, his perspective does not seem immune to controversies. First, his liberal predilection for 'democratic' deliberation could unnecessarily complicate a plain understanding of the Agreement. Although he tries to avert such sensitive nuances by focusing on a deliberative rather than representative element of democracy, a certain political or cultural backlash could still occur concerning what 'democracy' and 'democratic' actually mean. Arguably, a plausible alternative to this democratic premise can be found in the legal terrain. If one were to approach the SPS Agreement through an optic of 'fundamental principles of law,' such as good faith, consistency or the estoppel principle, various provisions in the Agreement related to Howse's

69. Howse, *Democracy*, *supra* note 6, at 2330.
70. *Id.*
71. *Id.*, at 2335 (quoting Cass R. Sunstein & Richard Pildes, *Experts, Economics, and Democrats*, *in* FREE MARKETS AND SOCIAL JUSTICE 128 (Cass R. Sunstein ed., 1997)) (emphasis added).
72. *Id.*, at 2336.

deliberation would come to be premised on legal obligations, rather than on political ideology, namely democracy.

Secondly, Howse's deliberation remains at a macro level—that is, between citizens and bureaucrat. Such deliberation becomes even more macro and complicated if both citizens and bureaucrats are situated outside the domestic territory. Even in a supranational structure, such as the European Union, a relationship between citizens and their government is hard to define. Yet, in an intergovernmental setting like the WTO, such a grand notion of deliberation would be hard to grasp mainly because so many deliberators, including individuals, NGOs, the civil society, governments and the Secretariat, are involved in different forms.

Furthermore, this macro, broad concept of deliberation tends to be politicized, converging not to a *right* answer, but to a *popular* answer. Howse underscores in another place the intuitive and practical wisdom of ordinary people, which Aristotle once labeled as 'phronesis.'[73] He places more priority on citizens' intuitive determinations regarding risk and its control than on the professional analysis of experts. However, in a sophisticated regulatory field where modern technology and science must play their due roles, merely a politically correct answer or regulatory popularism should not replace a scientifically desirable solution.[74] Scientists must brace themselves against unpopular and even hostile reactions to their findings, as Galileo did in medieval times. Also, it is the responsibility of a government to base such professional integrity on its risk assessment, instead of selectively accepting diverging opinion in a self-serving way to legitimize a policy direction that is politically pre-established.

At this juncture, it seems to be very important for scientific expertise and regulators, both domestic and international, to harmonize their views and opinions on sector-specific regulatory issues through 'functional deliberation,' as witnessed in the EU's 'Comitology' system.[75] In the EU, harmonization is essentially a 'decentralized' process since 'directives,' a main vehicle for harmonization, leave 'the choice of form and methods' to Member States.[76] However, despite their apparent merit, harmonization methods are problematic. First, the decision-making process can be inefficient. Although the current processes in many sectors have become subject to the so-called 'qualified majority voting' process, instead of 'unanimity,' complexities involving different institutions, such as the Commission, the Council and the Parliament, still remain.[77] Secondly, even if directives are issued,

---

73. *See* Howse, *Interface*, *supra* note 97, Chapter II, at 146.
74. In this line, Howse emphasizes 'openness' and 'trust' between citizens and expert regulators to prevent consumers from being obsessed by a 'deluded' belief regarding certain baseless risks. *See* Howse, *Democracy*, *supra* note 6, at 2338.
75. For a basic explanation of Comitology, *see generally* Francesca E. Bignami, *The Democratic Deficit in European Community Rulemaking: A Call For Notice and Comment in Comitology*, 40 HARV. INT'L L. J. 451, 456–59 (1999); Peter L. Lindseth, *Democratic Legitimacy and the Administrative Character of Supranationalism: The Example of the European Community*, 99 COLUM. L. REV. 628, 689–91 (1999).
76. Renaud Dehousse, *Regulation by Networks in the European Community: The Role of European Agencies*, 4 J. EUR. PUB. POL'Y 246, 248 (1997) [hereinafter Dehousse, *European Agencies*].
77. SHAW, *supra* note 253, Chapter II, at 145–55 (regarding the 'old' procedure, the cooperation procedure, Council-Parliament co-decision and the assent procedure); EU LAW, *supra* note 254, Chapter II, at 129–42 (regarding 'six' legislative procedures involving different institutions such as the Commission, the Council, and the Parliament under complicated matrices).

transposition by Member States can be incomplete.[78] Thirdly, even if Member States transpose directives using their best efforts, 'divergences' in detailed procedures can still be serious obstacles to trade.[79]

Against this background, the Comitology web, which gathers various sector-specific national experts and officials, has emerged as a measure for achieving in-depth compliance through converging their implementations of the Community law.[80] In fact, the original rationale of Comitology derived from the Council's concern regarding the 'principal-agent theory,' as well as from its intention to check excessive bureaucratic discretion by the Commission in exercising its legislative function, such as the right to propose a directive.[81] However, due mainly to the working-level composition of Comitology committees[82] and the consequent epistemic *ethos*, Comitology has contributed immensely to the Community's regulatory cooperation and convergence. As Professor Joseph Weiler pointedly observed, 'a distinct and powerful constructivist identity and culture (or subculture) obliterate the plenipotentiary and delegatory aspects of Committee membership.'[83] Here, psychological aspects, such as 'epistemic beliefs' and 'confidence building,' are critical for the success of Committees.[84] This *ethos* eventually facilitates the adoption of common solutions, transcending narrow parochial interests.[85] Therefore, the Comitology web contributes to the 'cooperative convergence' of regulatory behaviors while the decentralizing aspect of harmonization is still intact.[86]

Although scientific uncertainty often makes it harder for even scientists to agree fully on the existence of certain risks and their controls in a multilateral level rather

78. Dehousse, *European Agencies*, *supra* note 76, at 251.
79. *Id.*
80. *Id.*, at 254.
81. Michelle Egan and Dieter Wolf, *Regulation and Comitology: The EC Committee System in Regulatory Perspective*, 4 COLUM. J. EUR. L. 499, 519 (1998).
82. Comitology committees consist of national experts and government officials from each Member state, chaired by Commission representatives. Bignami, *supra* note 75, at 457. The Council intervenes in this process only indirectly when the Commission and committee members are unable to agree. *Id.*
83. *See notably* Joseph H. H. Weiler, *Epilogue: 'Comitology' as Revolution—Infranationalism, Constitutionalism and Democracy*, *in* EU COMMITTEES: SOCIAL REGULATION, LAW AND POLITICS 342 (Christian Joerges & Ellen Vos eds. 1999) [hereinafter *'Comitology' as Revolution*].
84. Dehousse, *European Agencies*, *supra* note 76, at 254.
85. Egan & Wolf, *supra* note 81, at 591. *See also 'Comitology' as Revolution*, *supra* note 83, at 342. (portraying this dynamic as 'functional deliberation').
86. *Id.* In the same context, Professor Majone highlighted vast 'issue networks,' consisting of both public and private experts, and even academics, as a characteristic of Comitology. Giadomenico Majone, *The Rise of the Regulatory State in Europe*, 17 W. EUR. POL. 77, 90 (1994); Lindseth, *supra* note 75, at 685–86. In those networks, 'innovative regulatory solutions' tend to be favored over political positions following national lines. Majone, *supra*, at 90; Lindseth, *supra* note 75, at 686 (describing this problem-solving *ethos* as 'policy entrepreneurship'). Of course, criticism from the perspective of preserving Member States' control also abounds. One problem has been dubbed 'Community capture,' and refers to 'a subtle shift in loyalties on the part of the national regulators serving on the various committees at the Community level, from champions of national interests to 'representatives of a Europeanized interadministrative discourse.' Lindseth, *supra* note 75, at 690; Christian Joerges and Jürgen Neyer, *From Intergovernmental Bargaining to Deliberative Political Processes: The Constitutionalization of Comitology*, 3 EUR. L. J. 273, 291 (1997). In contrast, Pollack argues that 'agency behavior that at first glance seems autonomous may in fact be subtly influenced by the preference of principals, making genuine agency autonomy exceedingly difficult to measure.' Mark A. Pollack, *Delegation, Agency, and Agenda Setting in the European Community*, 51 INT'L ORG. 99, 110 (1997); Lindseth, *supra* note 75, at 690.

than a regional level, such functional deliberation is still critical. This functional deliberation would provide citizens and their governments with a better picture about risks and their control, educate and enlighten them, and finally help them select reasonable and rational policy options. Moreover, this functional deliberation would also produce a better scientific conclusion through brainstorming, discussion and further research among the scientific expertise and regulators. For this purpose, governments should encourage and facilitate these activities through formal and informal channels. Relevant international organizations, such as the WTO (SPS Committee), the OECD and the APEC, as well as other informal forums can contribute to these activities. It is now high time that Members should use their political capital to nurture these apolitical activities.

3.1.3 Agreement on Technical Barriers to Trade (TBT)

3.1.3.1 Basic structure

The Agreement on Technical Barriers to Trade (TBT) is, like the SPS Agreement, one of the harmonization initiatives of the WTO. In fact, a similar agreement having the same title existed under the old GATT (GATT 1947) system. However, the old agreement was a 'plurilateral' agreement that bound only voluntary members, and its dispute settlement procedures were also separated from GATT Article XXIII. As a result of this disintegrated structure, the old GATT system was often called 'GATT a la carte.'[87] It was only with the launch of the new WTO system that the TBT Agreement was fully integrated into the WTO as one of the 'multilateral agreements on trade in goods.'[88] Now the Agreement legally binds every Member, and all related disputes are handled under the Dispute Settlement Understanding (DSU).[89]

The Agreement covers 'technical regulations' and 'standards,' except for sanitary or phytosanitary regulations.[90] According to the definitions of Annex A, a technical regulation is signified by a 'document which lays down product characteristics or their related processes and production methods, including the applicable administrative provisions, with which compliance is *mandatory*.'[91] Technical regulations 'may also include or deal exclusively with terminology, symbols, packaging, marking or labeling requirements as they apply to a product, process or production method.'[92] On the other hand, a standard is signified by a similar document with which compliance is *voluntary*. The Agreement also covers so-called 'process or production methods,' (PPMs) which are not covered by GATT Article III according to the conventional GATT jurisprudence. Yet, only *product*-related PPMs, which are related to product characteristics, are covered by the Agreement, excluding *process*-

87. Jackson et al., International Economic Relations, supra note 51, Chapter II, at 297.
88. WTO Agreement, *supra* note 1, Introduction, Annex 1 A.
89. DSU, *supra* note 106, Chapter II, art. 1.
90. TBT Agreement, *supra* note 7, Introduction, art. 1.5.
91. *Id.*, Annex 1, ¶ 1 (emphasis added).
92. *Id.*

related PPMs, such as mandatory labeling requirements on 'dolphin-free tuna' or on 'turtle-free shrimp.'

Like the SPS Agreement, the TBT Agreement also purports to overcome a pro-trade bias and dichotomy embedded in the GATT, thereby attempting to harmonize trade and regulatory values. In the Preamble, Members desire to 'further the objectives of GATT 1994,' and recognize that 'no country should be prevented from taking measures necessary ... for the protection of human, animal or plant life or health, of the environment, or for the prevention of deceptive practices, at the levels it considers appropriate.'[93] However, as the title of the TBT Agreement itself includes the term 'barriers to trade,' free market considerations abound in the Agreement, though they do not lead to the pro-trade bias. Finally, the TBT Agreement places more weight on 'conformity assessment' than the SPS Agreement does. For instance, Article 5 of the TBT Agreement specifically addresses the conformity assessment procedures by central government bodies with respect to technical regulations and standards.[94] This is apparently because technical regulations are generally more sophisticated and complicated than sanitary or phytosanitary measures.

3.1.3.2 Harmonization

The nature and features of harmonization are virtually the same as were discussed in terms of the SPS Agreement. Harmonization is brought about through soft law, namely international standards. Article 2.4 provides that:

> Where technical regulations are required and relevant international standards exist or their completion is imminent, Members shall use them, or the relevant parts of them, as a basis for their technical regulations, ...[95]

Article 2.5, like SPS Article 3.2, gives an incentive for using international standards. It provides that:

> Whenever a technical regulation is prepared, adopted or applied for one of the legitimate objectives explicitly mentioned in paragraph 2, and is in accordance with relevant international standards, it shall be rebuttably presumed not to create an unnecessary obstacle to international trade.[96]

In addition, Article 2.6 (technical regulation) and 5.5 (conformity assessment procedures) provide the same hortatory requirement, as in SPS Article 3.4, to 'play a full part' in the preparation of international standards. Negative harmonization, i.e., equivalence, is also provided in terms of technical regulations[97] and conformity assessment procedures.[98]

---

93. *Id.*, pmbl.
94. *Id.*, art. 5.
95. *Id.*, art. 2.4.
96. *Id.*, art. 2.5.
97. *Id.*, art. 2.7.
98. *Id.*, art. 6.1.

3.1.3.3 Administrative obligations

The TBT Agreement provides obligations mainly for technical regulations. In case of standards, Article 4 only refers to the 'Code of Good Practice' in Annex 3. Yet, obligations related to conformity assessment procedures are applied to both technical regulations and standards.

Internal obligations

Free market disciplines
As discussed above, trade considerations in the TBT Agreement are conspicuous, though that does not necessarily mean that the Agreement is tilted toward trade values vis-à-vis regulatory values. First, the title of the Agreement itself underscores that it purports to address 'barriers to trade.' Secondly, the Preamble is devoted first to trade and then to regulatory concerns. The Preamble reads as follows:

> *Members,*
> ...
> *Recognizing* the important contribution that international standards and conformity assessment systems can make in this regard by improving efficiency of production and facilitating the conduct of international trade; ...
> *Desiring* however to ensure that technical regulations and standards, including packaging, marking and labelling requirements, and procedures for assessment of conformity with technical regulations and standards do not create unnecessary obstacles to international trade;
> *Recognizing* that no country should be prevented from taking measures necessary to ensure the quality of its exports, or for the protection of human, animal or plant life or health, of the environment, or for the prevention of deceptive practices, at the levels it considers appropriate, subject to the requirement that they are not applied in a manner which would constitute a means of arbitrary or unjustifiable discrimination between countries where the same conditions prevail or a disguised restriction on international trade, and are otherwise in accordance with the provisions of this Agreement; ... (underlining added)

Thirdly, Article 2.8 requires Members to establish technical regulations related to product requirements in terms of 'performance' rather than 'design or descriptive characteristics.'[99] This provision purports to prevent any protectionist or trade restrictive effect that can be caused by unnecessary and confusing requirements that focus on trivial features of certain products without any regulatory value. The same obligation can be found in a number of different, but similar sources, such as the WTO Government Procurement Code ('Agreement on Government Procurement'). The Code also requires technical specifications prescribed by procuring entities to be

99. *Id.*, art. 2.8.

in terms of performance rather than design or descriptive characteristics.[100] In fact, this performance-oriented requirement is reminiscent of the doctrine of mutual recognition or equivalence principle in that in both cases 'functional,' rather than 'cosmetic,' aspects of products really matter in assessing the regulatory value of certain regulations.

Fourthly, the TBT Agreement stresses free market values by reflecting GATT Article III:4 (National Treatment in Domestic Regulation) and XI:1 (Prohibition on Quantitative Restrictions or Measures Equivalent to Quantitative Restrictions) in its own text. For instance, echoing the National Treatment principle, both Article 2.1, in terms of technical regulation, and Article 5.1.2, in terms of conformity assessment procedures, require Members to accord to imported products treatment *no less favorable* than that accorded to *like domestic products.*[101] Also, echoing the Market Access principle, both Article 2.2, in terms of technical regulation, and Article 5.1.1, in terms of conformity assessment procedures, require Members to ensure that such regulations or procedures are not 'prepared, adopted or applied with a view to or with the effect of creating unnecessary *obstacles* to international trade.' (emphasis added)

However, the forgoing free market considerations do not necessarily lead the TBT Agreement to be biased toward trade values vis-à-vis regulatory values. In fact, a careful reading of the Agreement would soon detect a certain safety valve to prevent such pro-trade bias and eventually to harmonize trade and regulatory concerns. As seen in the SPS Agreement, a dichotomy between general obligations, such as National Treatment obligation, and regulatory exceptions, as seen in GATT Article XX, does not exist in the TBT Agreement. In the preamble, Members recognize that 'no country should be prevented from taking measures necessary ... for the protection of human, animal or plant life or health, of the environment, or for the prevention of deceptive practices.'[102] This manifestation of regulatory authority on legitimate policy objectives is further elaborated in Article 2.2, which reads that:

> Such legitimate objectives are, *inter alia*, national security requirements; the prevention of deceptive practices; protection of human health or safety, animal or plant health, or the environment.

Remarkably, the Article uses the term '*inter alia*,' thereby making the list of these legitimate objectives illustrative, not exhaustive. In other words, any other policy objective that can be deemed legitimate from the perspective of a regulating Member can fall under the rubric of the TBT Agreement, though it may not belong to one of the exhaustive exception clauses of GATT Article XX. This textual expansion of legitimate objectives mirrors the principle of 'mandatory requirement' in the *Cassis de Dijon* (1979) case,[103] which tempered the strong pro-trade bias established in the *Dassonville* (1974) precedent.[104] Thanks to this provision, the

100. Agreement on Government Procurement, Annex 4, WTO Agreement, *supra* note 1, Introduction, art. 6.2.
101. TBT Agreement, *supra* note 7, Introduction, art. 2.1, 5.1.2.
102. *Id.*, pmbl.
103. *Cassis de Dijon, supra* note 267, Chapter II, ¶ 8.
104. *Dassonville, supra* note 266, Chapter II, ¶ 5.

problematic lacuna of GATT Article XX are mended, at least in terms of technical regulations.

Risk assessment

Unlike the SPS Agreement, the TBT Agreement does not use the term 'risk assessment.' Yet, a similar provision can be found in Article 2.2. In ensuring that technical regulations shall not be more trade-restrictive than necessary to fulfill a legitimate objective, Article 2.2 requires Members to 'take account of the risks non-fulfillment would create.'[105] Then, it exemplifies certain elements considered in the risk assessment, including 'available scientific and technical information, related processing technology or intended end-uses of products.'[106]

As in the SPS Agreement, it can be logically inferred that the 'existence' of such risk assessment is required when adopting, applying or enforcing any technical regulation, in addition to the basic requirement that these regulations be 'based on' the risk assessment. In conducting the risk assessment, the TBT Agreement requires Members to take into account an open list of factors to guarantee its better outcome. Article 2.2, for example, requires them to consider available 'scientific' factors, such as 'available scientific and technical information,' or 'related processing technology.' Markedly, no element implying an 'economic' consideration is expressed in this list, while the SPS Agreement expressly regards potential economic consequences as relevant to the risk assessment. Yet, considering that this is an open list and reflects a broader context compared with the SPS Agreement, it should be understood that such economic consequences are also taken into account in the risk assessment for technical regulations.

Importantly, Article 2.3 stresses a *dynamic* perspective of technical regulation by providing that:

> Technical regulations shall not be maintained if the circumstances or objectives giving rise to their adoption *no longer exist* or if the *changed* circumstances or objectives can be addressed in a less trade-restrictive manner.[107]

This provision reflects the ever-changing nature of technical regulations due to modern technological development and scientific findings. Thus, it should be interpreted as requiring Members to conduct a risk assessment on a periodic, regular basis.

External obligations

As in the SPS Agreement, certain procedural obligations in the TBT Agreement may be termed 'external' in that they mainly require Members to inform other Members of the new establishment or revision of technical regulations or conformity assessment procedures so that the trade restrictive effects of these measures are

---

105. TBT Agreement, *supra* note 7, Introduction, art. 2.2.
106. *Id.*
107. *Id.*, art. 2.3 (emphasis added).

minimized, and at the same time, so that other Members can be provided opportunities to question the validity of these measures. Various obligations regarding 'transparency' and 'reason-giving requirements' are scattered in relevant places,[108] often employing the same language as the SPS Agreement. Interestingly, the provision regarding an 'enquiry point' is far more detailed than the corresponding SPS provision, possibly reflecting the more technical nature of the TBT Agreement.[109]

3.2 Derivative jurisprudence

3.2.1 The SPS Agreement

3.2.1.1 Prelude

Three cases

Since the launch of the new WTO dispute settlement system, three cases involving the SPS Agreement have been adjudicated thus far: *Hormones* (1997); *Australian Salmon* (1998); and *Japanese Agricultural Products* (1999), dealing with 'human' health, 'animal' health and 'plant' health, respectively. These three cases have developed an integrated and synergistic jurisprudence on the SPS Agreement as subsequent cases have systematically followed and cited the preceding cases. Moreover, it seems apparent that this jurisprudence will continue in the future to guide the development of case law in this field.

Factual aspects

Hormones (1997)
The European Communities, through the series of Directives 81/602/EEC, 88/146/EEC, 88/299/EEC and 96/22/EC, has banned the importation of meat and meat products from animals to which any of six specific hormones have been administered for purposes of promoting the growth of animals. The six hormones are three natural hormones, oestradiol-17 ß (responsible for female characteristics), testosterone (responsible for male characteristics), progesterone, (responsible for maintaining pregnancy), and three synthetic hormones, zeranol, trenbolone, and melengestrol acetate (MGA), which mimic the actions of the three natural hormones, respectively.[110] The US, one of the largest exporters of hormones-treated beef,

108. *See e.g.*, *id.*, arts. 2.5, 2.9, 5.2.2., 10.
109. *Compare* TBT Agreement, *supra* note 7, Introduction, art. 10 *with* SPS Agreement, *supra* note 6, Introduction, art. 7, Annex B.
110. *Hormones*, Panel Report, *supra* note 8, Introduction, ¶ 8.1.

challenged the EC's import ban as a violation of GATT 1994 Articles I, III, as well as SPS Articles 2, 3 and 5.

Australian Salmon (1998)

Under the pretext of enforcing a quarantine, Australia banned the importation of fresh, chilled or frozen salmon according to the 'Quarantine Proclamation 86 A' (QP 86 A) and the subsequent administrative legislation, such as '1988 Conditions' and '1996 Requirements.' Canada, one of the largest exporters of these salmon, challenged these measures before the WTO Panel, arguing that they violated the SPS Article 2, 3 and 5, as well as GATT 1994 Article XI.

Japanese agricultural products (1999)

Japan prohibits the importation of eight agricultural products—apples, cherries, peaches (including nectarines), walnuts, apricots, pears, plums and quince—originating from, *inter alia*, the United States, on the grounds that they are potential hosts of codling moth, a pest, which poses a serious threat to Japanese produce. The only allowable alternative quarantine treatment is fumigation with methyl bromide, or a combination of methyl bromide fumigation and cold storage. In 1987, Japan developed two guidelines for this alternative quarantine treatment, one of which is the 'Experimental Guide for Cultivar Comparison Test on Insect Mortality—Fumigation' (the 'Experimental Guide'). This Guide imposes the testing requirement for approval of additional *varieties* of that product. In bringing a claim before the WTO dispute settlement body, the United States claimed that this 'varietal testing requirement' violated certain provisions of the SPS Agreement.

Jurisprudence

Relationship between the SPS Agreement and GATT

Hormones (1997)

Since the WTO system took effect, many scholars and practitioners have debated the legal relationship between the SPS Agreement and GATT. The WTO Charter does not say much about this issue, except for Annex 1A, which states that when a provision of GATT and that of the side agreements conflict with each other, the latter prevails for the purpose of resolving such conflict.[111] However, this provision seems to give little help in adjudicating actual cases since such conflict can be expected to occur only rarely. Moreover, in close cases, panelists and Appellate Body members alike can be expected to rule in such a way as to avoid finding such conflict between the provisions of GATT and the SPS Agreement. On the other hand, the SPS Agreement itself embodies slightly more precise language. In the Preamble, it expresses the rationale of the Agreement, i.e., to *elaborate* GATT provisions relating to sanitary or phytosanitary measures, particularly Article XX (b). Arguably, the SPS Agreement can be viewed as a *lex specialis* vis-à-vis GATT in light of Article XX (b). Yet, it would be hard to apply the same relationship to Article III (National Treatment).

111. Annex 1 A, WTO Agreement, *supra* note 1, Introduction.

Nevertheless, the *Hormone* Panel tried to highlight the difference, rather than the interrelationship, between GATT and the SPS Agreement. The Panel ruled that:

> Many provisions of the SPS Agreement impose 'substantive' obligations which go significantly beyond and are additional to the requirements for invocation of Article XX(b). ... They are not imposed, as is the case of the obligations imposed by Article XX(b) of GATT, to justify a violation of another GATT obligation (such as a violation of the non-discrimination obligations of Articles I or III).[112]
>
> We note in this respect that the general approach adopted in Article XX(b) of GATT is fundamentally different from the approach adopted in the SPS Agreement. Article XX(b), which is not limited to sanitary or phytosanitary measures, provides for a general *exception* which can be invoked to justify any violation of another GATT provision. The SPS Agreement, on the other hand, provides for specific *obligations* to be met in order for a Member to enact or maintain specific types of measures, namely sanitary and phytosanitary measures.[113]

Based on this fundamental difference, the Panel absolved itself from any obligation to establish a priority between GATT and the SPS Agreement,[114] but eventually examined the latter first based on the practical consideration that the latter 'specifically addresses the type of measure in dispute.'[115]

The Panel's approach, which was not appealed, is laudable in that it emphasizes the superior utility of the SPS Agreement vis-à-vis GATT. This superior utility is based on the fact that the SPS Agreement overcomes GATT's conventional dichotomy between general obligation and exceptions, which results in its pro-trade bias. Indeed, the SPS Agreement imposes substantive obligations, not mere exceptions for justification, which should be complied with through enactment or application of certain sanitary or phytosanitary measures.

On the other hand, the Panel essentially ducked the sensitive question of an eventual confrontation, albeit not conflict, between GATT and the SPS Agreement, in particular in terms of Article III:4. At the end of its report, the Panel refused to examine GATT on the ground of 'judicial economy.'[116] Nonetheless, the GATT scrutiny on Article III:4 need not be marginalized solely because of the existence of the SPS Agreement. This is especially so considering the concept of '*de facto* discrimination,' which is an equivalent of 'indistinctively applicable' measures in the ECJ jurisprudence, involving measures facially neutral but having disparate impacts on trade. In *Hormones* (1997), although the EU ban was an equally applicable measure, and thus *de jure* non-discriminatory, it would have fallen under the rubric of '*de facto* discrimination,' and therefore Article III:4, because it created a disparate impact on trade between 'hormone-treated US beef' and 'non hormone-treated EU

112. *Hormones*, Panel Report, *supra* note 8, Introduction, ¶ 8.38.
113. *Id.*, ¶ 8.39.
114. *Id.*, ¶ 8.41.
115. *Id.*, ¶ 8.42.
116. *Id.*, ¶ 8.272.

beef,' which would have distorted the equality of competitive opportunities established by the EU tariff binding on beef.

Burden of proof
Hormones (1997)
The AB virtually struck down the Panel's ruling on the burden of proof, which was based decidedly on the nature of harmonization through international standards. The Panel had originally interpreted Articles 3.1 and 3.3 as general obligations and exceptions, respectively. In other words, according to the Panel, it is a 'general obligation' that Members shall base their sanitary or phytosanitary measures on available international standards; and, on the other hand, it is an 'exception' to this general obligation that Members nonetheless depart from these international standards in order to establish a higher level of protection than is reflected in those standards. In the Panel's view, the presumption clause of Article 3.2 supported its logic. Accordingly, the Panel ruled that:

> It thereby suggests by implication that when a measure is not so based, the burden is on the respondent to show that the measure is justified under the exceptions provided for in Article 3.3.[117]

Nevertheless, the AB flatly rejected the Panel's logic. In particular, in an unusual and unnecessarily harsh tone, the AB condemned the Panel's invocation of Article 3.2 as a *non-sequitur* in that such presumption is merely an 'incentive,' the opposition of which does not amount to a 'penalty.'[118] It was the AB's view that the Panel had misinterpreted the relationship between Articles 3.1, 3.2 and 3.3, which differs qualitatively from the relationship between GATT Articles I or III and XX.[119] The AB ruled that:

> Article 3.3 recognizes the *autonomous right* of a Member to establish such higher level of protection, provided that that Member complies with certain requirements in promulgating SPS measures to achieve that level. (emphasis added)

In the end, the AB reversed the Panel's ruling on the burden of proof issue:

> In accordance with our ruling in *United States—Shirts and Blouses*, the Panel should have begun the analysis of each legal provision by examining whether the United States and Canada had presented evidence and legal arguments sufficient to demonstrate that the EC measures were inconsistent with the obligations assumed by the European Communities under each Article of the *SPS Agreement* addressed by the Panel, i.e., Articles 3.1, 3.3, 5.1 and 5.5. Only after such a *prima facie* determination had been made by the Panel may the

117. *Id.*, ¶ 8.86.
118. *Hormones*, AB Report, *supra* note 8, Introduction, ¶ 102.
119. *Id.*, ¶ 104.

onus be shifted to the European Communities to bring forward evidence and arguments to disprove the complaining party's claim.

Precautionary principle (Article 5.7)
Hormones (1997)

Agreeing with the Panel, the AB in this case took a rather cautious approach toward the 'precautionary principle.' Rejecting the EC's appeal, the AB expressed skepticism toward the view that the precautionary principle had obtained the status of 'general or customary principle of law,' though it acknowledged that the principle could arguably be a 'general principle of customary international *environmental* law.' [120] Yet, the AB neither denied that Article 5.7 contains a *reflection* of the precautionary principle, nor found that the Article exhausts the principle's relevance.[121]

Since the AB rejected the idea of the precautionary principle as a customary international law, it basically found that it had no duty to apply such principle, and instead focused on the text of the SPS Agreement according to the 'normal principles of treaty interpretation.' In conclusion, the AB agreed with the finding of the Panel that 'the precautionary principle does not override the provisions of Articles 5.1 and 5.2 of the SPS Agreement.'[122]

Japanese agricultural products (1999)

In this case, the AB decided a structural issue in affirming that 'Article 5.7 operates as a qualified *exemption* from the obligation under Article 2.2 not to maintain SPS measures without sufficient scientific evidence.'[123] In addition, the AB warned that 'an overly broad and flexible interpretation of that obligation would render Article 5.7 meaningless.'[124] Although the AB's interpretive approach here may be viewed as being in opposition to a general principle of law requiring a narrow and strict interpretation of exceptions, such approach seems to be motivated by a desire to broaden the scope of regulatory discretion for Members in the face of scientific uncertainty on modern regulatory subjects.

Nonetheless, at the same time, the AB emphasized that certain requirements should be met to invoke Article 5.7. Specifically, the AB extracted a 'four-prong test' from the text of Article 5.7. According to the first sentence of Article 5.7, a Member may provisionally adopt an SPS measure if this measure is:

> imposed in respect of a situation where 'relevant scientific information is insufficient'; and
> adopted 'on the basis of available pertinent information'.[125]

---

120. *Id.*, ¶ 123.
121. *Id.*, ¶ 124.
122. *Id.*, ¶ 125.
123. *Japanese Agricultural Products*, AB Report, *supra* note 10, Introduction, ¶ 80 (emphasis added).
124. *Id.*
125. *Id.*, ¶ 89.

According to the second sentence of Article 5.7, such a provisional measure may not be maintained unless the Member that adopted the measure:

> seek[s] to obtain the additional information necessary for a more objective assessment of risk'; and
> review[s] the ... measure accordingly within a reasonable period of time.[126]

The first two requirements, stipulated in the first sentence of Article 5.7, relate to an *ex ante* situation, while the remaining two requirements, stipulated in the second sentence of the Article, concern an *ex post* situation in terms of launching a provisional measure. Japan, in its appeal, took the narrow view that Members only have to fulfil the first two requirements to regard a provisional measure without sufficient scientific information as an exception to Article 2.2.[127] However, the AB rejected such a proposition by highlighting that 'Article 2.2 refers to Article 5.7 as a whole and Article 5.7 links the first and second sentence with the words "[i]n such circumstances".'[128]

In conclusion, the AB ruled that:

> Although the obligation 'to review' the varietal testing requirement has only been in existence since 1 January 1995, we agree with the Panel that Japan has not reviewed its varietal testing requirement 'within a reasonable period of time.[129]

The foregoing jurisprudence is quite significant in that the AB established a balanced discipline on the provisional measure based on a precautionary principle in the context of the SPS Agreement. While *ex ante* offering ample opportunities in initiating those provisional measures in respect of the first two requirements, the AB nonetheless *ex post* disciplined the maintenance of the measures by imposing the surveillance obligation on Members initiating the measures. In sum, though Japan initiated the provisional measure in question, i.e., the 'varietal testing requirement' back in 1987 before the launch of the WTO, it still should have complied with the SPS Agreement, which entered into force in January 1995, by implementing the positive duties stipulated in the second sentence of Article 5.7.

Harmonization through international standards (Article 3)

Hormones (1997)

As discussed above, the Panel in this case put too much weight on Article 3.1, which requires Members to base their sanitary or phytosanitary measures on international standards, labelling it as a general obligation. Accordingly, in the view of the Panel, Article 3.3, which provides a way for Members to deviate from such international standards, must be defined as an exception. This approach was deterministic of the

126. *Id.*
127. *Id.*, ¶ 90.
128. *Id.*
129. *Id.*, ¶ 93.

burden of proof, eventually requiring the defendant (the EC) to demonstrate that the measures in dispute met the requirements imposed by the SPS Agreement. As we have seen, the AB rejected the Panel's approach and reversed the latter's ruling on this point.

Behind these starkly contrasting conclusions lies a fundamental disagreement between the Panel and the AB regarding how to weigh harmonization (through international standards) in the SPS Agreement. The Panel took the Article 3.1 obligation seriously, and thus interpreted the term 'based on' narrowly, equating it with 'conform to.' Therefore, if a sanitary measure implied a different level of protection from that an international standard reflects, that measure was not based on the international standard.[130] This interpretation would have caused Members a tremendous burden in adhering very closely to international standards with respect to every new sanitary regulation, thereby suffocating their regulatory autonomy. On the other hand, this interpretation might have contributed to a lessening of the trade restrictive impact caused by the diverging sanitary measures of Members. In sum, one may reasonably speculate that the Panel's interpretation placed an implicit priority upon trade concerns over regulatory concerns.

However, the AB warned that the Panel's interpretation of Article 3.1 would 'transform those standards, guidelines and recommendations into binding *norms*.' To the AB, harmonization through international standards in the SPS Agreement is a dynamic, long-term goal, not an obligation respected here and now. Against this backdrop, the AB reinterpreted Articles 3.1, 3.2 and 3.3 as follows, respectively:

> Under Article 3.2 of the *SPS Agreement*, a Member may decide to promulgate an SPS measure that conforms to an international standard. Such a measure would embody the international standard completely and, for practical purposes, converts it into a municipal standard. Such a measure enjoys the benefit of a presumption (albeit a rebuttable one) that it is consistent with the relevant provisions of the *SPS Agreement* and of the GATT 1994.[131]
>
> Under Article 3.1 of the *SPS Agreement*, a Member may choose to establish an SPS measure that is based on the existing relevant international standard, guideline or recommendation. Such a measure may adopt some, not necessarily all, of the elements of the international standard. The Member imposing this measure does not benefit from the presumption of consistency set up in Article 3.2; but, as earlier observed, the Member is not penalized by exemption of a complaining Member from the normal burden of showing a *prima facie* case of inconsistency with Article 3.1 or any other relevant article of the *SPS Agreement* or of the GATT 1994.[132]
>
> Under Article 3.3 of the *SPS Agreement*, a Member may decide to set for itself a level of protection different from that implicit in the international standard, and to implement or embody that level of protection in a measure not 'based on' the international standard. The Member's appropriate level of

130. *Hormones*, Panel Report, *supra* note 8, Introduction, ¶ 8.72.
131. *Hormones*, AB Report, *supra* note 8, Introduction, ¶ 170.
132. *Id.*, ¶ 171.

> protection may be higher than that implied in the international standard. The right of a Member to determine its own appropriate level of sanitary protection is an important right.[133]

It may be true that the AB's approach was more politically correct than the Panel's in that the former gave more sympathy to the defendant's position in this highly sensitive case. Indeed, that the AB's approach might have involved a degree of political deliberation would be understandable to some extent, considering that the WTO was only two years old when this case was adjudicated, and that both the plaintiff (the US) and the defendant (the EU) were big players in the WTO system. However, even apart from its political sensitivity, the AB's approach was still comprehensible in that those international standards were originally meant to be 'non-binding.' If the Panel's approach were to be followed, those international standards would, indeed, have been virtually converted into 'binding' norm through the SPS Agreement, which was hardly the Members' intention. This interpretation would have been tantamount to an 'authoritative interpretation', which only Members can render.[134]

Moreover, the AB's approach appeared more faithful also to the rationale of the SPS Agreement than did that of the Panel. As discussed above, the Panel's strict view on harmonization through international standards seemed to be biased, albeit impliedly, toward free market considerations because the Panel's concern was oriented towards ensuring a better flow of international trade, even at the expense of restricting the regulatory leeway of Members. Yet, the SPS Agreement purports to overcome the pro-trade bias embedded in GATT's 'dichotomy' between general obligations (national treatment) and exceptions (protection of human health), and reinstate the regulatory autonomy of Members by acknowledging their *rights* to adopt and apply sanitary measures. This purpose is paralleled by the AB's approach.

Lastly, the Panel's narrow and strict perspective on harmonization would have undermined the legitimacy as well as effectiveness of the SPS Agreement. As discussed above, the approval procedures for those international standards in relevant international organizations are not necessarily consensus-based. Sometimes, a standard may be approved by a slight majority. If such a standard ever ended up being binding through the SPS Agreement, it would amount to a circumvention of the normal treaty-making process since what a small number of faceless professionals and regulators decided among themselves would become law. This circumvention would risk de-legitimizing the operation of the SPS Agreement. Furthermore, Members would feel more cautious and even reluctant to adopt those standards once they realize those standards would soon turn into binding norms through the SPS Agreement. Such misgivings would make the Agreement ineffective since they would likely lead to frustration of the very goal of harmonization through international standards.

133. *Id.*, ¶ 172.
134. WTO Agreement, *supra* note 1, Introduction, art. IX:2.

Risk assessment (Article 5.1)
The risk assessment requirement is the core of the SPS Agreement, and both the Panel and the AB in the *Hormones* (1997) case exerted considerable interpretive energy on behalf of this issue. It should thus come as no surprise that the jurisprudence developed in the *Hormones* case has played a guiding role in subsequent SPS cases, notably *Australian Salmon* (1998) and *Japanese Agricultural Products* (1999).

Preliminary issues

Hormones (1997)
In this case the Panel dealt with two preliminary issues with respect to risk assessment before examining the substance of the dispute. First, the Panel viewed the risk assessment requirement as a 'specific application of the basic obligations' in Article 2.2, such as the requirement of being 'based on scientific principles.'[135] The AB agreed with the Panel on this point, and further stressed that:

> Articles 2.2 and 5.1 should constantly be read together. Article 2.2 informs Article 5.1: the elements that define the basic obligation set out in Article 2.2 impart meaning to Article 5.1.[136]

The second preliminary issue related to the Panel's conceptual distinction between 'risk assessment' and 'risk management.' First, the Panel grouped a series of obligations, namely Articles 5.1 (the requirement of being *based on* risk assessment), 5.2 (the requirement of considering various *scientific* factors in risk assessment) and 5.3 (the requirement of considering various *economic* factors in risk assessment), as 'risk assessment.'[137] Then, the Panel grouped another series of obligations, namely Articles 5.4 (the requirement of minimizing negative trade effects in the *determination* of the appropriate level of protection), 5.5 (the consistency requirement in the *application* of the appropriate level of protection) and 5.6 (the less trade-restrictive means requirement), as 'risk management.'[138] The Panel observed that risk assessment concerns an objective analysis of 'scientific' data,[139] while risk management focuses on a 'social' judgment involving policy determination and application.[140]

The AB summarily rejected the Panel's conceptual distinction on the grounds that it enjoyed no textual basis.[141] The AB's concern was that such a distinction would unduly restrict the scope of risk assessment:[142] it implied that risk assessment may include more than an objective, scientific analysis. Yet the AB's ruling on this point seems controversial for the following reasons. First, the SPS Agreement does

135. *Hormones*, Panel Report, *supra* note 8, Introduction, ¶ 8. 93.
136. *Hormones*, AB Report, *supra* note 8, Introduction, ¶ 180.
137. *Hormones*, Panel Report, *supra* note 8, Introduction, ¶ 8. 93.
138. *Id.*, ¶ 8. 96.
139. *Id.*, ¶ 8. 94.
140. *Id.*, ¶ 8. 97.
141. *Hormones*, AB Report, *supra* note 8, Introduction, ¶ 181.
142. *Id.*

distinguish between 'risk assessment' and 'determination/application of the appropriate level of sanitary or phytosanitary protection.'[143] Secondly, the distinction was not of the Panel's invention, but of the Parties' use.[144] Thirdly, outside the WTO, such a distinction is widely used.[145]

Japanese agricultural products (1999)
After reaffirming that Article 2.2 (scientific justification requirement) represents a *basic* obligation of which Article 5.1 (risk assessment requirement) is a *specific* application,[146] the AB viewed that 'there is a "scientific justification" for an SPS measure, ... if there is a *rational relationship* between the SPS measure at issue and the available scientific information.'[147]

Risks

Hormones (1997)
The Panel elaborated the risk assessment into a 'two-step' process: *identification* of the adverse effects resulting from the use of the hormone and *evaluation* of the potential probability of such an occurrence.[148] Regarding this 'identifiable' risk, the AB agreed with the Panel that 'theoretical uncertainty' is not the kind of risk which is to be assessed under the SPS Agreement.[149] Yet the AB objected to the Panel's notion of identifiable risk to the extent that it contemplated a 'quantitative requirement,' i.e., a demonstration of a certain 'magnitude or threshold level of risk.'[150]

In the same context, the AB emphasized that:

> the risk that is to be evaluated in a risk assessment under Article 5.1 is not only risk ascertainable in a science laboratory operating under strictly controlled conditions, but also risk in human societies as they actually exist, in other words, the actual potential for adverse effects on human health *in the real world where people live and work and die*.[151]

The AB's perspective, accentuating a 'practical,' not necessarily 'scientific' perspective on risks, is a double-edged sword. First, this practical perspective on risk could serve to widen Members' regulatory autonomy, which might otherwise be narrowed due to an obsession with textbook or laboratory-borne scientific conclusions, by justifying a preventive regulatory move by a Member in the face

143. *Compare* SPS Agreement, *supra* note 6, Introduction, arts. 5.5, 5.6 *with* art. 5.1.
144. *Hormones*, Panel Report, *supra* note 8, Introduction, ¶ 8. 95.
145. *See e.g.*, OECD, Report of the OECD Workshop on Risk Assessment and Risk Communication in the Context of Chemical Accident Prevention, Preparedness and Response, *available at* <http://www.oecd.org//ehs/ehsmono/07E72653.DOC/ (last visited on August 6, 2001).
146. *Japanese Agricultural Products*, *supra* note 10, Introduction, ¶ 82.
147. *Id.*, ¶ 79 (emphasis added).
148. *Hormones*, Panel Report, *supra* note 8, Introduction, ¶ 8.98.
149. *Hormones*, AB Report, *supra* note 8, Introduction, ¶ 186.
150. *Id.*; n.331.
151. *Hormones*, AB Report, *supra* note 8, Introduction, ¶ 187 (emphasis added).

of a given health risk that may be causing panic among its citizens. On the one hand, this move is rational in that it is people who actually *feel* the risk. This parallels with Aristotle's *phronesis*, and also with the precautionary principle. On the other hand, this move is politically correct, and even legitimate, in that every government should respond to people's actual demand. It was in reliance upon this logic that the AB rejected the Panel's narrow conceptualization of 'risk assessment,' which focused on 'scientific' examination, thereby leaving a certain amount of room for practical consideration of risks.

Nevertheless, it should be noted that this pragmatic approach to risk always carries with it the potential for misuse or abuse. In other words, governments could use this perspective as an effective subterfuge for bypassing relevant and even necessary regulatory processes of investigation, analysis and discussion. Governments would be tempted to rely on popular belief clad only in practical wisdom since such belief or wisdom better serves their political purposes in that it tends to be more malleable than hard facts. Disguised protectionism flourishes under such circumstances. Responsible governments should endeavour to enlighten and educate their people based on sound scientific information, instead of yielding to or pandering to the often unnecessarily escalated fears of some citizens.

Therefore, the *Hormone* case, with its practical perspective on risks, should be followed by subsequent panels or the AB in a subtle and nuanced way, taking full account of the opposite edge of this particular sword.

Risk assessment

Hormones (1997)

On this point the Panel found in Article 5.1, which requires that measures be *based on* risk assessment, two separate obligations: one procedural and the other substantive. As for the procedural obligation, the Panel opined that there should be a minimum procedural requirement of demonstrating that a regulating Member *actually* took into account a risk assessment.[152] The Panel ruled that the EC had failed to meet this requirement since 'none of the preambles to the EC measures at issue mention any of the scientific studies referred to by the European Communities.'[153] As for the substantive obligation, the Panel expressed its view that the scientific conclusions shaping the EC measures should be 'in conformity with' at least some of those reached in the studies cited by the European Communities.[154]

The AB rejected the Panel's interpretation on the minimum procedural requirement, and ruled that 'the SPS measure might well find its objective justification in a risk assessment carried out by another Member, or an international organization.'[155] However, as for the substantive requirement, which the AB posited as a 'rational relationship' between an SPS measure and a risk assessment, the AB agreed with the finding of the Panel that the EC had merely dealt with the condition that hormones be administered 'in accordance with good practice' 'without further

152. *Hormones*, Panel Report, *supra* note 8, Introduction, ¶ 8. 113.
153. *Id.*, ¶ 8. 114.
154. *Id.*, ¶ 8. 117.
155. *Hormones*, AB Report, *supra* note 8, Introduction, ¶ 190.

providing an assessment of the potential adverse effects related to non-compliance with such practice.'[156] Therefore, the AB concluded that:

> The absence of such a risk assessment, when considered in conjunction with the conclusion actually reached by most, if not all, of the scientific studies relating to the other aspects of risk noted earlier, leads us to the conclusion that no risk assessment that *reasonably supports* or *warrants* the import prohibition embodied in the EC Directives was furnished to the Panel.[157]

Here again, the AB seems to have been concerned about the undue loss of Members' regulatory autonomy. The AB provided Members with more room to manoeuvre in establishing a sanitary or phytosanitary regulation by relieving them of the obligation of an actual implementation of their own risk assessment. Moreover, the AB stressed that the actual outcome of risk assessment may reflect a 'divergent,' not a 'mainstream,' scientific conclusion.[158] The AB's reading of Article 5 may be appealing from the perspective of ensuring Members' regulatory autonomy. However, the AB itself seemed to acknowledge, albeit impliedly, a bottom-line requirement of the 'existence' of risk assessment. The AB depicted the EC's deficient procedure as the 'beginning' of risk assessment,[159] and also found that the EC did 'not actually proceed to' a risk assessment.[160] In the absence of such a bottom-line procedural requirement, a losing Member could be tempted to *ex post* justify its measure, after it had been struck down, through managing to employ a self-serving minority view, which the EC did attempt when it lost the case.[161] Therefore, in order to prevent such jurisprudential misuse, at least a certain procedural requirement seems necessary to warrant an *ex ante* 'existence' of risk assessment, whether such risk assessment is conducted directly by a regulating Member, or borrowed from other institutions.

Australian Salmon (1998)

In dealing with the risk assessment issue, the Panel faithfully followed the interpretive track established in the *Hormones* (1997) case. It began with a scrutiny of the definition of 'risk assessment' provided in Annex A, deconstructing the text and creating a 'three-prong test,' which the AB also adopted.[162]

> (1) *identify* the diseases whose entry, establishment or spread a Member wants to prevent within its territory, as well as the potential biological and economic

156. *Id.*, ¶ 207. *See* Victor, *supra* note 16, at 901–2.
157. *Hormones*, AB Report, *supra* note 8, Introduction, ¶ 208 (emphasis added).
158. *Id.*, ¶ 194.
159. *Id.*, ¶ 207.
160. *Id.*, ¶ 208.
161. *See EU to Pursue New Risk Studies for Hormone Treated Beef*, BRIDGES WEEKLY TRADE NEWS DIGEST, VOL. 2, No. 9, Mar. 16, 1998, *available at* <http://www.newsbulletin.org/bulletins/getbulletin.cfm?browse=1&Issue_ID=389&Bulletin_ID=14&SID=#EU TO PURSUE NEW RISK STUDIES FOR HORMONE TREATED BEEF> (last visited on March 12, 2001).
162. *Australian Salmon*, Panel Report, *supra* note 9, Introduction, ¶ 8. 72; *Australian Salmon*, AB Report, *supra* note 9, Introduction, ¶ 121.

> consequences associated with the entry, establishment or spread of these diseases; (2) *evaluate the likelihood* of entry, establishment or spread of these diseases, as well as the associated potential biological and economic consequences; and (3) evaluate the likelihood of entry, establishment or spread of these diseases *according to the SPS measures which might be applied.*[163]

Surprisingly, however, the Panel took such a soft stance in examining whether Australia fulfilled the risk assessment requirement that it basically 'assumed,' rather than actually found, that the 1996 Final Report met the risk assessment requirements stipulated in Articles 5.1 and 5.2 of the SPS Agreement. The Panel ruled that:

> Referring to our findings in paragraphs 8.73, 8.75, 8.80 and 8.88 and to our *assumptions* in paragraphs 8.83 and 8.91, we recall that the 1996 Final Report identifies the diseases of concern as well as the associated biological and economic consequences. It does so on a disease-by-disease basis. To *some* extent it also addresses elements of probability of occurrence of the identified risk. It analyzes risk reduction factors on a disease-by-disease basis and identifies five quarantine options to reduce the total disease risk. For the purpose of our further examination we shall, therefore, *assume—without making a finding on this issue*—that the 1996 Final Report meets the requirements of a risk assessment set out in Articles 5.1 and 5.2.[164]

The AB attempted to preserve the rigor of the risk assessment requirement by striking down this lenient approach by the Panel. As for the second element, the AB emphasized that '*some* evaluation of the likelihood is not enough.'[165] In particular, the AB problematized the Panel's ruling on the second element by highlighting the Panel's own factual findings diverged from expert opinions which stated congruently that the 1996 Final Report fell short of a risk assessment.[166] Therefore, the AB concluded that:

> the 1996 Final Report meets neither the second nor the third requirement for the type of risk assessment applicable in this case, and, therefore, that the 1996 Final Report is *not a proper risk assessment* within the meaning of Article 5.1 and the first definition in paragraph 4 of Annex A.[167]

Inasmuch as we have found that the 1996 Final Report is not a proper risk assessment, and since it was the only risk assessment put forward by Australia, we conclude that the measure at issue, i.e., the import prohibition on fresh, chilled or frozen salmon, is *not based on a risk assessment* as required by Article 5.1 of the SPS Agreement, and, therefore, that Australia has acted inconsistently with Article 5.1 of the SPS Agreement.[168]

163. *Australian Salmon*, AB Report, *supra* note 9, Introduction, ¶ 121.
164. *Australian Salmon*, Panel Report, *supra* note 9, Introduction, ¶ 8. 92 (emphasis added).
165. *Australian Salmon*, AB Report, *supra* note 9, Introduction, ¶ 121.
166. *Id.*, ¶ 129.
167. *Id.*, ¶ 135 (emphasis added).
168. *Id.*, ¶ 136 (emphasis added).

The Panel's lenient stance on the existence of the risk assessment seems to originate from the *Hormones* case law. The AB in the *Hormones* case focused on the requirement of a 'rational relationship' between an SPS measure and a risk assessment rather than on the existence of such risk assessment itself. The Panel in the *Australian Salmon* case also seemed to follow this track finding that the measure at issue was not based on a risk assessment,[169] once it merely assumed the existence of the risk assessment. To the *Australian Salmon* Panel, the existence of a risk assessment might be just an auxiliary element to base a more important requirement, namely a 'rational relationship' requirement. Yet, by contrast, the AB in the *Australian Salmon* case brought to the interpretive forefront the requirement of the existence of a risk assessment through the 'three-prong test.' As a result, Members are now required to demonstrate two separate requirements, the existence of a risk assessment, *and* a rational relationship between an SPS measure and such a risk assessment, in order to comply with Article 5.1. This interpretive development, from *Hormones* to *Australian Salmon*, can be taken as an example of jurisprudential 'evolution' since jurisprudence becomes more precise and sophisticated case after case.

Japanese agricultural products (1999)

In defending the regulations in question, Japan argued that its varietal testing requirement was based on the 1996 Pest Risk Assessment of Codling Moth (the '1996 Risk Assessment'). However, the AB observed that the 1996 Risk Assessment failed to 'discuss or even refer to' the varietal testing requirement or to any other phytosanitary measure to reduce the risk, thereby falling short of a risk assessment within the meaning of Article 5.1.[170]

Consistency (Article 5.5)
Three elements

Hormones (1997)

Article 5.5 requires the consistency in levels of protection and prohibits resultant discrimination or disguised restriction on international trade. In Article 5.5 the Panel found three elements, namely, 'different levels of protection in different situations,' 'arbitrary or unjustifiable distinctions in the treatment of different situations,' and 'the arbitrary or unjustifiable differences resulting in discrimination or disguised restriction on international trade.'[171] According to the Panel, these three elements are cumulative in that 'all three elements need to be present' 'to find a sanitary measure to be inconsistent with Article 5.5.'[172] The AB agreed with the Panel on this basic structure of Article 5.5.[173]

---

169. *Australian Salmon*, Panel Report, *supra* note 9, Introduction, ¶ 8. 99.
170. *Japanese Agricultural Products*, AB Report, *supra* note 10, ¶ 113.
171. *Australian Salmon*, Panel Report, *supra* note 9, Introduction, ¶ 8. 174.
172. *Id.*
173. *Australian Salmon*, AB Report, *supra* note 9, Introduction, ¶ 214.

Australian Salmon (1998)

The *Australian Salmon* Panel also followed the *Hormones* case law regarding three elements in Article 5.5,[174] and the AB examined the Panel's interpretations based on these three elements.[175]

The first element: 'different levels of protection in different situations'

Hormones (1997)

Regarding the first element, the Panel interpreted the term 'different' as 'comparable.'[176] The AB agreed on this interpretation, stating that comparable situations present some common element(s), but are not totally different from each other.[177] Markedly, this test on 'difference' or 'comparability' mirrors the 'like product' test in the conventional GATT jurisprudence. Under the like product test, likeness between products in comparison is determined partly by their properties, including physical characteristics or end-uses. Likewise, in interpreting 'different situations,' comparability is determined by certain substantial elements defining those situations, including the biochemical nature of hormones and their health risks. In this regard, the AB noted the Panel's findings of several different levels of protection in different (comparable) situations, which were 'in respect of natural hormones and synthetic hormones (zeranol and trenbolone) when used for growth promotion,' 'in respect of natural hormones occurring endogenously in meat and other foods,' 'in respect of natural hormones when used for therapeutic or zootechnical purposes,' and 'in respect of carbadox and olaquindox.'[178]

The EC appealed on this arguably narrow criterion that the Panel used in determining 'different situations.' To the EC, regardless of the presence of some common features, such as the health risk, a fundamental line must be drawn between situations that are by nature incomparable. The EC argued that:

> Science and the regulatory practices of Members do not treat man-made risks, such as the risks created by hormones used for growth promotion, and naturally-occurring risks, such as those arising from the presence of hormones in meat, milk, cabbage or broccoli, in the same way.[179]

The EC's position on this issue seems attention-grabbing in that it reflects the 'phronesis' aspect discussed above. In other words, to the EC, one just cannot compare man-made risks with naturally-occurring risks because they are totally or fundamentally different in nature. In fact, this perspective was accepted by the AB when interpreting the second element, and thus came to reverse the Panel's ruling on Article 5.5.[180]

174. *Australian Salmon*, Panel Report, *supra* note 9, Introduction, ¶ 8. 108.
175. *Australian Salmon*, AB Report, *supra* note 9, Introduction, ¶ 142.
176. *Hormones*, Panel Report, *supra* note 8, Introduction, ¶ 8. 176.
177. *Hormones*, AB Report, *supra* note 8, Introduction, ¶ 217.
178. *Id.*, ¶ 218.
179. *Id.*, ¶ 32.
180. *Id.*, ¶ 221.

Australian Salmon (1998)

Following the ruling by the AB in the *Hormones* case, the Panel defined comparable situations as those involving '*either* a risk of entry, establishment or spread of the same or a similar disease *or* the same or similar associated biological and economic consequences.'[181] Based on this definition, the Panel found that the import prohibition on fresh, chilled or frozen salmon for human consumption and other situations, such as the admission of imports of 'herring used as bait' and 'live ornamental finfish,' were 'different' situations which can be compared under Article 5.5 of the SPS Agreement.[182] However, Australia appealed, based on the definition of a risk assessment in Annex A, that comparable situations should involve the risk of '*both* the entry, establishment or spread of a disease *and* the associated potential biological and economic consequences.'[183]

The AB rejected the Australian appeal aiming to narrow down the scope of comparable situations and eventually exclude its measure from the grip of the SPS Agreement. The AB ruled that either situation with a risk of entry, establishment or spread of the same or a similar disease, or with a risk of the same or similar associated biological and economic consequences had 'some common elements sufficient to render them comparable under Article 5.5.'[184] Furthermore, the AB stressed that 'for situations to be comparable under Article 5.5, it is sufficient for these situations to have in common a risk of entry, establishment or spread of *one* disease of concern.'[185] Obviously, it seemed that the AB tried to maintain a rather broad reach for Article 5.5, at least in light of the first element.

The second element: 'arbitrary or unjustifiable distinctions in the treatment of different situations'

Hormones (1997)

Based on its interpretation of the first element, the Panel found with little difficulty that the EC's different levels of sanitary protection under those comparable situations was 'arbitrary and unjustifiable.' In particular, the Panel found such arbitrariness or unjustifiability on the grounds that the EC permitted a 'no residue' level of protection (an import ban) in respect of natural and synthetic hormones when used for growth promotion, while it permitted an 'unlimited' level of protection (no regulation) in respect of natural hormones occurring endogenously in meat and other foods, as well as in respect of carbadox and olaquindox.

However, the AB struck down and reversed the Panel's finding in respect of natural hormones occurring endogenously in meat and other foods. The AB ruled that:

181. *Australian Salmon*, Panel Report, *supra* note 9, Introduction, ¶ 8. 117 (underlining added).
182. *Australian Salmon*, AB Report, *supra* note 9, Introduction, ¶ 144.
183. *Id.*, ¶ 145.
184. *Id.*, ¶ 146.
185. *Id.*, ¶ 152.

> [W]e consider there is a *fundamental distinction* between added hormones (natural or synthetic) and naturally-occurring hormones in meat and other foods. In respect of the latter, the European Communities simply takes no regulatory action; to require it to prohibit totally the production and consumption of such foods or to limit the residues of naturally-occurring hormones in food, entails such a comprehensive and massive governmental intervention in nature and in the ordinary lives of people as to *reduce the comparison itself to an absurdity*.[186]

Similarly, the AB examined 'whether the difference in the levels of protection set by the European Communities in respect of natural hormones used as growth promoters and in respect of the same hormones when used for therapeutic or zootechnical purposes, is justified,' an issue which the Panel ignored.[187] Taking into account the EC's argument regarding two important differences between the administration of hormones for growth promotion purposes and their administration for therapeutic and zootechnical purposes, namely 'the frequency and scale of the treatment' and 'the mode of administration of hormones,'[188] the AB also ruled that:

> [O]n balance, the difference in the levels of protection concerning hormones used for growth promotion purposes, on the one hand, and concerning hormones used for therapeutic and zootechnical purposes, on the other, is not, *in itself*, 'arbitrary or unjustifiable.' (emphasis added)

The AB's almost total rejection of the Panel' s ruling was apparently motivated by the EC's argument, discussed above, which maintained that there was a fundamental difference between 'man-made risks,' such as the risks created by hormones used for growth promotion, and 'naturally-occurring risks,' such as those arising from the presence of hormones in meat, milk, cabbage or broccoli.[189] In this context, it would have been clearer and more consistent if the AB had dealt with this issue at the earlier stage when it interpreted the first element, rather than it did at the second stage.

Yet, more critically, the AB's conclusion on the second element, albeit understandable from the standpoint of the Aristotelian 'phronesis,' still leaves certain controversies unresolved. Although it may fall into the realm of intuition and common sense whether or not 'man-made risks' and 'naturally-occurring risks' are comparable, this question must nonetheless be scanned by a scientific lens because it is the rationale of the SPS Agreement to maintain scientific prudence in regulating SPS matters, which are otherwise vulnerable to whim and irrationality. In fact, many scientific revelations on risks are 'counter-intuitive.' This counter-intuitive ground of modern risks has been raised in a recent WTO symposium:

---

186. *Hormones*, AB Report, *supra* note 8, Introduction, ¶ 221 (emphasis added).
187. *Id.*, ¶ 222.
188. *Id.*, ¶¶ 223, 224.
189. *Id.*, ¶ 32.

> *Human perception of risks is an important consideration*, since in many societies people are more afraid of food risks than other incidents which actually kill many more people, such as automobile accidents. Humans also perceive risks differently if they are from hereditary or non-hereditary diseases, from voluntary or forced risks, and from pharmaceuticals versus food-borne risks. There is a marked tendency to focus on novel risks, although traditional products may be at least as dangerous. In general, the public accepts some foods that scientists do not consider to be safe, but do not accept all foods that scientists know to be safe. Therefore, from a public health point of view, there is *a gap to be filled between perceived risks and real risks as well as between accepted and unaccepted risks*.[190]

In this line, the logic, which the AB employed when it rejected the Panel's ruling, may be questionable. The Panel originally found arbitrariness between the 'no residue' level of protection regarding the risks created by hormones used for growth promotion, and the 'unlimited residue' level of protection regarding the risks from hormones naturally occurring in normal foods. Yet, the AB highlighted the impracticability of regulatory intervention in the type of massive occasions in which growth promotion hormones naturally occur, and considered this regulatory impracticability to be the factor that renders absurd comparison with other occasions in which the same or similar hormones are used for the purpose of promoting the growth of beef.

Nevertheless, the criterion of comparison here should be the adverse health *risks* resulting from the hormones themselves, not the regulatory *measures* to be used to tackle such risks. In other words, the impracticability of risk-avoiding measures of one side should not halt the comparison itself between both *risks* since our attention must be focused on *risks* that are compared. To take an analogy, we do not ban the use of cellular phones, even though some contend that electronic waves flowing from the phone may cause a serious health risk. One of the main reasons for such absence of regulation stems from the fact that we are surrounded by electronic waves that most electronic devices, such as TVs and refrigerators, emit, and that naturally exist even in the air. Those electronic waves are not fatal to human health, and besides, governments cannot realistically be expected to intervene with regulation in all of those areas. Yet, regulatory impracticability still does not make it absurd to compare two kinds of risks resulting from electronic waves in respect of the use of cellular phones, on the one hand, and those naturally-occurring, on the other.

In this context, the persuasive logic of the Panel's original ruling on this issue, which was struck down by the AB, still reverberates:

> [A]ll scientific experts advising the Panel have concluded that residues of the three natural hormones present endogenously in meat and other foods or administered for therapeutic or zootechnical purposes are qualitatively the

190. Kazuaki Miyagishima, Summary Reports by the Moderators, Symposium on Issues Confronting the World Trading System, World Trade Organization, Geneva, Switzerland, 6 and 7 July 2001, *available at* <http://www.wto.org/english/forums_e/ngo_e/ngo_symp2001_repsps_e.htm> (last visited on Sep. 15, 2001) (emphasis added).

same as the residues of these hormones administered for growth promotion and that if any differences between these hormones could exist (e.g., differences in pathways taken or metabolites), these differences would in any event not have consequences for the potential adverse effects of these hormones. Therefore, even if these hormones would not be totally identical substances, they pose, in any event, the *same adverse health effect* and can, therefore, . . ., be considered as comparable situations for the purposes of Article 5.5.[191]

Australian Salmon (1998)

The Panel first noted that the difference in the levels of protection between the salmon products in question, and other fish and fish products, such as herring as a bait and live ornamental finfish, called for some justification, such as a *higher* risk from the former.[192] Furthermore, the Panel noted that all the evidence before it demonstrated that the latter, with a lower level of protection, represented at least as high a risk, if not higher, than the former.[193] Therefore, the Panel found that the distinctions in the levels of protection between the salmon products in question and other fish and fish products, such as herring as a bait and live ornamental finfish, were 'arbitrary or unjustifiable' in the sense of the second element of Article 5.5.[194] The AB upheld the Panel's finding.[195]

In fact, this ruling revealed the same pattern as seen in the *Hormones* Panel report, which viewed that the distinction in the levels of protection between man-made risks and naturally-occurring risks, which led to a zero-tolerance and no regulation, respectively, was arbitrary or unjustifiable. Although this *Hormones* Panel's finding was rejected by the AB on the grounds that these two risks were fundamentally incomparable, its basic approach, which based 'arbitrariness and unjustifiability' on the lack of justification in the face of regulatory difference, was deemed still relevant by the subsequent *Australian Salmon* Panel and the AB.

The third element: 'arbitrary or unjustifiable differences resulting in discrimination or disguised restriction on international trade'

Hormones (1997)

It is important to note that, for reasons related to the text of Article 5.5, 'arbitrariness or unjustifiability' should necessarily be accompanied by another element of 'discrimination or disguised restriction on international trade.' This cumulative structure tends to make it harder to find a violation of the Article, as compared to a hypothetical situation in which these two elements were to exist alternatively, that is 'arbitrary or unjustifiable discrimination in the levels of protection' *or* 'disguised restriction on international trade.'

According to the rationale of the SPS Agreement, which purports to discipline the 'manner' in which sanitary or phytosanitary measures are applied, even as it

191. *Hormones*, Panel Report, *supra* note 8, Introduction, ¶ 8. 187 (underlining added).
192. *Australian Salmon*, Panel Report, *supra* note 9, Introduction, ¶ 8. 133.
193. *Id.*, ¶ 8. 134.
194. *Id.*, ¶ 8. 141.
195. *Australian Salmon*, AB Report, *supra* note 9, Introduction, ¶ 158.

enshrines the adoption of such measures as the exercise of autonomous regulatory rights, 'arbitrary or unjustifiable discrimination in the levels of protection' should itself be regarded as a flaw in the regulatory process, and thus as a violation of the Agreement, regardless of its actual trade effect. As a matter of fact, the Preamble of the Agreement also follows this approach by means of language, making the application of sanitary or phytosanitary measures 'subject to the requirement that these measures are not applied in a manner which would constitute a means of arbitrary or unjustifiable discrimination between Members where the same conditions prevail *or* a disguised restriction on international trade.'[196]

Confronted with this textual dilemma, the Panel attempted to dilute the significance of the third element by basing the interpretation of the third element directly on the interpretation of the second element. In other words, the Panel employed its main finding in the interpretation of the second element—that is, the 'significance of difference' between a 'no residue' and an 'unlimited' level of protection—for the purpose of interpreting the third element. In the Panel's view, a wide discrepancy in the level of protection indicated the presence of discrimination or a disguised restriction on international trade.[197]

Interestingly, in support of this line of reasoning the Panel engaged in an analysis that echoed the approaches set forth in GATT Article XI:1 ('obstacle' test) and Article III:1 and 4 ('aim and effect' test). First, the Panel highlighted the fact that the EC had given no justification for the restriction on international trade that had resulted from the significant difference leading to the import ban.[198] The obverse side of this finding is that the existence of such a significant difference and resultant import ban is *ipso facto* a restriction on international trade that can only be justified *ex post* to avoid an eventual violation. This analysis mirrors that found in GATT Article XI:1. In addition, in support of its finding the Panel invoked the EC's protectionist intent, which was evidenced by some of the objectives of the import ban, that is 'providing more favourable treatment to domestic producers,' as well as by the effect of *de facto* discrimination against US meat in favour of EC meat after the ban.[199] This analysis mirrors the aim and effect test derived from GATT Article III:1 and 4.

The AB, however, rejected the Panel's findings as well as its supporting reasoning. First, the AB took the view that the degree of difference in the levels of protection is 'only one kind of factor which, along with others, may cumulatively lead to the conclusion.'[200] Accordingly, the AB ruled that:

> [W]e do not think that the difference between a 'no residues' level and 'unlimited residues' level is, together with a finding of an arbitrary or unjustifiable difference, sufficient to demonstrate that the third, and most important, requirement of Article 5.5 has been met.[201]

196. SPS Agreement, *supra* note 6, Introduction, pmbl. (emphasis added).
197. *Hormones*, Panel Report, *supra* note 8, Introduction, ¶ 8. 203.
198. *Id.*
199. *Id.*, ¶ 8. 205.
200. *Hormones*, AB Report, *supra* note 9, Introduction, ¶ 240.
201. *Id.*

As for the additional factors that the Panel invoked to back up its finding, the AB disagreed with the Panel's findings, and instead determined that the EC's import ban was legitimate, considering the 'depth and extent of the anxieties experienced within the EC on hormones,' as well as the 'intense concern of consumers within the EC over hormone-free beef.'[202] Therefore, the AB concluded that:

> We are unable to share the *inference* that the Panel apparently draws that the import ban ... were not really designed to protect its population from the risk of cancer, but rather to keep out US and Canadian hormone-treated beef and thereby to protect the domestic beef producers in the European Communities. (emphasis added)

Of course, the AB's perspective is understandable in that it respected the EC's legitimate policy objective—protection of its internal market from the inflow of hormone-treated beef—rather than second-guessing its legislative intent or trying to infer protectionist aims from the language of the Directives in question.[203] In a sense, the Panel's flat accusation that the EC was cheating, which was certainly embarrassing to the EC, could easily be viewed as politically incorrect from a legal realist's standpoint. Therefore, the AB might have felt a necessity to help the EC save face by rejecting the Panel's accusation and instead affirming the legitimacy of the EC's import ban. Nonetheless, it should be noted that such face-saving gestures involve the risk of abetting hidden protectionist policies under the guise of a legitimacy objective.[204]

Australian Salmon (1998)

Unlike the *Hormones* Panel, which used the second element ('arbitrary or unjustifiable distinction') as a decisive factor in interpreting the third element ('resulting in discrimination or a disguised restriction on international trade'), the *Australian Salmon* Panel took a *cumulative* approach in examining the third element. In other words, the Panel identified various 'warning signals' and 'additional factors,' which cumulatively contributed to the decision of the third element.[205] The AB endorsed such an approach and largely upheld the Panel's findings based on this approach.[206]

However, this approach seems problematic in many aspects. First of all, this approach tends to undermine the credibility of the Panel's ruling because it was not supported by 'evidence' but a mere collection of 'warning signals and additional factors.' Critically, all of those signals and factors failed to amount to the status of a piece of 'evidence' in itself. For instance, in respect of one additional factor, the AB ruled that the Panel merely stated its *doubts*, but that such doubts could nonetheless be taken into account in the examination under the third element of Article 5.5.[207]

202. *Id.*, ¶ 245.
203. *See* Victor, *supra* note 16, at 904.
204. *See id.*
205. *Australian Salmon*, Panel Report, *supra* note 9, Introduction, ¶¶ 8. 149, 8. 158.
206. *Australian Salmon*, AB Report, *supra* note 9, Introduction, ¶ 178.
207. *Id.*, ¶ 176.

Moreover, all three warning signals, namely 'the arbitrary or unjustifiable character,' 'the rather substantial difference in levels of protection' and 'no risk assessment,' were not independent considerations that firmly evidenced discrimination or a disguised restriction, but were merely inferences from the findings on other elements and provisions. It is quite possible that the dependent status of the third element implies its structural weakness under the SPS Agreement in that it stands for a *result*-oriented element (discrimination or a disguised restriction on international trade), while the Agreement focuses more on regulatory *process* itself. In other words, the status of the third element cannot help being diminished under the SPS Agreement.

Yet the second additional factor, namely 'the substantial, but unexplained' change in conclusion between the 1995 Draft Report (which recommended allowing the importation of ocean-caught Pacific salmon under certain conditions) and the 1996 Final Report (which recommended continuing the import prohibition), seems rather critical in demonstrating a regulatory flaw embedded in the Australian import restrictions. The Panel attributed this sudden change to a protectionist motivation and determined that it could be taken into account in examining the third element.[208] In contrast to its decision in the *Hormones* case, the AB upheld the Panel's ruling which implied that Australia was cheating.[209] It is fair to say that this finding appears most plausible, out of all warning signals and additional factors, as a means for substantiating the third element (discrimination or a disguised restriction on international trade). Nonetheless, it would have been more consistent with the rationale of the SPS Agreement, which tends to emphasize a prudent regulatory process over any actual impact on trade, if this erratic regulatory process—the substantial, but unexplained change in conclusion between the two Reports—had been examined under the second element without the necessity of reaching the third one.

Less trade-restrictive means (Article 5.6)

Australian Salmon (1998)

For the first time, the *Australian Salmon* Panel interpreted Article 5.6. The Panel, focusing on the definition provided in the footnote to Article 5.6, viewed that an SPS measure is 'more trade-restrictive than required' only if there is another SPS measure that:

(1) is 'reasonably available taking into account technical and economic feasibility';
(2) 'achieves [Australia's] appropriate level of sanitary ... protection'; and
(3) is 'significantly less restrictive to trade' than the contested measure.[210]

Applying this three-prong test, the elements of which are cumulative in nature,[211] to the facts in this case, the Panel concluded that Australia had violated Article 5.6 because there were other technically or economically reasonable policy options, such

208. *Australian Salmon*, Panel Report, *supra* note 9, Introduction, ¶ 8. 154.
209. *Australian Salmon*, AB Report, *supra* note 9, Introduction, ¶ 173.
210. *Australian Salmon*, Panel Report, *supra* note 9, Introduction, ¶ 8. 167.
211. *Id.*

as 'certification, inspection, evisceration and filtering,' other than an 'outright prohibition.'[212]

The AB, though it endorsed the use of the Panel's three-prong test, rejected the Panel's premise in the second element that 'the *level* of protection implied or reflected in a sanitary *measure* or regime imposed by a WTO Member can be presumed to be at least as high as the level of protection considered to be *appropriate* by that Member.'[213] This seemingly trivial issue was nonetheless of great significance to the AB in terms of preserving the Members' regulatory autonomy, which is the rationale of the SPS Agreement. After showing that the level of protection *reflected* in the SPS measure at issue, which was a 'zero-risk level,' was not the same as the level of protection that Australia had *determined explicitly* as appropriate, which was 'very low levels,'[214] the AB stressed that such determination is a '*prerogative* of the Member concerned and not of a panel or the Appellate Body.'[215] In sum, the AB determined that:

> The 'appropriate level of protection' established by a Member and the 'SPS measure' have to be clearly distinguished. They are not one and the same thing. The first is an *objective*, the second is an *instrument* chosen to attain or implement that objective.[216]

Nonetheless, at the same time the AB tried to check this autonomous regulatory right of Members by imposing a certain minimum requirement. The AB opined that:

> We recognize that the SPS Agreement does not contain an *explicit* provision which obliges WTO Members to determine the appropriate level of protection.[217]
>
> We thus believe that the SPS Agreement contains an *implicit* obligation to determine the appropriate level of protection. We do not believe that there is an obligation to determine the appropriate level of protection in quantitative terms. This does not mean, however, that an importing Member is free to determine its level of protection with such *vagueness* or *equivocation* that the application of the relevant provisions of the SPS Agreement, such as Article 5.6, becomes impossible . . . .[218]

Although the AB did not complete its finding on the merits since it found insufficient factual information at hand,[219] the basic architecture of the interpretation of Article

212. *Id.*, ¶¶ 8. 171, 181, 182.
213. *Australian Salmon*, AB Report, *supra* note 9, Introduction, ¶ 196.
214. *Id.*, ¶ 197.
215. *Id.*, ¶ 199.
216. *Id.*, ¶ 200.
217. *Id.*, ¶ 205 (emphasis added).
218. *Id.*, ¶ 206 (emphasis added).
219. *Id.*, ¶¶ 209–212.

5.6 that the AB established in this case seems to have been followed in future cases.[220]

Japanese agricultural products (1999)

The US argued that 'testing by product' of the efficacy of the quarantine treatment is a reasonably available alternative to the varietal testing requirement within the meaning of Article 5.6.[221] The Panel also agreed with the US that testing by product is significantly 'less trade-restrictive' than the varietal testing requirement, taking into account technical and economic feasibility.[222] Nonetheless, the Panel found that there was not sufficient evidence to prove that such an alternative would achieve Japan's appropriate level of protection for any of the products at issue.[223] When the US appealed, the AB upheld the Panel's decision based on the view that the Panel's findings were part and parcel of the 'weighing of the evidence,' which falls outside the scope of appellate review under Article 17.6 of the DSU.[224]

One might reasonably speculate from this ruling that the second element, namely 'to achieve the Member's appropriate level of protection,' would be harder to meet than the other two elements under Article 5.6 in that it involves a regulatory prerogative of the Members.

Transparency (Article 7 and paragraph 1 of Annex B)

Japanese agricultural products (1999)

Regarding this issue, the Panel found that Japan had violated Article 7 and paragraph 1 of Annex B because it had not published the varietal testing requirement.[225] Japan appealed this finding, arguing that the 'regulations,' which are subject to the publication requirement under the paragraph 1 of Annex B, should be limited to 'legally enforceable instruments.'[226] The AB rejected Japan's appeal by observing that:

> The scope of application of the publication requirement is not limited to 'laws, decrees or ordinances', but also includes, in our opinion, other instruments which are applicable generally and are similar in character to the instruments explicitly referred to in the illustrative list of the footnote to paragraph 1 of Annex B.[227]
>
> The *object and purpose* of paragraph 1 of Annex B is 'to enable interested Members to become acquainted with' the sanitary and phytosanitary regulations adopted or maintained by other Members and thus to enhance

220. Although the *Hormones* case did not involve any discussion of Article 5.6, it could have been argued that a 'mandatory labeling' requirement would be a less trade-restrictive means within the meaning of Article 5.6.
221. *Japanese Agricultural Products*, Panel Report, *supra* note 10, Introduction, ¶ 8. 78.
222. *Id.*, ¶ 8. 79.
223. *Id.*, ¶ 8. 84.
224. *Japanese Agricultural Products*, AB Report, *supra* note 10, Introduction, ¶ 98.
225. *Japanese Agricultural Products*, Panel Report, *supra* note 10, Introduction, ¶ 8. 116.
226. *Japanese Agricultural Products*, AB Report, *supra* note 10, Introduction, ¶ 104.
227. *Id.*, ¶ 105.

> transparency regarding these measures. In our opinion, the scope of application of the publication requirement of paragraph 1 of Annex B should be *interpreted in the light of the object and purpose* of this provision.[228]

This ruling is significant and propitious in that it represents the first attempt under the SPS Agreement to develop jurisprudence on procedural discipline in the area of notification and publication. On the one hand, this procedural discipline provides Members with ample opportunities to be warned against any sudden trade-restrictive impact that any SPS measure by other Members may cause. Thanks to this notification and publication, Members that are potentially influenced by the measure are also given opportunity to request an explanation or justification from regulating Members. On the other hand, this procedural discipline tends also to benefit regulating Members, which can receive informative feedback from other Members and improve their original measure in a way that eliminates or mitigates unintended negative side effects. From the standpoint of regulating Members, this feedback process possibly leads to effective 'regulatory reform.' In conclusion, this procedural discipline can contribute to the achievement of the dual goals of free trade and effective regulation in a more economically efficient way since this discipline purports to prevent *ex ante*, rather than correct *ex post*, problematic SPS measures.

Against this background, the AB rejected Japan's narrow interpretation, which had attempted to restrict the scope of this procedural discipline to 'legally enforceable instruments,' by highlighting the 'object and purpose' of this important provision, the eventual effect of which will be to enhance the 'transparency' of SPS measures.

3.2.2 The TBT Agreement

There have been no decisions under the WTO dispute settlement system regarding the TBT Agreement, except for one panel and the AB decision in the *Asbestos* (2001) case concerning the *application* of the Agreement.

3.2.2.1 Conflicting arguments

In this case Canada maintained that a French Decree was a 'technical regulation' within the meaning of Annex 1.1 to the TBT Agreement in that the Decree sought to lay down characteristics of asbestos and asbestos-containing products, their PPMs (process and production methods) and administrative provisions applicable to those asbestos and asbestos-containing products.[229] However, the EC counter-argued that the Decree could not be considered a 'technical regulation' under the TBT Agreement because the Agreement does not cover 'general prohibitions on the use of a product for reasons to do with the protection of human health, which come under

228. *Id.*, ¶ 106 (emphasis added).
229. *Asbestos*, Panel Report, *supra* note 16, Introduction, ¶ 8. 20.

the GATT 1994.'[230] For the EC, the Decree prohibits asbestos fibers 'at all stages,' and does not specify additional information, such as characteristics, PPMs and relevant administrative provisions.[231] More fundamentally, for the EC, the rationale of the TBT Agreement is to handle technical regulations and standards, not to address 'market access' problems related to general prohibitions.[232]

3.2.2.2 The panel's view

In deciding this 'threshold' issue,[233] the Panel took a 'two-tier' approach: first, it addressed the part of the Decree *banning* asbestos and asbestos-containing products in all circumstances; then, it examined the exceptions in the Decree *permitting* asbestos to be marketed under certain conditions.[234]

Regarding the banning provisions, the Panel conducted its analysis based on a classic interpretive guide, namely Article 31:1 (General Rule of Interpretation) of the Vienna Convention on the Law of the Treaties. First, in light of the 'ordinary meaning' of the term, the Panel, noting that the definition of a 'technical regulation' used the word *product*, concluded that a technical regulation is 'a regulation which sets out the specific characteristics of one or more identifiable products in comparison with general characteristics that may be shared by several unspecified products.'[235] Secondly, in light of the 'object and purpose' of the TBT Agreement, the Panel observed that the Agreement purports to prevent 'more complex situations than a straightforward unconditional ban on a product, which is covered by the very strict provisions in Article XI:1 of GATT 1994.'[236] Lastly, in light of the 'context,' the Panel agreed with the EC that 'Canada's interpretation of the TBT Agreement would be equivalent to nullifying the effect of Articles I and III of the GATT 1994.'[237]

In sum, the Panel adopted the view that a measure constitutes a 'technical regulation' under the TBT Agreement if:

(a) the measure affects one or more given products;
(b) the measure specifies the technical characteristics of the product(s) which allow them to be marketed in the Member that took the measure;
(c) compliance is mandatory[238]

The Panel, therefore, found that the part of the Decree *banning* asbestos and asbestos-containing products did not constitute a 'technical regulation' under the TBT Agreement.[239]

---

230. *Id.*, ¶ 8. 22.
231. *Id.*, ¶ 8. 23.
232. *Id.*, ¶ 8. 25.
233. *Asbestos*, AB Report, *supra* note 16, Introduction, ¶ 60.
234. *Asbestos*, Panel Report, *supra* note 16, Introduction, heading (a) on p. 404 and heading (b) on p. 411.
235. *Id.*, ¶ 8. 39.
236. *Id.*, ¶ 8. 49.
237. *Id.*, ¶ 8. 56.
238. *Id.*, ¶ 8. 57.
239. *Id.*, ¶ 8. 58.

In contrast, the Panel took an opposite view in the exception part of the Decree *permitting* the marketing of asbestos and asbestos-containing products. The Panel basically found that the exception part of the Decree met the foregoing three elements to become a 'technical regulation' under the TBT Agreement.[240] For instance, the Panel determined that certain provisions address the characteristics of one or more given products or their PPMs as well as relevant administrative provisions, and that those provisions are mandatory since their compliance is required and enforced by penalties.[241]

3.2.2.3 The AB's view and its critique

Canada appealed the Panel's finding on this point, arguing that the Panel should have examined the French Decree as a 'single, unified' measure, instead of taking a 'two-tier' approach.[242] The AB accepted this appeal and reversed the Panel's two-tier approach, observing that the measure in question is a mix of both prohibition and permission on the use of asbestos fibers.[243] Then, the AB ruled that:

> Viewing the measure as an *integrated* whole, we see that it lays down 'characteristics' for all products that might contain asbestos, and we see also that it lays down the 'applicable administrative provisions' for certain products containing chrysotile asbestos fibres which are excluded from the prohibitions in the measure. Accordingly, we find that the measure is a 'document' which 'lays down product characteristics ... including the applicable administrative provisions, with which compliance is mandatory.' For these reasons, we conclude that the measure constitutes a 'technical regulation' under the TBT Agreement.[244]

Unfortunately, however, the AB intentionally avoided a more substantial and critical analysis of the TBT Agreement. The AB seemed basically to duck the question of which provisions the Decree might violate. First, it viewed the TBT as a *lex specialis* vis-à-vis the GATT, observing that 'the TBT Agreement imposes obligations on Members that seem to be *different* from and *additional* to the obligations imposed on Members under GATT 1994.'[245] The AB attempted to justify its position by pointing to the text of the Preamble of the TBT Agreement, which provides that the Agreement is intended to 'further' the objectives of GATT 1994.[246] However, this logic seems too weak to support the AB's position because 'to further the objectives of GATT 1994' does not necessarily mean the creation of an 'exclusive, separate' legal regime other than GATT 1994. On the contrary, the framers of the WTO system would want to establish an 'interdependent' relationship between GATT 1994 and the TBT Agreement.

---

240. *Id.*, ¶ 8. 70.
241. *Id.*, ¶ 8. 69.
242. *Asbestos*, AB Report, *supra* note 16, Introduction, ¶ 62.
243. *Id.*, ¶ 64.
244. *Id.*, ¶ 75 (emphasis added).
245. *Id.*, ¶ 80.
246. *Id.*

The AB finally ruled that:

> As the Panel decided not to examine Canada's four claims under the *TBT Agreement*, it made no findings, at all, regarding any of these claims. Moreover, the meaning of the different obligations in the *TBT Agreement* has not previously been the subject of any interpretation or application by either panels or the Appellate Body. Similarly, the provisions of the Tokyo Round *Agreement on Technical Barriers to Trade*, which preceded the *TBT Agreement* and which contained obligations similar to those in the *TBT Agreement*, were also never the subject of even a single ruling by a panel.[247]
>
> In light of their novel character, we consider that Canada's claims under the *TBT Agreement* have not been explored before us in depth. As the Panel did not address these claims, there are no 'issues of law' or 'legal interpretations' regarding them to be analyzed by the parties, and reviewed by us under Article 17.6 of the DSU. We also observe that the sufficiency of the facts on the record depends on the reach of the provisions of the *TBT Agreement* claimed to apply – a reach that has yet to be determined.[248]

This final ruling by the AB seems even more controversial and unacceptable than the first ruling on the nature of the TBT Agreement vis-à-vis GATT 1994. First, even though the Panel decided not to examine Canada's claims under the TBT Agreement, there existed sufficient grounds on which the AB could have completed the substantial analysis on which the French Decree violated the TBT Agreements. In fact, as the AB itself confessed, it had done so many times in the past.[249] Secondly, the fact that 'the TBT Agreement has not previously been the subject of any interpretation or application by either panels or the Appellate Body' could and should not be a ground for the AB's passive stance on this issue. On the contrary, the AB could have thought that it would be a good opportunity to interpret the key provisions of the TBT Agreement here for the first time in WTO history. Lastly, although the AB took the view that there were no 'issues of law' or 'legal interpretations' falling within the scope of appellate review under DSU Article 17.6, it is undeniable that 'the applicability of the TBT' itself is an 'issue of law' subject to 'legal interpretations.'

Yet frustratingly, the AB failed to seize the moment to utilize for the first time the TBT Agreement's novel legal innovations, including various *due process*-related obligations, which could have served to effectively discipline technical regulations, such as the asbestos ban in this case. The alternative track, which may be dubbed the 'product-oriented' approach, is the conventional 'like product' test under GATT Article III:4. However, this approach is not well suited to the task since it is not a 'product,' but a 'measure' that most people would regard as deterministic in identifying the existence of protection or discrimination. Hence, it should have been the French ban (measure), as opposed to the asbestos itself (product), to which the

247. *Id.*, ¶ 81.
248. *Id.*, ¶ 82.
249. *Id.*, ¶ 78.

AB focused its interpretive energy. That is, the AB ought to have taken a 'measure-oriented' approach using various legal innovations under the TBT Agreement, such as the 'risk assessment requirement.'

In conclusion, an esoteric test symbolized by 'like products' should be replaced by an exoteric one represented by 'due process' or other general principles of law that is much easier and more to the point, if the AB's decisions are to invite more acceptability and emit legitimacy from the perspective of lay people.

3.3 Comparative insight

3.3.1 HARMONIZATION: A SKETCH

The interface of trade and regulation can be seen not only in the global (i.e., WTO) context, but also in the regional (e.g., the EU) as well as the federal (e.g., the US) context. For instance, the integrative *telos* of the European Common Market has been continuously challenged by differing domestic regulations of Member States that have tried to expand their regulatory autonomy vis-à-vis the European Union. Likewise, the *Ideatypus* of a single federal marketplace in the US has been frustrated by various state regulations and their centrifugal impact. This changing landscape of trade and regulation has caused a dilemma for each trade regime. If diverging and heterogeneous local regulations were left to expand with no action, economic integration could not be attained (trade failure). On the other hand, if local regulatory demands were ignored for reasons of market efficiency alone, any trading regime could easily become illegitimate as a result of a failure to reflect the *vox populi* (regulatory failure).

The most conventional yet direct approach to addressing this dilemma is to 'harmonize' different local regulations. In general, this 'legislative' methodology has been prevalent under different trade regimes. For instance, the US started to mass-produce federal statutes, beginning in the late thirties, after the Supreme Court struck down *Lochnerism*.[250] As a growing number of 'federal' regulations that could trump any conflicting state regulations were enacted, economic integration at the federal level became more intense than ever before. Likewise, after overcoming the stalemate of the Luxembourg Compromise[251] through amendments to the Treaty of Rome, the EC was also able to mass-produce 'secondary laws' such as 'regulations' and 'directives,' which purported to harmonize diverging Member State regulations in certain regulatory areas such as health and environment. Only through harmonization could Member States finally remedy the problem of market

250. Regarding the birth and the demise of *Lochnerism*, *see generally* LAURENCE H. TRIBE, AMERICAN CONSTITUTIONAL LAW 1342–71 (3d ed. 2000); *but see* Cass Sunstein, *Lochner's Legacy*, 87 COLUM. L. REV. 873(1987) (suggesting that 'the case should be taken to symbolize not merely an aggressive judicial role, but an approach that imposes a constitutional requirement of neutrality, and understands the term to refer to preservation of the existing distribution of wealth and entitlements under the baseline of the common law').

251. *See* SHAW, *supra* note 253, Chapter II, at 35–7; EU LAW, *supra* note 254, Chapter II, at 13–6.

fragmentation that the negative integrationist approach embodied in judicial innovation (e.g., 'mutual recognition') had failed to resolve completely.

Critically, the harmonization methodology in the EC underwent a major shift in the eighties. Before the Single European Act of 1987, harmonization instruments of the European Community, namely directives and regulations, focused mainly on product specifications, which made harmonization so hard. However, with the launch of the so-called 'New Approach,' harmonization came to address only 'essential requirements' related to function or performance of regulatory subjects, leaving other unessential elements to the Member States.[252] This represented a Copernican change in perspective and was one of the main reasons behind the increasing numbers of directives and regulations that contributed to broadening, as well as deepening, the extent of harmonization in the EU context.

3.3.2 Procedural Requirements

Under both the SPS and TBT Agreements, various provisions are provided concerning certain procedural requirements, such as notification, reason-giving and transparency in general. These requirements, which are part of 'administrative law,' can be found in other trading regimes. For instance, in the current European administrative culture, the desire for transparency and participation in the administrative process has been growing fast reflecting a deeper skepticism of the Eurocrats' problem-solving capacity.[253] In this regard, it has been suggested that the 'giving reasons requirement' in ex Article 190 EEC should be highlighted not only as a solid administrative law but also as a constitutional doctrine that can be adopted by the ECJ to invalidate any improper Commission or Council action.[254] Significantly, this development of procedural administrative or constitutional law doctrine in the EU reflects the recent phenomenon of the 'multiplicity of actors and interests' at the supranational level.[255] In the same context, 'scientific reasoning,' not political bargaining, has become one of the most critical attributes in the Comitology committees.[256]

One critical virtue of this transformation of procedural requirements into more doctrinal administrative or constitutional law principles is that it can catalyze the 'convergence' of administrative practices of different trade regimes. In this regard,

252. Giandomenico Majone, *Comparing Strategies of Regulatory Rapprochement*, *in* Regulatory Cooperation for an Interdependent World, 155, 163–5 (1994). Regarding the 'New Approach' to technical harmonization and standardization, *see* European Commission, *Guide to the Implementation of Directives Based on the New Approach and the Global Approach* 7, *available at* <http://europa.eu.int/comm/enterprise/newapproach/legislation/guide/document/1999_1282_en.pdf> (last visited on Feb. 4, 2001).

253. Martin Shapiro, *Codification of Administrative Law: The US and the Union*, 2 Eur. L. J. 26, 40 (1996) [hereinafter Shapiro, *Codification*]. *Cf.* CIA Security International SA v Signalson SA and Another, Case 194/94, 30 April 1996, [1996] All ER (EC) 557, [1996] 2 CMLR 781 (ruling that 'the effectiveness of Community control will be that much greater if the directive is interpreted as meaning that breach of the obligation to notify constitutes a substantial procedural defect such as to render the technical regulations in question inapplicable to individuals.')

254. Shapiro, *Codification*, *supra* note 253, at 44.

255. Egan & Wolf, *supra* note 81, at 521.

256. *Id.*

Martin Shapiro has offered an interesting hypothesis that 'the Union administrative law was likely to move in the directions that American administrative law did in the 1960s, '70s and '80s.'[257] The cause of convergence, according to this view, lies in the fact that European administrative culture was subject to the same forces, i.e., strong demand for transparency and participation, which conditioned American law during the same periods. For Shapiro, ex Article 190 EEC (the 'reason-giving' requirement) was a 'test of convergence.'[258]

Likewise, Francesca Bignami has also put forward a reform proposal for the Community adopting the basic features of the US 'notice and comment' process in administrative rule-making in order to attain the dual goals of 'accountability' and 'pluralist interest group participation.'[259] She justifies her proposal for convergence with the US administrative rules by emphasizing that the Community's government structure mirrors that of the US in terms of shared powers (checks and balance) and independent regulatory branches.[260]

A similar, yet even stronger, argument for convergence with US administrative rules has been advanced by Giandomenico Majone. Inspired by the US experience with the Administrative Procedure Act (APA) of 1946, which stipulated procedural discipline without harming agency discretion, Majone recommends the enactment of a 'European APA' to improve both the efficiency and legitimacy of Community policy-making.[261] Then, in still bolder fashion, he extends the same recommendation to the WTO and other international organizations to achieve transparency and accountability in these institutions.[262] The prototype for his 'Global APA' includes the requirement of 'reason-giving' by regulators, which activates further obligations such as 'notice-and-comment' and 'public participation and debate.'[263] The concept of a Global APA is not intended to be a universal prescription, but rather a general reference. As a general reference for administrative behaviors, a Global APA is expected to enhance transparency and public participation, which would eventually contribute to increased legitimacy for the administrative behaviors of supranational as well as domestic governments.[264]

In fact, harbingers of this type of Global APA have recently been detected in various places. Since 1993, for example, the 'OECD Procedural Guidelines on Trade and Environment' have guided Member Countries regarding ways of attaining both trade and environmental goals in a coherent and mutually reinforcing fashion.[265]

257. Shapiro, *Codification*, *supra* note 253, at 44.
258. *Id.*
259. *See* Bignami, *supra* note 75, at 451.
260. *Id.*, at 514.
261. Giandomenico Majone, *Democracy and Constitutionalism in the European Union* 13 ECSA REV. FORUM 4–5 (2000).
262. *Id.*
263. *Id.*
264. *See* Daniel Bodansky, *The Legitimacy of International Governance: A Coming Challenge for International Environmental Law?*, 93 AM. J. INT'L L. 596, 619 (1999) (arguing that 'administrative procedure requirements such as notice and comment rulemaking would provide at least some measure of accountability to the public and therefore have the potential to serve the same legitimating functions as they do domestically').
265. *See* OECD, Report on TRADE AND ENVIRONMENT (COUNCIL AT MINISTERIAL LEVEL), 26–27 May 1999, C/MIN(99)14.

These Guidelines set forth appropriate administrative procedures such as 'transparency and consultation with civil society,' 'review of trade and environmental policies and agreements from the perspective of the other policy area,' and 'international cooperation in environmental policies.'[266] Then, the 'Joint Working Party on Trade and Environment' (JWP) reviews actual implementations of these Guidelines by the Member Countries based on their procedures and publications.[267] Though these peer review processes may not be formally binding *per se*, they still carry a normative value since they assist and facilitate Member Countries to implement the relevant Guidelines. As another example, the recently concluded 'Cartagena Protocol on Biosafety' requires Members to give notice of any change in its original regulatory decision and to explain the reasons.[268] This mechanism tends to supply a degree of procedural discipline to Parties' regulatory behaviors, thereby preventing arbitrary and capricious decisions.

3.3.3 NAFTA (CUSFTA) CHAPTER VII

Procedural requirements of regulations can also be found in the Canada United States Free Trade Agreement (CUSFTA) and the North American Free Trade Agreement (NAFTA). Under the CUSFTA, for instance, Chapter VII specified concrete provisions regarding technical regulations and standards on agricultural goods.[269] Likewise, under the NAFTA, Chapter VII provides detailed provisions regarding technical regulations and standards on agricultural goods.[270] Those provisions in Chapter VII of both CUSFTA and NAFTA, like the SPS, crystallize the spirit of the chapeau in GATT 1994 Article XX (i.e., procedural disciplines in regulatory process). This structural similarity and commonality tends to guarantee the same interpretive proclivity toward prioritizing detailed and precise procedural regulatory requirements when reviewing measures in question.

On the basis of this concretizing textual structure, the *UHT Milk* (1993) Panel, which was established under the CUSFTA, was able to base its determinations on more specific provisions (i.e., Chapter VII of the CUSFTA) rather than on general provisions of the GATT (i.e., Article III and XX). This case concerned a Canadian complaint against Puerto Rican regulations on the importation, distribution, and sale of Ultra-High Temperature (UHT) milk from Quebec. In a departure from the conventional GATT 1947 approach highlighting the content of a questioned

266. *Id.*
267. *Id.*
268. *See* Cartagena Protocol on Biosafety to the Convention on Biological Diversity, art. 12, *available at* <http://www.biodiv.org/biosafe/Protocol/html/Biosafe-Prot.html> (last visited on March 12, 2001) (emphasis added):

    Article 12 (Review of Decisions)

    1. A Party of import may, at any time, in light of new scientific information on potential adverse effects on the conservation and sustainable use of biological diversity, taking also into account the risks to human health, review and change a decision regarding an intentional transboundary movement. In such case, the Party shall, within thirty days, *inform* any notifier that has previously notified movements of the living modified organism referred to in such decision, as well as the Biosafety Clearing-House, and shall set out the *reasons for its decision.*
269. CUSFTA, *supra* note 62, Chapter II, ch. VII.
270. NAFTA, *supra* note 13, Introduction, ch. VII.

regulation, the Panel focused on the 'good faith' or 'best efforts' of the U.S. in its regulatory process on the importation, distribution, and sale of UHT milk, and more specifically on the 'equivalency' test based on Article 708.1 and 708.2.[271] The Panel held that the US acted in a manner consistent with the CUSFTA after it concluded, from regulatory documents and letters, that the US had exerted its best efforts in checking whether the Canadian UHT milk was processed in conditions 'substantially equivalent' with those of the US standard so that the Canadian UHT milk could enter the US market.[272]

Facing an alternative claim, the Panel considered whether such prohibition nullified or impaired benefits that Canada reasonably expected would accrue under the CUSFTA.[273] Even in dealing with this 'non-violation' nullification or impairment claim, the Panel also focused on the *manner* of its *application*, not on the adoption of a certain measure ('Grade A Pasteurized Milk Ordinance') itself.[274] After re-iterating the rationale of the CUSFTA, namely 'entailing integration of two separate trading communities,' the Panel concluded that Canada did have a reasonable expectation that the US would not unilaterally close its market to Canadian UHT milk before the issue was resolved between the Parties on the basis of the CUSFTA.[275]

3.4 Summary and prospect

3.4.1 Summary

A logical way to overcome the aforementioned pro-trade bias and fully materialize the new jurisprudence through rectifying the locus of burden of proof would be for the GATT/WTO system to discard the current dichotomy and adopt instead a 'unitary' mode in the interpretation of Article III (national treatment) and Article XX (general exceptions). Yet, a legislative option, namely the amendment of the GATT 1994 in this direction, should be rejected, at least in the short-run, in view of the current strict decision-making mechanism in the WTO Agreement (i.e., consensus[276] and super-majority rule[277]), not to mention the political difficulties that would surely accompany any attempt to initiate such an amendment.

Another option might be a judicial innovation, which was exercised by the ECJ when it constructed the rule of reason throughout the *Dassonville* (1974) and *Cassis de Dijon* (1979) cases. Such interpretive innovation could overcome the problematic dichotomy enshrined in the GATT/WTO by de-exceptionalizing legitimate social

271. *See* In the Matter of Puerto Rico Regulations on the Import, Distribution and Sale of U.H.T. Milk from Qebec, USA-93-1807-01, ¶¶ 5.27–5.50 [hereinafter *UHT Milk* (1993)].
272. *Id.*, at ¶¶ 5.48–5.50.
273. *Id.*, at ¶ 5.52.
274. *Id.*, at ¶ 5.58.
275. *Id.*, at ¶¶ 5.61, 5.62.
276. WTO Agreement, *supra* note 1, Introduction, art. IX, ¶ 1.
277. *Id.*, art. IX, ¶¶ 1–4.

values, while at the same time mending the lacuna of the limited and outdated list of Article XX (a)–(j). However, this sort of teleological movement might be vulnerable to potential criticism with regard to the role of the WTO panel and the Appellate Body. Indeed, such a bold innovation might be seen as amounting to a *de facto* amendment or at least an 'authoritative interpretation'[278]—in other words, as encroaching upon legislative functions reserved exclusively for Member States. In addition, though reinforced in the Uruguay Round, the institutional status of the WTO panels and the Appellate Body is not as strong as that of the ECJ. Strictly speaking, panels and the Appellate Body still deliver 'recommendations,' not 'decisions' as the WTO system does not have its own court *per se*.

Nonetheless, the WTO system has attempted to overcome this dichotomy and pro-trade bias by establishing some sector-specific side agreements, such as the Agreement on the Application of Sanitary and Phytosanitary Measures (SPS) and the Agreement on Technical Barriers to Trade (TBT). Although both side agreements base their *raison d'etre* on the GATT 1994,[279] they take a far different stance from the GATT 1994 in terms of the regulatory autonomy of Member States. While legitimate non-trade regulatory concerns are treated merely as 'exceptions' to general obligations under the GATT 1994, the Preambles of both the SPS and the TBT Agreements emphasize that *no* country should be *prevented* from taking measures for the protection of human health or the environment.[280] Considering that the use of exceptions was discouraged under the old GATT jurisprudence,[281] such *expressive verbis* in the Preambles reflects a remarkable change in perspective. This change is essentially an advancement from a narrow (pro-trade) GATT 1994 objective to a more mature terrain of free trade modified by a greater concern with regulatory autonomy.[282]

A structural examination of the provisions of both side agreements reveals this change in perspective more vividly. First of all, the lacunae inherent in Article XX of GATT 1994[283] were addressed in the TBT. The ten paragraphs (a–j) of Article XX were created in the 1940's, and naturally reflect the regulatory concerns of that time. Now, a half century later, many of those concerns are inevitably obsolete. Moreover, except for a few paragraphs, such as paragraphs (b),[284]

278. *Id.*, art. IX, ¶ 2.

279. TBT Agreement, *supra* note 7, Introduction, pmbl. ('*Desiring* to further the objectives of GATT 1994.'); SPS Agreement, *supra* note 6, Introduction, pmbl. ('*Desiring* therefore to elaborate rules for the application of the provisions of GATT 1994 which relate to the use of sanitary or phytosanitary measures, in particular the provisions of Article XX(b).').

280. TBT Agreement, *supra* note 7, Introduction, pmbl. ('*Recognizing* that no country should be prevented from taking measures necessary to ensure the quality of its exports, or for the protection of human, animal or plant life or health, of the environment.'); SPS Agreement, *supra* note 6, Introduction, pmbl. ('*Reaffirming* that no Member should be prevented from adopting or enforcing measures necessary to protect human, animal or plant life or health.').

281. *See supra* text accompanying note 95, Chapter II.

282. TBT Agreement, *supra* note 7, Introduction, art. 2.2. *Cf.* Howse & Regan, *supra* note 246, Chapter II, at 289 (suggesting that the broad anti-discrimination norm in GATT Article III (National Treatment) could be replaced by more specific rules in the TBT and the SPS).

283. *Aim and Effects*, *supra* note 29, Chapter II, at 638.

284. GATT 1994, *supra* note 2, Chapter II, art. XX, ¶ (b) ('necessary to protect human, animal or plant life or health').

(d),[285] and (g),[286] other paragraphs were little used, and essentially became fossils. However, according to the new WTO Standard Code (TBT), a list of legitimate policy objectives addressed by various technical regulations is not *exhaustive* but *exemplary*, which means that a Member State can uphold any type of social regulation that it deems to be legitimate.[287] In this context, it is worth noting that a regulatory objective for consumer protection, such as 'the prevention of deceptive practices' is explicitly included in the exemplary list of TBT Article 2.2, representing a salient change vis-à-vis GATT Article XX.

On top of this improvement, in both the TBT and the SPS Agreement, legitimate regulatory concerns are no longer marginalized as mere 'exceptions,' but redefined as 'rights.' For instance, SPS Article 2.1 specifies that 'Members have the *right* to take sanitary and phytosanitary measures necessary for the protection of human, animal or plant life or health, provided that such measures are not inconsistent with the provisions of this Agreement.'[288] Considering that the SPS is designed to 'elaborate' rules for the application of the provisions of GATT 1994 relating to the use of sanitary or phytosanitary measures, in particular the provision of 'Article XX(b) *plus* the chapeau,'[289] the use of 'right' is not accidental and is thus especially significant in elucidating the perspectival change from the old GATT position of exceptionalization. In parallel with this, the AB in the *Hormones* (1998) case struck down the Panel's view[290] that SPS Article 3.3[291] provides an 'exception' to the general obligation contained in Article 3.1,[292] and reaffirmed that Article 3.3 recognizes the autonomous 'right' of a Member.[293]

Of course, autonomous rights are not unlimited as the AB in *Hormones* (1998) rightly observed. Such rights are juxtaposed by various obligations, including SPS Articles 3.3 (the requirement of 'scientific justification'), 5.1 (the requirement of 'risk assessment') and 5.5 (the requirement of 'avoiding arbitrary and unjustifiable distinctions'). These obligations are designed to ensure that a Member respects and follows certain procedural requirements ('manners') in exercising their autonomous regulatory rights regarding sanitary and phytosanitary measures.

Moreover, the observance of such obligations is closely related to the 'application' of a questioned measure, rather than to the 'content' of the measure itself. The Preamble of the SPS Agreement clarifies that Member's regulatory autonomy should be subject to the requirement that these (sanitary or phytosanitary) measure are not 'applied' in a manner which would constitute a 'means' of arbitrary or unjustifiable

285. *Id.*, art. XX, ¶ (d) ('necessary to secure compliance with laws or regulations which are not inconsistent with the provisions of this Agreement . . .').
286. *Id.* art. XX, ¶ (g) ('relating to the conservation of exhaustible natural resources if such measures are made effective in conjunction with restrictions on domestic production or consumption').
287. TBT Agreement, *supra* note 7, Introduction, art. 2.2.
288. SPS Agreement, *supra* note 6, Introduction, art. 2.1 (emphasis added).
289. *Id.*, pmbl.
290. *Hormones*, Panel Report, *supra* note 8, Introduction, ¶ 8.86.
291. SPS Agreement, *supra* note 6, Introduction, art. 3.3.
292. *Id.*, art. 3.1.
293. *Hormones*, AB Report, *supra* note 8, Introduction, ¶ 104. The Appellate Body stressed that the relationship between Articles 3.1, 3.2 and 3.3 is qualitatively different from that between Article III and XX of the GATT 1994. *Id.* Likewise, the Appellate Body in *Asbestos* (2001) could and should have based its ruling on the TBT. *See Asbestos*, AB Report, *supra* note 16, Introduction, pt. V.

discrimination, and thus confirms that one of the objectives of the SPS is to elaborate upon the chapeau of GATT 1994 Article XX, which contains the same language ('arbitrary or unjustifiable discrimination').[294] In addition, SPS Articles 2.2 and 2.3 respectively stipulate that any sanitary or phytosanitary measure shall be 'applied' only to the extent necessary to protect human, animal or plant life or health, and that such measures shall not be 'applied' in a manner which would constitute a disguised restriction on international trade.[295]

This crystallization of the chapeau into a precise and detailed set of material obligations in the SPS context provides a huge benefit for the WTO panel and the Appellate Body, as reliance on such clear provisions tends to mitigate the interpretive burden that may result from having to extend or 'teleologize' the chapeau beyond its original bounds. Indeed, if the Appellate Body had relied solely upon the provisions of GATT 1994, their underlying reasoning would very likely have been strained since it would have had to stretch the simplistic language of the chapeau to serve a purposeful interpretation. Importantly, this structural attribute (i.e., crystallization of the chapeau) of the SPS also has practical implications for the burden of proof issue. Under the SPS, as reaffirmed by the Appellate Body in *Hormones* (1998), the complainant, rather than the regulating state (defendant), bears the burden of proof.[296] Considering the opposite situation obtained under GATT 1994,[297] such transposition of the burden of proof contributes to extending more regulatory leeway to Member States, and thus to mending the pro-trade dichotomy and exceptionalizing tendencies in Article XX of GATT 1994.

3.4.2 Prospect

So far, we have found that the clash between the free market ideology and state regulation under the WTO system has been more effectively addressed through legislative initiative in a set of new side agreements and their derivative jurisprudence than solely under the jurisprudential evolution of GATT. Nevertheless, even if various efforts in the WTO treaties seek to reconcile the clash between trade and regulatory values, and even if the more mature, intellectually refined GATT/WTO jurisprudence tends to produce decisions that safeguard the coherence of these concerns, such reconciliation cannot be attained without the actual behavioral change on the part of Members. In other words, the discussion to this point has been limited to the 'international dimension.' Yet it is in the 'domestic' sphere that the detailed behavioral changes take place, changes which are necessary if the dual mission of free markets and state regulation is to be accomplished in a coherent fashion. Therefore, the next Chapter deals with issues concerning 'compliance' and 'implementation.'

294. SPS Agreement, *supra* note 6, Introduction, pmbl., n.1.
295. *Id.*, arts. 2.2, 2.3.
296. *Hormones*, AB Report, *supra* note 8, Introduction, ¶ 109.
297. *A GATT's-Eye View*, *supra* note 93, Chapter II, at 1420–21.

Chapter IV
Compliance pull

4.1 Overview

The argument set forth in previous Chapters of this book has largely been confined to the 'international' dimension. However, it is in the 'domestic' sphere and through domestic legal mechanisms that desired behavioral changes, which are necessary to accomplish the dual mission of free markets and adequate regulatory intervention in a coherent fashion, actually take place. In other words, each national government is ultimately responsible for ensuring that its domestic regulation is not trade restrictive while still preserving its own regulatory autonomy.

The project of putting various features of international trade law into actual practice within the domestic legal system can be defined as 'compliance.' Although traditional international law scholarship has long wrestled with the issue of compliance,[1] it is only recently that trade scholars have begun to tackle the issue seriously, largely in response to trade conflicts involving compliance with the WTO Appellate Body (AB) Reports pertaining to the *Banana III* (1997) and *Beef-Hormones* (1998)[2] disputes.

Against this background, Chapter IV deals with, firstly from a broad, long-term perspective, issues concerning implementation and nationalization. It examines how the SPS and TBT Agreements, as well as certain aspects of the GATT jurisprudence, which have been discussed so far as a potential means for reconciling the clash, should be understood, incorporated and put into practice by Members. From a narrow, short-term perspective, Chapter IV also examines post-adjudicative issues concerning how a losing party must accept, often reluctantly, a specific formula for reconciling a particular clash between free markets and state regulation, as prescribed by the panel and the AB decisions.

---

1. *See notably* Louis Henkin, How Nations Behave (2d ed. 1979); Chayes & Chayes, *supra* note 202, Chapter II; Harold Hongju Koh, *Why Do Nations Obey International Law*, 106 Yale L. J. 2599 (1997) [hereinafter *Obey International Law*]; Jose E. Alvarez, *Why Nations Behave*, 19 Mich. J. Int'l L. 303 (1998); *see also* Harold K. Jacobson & Edith Brown Weiss, *Strengthening Compliance with International Environmental Accords: Preliminary Observations from a Collaborative Project*, 1 Global Governance 119, 119 (1995) (examining 'how and the extent to which countries implement and comply with international environmental treaties').
2. *See e.g.*, Joel P. Trachtman, *Bananas, Direct Effect and Compliance*, 10 Eur. J. Int'l L. (1999) [hereinafter Trachtman, *Compliance*]; Joost Pauwelyn, *Enforcement and Countermeasures in the WTO: Rules are Rules—Toward a More Collective Approach*, 94 Am. J. Int'l L. 335 (2000) (focusing on a 'narrow' concept of compliance in the WTO context). *Cf.* Implementing the Uruguay Round (John H. Jackson & Alan O. Sykes eds. 1997) (addressing a 'broad' concept of compliance with, *i.e.*, *implementation* of, the Uruguay Round by representative Member States).

4.2 Broad, long-term perspective

4.2.1 Concept

We have thus far observed that a refined set of jurisprudence as well as sophisticated harmonization agreements have been developed to reconcile a clash between free markets and state regulation, thereby overcoming a dual crisis of trade and regulatory failure under the GATT/WTO system. Yet, compliance with this jurisprudence and these agreements by Members is not a simple task to be accomplished overnight.[3] Although this transformation might be expected to benefit domestic economies in the long run, it is nevertheless a daunting task to transform domestic legal infrastructure, including statutes and institutions, to accommodate far-reaching changes—particularly changes viewed as mandated by external authorities like the WTO.

Time and again, this transformation invites a bitter political battle since deep-rooted domestic interest groups tend to resist any sort of transformation that threatens to undermine their interest base. Such transformation also requires a vast amount of administrative resources in various governmental sectors and sub-sectors. As a result, the pace of the transformation may be gradual and incremental, trudging along by trial and error. In sum, compliance with the WTO's prescription to achieve both free trade and regulatory values, which consist of jurisprudence and agreements, tends to involve 'broad' as well as 'long-term' domestic efforts.

It is critical that Members comply with a given prescription in good faith if they expect the prescription to deliver on its promise of contributing to the sustainable development of the global trading system. Mere superficial or mechanical implementation tends to result in a limited level of achievement, which can itself lead to further disputes among Members. Undoubtedly, this shallow level of implementation cannot address contemporary regulatory challenges that become increasingly complicated and sophisticated, nor can it ensure the free flow of international commerce that has been continuously threatened by those challenges. This problem can be solved only by a more proactive yet diffuse mode of implementation that eventuates in-depth implementation.

4.2.2 Modalities and sequence: legislative and administrative implementation

Domestic 'legislation' is the most conventional modality of implementation and is often considered as the first step in the whole process. Legislative implementation transposes prescriptions that originate at the international level, e.g., the SPS Agreement, to local contexts. Traditionally, legislative implementation is carried out by certain 'acts of transformation' relying on a local constitutional structure.[4]

---

3. *See* Victor, *supra* note 16, Chapter III, at 895.
4. *See* John H. Jackson, *National Constitutions, Transnational Economic Policy and International Economic Law: Some Summary Reflections*, *in* National Constitutions and International Economic Law 576 (M. Hilf & E.U. Petersmann eds., 1993).

Under certain constitutional regimes, international treaties, such as GATT or the SPS Agreement, become part of the domestic legal order automatically without any implementing legislation ("monism').[5] Under this monistic legal structure, an individual can sue other parties in the domestic court for the violation of material obligations in the WTO Agreement.[6] In most jurisdictions, however, certain kinds of 'implementing legislation' are required to effectuate those treaties ('dualism').[7] Under this dualistic structure, an individual is usually prohibited from suing other parties directly for alleged violations of such international agreements in domestic court[8] unless certain exceptions apply, as in the case of 'direct effect'[9] or 'self-executing treaties.'[10] In sum, transformative legislation is required to implement treaties, though such transformation does not necessarily ensure direct invocability in the domestic court system.

As a next step, 'administrative' implementation follows legislative implementation. The normative impact of treaties would be limited without actual execution of those implementing or transposing legislation. Sector-specific departments or agencies, such as the Treasury or the Commerce Department, are involved in the administrative implementation that often requires a set of sub-legislation, such as decrees and other administrative regulations.

Critically, these departments or agencies tends to play a pivotal role in determining the success of the foregoing prescription, such as GATT/WTO jurisprudence or agreements to attain both free trade and regulatory goals, since they directly influence domestic markets and regulatory fields in which the effects of the prescription should eventually be observed. It must be noted that a subtle and circumspect application and enforcement of a given implementing statute tends to lead to an in-depth compliance with the prescription. This point can hardly be overemphasized because a single statute is capable of producing different *applications* depending on the administrative organ that is charged with its application. Therefore, even a problematic domestic statute, which reflects a poor legislative implementation on its face, can still realize an eventual in-depth implementation through nuanced and sophisticated administrative execution.

---

5. Ian Brownlie, Principles of Public International Law 31–33 (5th ed. 1998). *See also* J.G. Starke, *Monism and Dualism in the Theory of International Law*, 17 Brit. Y.B. Int'l L. 66 (1936); John H. Jackson, *Status of Treaties in Domestic Legal Systems: A Policy Analysis*, 86 Am. J. Int'l L. 310, 313–15 (1992).
6. *See e.g.*, Case C-53/96 Hermes International v. FHT Marketing Choice BV, 1998 ECR I-3603.
7. Brownlie, *supra* note 5, at 31–33.
8. Uruguay Round Agreements Act, Pub. L. No. 103–465, § 102(c)(1), 108 Stat. 4809 (1994):
   (c) Effect of Agreement With Respect to Private Remedies
   (1) Limitations—No Person other than the United States
   (A) shall have any cause of action or defense under any of the Uruguay Round Agreements or by virtue of congressional approval of such an agreement, or
   (B) may challenge, in any action brought under any provision of law, any action or inaction by any department, agency, or other instrumentality of the United States, any State, or any political subdivision of a State on the ground that such action or inaction is inconsistent with such agreement.
9. *See notably* Joseph H. H. Weiler, *The Transformation of Europe*, 100 Yale L.J. 2403, 2413–4 (1991) [hereinafter *Transformation*].
10. *See generally* Carlos Manuel Vázquez, *The Four Doctrines of Self-Executing Treaties*, 89 Am. J. Int'l L. 695 (1995). *See also* Edith Brown Weiss, *The Rise or the Fall of International Law?*, 69 Fordham L. Rev. 345, 357 (2000).

4.2.3 A RADICAL SOLUTION FOR COMPLIANCE: DIRECT EFFECT?

4.2.3.1 Direct effect

Heated discussions have surrounded the adoption of the so-called 'direct effect' or 'self-executing effect' to enhance compliance with the WTO system. Those who favor the 'constitutionalization' of international trade law might believe that a domestic judicial system can and should *serve* to materialize certain fundamental treaty provisions, always allowing individuals to sue their own governments for damages they have incurred as a result of the violation by the government of specific treaty provisions.[11] Yet regardless of its value as a legal *Ideatypus*, this argument lacks a practical foundation at the present time: it is simply too radical.[12]

First, the determination of how to incorporate and accommodate treaty obligations into a given domestic judicial system depends largely on the domestic constitutional framework. Some countries may absorb treaties immediately and unconditionally into their domestic legal system without any need of an act of transformation (*monism*); other countries may require treaties to be nationalized through independent domestic legal instruments in order to achieve domestic legal effect (*dualism*).[13] One may reasonably speculate that in a dualistic regime, a direct effect would be most improbable. Secondly, the task of making operational a system of direct effect necessitates a solid constitutional or supranational infrastructure, as is the case with the EU. In an institutional vacuum in which such infrastructure is lacking, which is the case under the current WTO regime, hasty adoption of direct effect sounds implausible at best and counterproductive at worst.[14]

---

11. *See e.g.*, Ernst-Ulrich Petersmann, *How to Constitutionalize International Law and Foreign Policy for the Benefit of Civil Society?*, 20 MICH. J. INT'L L. 1, 30 (1998) (arguing that 'European integration law and WTO law confirm the Kantian insight that rule of law requires compulsory judicial protection of freedom and non-discrimination at home and abroad').
12. *But cf.* Trachtman, *Compliance*, *supra* note 2, at 657 (arguing that direct effect can strengthen *compliance* through 'deputizing' or 'coopting' the domestic legal system, or make the domestic rule of law 'hostage' to compliance with international law). Importantly, opposition to the generalization of direct effect to induce or enhance compliance with international trade law should not be misconstrued as generalized opposition to direct effect. On the contrary, in a given trading unit in which sufficient legal infrastructure is established, direct effect tends to serve as a means to 'interconnect' different trading units. *See generally* Piet Eeckhout, *The Domestic Legal Status of the WTO Agreement: Interconnecting Legal Systems*, 34 COMMON MKT. L. REV. 11 (1997).
13. *See* BROWNLIE, *supra* note 5.
14. As a matter of fact, most supporters of direct effect in international law take a cautious and incremental approach. *See* Thomas Cottier & Krista Nadakavukaren Schefer, *The Relationship between World Trade Organization Law, National and Regional Law*, 1 J. INT'L ECON. L. 83, 118–19 (1998) (arguing that 'we might succeed with a step-by-step, provision-by-provision approach to negotiations, achieving a gradual direct effect of most, if not all, of the WTO Agreements.'); Ronald A. Brand, *Direct Effect of International Economic Law in the United States and the European Union*, 17 NW. J. INT'L L. & BUS. 556, 608 (1996–97) (suggesting that 'while the global system is not yet ready for the wholesale application of these developments, it is important that we realize the need to move in a similar direction').

4.2.3.2 *A more nuanced approach to judicial implementation*

As a more promising approach, judicial implementation of the WTO-prescribed jurisprudence and agreements could take place without any imposing doctrine such as direct effect so long as domestic courts 'sympathized with' the prescription, and adapted their legal reasoning to such an orientation.[15] In other words, domestic judges can adjudicate domestic cases, in which free trade and regulatory concern are intertwined, in such a way that their decisions are coherent and harmonious with the object and purpose (*telos*) of the global trading system, which can be portrayed as 'integration,' 'anti-unilateralism' or 'sustainable development.'

Domestic judges can effectively deliver these teleological decisions by employing certain domestic 'legal anchors,' namely, fundamental legal doctrines or principles. Obviously, the constitutional or other administrative statutes of most domestic legal regimes include such basic and fundamental provisions. One finds the most promising candidates for these legal anchors in the 'Commerce Clause'[16] and 'Due Process Clause'[17] from US law, as well as in the 'Non-Discrimination' principle[18] or 'Due Process' provision[19] from EU law. These legal anchors in fact represent 'general principles of law,'[20] which base the chapeau test and other process-oriented

15. *Cf.* Bradford R. Clark, *Federal Common Law: A Structural Reinterpretation*, 144 U. PA. L. REV. 1245, 1276 (1996) (arguing that the law applied by the Supreme Court in *Swift v. Tyson* (1842) was a 'customary body of rules' derived from *jus gentium* and that no court is free to establish its own hermeneutics in departure from it); *see also* Alec Stone Sweet, *The New GATT: Dispute Resolution and the Judicialization of the Trade Regime in* LAW ABOVE NATIONS: SUPRANATIONAL COURTS AND THE LEGALIZATION OF POLITICS 138 (Mary L. Volcansek ed., 1997) (suggesting that 'WTO legal norms gradually embed themselves within national legal systems, either by domestic legislative actions or judicial decisions'). From a congruent standpoint, Justice O'Connor advocates that domestics courts should 'faithfully recognize the obligations imposed by international law' as seen in *Murray v. Charming Betsy* and the *Paquete Habana. See* Sandra Day O'Connor, *Federalism of Free Nations*, 28 N.Y.U.J. INT'L L. & POL. 35, 38–41, (1995–96). She emphasizes the federalist ideal of healthy dialogue and mutual trust which may be formed between domestic courts and transnational tribunals, which might be depicted in terms of Kant's 'federalism of free nations.' *Id. See also* Sandra Day O'Connor, *Broadening Our Horizons: Why American Lawyers Must Learn about Foreign Law*, 45–SEP Fed. Law. 20, 20–1 (1998), (highlighting the flexibility and dynamism of the common law tradition which enables the borrowing of new ideas form other legal systems and permits the 'civilizing fiction of constitutional law'); Bruce Ackerman, *The Rise of World Constitutionalism*, 83 VA. L. REV. 771, 775 (1997) (advising his readers strongly to 'look upon the American experience as a special case, not as the paradigmatic case'); Roger J. Miner, *The Reception of Foreign Law in the U.S. Federal Courts*, 43 AM. J. COMP. L. 581, 581 (1995) (observing that the U.S. federal courts tend to 'duck and run' in the face of foreign law issues despite that they are beginning to 'form a significant part of the business of the federal courts'); Mark Tushnet, *The Possibilities of Comparative Constitutional Law*, 108 YALE L. J. 1225, 1228 (1999) (introducing a 'more systematic approach to the possibility of learning from constitutional experience elsewhere'); Richard M. Goodman & John M. Frost, *International Economic Agreements and the Constitution*, THE INSTITUTE FOR INTERNATIONAL ECONOMICS WORKING PAPER (No. 00-2) 2 (2000), *available at* <http://207.238.152.36/CATALOG/WP/2000/00-2.pdf> (last visited on Apr. 10, 2001) (arguing that 'international agreements, such as GATT and NAFTA, can serve as useful interpretive guidelines for the Court where the challenged state measure restricts the cross-border flow of goods or services').
16. U.S. CONST. art I, § 8, cl. 3.
17. U.S. CONST. amend. XIV.
18. EC TREATY, *supra* note 12, Introduction, art. 12.
19. *Id.*, art. 230.
20. *See, e.g.*, Wolf Sauter, *The Economic Constitution of the European Union*, 4 COLUM. J. EUR. L. 27, 41 (1998). In an interesting development that may prove inspirational to international trade law scholars, Chiquita recently filed a lawsuit for $525 million in damages against the European

requirements on the SPS Agreement, which represent the WTO prescription for reconciling clashes between free trade and regulatory concerns. Accordingly, through the intermediation of general principles of law, domestic judges can contribute to judicial implementation of the WTO prescriptions as they employ these legal anchors in individual cases before them. As a result, these domestic legal anchors function to prevent domestic court decisions from plunging into a narrow-minded parochialism since they also represent clear and certain constitutional principles that resist any discriminatory treatment to the detriment of foreign producers.[21]

Under these circumstances, even foreign investors or importers may sue a host country government in their resident courts for its discriminatory regulation on the grounds of these legal anchors. As a matter of fact, some domestic courts have already begun to invoke those legal anchors in dealing with certain cases in which free trade and regulatory issues are intertwined.[22] For instance, in *Goya De Puerto Rico Inc. v. Neftali Santiago* (1999),[23] the Puerto Rico Department of Agriculture adopted a regulation mandating the 'inspection and the exaction of an inspection fee' on all imported pigeon peas for a sanitary reason.[24] The inspection was to be performed by Puerto Rico Department of Agriculture personnel, and the inspection cost was to be paid to the Department by the plaintiff Goya.[25] According to the adopted regulation, if Goya failed to pay the fee, it would lose its business license in Puerto Rico.[26] The US Federal Court struck down this regulation on the grounds that it violated the 'Commerce Clause.' The court ruled that this regulation 'facially discriminates against interstate commerce' because it 'imposes significant costs on pigeon pea importers which are not borne by their local counterparts.'[27] The Court

---

contd

Commission in the ECJ, arguing that the EC's failure to comply with the WTO rulings (*Banana III*) violated the 'fundamental rights and general principles of European Community law, such as non-discrimination and the freedom to pursue a trade or business.' *See Chiquita Sues EC over Banana Regime*, Bridges Weekly Trade News Digest, Vol. 5, No. 3, Jan. 30, 2001, *available at* <www.ictsd.org/html/weekly/story6.30-01-01.htm> (last visited on March 12, 2001).

21. *Cf.* Meinhard Hilf, *The Role of National Courts in International Trade Relations*, 18 Mich. J. Int'l L. 321, 346–47 (1997) [hereinafter *The Role of National Courts*] (observing in the EU context that 'national courts tend to interpret the relevant implementing legislation in a manner which avoids conflicts with existing GATT law'). Such teleological hermeneutics can also be found in the *Charming Betsy* doctrine in which the US Supreme Court interpreted even facially unambiguous text against its language if textual interpretation would violate the law of nations or international law. *See* Ralph G. Steinhardt, *The Role of International Law as a Canon of Domestic Statutory Construction*, 43 Vand. L. Rev. 1103, 1197 (1990).

22. *See e.g.*, Territory of Hawaii v. Harry M. Y. Ho, 1957 WL 10599 (Hawai'I Terr.), 1 (1957) (ruling that a Hawaiian law requiring 'a display of a placard of origin in connection with the sale or offering for sale foreign eggs' violated the GATT and was void according to the Supremacy Clause); *See also* Crosby v. Nat'l Foreign Trade Council, 530 U.S. 363, 120 S.Ct. 2288, 2293–2302 (2000) (rejecting the 1996 Massachusetts law barring state entities from purchasing goods or services from companies doing business with Burma on the ground that the state Act was 'preempted,' and its application 'unconstitutional, under the Supremacy Clause'); United States—Measure Affecting Government Procurement; Request for Consultations by the European Communities, WTO Doc. WT/DS88/1 (June 26, 1997).

23. 59 F. Supp. 2d 274 (1999).

24. *Id.*, at 276.

25. *Id.*

26. *Id.*

27. *Id.*, at 277.

also observed that Puerto Rico failed to show that the challenged regulation 'serves a legitimate local interest,' emphasizing that the Puerto Rico Department of Agriculture 'could have adopted the same safety measures that it implements with regard to the locally grown pigeon peas.'[28]

This domestic case, involving an 'international trade' issue, i.e., the importation of pigeon peas, and a 'regulatory' issue, i.e., an inspection and an extraction of an inspection fee, could have been adjudicated under the WTO dispute settlement system, if countries exporting pigeon peas had challenged the Puerto Rican regulation before the WTO Panel. In such a case, the Panel and the AB would have relied on GATT Articles III:4 (National Treatment) and XX (General Exception) as well as other articles under the SPS Agreement. Yet, despite this reliance on different textual bases, the Panel's or the AB's ruling would have still been practically the same as that of the US court. In the actual dispute, the legal reasoning employed by the US court seemed, in particular, to have been based on a test similar to the 'chapeau' test under the GATT/WTO or the 'arbitrariness or unjustifiability' test under the SPS Agreement. The court highlighted the 'inconsistency' of the regulation by observing that domestic pigeon peas as well as other similar peas imported, such as chicken peas, were all immune to such burdensome inspection. Had the dispute been adjudicated under the WTO dispute settlement system, the panel or the AB would have presumably reached the same conclusion by invoking either the chapeau test under GATT Article XX or Article 5.5 (the prohibition of arbitrary or unjustifiable distinction) under the SPS Agreement.

In sum, the US court took the same track as the WTO prescription in addressing the interface between free trade and state regulation in its domestic context. Although, the outcome would have been substantially similar under the WTO dispute settlement system, a domestic adjudication tends to offer certain merits that an international adjudication cannot provide. First, in this case, the exporters or producers of pigeon peas did not need to lobby their governments to sue the US before the WTO. Secondly, the remedy would be more immediate and direct than under the WTO system because the US court ruling is enforced under the US judicial system. In conclusion, by employing domestic legal anchors domestic judges can ensure compliance with the WTO jurisprudence and agreements when adjudicating domestic cases in which trade and regulation are interfaced, without the need of having recourse to an artificial and intrusive doctrine such as direct effect.[29]

---

28. *Id.*, at 278.
29. *Cf.* Martin A. Rogoff, *Interpretation of International Agreements by Domestic Courts and the Politics of International Treaty Relations: Reflections on Some Recent Decisions of the United States Supreme Court*, 11 AM. U. J. INT'L L. & POL'Y 559, 684–85 (1996). He concluded that:

> While cases involving the interpretation of international agreements by national courts represent only one small part of the flow of decisions that impact law in the international community, they are nonetheless a highly significant part, for they represent the efforts of the states to harmonize their actions and to settle their differences, as well as differences involving their nationals, on the basis of principles rather than politics. The extent to which national courts contribute to the enlargement of this legal enclave, this sphere of legality, in the international political process serves the interests of all states and their leaders in the construction of a more stable, predictable, and less contentious, and ultimately more peaceful, efficient, and harmonious international order.

Concomitantly, the fact that general principles of law or other constitutional principles flowing from those domestic legal anchors[30] mirror key legal precepts embedded in the GATT/WTO jurisprudence and agreements, which have been developed as a prescription to address the interface of free trade and state regulation, tends to contribute to the effectiveness and legitimacy of such prescription, thus enhancing its compliance pull.[31]

4.2.4 Monitoring compliance: surveillance

Compliance is not an ephemeral or one-shot phenomenon. Instead, it is a gradual, on-going and even evolutionary process. In fact, there can be many situations where a distinction between compliance and non-compliance or violation is blurred. There can also be many situations where non-compliance has not yet resulted in a dispute. These regulatory irregularities, which cause trade frictions, are deep-rooted and hidden, and therefore tend not to develop quickly into formal disputes. Although such trade frictions may not cause more serious trade distortions immediately, they can still harm free trade, generally in a cumulative way. To address these trade frictions and thus to prevent them from developing into trade distortions, a *managerial* model seems effective, such as the 'Trade Policy Review Mechanism' (TPRM).[32]

The TPRM is a post-nationalization mechanism that monitors and supervises Members' compliance with the WTO obligations. The purpose of the TPRM is to 'contribute to improved *adherence* by all Members to rules, disciplines and commitments'[33] under the WTO system. For this purpose, the 'Trade Policy Review Body,' (TPRB) which is another name of the General Council, was established to carry out periodic reviews on Members' trade and trade-related policies.[34] In addition, each Member must report its trade policies and practices on a regular basis to the TPRB.[35] Although the TPRM, in carrying out these policy reviews, engages in

---

30. *See* Hersche Lauterpacht, Private Law Sources and Analogies of International Law viii (1970) (arguing that 'general principles of law, recognized by civilized States and adopted by customary and conventional international law as a source of decision in international disputes, are for the most part identical with generally recognized principles of *private* law') (emphasis added); Raul Emilio Vinuesa, *The New Role of Equity as a Source of International Law*, *in* Thesaurus Acroasium of the Institute of Public International Law and International Relations of Thessaloniki 'Peace Messenger of the UN (A42/487) (Vol. XIX) 451 (1992).
31. *Cf. The Role of National Courts*, *supra* note 21, at 346–47 (arguing that a major effort made at both national and international levels to provide for more efficient application of GATT law would boost the efficiency of the WTO system as a whole and reinforce its *legitimacy*).
32. *See* TPRM, *supra* note 11, Introduction; WTO, Trade Policy Reviews: Enhancing Transparency, Trading into the Future: Introduction to the WTO, *available at* <http://www.wto.org/english/thewto_e/whatis_e/tif_e/agrm10_e.htm> (last visited on March 12, 2001) (hereinafter WTO, Trade Policy Reviews):

    Individuals and companies involved in trade have to know as much as possible about the conditions of trade. It is therefore fundamentally important that regulations and policies are transparent. In the WTO, this is achieved in two ways: governments have to inform the WTO and fellow-members of specific measures, policies or laws through regular 'notifications'; and the WTO conducts regular reviews of individual countries' trade policies—the trade policy reviews.

33. TPRM, *supra* note 11, Introduction, ¶ A (Objectives) (emphasis added).
34. *Id.*, ¶ C (Procedures for Reviews).
35. *Id.*, ¶ D (Reporting).

the evaluation of Members' regulations and policies for 'consistency' with the WTO system, it is a 'managerial,' rather than 'enforcement,' mechanism. In other words, it basically amounts to a 'peer review' process.[36]

Yet, despite this managerial nature, Members can effectively adapt, through the TPRM, their own way of addressing the interface between free trade and state regulation to the WTO prescriptions manifest in WTO agreements and jurisprudence. In other words, Members can seize the initiative in identifying problems in their trade and trade-related policies, and then rectify them in a way consistent with the WTO regime as they respond to other Members' questions on their policies and try to provide relevant justifications. Over time, this positive feedback process tends to improve the level of Members' compliance, thereby preventing future disputes.[37]

4.2.5 CAPACITY GAP PROBLEM

4.2.5.1 Development issue

Thus far, discussions on issues of broad and long-term compliance have been premised on an implied proposition that all Members are 'equally' capable of implementing the WTO jurisprudence and agreements that have been prescribed to reconcile the clash between free trade and state regulation. In reality, however, Members hold different levels of implementing capacity depending on their developmental stages.[38] For instance, some developing countries cannot afford the financial and technical resources necessary for complying with or implementing certain obligations under the SPS Agreement.[39] A participant in the recent WTO symposium expressed the developing country concerns on the capacity gap as follows:

> Before 1999, many developing countries had no knowledge at a technical level of the SPS Agreement. Since 1999, there had been some workshops and training, not always well coordinated. Developing countries remained concerned about the absence of new market access, insufficient modernization

36. WTO, TRADE POLICY REVIEWS, *supra* note 32. *See also* TPRM, *supra* note 11, Introduction, ¶ A (Objectives) ('It is not, however, intended to serve as a basis for the *enforcement* of specific obligations under the Agreements ...') (emphasis added).
37. *See* Victor, *supra* note 16, Chapter III, at 918.
38. Often, this developmental gap appears in a much more thorny fashion when it is intertwined with socio-cultural characteristics, thereby complicating the implementation issue. This complexity has been detected in the area of intellectual property obligations. For instance, as Professor Alford eloquently pointed out, it is not realistic at the present time to expect the Chinese people to 'establish and maintain a complex and costly legal framework for the protection of intellectual property rights.' William P. Alford, *Intellectual Property, Trade and Taiwan: A GATT-Fly's View*, 1992 COLUM. BUS. L. REV. 97, 107 (1992). Such attempt has consistently been futile no matter when or where it has been initiated. *See, e.g.*, WILLIAM P. ALFORD, TO STEAL A BOOK IS AN ELEGANT OFFENSE: INTELLECTUAL PROPERTY LAW IN CHINESE CIVILIZATION 30–55, 97, 112–23 (1995). To make matters worse, this futile attempt tends to create the 'false impression' that a mere body of law can rapidly change legal consciousness in China as well as escalate mutual 'distrust' between parties concerned. William P. Alford, *Making the World Safer for What?: Intellectual Property Rights, Human Rights and Foreign Economic Policy in the Post-European Cold War World*, 29 N.Y. U. J. INT'L L. & POL. 135, 151 (1996–97).

> of laws and institutions, non use of risk analysis, lack of knowledge and involvement with standard-setting organizations, and insufficient technical assistance.
>
> ... given the high costs for developing countries of setting up structures and institutions to implement the SPS Agreement, their implementation should be made *conditional* upon technical and financial assistance being made available to them.[40]

As the global trading community becomes more integrated, this 'inequality' will also become less and less tolerable.[41] Critically, this gap must be filled in by 'development assistance' based on an appropriate developmental perspective that enables the dual goals of free markets and adequate regulation to be achieved in a just and sustainable way.[42] Otherwise, the global trading community remains caught in a dual crisis of trade and regulatory failure since poor countries can neither improve their access to rich countries' markets nor implement necessary obligations under the WTO regulatory regime.

4.2.5.2 Problematizing an old model of development assistance (GSP)

Under the old GATT, development assistance was concentrated in temporary and transient 'special and different treatment' measures such as the 'Generalized System of Preferences' (GSP).[43] However, since the nature of the GSP is not only temporary but

---

39. In this context, WTO Director General Moore warns that 'the growth of the Internet can also increase the marginalisation of the world's poor, unless we take steps to ensure they get access to the Internet too.' WTO, *WTO News: Speeches—DG Mike Moore (31 October 2000), Opening Remarks—E-Commerce Conference, ITC, available at* <http://www.wto.org/english/news_e/spmm_e/spmm40_e.htm> (last visited on March 12, 2001).
40. Kazuaki Miyagishima, *Summary Reports by the Moderators, Symposium on Issues Confronting the World Trading System, World Trade Organization, Geneva, Switzerland, 6 and 7 July 2001, available at* <http://www.wto.org/english/forums_e/ngo_e/ngo_symp2001_(last visited on Sept. 20, 2001) (emphasis added).
41. *See* Amartya Sen, Global Doubts, Harv. Mag. 68 (Sep.–Oct. 2000).
42. *See generally* Frank. J. Garcia, *Trade and Inequality: Economic Justice and the Developing World*, 21 Mich. J. Int'l L. 975 (2000). UN Secretary-General Kofi Annan called for a new 'development round' of global trade negotiations to bridge the gap between the world's rich and poor. *Development: Annan Calls For 'Development Round' Of Trade Talks*, UN Wire, September 19 2000, *available at* <http://www.unfoundation.org/unwire/archives/UNWIRE000919.cfm#13> (last visited on March 12, 2001). World Bank President James Wolfensohn also warned that:

    > global poverty and the resulting social unrest threatens to destabilize developed countries and that 'it is in their interest to bring about poverty alleviation in the developing world because we are one world and, unless we get stability and growth in the developing world, we are not going to have a peaceful world.

    IMF/World Bank: Wolfensohn Promotes Equitable Growth, UN Wire, September 22 2000, *available at* <http://www.unfoundation.org/unwire/archives/UNWIRE000922.cfm#16> (last visited on March 12, 2001). *Cf.* Frederick M. Abbott, *The Enduring Enigma of TRIPs: A Challenge for the World Economic System*, 1 J. Int'l Econ. L. 497 (1998) (arguing that developed countries' emphasis on the *static* protection of intellectual property rights is misplaced and that such emphasis on maintaining a technological advantage is a 'beggar-thy-neighbor' approach incompatible with an integrating world economy).
43. The Enabling Clause, officially titled the 'Decision on Differential and More Favourable Treatment, Reciprocity and Fuller Participation of Developing Countries' that was adopted under GATT in 1979 is the WTO legal basis for the 'Generalized System of Preferences' (GSP). *See generally* WTO,

also unilateral and conditional, its actual effect as development assistance has often been questioned. In particular, developed countries tend to link the GSP benefit with other economic or non-economic conditions (e.g., security) that are favorable to them but may be detrimental to recipient countries.[44] This conditionality nurtures a supportive climate for protectionist regimes such as the 'Multi-Fiber Agreement' (MFA), which endorses and maintains numerous quantitative restrictions on textiles despite their fatal global market-distorting effect. In other words, developing countries are forced to give up their comparative advantage in textiles in return for temporary benefits from the GSP on other products.[45] This short-sighted bargain tends to yield long-term pathologies akin to those that some have identified in connection with affirmative action programs. As developing countries accept disadvantaged terms of trade on products in which they would otherwise enjoy a comparative advantage in exchange for the temporary relief of measures such as the GSP, they are deprived of critical potential for their long-term development. In other words, their economic structure is prevented from reaching higher developmental stages since the necessary springboards for such jumps are lacking.

Problematic aspects of conventional development assistance can be portrayed as 'supply-oriented' and 'negative.' First, as seen in the GSP, trade aids are unilateral and conditioned by terms that donors would impose. Producers insulated from competition by developing countries in return for the grant of GSP are usually powerful domestic constituencies that can lobby their governments for their benefit. Secondly, under the old GATT 1947 most development assistance was designed in a negative fashion, i.e., 'reduction and elimination of barriers,'[46] rather than as 'positive' programs, such as technical assistance. Not surprisingly, the effectiveness

---

cont.

Development: Main Legal Provisions, *available at* <http://www.wto.org/english/tratop_e/devel_e/d2legl_e.htm> (last visited on March 12, 2001). Under the Generalized System of Preferences, developed countries offer 'non-reciprocal preferential treatment,' such as low or zero duties on imports to products originating in developing countries, but developed countries (preference-giving countries) *unilaterally* determine the recipient (which countries) as well as the subject (which products) of the GSP schemes. *Id.* For instance, The U.S. Generalized System of Preferences (GSP) provides preferential duty-free entry for more than 4,650 products from approximately140 designated beneficiary countries and territories. USTR, *A Guide to the United States Generalized System of Preferences*, *available at* <http://www.ustr.gov/reports/gsp/index.html> (last visited on March 12, 2001). The U.S. GSP program was instituted on January 1, 1976, and authorized under Title V of the Trade Act of 1974 (19 U.S.C. 2461 et seq.) for a 10-year period, and the authorization was renewed four times (July 4, 1993, by the Trade and Tariff Act of 1984; July 31, 1995, by the Uruguay Round Agreement Act; May 31, 1997, by the Small Business Act of 1996; June 30, 1998, by the Budget and Reconciliation Act of 1997). *Id.*

44. *See* Frieder Roessler, *Domestic Policy Objectives and the Multilateral Trade Order: Lessons from the Past*, 19 U. Pa. J. Int'l Econ. L. 513, 520–21 (1998) (remarking critically that 'the nonreciprocal nature of preferences thus turned out to be an illusion').

45. In the same context, it has been noted that potential benefits from 'special and differential' (S&D) treatments for developing countries might have been outweighed by exemptions that had in practice favored developed countries: something that may be called 'reverse S&D.' WTO, *Development: Closing Remarks (by Mr. Ouedraogo, Deputy Director-General), Seminar on Special and Differential Treatment for Developing Countries*, *available at* <www.wto.org/english/tratop_e/devel_e/sem01_e/sdtrem_e.htm>(last visited on March 12, 2001).

46. GATT 1947, *supra* note 4, Introduction, art. 37:

> 1. The developed contracting parties shall to the fullest extent possible—that is, except when compelling reasons, which may include legal reasons, make it impossible—give effect to the following provisions:

of these conventional trade aids has been severely questioned in recent times amid a widening income and technology gap between North and South, leading to increasing criticism of globalization as well as of the WTO itself.[47] Certainly, if the global trading community wished to prevent any further economic marginalization of developing and least-developed countries from the mainstream of international commerce, developed countries should change their conventional perspective on trade aids and embrace developing countries as 'partners,'[48] not merely as 'recipients.'[49] In this regard, what most less developed countries need right now is more consistent and constructive 'assistance,' both financial[50] and technical,[51] by which they can establish a solid infrastructure for their long-term development.

4.2.5.3 *A new model of development assistance: 'capacity-building'*

Fortunately, in the new WTO setting, technical assistance has been emphasized, reflecting Members' realization that without such assistance developing countries

---

cont.

(*a*) accord high priority to the *reduction and elimination of barriers* to products currently or potentially of particular export interest to less-developed contracting parties, including customs duties and other restrictions which differentiate unreasonably between such products in their primary and in their processed forms;

(*b*) *refrain from introducing, or increasing the incidence* of, customs duties or non-tariff import barriers on products currently or potentially of particular export interest to less-developed contracting parties; and ... (emphasis added).

47. *See Hunger-striking Protesters Slam Globalization at ASEAN Meeting*, WTOWATCH, July 25 2000, *available at* <www.wtowatch.org/news/index.cfm?ID=2143> (last visited on March 12, 2001); *WTO: Trade Body Protests 'Nightmare' Reports*, UN WIRE, August 25 2000, *available at* <http://www.unfoundation.org/unwire/archives/UNWIRE000825.cfm#9> (last visited on March 12, 2001); *UN Trade Conference Calls for 'Fairer' Economic System*, CNN.com, February 18 2000, *available at* <www.cnn.com/2000/ASIANOW/southeast/02/18/world.trade.02/index.html> (last visited on March 12, 2001); *White Man's Shame*, THE ECONOMIST, September 24 1999, *available at* <www.economist.com/editorial/freeforall/current/fn2116.html> (last visited on March 12, 2001); *G-77: Poor Countries Call for Fair Trade*, UN WIRE, April 17, 2000, *available at* <http://www.unfoundation.org/unwire/archives/UNWIRE000417.cfm#14> (last visited on March 12, 2001); *Technology: UN Urged to Narrow Global Digital Divide*, UN WIRE, April 24 2000, *available at* <http://www.unfoundation.org/unwire/archives/UNWIRE000424.cfm#15> (last visited on March 12, 2001); *WTO: UN Report Charges Bias against Poorer Nations*, UN WIRE, August 14 2000, *available at* <http://www.unfoundation.org/unwire/archives/UNWIRE000814.cfm#14;Poverty> (last visited on March 12, 2001); *Little Improvement for World's Poor in 1990s—World Bank*, UN WIRE, August 4 2000, *available at* <http://www.unfoundation.org/unwire/archives/UNWIRE000804.cfm#15> (last visited on March 12, 2001).
48. 'Development, in the knowledge era, must mean partnerships based on sustainable systems of innovation in both developed and developing nations for equity to be achieved.' *Globalization: Neither a Devil Nor a Panacea*, OECD OBSERVER, Jun. 27 2000, *available at* <www.oecdobserver.org/news/fullstory.php3/aid/268> (last visited on March 12, 2001) (citing the statement by Baldwin Sipho Ngubane, South African Minster for Art, Culture, Science and Technology).
49. *See* WTO, *Press Release, Speech by the Director General Mike Moore, National Conference on the Millennium Round (Rome, November 11, 1999)*, *available at* <www.wto.org/wto/speeches/mm14.htm> (last visited on March 12, 2001).
50. As is the case with the EU, 'substantial transfer payments' are necessary for less developed countries to implement higher regulatory standards. *See* William P. Alford, *Introduction: The North American Free Trade Agreement and the Need for Candor*, 34 HARV. INT'L L. J. 293, 297 (1993).
51. *See e.g.*, *ECOSOC: Chinese Official Calls on UN for Info Tech Help*, UN WIRE, July 22, 2000, *available at* <http://www.unfoundation.org/unwire/archives/UNWIRE000722.cfm#15> (last visited on March 12, 2001).

would never be able to 'implement' new obligations flowing from the WTO agreements, such as the SPS, the TBT and the GATS.[52] In this regard, the SPS Agreement provides certain examples of technical assistance, such as 'research and infrastructure,' 'establishment of national regulatory bodies' and 'technical expertise, training and equipment.'[53] The TBT and the GATS also follow suit.[54]

Furthermore, more recently, a new paradigm of development assistance in the form of 'capacity-building' or 'confidence-building' has emerged.[55] This is a new developmental strategy for building capacity to implement WTO agreements.[56] The new paradigm aims to provide 'tailor-made' packages of technical assistance for developing countries through a survey of their needs and an evaluation of existing international cooperation schemes,[57] and is already reflected in recent rule-making actions in important regulatory fields including 'biosafety.'[58] A

---

52. *See* Philippe Cullet, *Differential Treatment in International Law: Towards a New Paradigm of Inter-State Relations*, 10 Eur. J. Int'l L. 549–551 (1999) (defining 'technology transfer' or 'aid mechanisms' to foster the implementation of treaties by less developed countries as the application of 'different treatment').
53. SPS Agreement, *supra* note 6, Introduction, art. 9.
54. TBT Agreement, *supra* note 7, Introduction, art. 11*; see also* WTO, *WTO News: 2000 News Items, Developing Countries Call for More Help in the Area of Technical Barriers to Trade* (Jul. 20, 2000), *available at* <www.wto.org/english/news_e/news00_e/chairs_e.html> (last visited on March 12, 2001); WTO, *WTO News: 2000 News Items, Workshop on Technical Assistance and Special and Different Treatment in the Context of the TBT Agreement* (Jul. 20, 2000), *available at* <www.wto.org/english/news_e/news00_e/chairs_e.htm> (last visited on March 12, 2001). Regarding GATS, most developing countries want specific mechanisms for 'effective implementation' or even 'operationalization' of Article IV. *See WTO's Draft Guidelines for Services Talks Strive for Inclusiveness*, Bridges Weekly Trade News Digest, Vol. 5, No. 3, Jan. 30, 2001, *available at* <www.ictsd.org/html/weekly/story6.30-01-01.htm> (last visited on March 12, 2001).
55. APEC, *Statement of Chair, Meeting of APEC Ministers Responsible for Trade (Darwin, Australia, June 6-7, 2000)*, *available at* <http://www.apecsec.org.sg/whatsnew/press/rel27_2000.html> (last visited on March 12, 2001).
56. *Id.*
57. *Id.* For additional empirical confirmation based on similar approaches, *see e.g.*, WTO, *WTO News: 2000 Press Releases (22 June 2000), General Council Special Session on Implementation: 22 June 2000 Organization of Work and Indicative Schedule of Meetings—2000, available at* <www.wto.org/english/news_e/pres00_e/pr184_e.htm> (last visited on March 12, 2001); WTO, *WTO News: 2000 Press Releases (20 June 2000), Officials Examine How to Analyze Risk for Food Safety Measures, available at* <www.wto.org/english/news_e/press00_e/pr183_e.htm> (last visited on March 12, 2001); WTO, *WTO News: 2000 News Items (WTO Highlights January–August 2000), available at* <www.wto.org/english/news_e/news00_e/knote_e.htm> (last visited on March 12, 2001).
58. *See* Cartagena Protocol on Biosafety (in Convention on Biological Diversity), *available at* <http://www.biodiv.org/biosafe/Protocol/html/Biosafe-Prot.html> (last visited on Feb. 13, 2001):

    Article 20, paragraph 1 (A Biosafety Clearing-House)

    A Biosafety Clearing-House is hereby established as part of the clearing-house mechanism under Article 18, paragraph 3, of the Convention, in order to:

    (a) Facilitate the exchange of scientific, technical, environmental and legal information on, and experience with, living modified organisms; and

    (b) *Assist* Parties to *implement* the Protocol, taking into account the special needs of developing country Parties, in particular the least developed and small island developing States among them, and countries with economies in transition as well as countries that are centres of origin and centres of genetic diversity. (emphasis added)

    Article 22 (Capacity Building)

    1. The Parties shall cooperate in the development and/or strengthening of human resources and institutional capacities in biosafety, including biotechnology to the extent that it is required for biosafety, for the purpose of the effective *implementation* of this Protocol, in developing country Parties, in particular the least developed and small island developing States among them, and in Parties with economies in transition, including through existing global, regional, subregional

remarkable aspect of the Cartagena Protocol on Biosafety regarding the capacity-building and assistance initiative can be found in its 'country-specificity' approach. The Protocol emphasizes, *inter alia*, the 'special needs' of developing country Parties,[59] and therefore seeks to 'identify' the needs and involvement of Parties before it launches any assistance program.[60] Undoubtedly, this tailored and 'demand-oriented' development assistance will be more effective because it is a more direct and particularized response to the actual needs of developing countries than the foregoing 'supply-oriented' approach which tends to be vague and unspecific.

Another critical factor in this new paradigm of trade and development assistance is the 'integration' of discrete assistance activities conducted by different international institutions in order to maximize their effectiveness.[61] In this regard, collaboration among the WTO, the IMF, the World Bank and other UN agencies is important because such collaboration provides developing countries with more *coherent* trade-related technical assistance and capacity-building measures.[62] For instance, while the WTO assists developing countries to implement their legal obligations,[63] the World Bank focuses on assistance related to human and infrastructural capacity-building.[64] Against this background, representatives of the Six Core Agencies (International Monetary Fund, International Trade Center, United Nations Conference on Trade and Development, United Nations Development Program, World Bank and WTO) of the 'Integrated Framework for Trade-Related Technical Assistance to Least-Developed Countries' (IF)[65] have recently

---

cont.

and national institutions and organizations and, as appropriate, through facilitating private sector involvement.

2. For the purposes of implementing paragraph 1 above, in relation to cooperation, the needs of developing country Parties, in particular the least developed and small island developing States among them, for *financial resources* and access to and *transfer of technology* and know-how in accordance with the relevant provisions of the Convention, shall be taken fully into account for capacity-building in biosafety. Cooperation in capacity-building shall, subject to the different situation, capabilities and requirements of each Party, include scientific and technical training in the proper and safe management of biotechnology, and in the use of risk assessment and risk management for biosafety, and the enhancement of technological and institutional capacities in biosafety. The needs of Parties with economies in transition shall also be taken fully into account for such capacity-building in biosafety. (emphasis added)

59. *Id.*, art. 20.
60. *Id.*, Annex Item A (3) of decision V/1 of the Conference of the Parties.
61. The WTO becomes increasingly underbudgeted and understaffed in technical cooperation activities. WTO Committee on Trade and Development (Twenty-Seventh Session), WTO Programme for Technical Cooperation, October 15 1999, WT/COMTD/W/64.
62. WTO, *WTO News: 2000 News Items (WTO Highlights January–August 2000), available at* <www.wto.org/english/news_e/news00_e/knote_e.htm> (last visited on March 12, 2001).
63. To help developing countries to fulfill their legal obligation through implementation, legal training and advice is critical. *See* WTO, *WTO News: 2000 Press Releases (14 July 2000), 14th WTO Trade Policy Course Comes to an End, available at* <www.wto.org/english/news_e/pres00_e/pr187_e.htm> (last visited on March 12, 2001); Trade and Development Center, *An Advisory Center on WTO Law, available at* <www.itd.org/links/acwlintro.htm> (last visited on March 12, 2001).
64. *Id.*
65. *See* Integrated Framework for Trade-Related Technical Assistance to Least Developed Countries, *available at* <http://www.Idcs.org>(last visited on Feb. 14, 2001).

pledged to make the IF an effective mechanism for assisting in the delivery of trade-related technical assistance and capacity-building.[66]

Finally, one additional prerequisite must be met if this new paradigm of development assistance is to be successful in helping less developed countries to better implement the WTO prescription. That is, developed countries must relieve less developed countries of their chronic economic burden, i.e., their 'debts.'[67] Without sizable and significant debt relief, the capacity-building efforts of less developed countries will never crystallize into net economic growth. This is because repayment burdens are so heavy that any tangible benefit from development assistance is quickly eclipsed by such burdens, creating a 'vicious cycle of impoverishment.' For sustainable and equitable development, this vicious cycle must be broken. In this regard, debt relief becomes the moral obligation of developed countries as trading partners in the global trading community.[68] Fortunately, international efforts such as the 'Copenhagen plus 5'[69] initiative have recently been exerted in this direction. Nonetheless, the actual execution of debt relief programs, as opposed to mere verbal commitments to them, is what is most important.

4.3 Narrow, short-term perspective

4.3.1 Rationale: complementing the broad, long-term perspective

Compliance from a broad, long-term perspective denotes the so-called 'managerial' paradigm that primarily emits a cooperative and constructivist *ethos* rather than a

66. WTO, *WTO News: 2000 News Items, Joint Statement on the Mandated Review of the Integrated Framework for Trade-Related Technical Assistance to Least-Developed Countries (IF) by the Six Core Agencies (IMF, ITC, UNCTAD, UNDP, World Bank and WTO)*, *available at* <www.wto.org/english/news_e/new00_e/ifstat_e.htm> (last visited on March 12, 2001). This *integrated* pattern of efforts to help developing countries to build capacity through technical assistance to implement trade-related regulatory treaties such as the TBT and the SPS, can also be found in a recent decision of the WTO General Council. The General Council Decision on 'Implementation-Related Issues and Concerns' urged international standard-setting organizations to ensure participation of developing countries throughout *all* phases of standard of development. *See* WTO General Council Decision on Implementation-Related Issues and Concerns, Dec. 19 2000, WT/L/384.
67. *See Debt Relief: Oxfam Criticizes IMF, World Bank Efforts*, UN WIRE, August 21 2000, *available at* <http://www.unfoundation.org/unwire/archives/UNWIRE000821.cfm#14> (last visited on March 12, 2001); *Debt Relief: IMF Says Poor Nations' Debts Being Cancelled*, UN WIRE, August 18 2000, *available at* <http://www.unfoundation.org/unwire/archives/UNWIRE000818.cfm#13> (last visited on March 12, 2001); *Debt Relief: Former IMF Head Joins Vatican Campaign*, UN WIRE, August 8 2000, *available at* <http://www.unfoundation.org/unwire/archives/UNWIRE000808.cfm#15> (last visited on March 12, 2001); *G-8: Annan Assails Inaction on Debt Relief*, UN WIRE July 25, 2000, *available at* <http://www.unfoundation.org/unwire/archives/UNWIRE000725.cfm> (last visited on March 12, 2001).
68. 'There can be no real human development without a redistribution of wealth and a more equitable sharing of economic decision-making to help the poorest and most vulnerable.' OECD OBSERVER, *supra* note 130 (citing the statement by Fouad El-Hage, President of Caritas International).
69. *See Copenhagen+5: Final Declaration on Poverty Adopted*, UN WIRE, July 5 2000, *available at* <http://www.unfoundation.org/unwire/archives/UNWIRE000705.cfm#12> (last visited on March 12, 2001); *Copenhagen+5: Poverty Conference Opens in Geneva*, UN WIRE, June 26 2000, *available at* <http://www.unfoundation.org/unwire/archives/UNWIRE000626.cfm#10> (last visited on March 12, 2001).

coercive one. As Chayes and Chayes observed, this paradigm assumes that states have a general propensity to comply with international obligations under treaties.[70] The basic cause of non-compliance according to this view is the inherent ambiguity of treaty language or limitations of capacity.[71] Therefore, compliance can be managed and enhanced through non-coercive managerial instruments such as dialogue, persuasion, and technical or financial assistance.[72] This managerial approach fits well within the contemporary global economic situation, namely ever-growing interdependence and integration, which tends to encourage deep cooperation among trading nations.[73] As Wolfgang Friedmann has pointedly described, the current ambience of international law, in particular international trade law, is undergoing a transformation from 'co-existence' to 'co-operation.'[74]

Nevertheless, such a constructivist perspective does not necessarily apply to the 'narrow, short-term' aspect of compliance—that is, compliance with *an* adjudicated decision on a specific case. Adjudication by trade tribunals involves specific obligations and their actual applications. As far as the interface or conflict between free trade and state regulation is concerned, a primary function of the narrow, short-term aspect of compliance is provision of a *particular* prescription by a panel or the AB for a *particular* case at a given point of time. Yet, it is only through the accumulation of actual compliance by trading nations with these contextualized decisions that a solid jurisprudence with normative force is formed in the long-term, thereby ensuring the predictability of the global trading system. In this regard, a certain enforcement mechanism is a necessary evil in the dispute settlement system to ensure a narrow, short-term compliance with these adjudicated decisions.[75] Moreover, without this enforcement mechanism, the settlement of a dispute would also be hollow since implementation of any settlement would remain wholly at the mercy of the losing party. Only when the last resort of an enforcement mechanism protects a settlement can its fulfillment be ensured. Only then will settlement

70. Chayes & Chayes, *supra* note 202, Chapter II, at 3.
71. *Id.* at 10–15
72. *Id.*
73. However, Downs et al. highlighted the *rarity* of such deep cooperation (i.e., the 'selection' problem) using the analogy of an orchestral repertoire. If some treaties are more likely to be complied with than others or require more enforcement than others, this will almost certainly influence the choices that states make. In other words, just as orchestras will usually avoid a repertoire that seems difficult to perform, states will not spend a great deal of time and energy in negotiating an unpromising treaty whose outcome looks fruitless or abortive. Most states do not want to touch a 'hot potato.' This endogenous strategy in the selection of treaties explains why there exist so many fluid treaties which are close to mere 'declarations' or 'political commitments.' Under these treaties, compliance is not so hard an assignment because the required level of effort by states to comply is relatively low; that is, the degree of cooperation among states is relatively shallow. *See* George W. Downs et al., *Is the Good News about Compliance Good News about Cooperation?*, 50 Int'l Org. 379, 382–392 (1996).
74. Wolfgang Friedmann, The Changing Structure of International Law 60–62 (1964).
75. Such an enforcement system is not unique in the field of international trade law. For instance, in regulating international oil pollution by oil tankers, as described by Ronald Mitchell, the International Maritime Organization (IMO) was successful through establishing the International Convention for the Prevention of Pollution from Ships, in which tankers lacking the International Oil Pollution Prevention (IOPP) certificate could be *barred* from doing business or detained in port. Ronald B. Mitchell, International Oil Pollution at Sea: Environmental Policy and Treaty Compliance 291 (1994).

function as an effective instrument for ending disputes. In sum, the rationale of a narrow, short-term concept of compliance may be found in the adjudicative function of a dispute settlement mechanism: namely, review, determination, and enforcement.

4.3.2 THE MAIN MECHANISM: ADJUDICATION AND ENFORCEMENT

From a broad, long-term perspective, compliance with the WTO obligations is a long-term process as Members' efforts to implement those obligations cannot be completed overnight. Some Members may simply need more time than others in undertaking domestic legislative procedures to adopt implementing statutes. Some other Members should be given a considerable degree of technical and financial assistance from other Members due to their lack of capacity.

However, explanations of this model of compliance would not directly apply to a narrower dimension in which a violation of an obligation is disputed in a specific case and such a violation, once found, must be quickly remedied. As for the interface between trade and regulation, a violation stands for a case-specific inconsistency with the balance that the WTO has prescribed in its jurisprudence and agreements. Violations should be addressed promptly through adjudication,[76] and once adjudicated, the losing party should implement the decision without delay.[77] Both inefficiency in adjudicative processes and ineffectiveness in enforcing adjudicated results tend to undermine the credibility and vitality of the global trading system, leading to serious sclerosis in global trade flows over the long-term. In particular, businesspersons who favor a predictable and confidence-sustaining trading system would prefer that the system not be derailed by lingering violations resulting from non-compliance by losing parties. In this regard, sanctions[78] are mobilized to enforce the decisions of panels and the AB in the absence of voluntary compliance by losing parties. However, under the WTO dispute settlement system, the enforcement mechanism is indirect. No central authority, such as federal marshals, enforce the

76. *Cf.* Richard B. Bilder, *International Dispute Settlement and the Role of Adjudication, in* THE INTERNATIONAL COURT OF JUSTICE AT A CROSSROAD 165 (L. F. Damrosch ed., 1987). Where complex and difficult factual and technical questions are involved, the adjudicative process may facilitate a more orderly and thorough examination of the issues than might otherwise be the case. *Id.* This orderly and thorough examination, in turn, leads to a better understanding by the parties themselves of the respective merits of each other's positions concerning the issue in dispute, and to their own negotiation of a settlement. *Id.*

77. *But cf.*, Judith Hippler Bello, *The WTO Dispute Settlement Understanding: Less Is More*, 90 AM. J. INT'L L. 416 (1996) (arguing that the WTO dispute settlement system gives member States the 'choice' to compensate or obey their obligations); *but see* John H. Jackson, *The WTO Dispute Settlement Understanding—Misunderstandings on the Nature of Legal Obligations*, 91 AM. J. INT'L L. 60 (1997), refuting Bello's argument and re-emphasizing that 'the DSU clearly establishes a preference for an obligation to perform the recommendations; notes that the matter shall be kept under surveillance until performance has occurred; indicates that compensation shall be resorted to only if the immediate withdrawal of the measure is impracticable.'

78. Within the meaning of international trade law under the WTO, sanctions represent an enforcing mechanism. Yet, under public international law, sanctions may be non-violent in a broader spectrum. *See* MARGARET P. DOXEY, INTERNATIONAL SANCTIONS IN CONTEMPORARY PERSPECTIVE 10–12 (1987) (introducing a typology of non-violent sanctions containing diplomatic and political measures such as political protest, and cultural and communications measures such as cancellation of cultural exchanges).

adjudicated outcome; instead, prevailing parties are entitled to retaliate by suspending their concessions to the losing parties.[79]

Functionally, sanctions are intended to correct violative measures as well as deter future occurrence of similar violations.[80] Yet, the first function may fail if a settlement reached between an offender and a state affected by the violation compromises the offender's obligation, thus inflicting a separate harm upon third-party trading partners. Given this situation, sanctions function only as a potential license for private retaliation in cases where a bilateral settlement is not reached or implemented. Therefore, to maintain the corrective function of sanctions, which is to prevent trade rules from being compromised or circumvented by settlements, a reliable mechanism is necessary to ensure that any settlement should be compatible with obligations that concerned parties are required to respect.[81] A more important function of sanctions is 'deterrence.' Deterrence occurs in two forms: 'direct' and 'indirect.' Direct deterrence involves a case-specific impact. In other words, once sanctioned, an offender will not again disrupt the balance between free trade and state regulation that the WTO has prescribed, because it has learned that such action violates its obligation. On the other hand, indirect deterrence is achieved when third-party Members, which observe this process of adjudication and sanction, bring their policies and practices into a state of consistency with such balance in order to avoid similar sanctions in the future.[82]

4.4 Relationship between two perspectives

Although these two concepts of compliance—'broad, long-term' and 'narrow, short-term'—can be separated conceptually, their relationship should not be underestimated, in particular from a 'dialectical' standpoint. A sustained record of

---

79. DSU, *supra* note 106, Chapter II, art. 22 (Compensation and the Surveillance of Concession).
80. *See* Frederic L. Kirgis, Jr., International Organization in Their Legal Setting 554 (2d ed. 1993).
81. *See* DSU, *supra* note 106, Chapter II, art. 3, ¶ 5.
82. One disadvantage of sanctions is that they may impose a high cost upon the sanctioner. *See* Chayes & Chayes, *supra* note 202, Chapter II, at 33. Nevertheless, privatizing sanctions may substantially reduce such costs. As is the case with provisions for penalizing and confiscating specimens under the Convention on International Trade in Endangered Species of Wild Fauna and Flora (CITES), the use of domestic enforcement procedures is possible, and even desirable, in an increasing range of cases including environmental treaties, where international regimes ultimately aim at directly influencing private activities rather than state behaviors. Convention on International Trade in Endangered Species of Wild Fauna and Flora (CITES), Mar. 3, 1973, 27 U.S.T. 1087, 12 I.L.M. 1085 (entered into force July 1, 1975), art. VIII (Measures to be taken by the Parties), ¶ 1, *available at* <http://www.cites.org/CITES/eng/index.shtml> (last visited on March 13, 2001):

    1. The Parties shall take appropriate measures to *enforce* the provisions of the present Convention and to prohibit trade in specimens in violation thereof. These shall include measures:
    (a) to *penalize* trade in, or possession of, such specimens, or both; and
    (b) to provide for the *confiscation* or return to the State of export of such specimens. (emphasis added)

    See also Compliance Theory, *supra* note 173, Chapter II, at 22.

narrow compliance by Members with the panels and the AB reports eventually translates into compliance with the system as a whole. In the same vein, trade jurisprudence backed by records of compliance serves as a guide to future application and interpretation of trade and trade-related regulatory rules, thus encouraging in-depth implementation in the long-term.[83] On the other hand, a generally well-implemented and thus well-functioning trading system is in itself a positive influence encouraging Member States also to follow panel and the AB decisions in the short-term. In turn, this encouraged compliance tends to yield deeper compliance with and implementation of the system as a whole, thereby realizing a virtuous dialectical cycle of narrow (short-term) and broad (long-term) compliance.

Nonetheless, this relationship should not unduly blur the distinction between these two perspectives. For instance, lack of budget and technology may discourage a developing country from conducting a comprehensive evaluation of health risks associated with the importation of certain agricultural or fishery products that may carry certain diseases. As a result, that developing country tends to narrow down its regulatory options to drastic measures such as an import ban, instead of seeking a reasonable inspection policy, thereby making it hard for them to fully implement the SPS Agreement. In this hypothesis, if a Member, which exports those agricultural or fishery products, challenges the import ban before a WTO panel, it would be hard for the panel to rule that the importing country violated the SPS Agreement since the country adopted and applied its regulatory measure, i.e., the import ban, taking into account its own 'technical and economic feasibility.'[84] Under this situation, adjudication alone does not suffice to fully realize a dual goal of free markets and effective state regulation because a regulating Member has a limited level of capacity. The only way to overcome this predicament is to enhance such 'technical and economic feasibility' through technical and financial assistance offered by other Members. This, in turn, belongs to the broad, long-term dimension of compliance.

More critically, it should be cautioned that a mismatch of these two different types of compliance might damage the global trading system. Such a mismatch might occur when enforcing narrow compliance on an issue that should ideally be dealt with through broad compliance. Some cases are politically sensitive due to the complicated matrix of interests embedded in them; others are not ripe for adjudication due to a lack of information or the presence of significant scientific uncertainty. These cases should be approached from a broad, long-term perspective on compliance because more information, knowledge, education, cooperation and functional discussion-*cum*-deliberation are necessary to solve the problem. Ideally, these issues should be handled with care and patience without any political escalation or scandalization. Nonetheless, if these hard issues are adjudicated hastily

83. *See Compliance Theory*, *supra* note 173, Chapter II, at 3–4 (distinguishing between the 'compliance with a treaty's *explicit* obligations' and the 'treaty-induced compliance')

84. *Cf.* Victor, *supra* note 16, Chapter III, at 872 (observing that 'the latitude afforded to nations in setting their own food safety standards is so large that nearly all bona fide attempts to protect food safety will be consistent with the SPS Agreement').

or prematurely from a narrow, short-term perspective on compliance, institutional damage to the trading system might be expected.[85]

An apt example of such a 'wrong case'[86] can be found in the aftermath of *Hormones* (1997) case. The WTO dispute settlement system failed to induce compliance from the EC in this case.[87] In fact, the adjudication was no more than 'dragging out a dispute' which 'afforded an additional two or three years of protectionism.'[88] As Robert Hudec trenchantly observed, such a strategy would be to 'temporize' the dispute, not to 'solve' it.[89] The *Hormones* case could have been effectively addressed through a non-adjudicative solution, including an appropriate 'labeling' system, nurtured by a constructive transatlantic regulatory dialogue, which falls within the rubric of a broad, long-term perspective in compliance.[90] As actually adjudicated, however, the case seems to have served little purpose aside from fueling public concern and skepticism about the WTO system as a whole.[91]

Moreover, even if losing parties are forced to follow the Panel and the AB decisions under the situation of these 'wrong cases', such compliance could fail to achieve both free trade and adequate regulation and could even undermine both goals. For instance, in the aftermath of *Hormones* (1997), the EC attempted to tighten the regulation on other carcinogens (carbadox and olaquindox), which were in comparison with hormones in dispute, in order to create 'consistency' that the AB

---

85. *Cf.* ORAN R. YOUNG, COMPLIANCE AND PUBLIC AUTHORITY: A THEORY WITH INTERNATIONAL APPLICATIONS 106 (1979) (observing that even states who acknowledge the authoritativeness of a treaty and generally favor the existence of specific behavioral prescriptions frequently find it advantageous to violate them in practice).
86. Robert E. Hudec, *GATT Dispute Settlement after the Tokyo Round: An Unfinished Business*, 13 CORNELL INT'L L.J. 145, 159 (1980); *see also* William J. Davey, *Dispute Settlement in GATT*, 11 FORDHAM INT'L L.J. 51, 67–78 (1987). These wrong cases may also be dubbed 'big cases,' which cannot be handled properly by adjudication. *See* John H. Jackson, *The Jurisprudence of International Trade: The DISC Case in GATT*, 72 AM. J. INT'L L. 747, 779–80 (1978) [hereinafter Jackson, *The DISC Case*].
87. *See WTO Beef Deadline Passes: U.S., Canada to Seek Retaliatory Sanctions*, BRIDGES WEEKLY TRADE NEWS DIGEST, VOL. 3, NO. 19, May 17, 1999, *available at* <http://www.newsbulletin.org/bulletins/getbulletin.cfm?browse = 1&Issue_ID = 1341&Bulletin_ID = 14&SID = #WTO Beef Deadline Passes: U.S., Canada To Seek Retaliatory Sanctions> (last visited on March 12, 2001).
88. Victor, *supra* note 16, Chapter III, at 922.
89. Robert E. Hudec, *'Transcending the Ostensible': Some Reflections on the Nature of Litigation between Governments*, 72 MINN. L. REV. 211, 217–18 (1987).
90. *See* Victor, *supra* note 16, Chapter III, at 921.
91. Most wrong cases are, in a sense, 'polycentric' in that they 'create a different complicated pattern of tensions' and notably involve 'allocation of economic resources.' *See* Lon L. Fuller, *The Forms and Limits of Adjudication*, 92 HARV. L. REV. 353, 394–404 (1978). For instance, *Hormones* (1997), adjudicated under the new WTO dispute settlement system, represented a highly sensitive problem of global income distribution between the European and the U.S. agricultural industries, though it appeared to involve more scientific and regulatory issues as a legal dispute. Naturally, this case had already been highly politicized before it finally came to the WTO panel and ended in serious non-compliance with the adjudicative outcome by the losing party (the European Communities), which hurt the WTO system as a whole. In hindsight, such a dispute should have been dealt with by non-adjudicative efforts, such as deliberation or even diplomatic solution. *Cf.* C.W. Jenks, *Craftsmanship in International Law*, *in* INTERNATIONAL LAW IN THE TWENTIETH CENTURY 75, 80 (Leo Gross ed., 1969) (maintaining that 'a jurisprudence which . . . ignores and belittles the limitations with which the rule of law operates in practice in international affairs in the present stage of development of the law, and a jurisprudence which rationalizes, defends and even idealizes these limitations, are equally unhelpful and unserviceable').

prescribed.[92] Likewise, in the aftermath of *Australian Salmon* (1998), the Australian government reviewed its rules to govern the importation of ornamental fish, which was in comparison with salmon in dispute, for the same purpose as the EC pursued in the post-*Hormones* process.[93] In the end, this short-term compliance results in erecting new trade barriers in the territories of the losing parties. In the above situations, domestic as well as international commerce involving carbadox and ornamental fish would decrease due to the new barriers (trade failure). Moreover, these new regulations adopted for the sole purpose of maintaining other regulations would eventually result in 'over-regulation' (regulatory failure). In sum, instead of attaining a dual goal of free trade and adequate regulation, this narrow, short-term compliance created a new crisis in terms of trade and regulatory failure. Under these circumstances, to streamline domestic regulatory procedures on hormones or salmon through 'internal alignment of risks'[94] would contribute to achieving the dual goal, which the SPS Agreement eventually denotes. This in-depth compliance could only be obtained from a broad, long-term perspective.

Lastly, but not least, even if these 'wrong cases' are adjudicated and their decisions are temporarily enforced, similar disputes are likely to resurface under different names and faces, as was the case with the notorious *DISC* (1977) case under the old GATT panel[95] and the *FSC* (2000) case under the new WTO dispute settlement system,[96] both concerning a problematic US tax-cutting practice for overseas shell companies, which are tantamount to prohibited subsidies.

4.5 Summary

Even if various efforts associated with the WTO treaties seek to reconcile the clash between free trade and regulatory values, and even if the more mature, intellectually refined GATT/WTO jurisprudence tends to produce decisions that safeguard the coherence of these concerns, such reconciliation cannot be attained without actual behavioral change on the part of Members. In other words, Members must faithfully incorporate their international obligations into their respective domestic regimes, in addition to executing the changes prescribed by individual panel and the AB reports. Without such compliance, WTO treaties and jurisprudence will fail to accomplish

92. Victor, *supra* note 16, Chapter III, at 924–25.
93. *Id.*
94. *See id.*, at 921.
95. United States—Tax Legislation (DISC), Report of the Panel, Nov. 12, 1976, GATT B.I.S.D. (23rd Supp.) at 98 (1977), *available at* <http://www.wto.org/english/tratop_e/dispu_e/73discec.wpf> (last visited on March 13, 2001). *See generally* Jackson, *The DISC Case*, *supra* note 86; Robert E. Hudec, *Reforming GATT Adjudication Procedures: The Lessons of the DISC Case*, 72 MINN. L. REV. 1443 (1988).
96. United States—Tax Treatment for 'Foreign Sales Corporations,' WT/DS108/1, Appellate Body and Panel Report (as modified) adopted on Mar. 20, 2000, *available at* <http://www.wto.org/english/tratop_e/dispu_e.htm> (last visited on March 13, 2001). *See generally* Julie Elizabeth McGuire, *World Trade Organization Finds U.S. Foreign Sales Corporation Violates EU Trade Agreements*, 2 No. 7 LAWYERS J. 5 (2000).

the dual objective of fostering freer international trade as well as domestic regulatory sovereignty.

Here compliance has two dimensions. From a broad, long-term perspective, compliance concerns a wide spectrum of state activities devoted to implementing WTO treaties. These implementation activities may need a substantial amount of time and energy. Yet, some Members lack the capacity to implement certain rules despite their good faith intentions to do so. Under these circumstances, financial and technical assistance becomes an important instrument for inducing compliance with the WTO rules in that such assistance helps these countries to establish prudent regulatory policies, and that at the same time it avoids trade-restrictive measures like import bans. On the other hand, from a narrow, short-term perspective, compliance refers to whether a losing party respects and implements a specific adjudicative decision by panels or the AB. This dimension is accompanied by a retaliatory mechanism for enforcing those adjudicative reports as a way of ensuring compliance. The stability of the global trading system would be seriously damaged if losing parties were continuously to fail to comply with panel and AB decisions.

Finally, the conceptual distinction of these two modes of compliance bears practical significance. Adjudication alone cannot fully induce Members to implement the WTO obligations, in particular when Members lack necessary capacity. Moreover, without adequate managerial efforts to help implementation, to impulsively rely on adjudication with enforcement mechanism only tends to precipitate a negative outcome, as seen in 'wrong cases.' Therefore, a circumspect approach to these two types of compliance is required.

In conclusion, through both dimensions of compliance, legal obligations instilled in treaties and jurisprudence to reconcile free markets and state regulation will eventually be transformed into reality.

Chapter V
Convergence

5.1 The convergence phenomenon

5.1.1 Overview

In the previous Chapters, this book has explored, from a comparative perspective, how other trade regimes, such as the EU and the US, have attempted to reconcile, in each of their respective contexts, the clash between free markets and state regulation through jurisprudential as well as legislative efforts. This book began its comparative exploration by observing that a dual crisis of regulatory and trade failure has also existed in other trade regimes. Then, the thesis examined how their judicial organs have interpreted their basic charters, namely the constitution or treaties, to tackle this crisis within their own contextualized dimensions of integration. The thesis also reviewed harmonization (legislative) efforts in other trade regimes as a way of addressing the crisis.

Remarkably, this comparative inquiry reveals a considerable degree of similarity in terms of the approaches that different trade regimes have used for responding to the crisis. For example, a preceding discussion observed jurisprudential evolution under the EU and the US similar to that occurring under the WTO system.[1] It also demonstrated that similar legislative patterns appeared in the basic charters of different trade regimes to promote harmonization.[2] This similarity may serve as the basis for claiming 'convergence' in this field.[3] Nonetheless, convergence should never be identified with 'universalization.' On the contrary, convergence can be best observed from a comparative analysis and thus contribute to a better understanding of one's own system.[4] At the same time, a convergence thesis also admits 'methodological' difficulties resulting from 'cross-level' comparisons.[5]

1. *See supra* sub-sec. 2, Chapter II.
2. *See supra* sub-sec. 3, Chapter III.
3. *See* Joseph H. H. Weiler, *Cain and Abel—Convergence and Divergence in International Trade Law*, *in* The EU, the WTO and the NAFTA: Towards a Common Law of International Trade 1, 3–4 (Joseph H.H. Weiler ed., 2000) [hereinafter Weiler, *Convergence*].
4. *See* Renaud Dehousse, *Comparing National and EC Law: The Problem of the Level of Analysis*, 42 Am. J. Comp. L. 761, 781 (1994).
5. *Id. See* Mark L. Movsesian, *Sovereignty, Compliance, and the World Trade Organization: Lessons from the History of Supreme Court Review*, 20 Mich. J. Int'l L. 775, (1999) (viewing basically that the supranational judicial proceedings of the WTO cannot be tantamount to the U.S. Supreme Court review); *see also infra* sub-sec. 5.2.1.2.

5.1.2 POINTS OF CONVERGENCE

This convergence phenomenon is found in both jurisprudential and legislative dimensions. In the legislative dimension, for example, certain procedural requirements such as 'notification' and 'reason-giving,' are commonly found in the WTO, the EU and the US context.[6] Moreover, adoption of a similar regulatory model, such as a 'performance'-oriented approach rather than a 'design'-oriented approach, is reflected in the SPS and TBT Agreements as well as in the EU's New Approach.[7]

Yet, an even more dramatic manifestation of convergence can be observed in the area of jurisprudential development. In the previous chapters, it was observed that the core of this converging jurisprudence can be depicted as the shifting of the focus of judicial scrutiny from issues of 'substance' or 'content,' such as whether US environmental legislation itself is necessary to protect the environment, to issues of 'procedure' or 'manner,' such as whether the US actually applies its domestic law in a consistent way or enforces its own law as it is written. Against the background of this dramatic jurisprudential convergence lies the *telos* of 'integration,' which is a central ideology in any nation-building or community-building enterprise.[8] In pursuing this integrative *telos*, reconciliation of trade and non-trade values is essential, and the judicial organ has been a critical engine driving this enterprise. As Thomas Jefferson once observed, 'the judiciary branch is the instrument which, working like gravity, without intermission, is to press us at last into one consolidated mass.'[9]

5.1.3 CONTRIBUTING FACTORS

Myriads of explanations can be served as answers to the question why such a phenomenon takes place. Yet, two factors seem to prevail over others: one *internal* and the other *external.*

One factor driving convergence in the internal, domestic dimension lies in the 'constitutional' nature of the interface between free markets and state regulation. Addressing this interface or clash is an essential constitutional issue with which every polity or organization must wrestle. John Jackson has conceptualized this issue as a 'trade constitution,' which represents a 'very delicate mix of economic and governmental policies, political constraints, and above all an intricate set of constraints imposed by a variety of rules or legal norms in a particular institutional

6. *See supra* sub-sec. 3.3.2, Chapter III.
7. *See supra* sub-sec. 3.3.1, Chapter III.
8. *See e.g., Baldwin, supra* note 299, Chapter II, at 511 (regarding Cardozo's famous sentence: '[The Constitution] was framed upon the theory that the peoples of the several states must *sink or swim together.*' (emphasis added)); *Dassonville, supra* note 266, Chapter II, ¶ 5 ('All trading rules enacted by Member States which are *capable* of hindering, directly or *indirectly*, actually or *potentially*, intra-Community trade are to be considered as measures having an effect equivalent to quantitative restrictions.') (emphasis added).
9. Movsesian, *supra* note 5, at 775 (quoting from THOMAS JEFFERSON, LETTER FROM THOMAS JEFFERSON TO ARCHIBALD THWEAT (JAN. 19, 1821), *in* 12 THE WORKS OF THOMAS JEFFERSON 196 (Paul Leicester Ford ed. 1905)).

setting.'[10] In the same vein, Daniel Farber and Robert Hudec conducted a comparative study of the US Dormant Commerce Clause and GATT in which they offered the sharp observation that 'federalism,' far more than a 'peculiarly American institution,' is a 'special case of the more general problem of allocating power among geographic units' as seen in the European Union or the GATT.[11]

According to the trade constitution[12] approach, a judicial organ in a particular institutional setting tends to determine *how* a Member or a State exercises its regulatory power without undermining free market objectives by focusing on whether local regulators have executed regulations in a manner which fulfills basic requirements such as consistency and due process, which are often codified in their own legislation, instead of substituting whatever 'correct' regulatory solutions the court deems most appropriate. According to Farber and Hudec, adherence to a free trade standard based on a general principle of law such as equality should narrow the choice of governmental means only to the extent of requiring 'even-

10. John H. Jackson, The World Trading System: Law and Policy of International Economic Relations 339 (2d. 1997); Jackson, Constitution and Jurisprudence, *supra* note 1, Chapter III, at 101–4; John H. Jackson, *Reflections on International Economic Law*, 17 U. Pa. J. Int'l Econ. L. 17, 25–28 (1996); John H. Jackson, *Perspectives on Regionalism in Trade Relations*, 27 Law & Pol'y Int'l Bus. 873, 873 (1996). *See also* Antonio F. Perez, *WTO and U.N. Law: Institutional Comity in National Security*, 23 Yale J. Int'l L. 301, 316–24 (1998) (discussing Professor Jackson's constitutional premise of international trade law).
11. *A GATT's-Eye View*, *supra* note 93, Chapter III, at 1401–3.
12. However, this 'trade constitution' should be distinguished from 'constitutionalization.' For instance, Ernst-Ulrich Petersmann has argued more radically that 'European integration law and WTO law confirm the Kantian insight that rule of law requires compulsory judicial protection of freedom and non-discrimination at home and abroad.' Ernst-Ulrich Petersmann, *How to Constitutionalize International Law and Foreign Policy for the Benefit of Civil Society?*, 20 Mich. J. Int'l L. 1, 30 (1998). *Cf.* Ernst-Ulrich Petersmann, *How to Promote the International Rule of Law?: Contributions by the World Trade Organization Appellate Review System*, 1 J. Int'l Econ. L. 25, 32 (1998) (arguing that the ever-growing adjudication phenomenon in international economic law is an empirical confirmation of the necessity of a judicial dispute settlement system for the strengthening of the 'rule of law' and of more democratic 'checks and balances' for the benefit of the citizens). Yet, Howse and Nicolaidis criticize the 'constitutionalization' of the WTO in two respects. First, they object to constitutionalizing the WTO through a Madisonian liberal model in terms of 'pre-commitment by which politicians tie their hands in such a manner as to resist the depredation of economic rights by domestic interest groups.' They view this pre-commitment perspective as problematic in and of itself because 'it is an attempt to take politics out of the global equation when on the contrary it needs to be brought back in.' Similarly, they are also opposed to another constitutionalizing model based on 'constitutional politics.' An effort to bring politics back in to the picture, this model understands the function of constitutions as 'formalizing the distribution of power among governmental institutions while establishing a permanent link between these institutions and societies.' Howse and Nicolaidis, however, view this model as unsuited to the WTO because, unlike the EU, it lacks accountable integrative institutions to oversee and conduct the policy and value trade-offs. Notwithstanding this critique, and regardless of the symbolism that 'constitutionalism' or 'constitutionalization' may carry, it is difficult to deny that the current WTO system as a whole contains at least *some* aspects of the foregoing two constitutionalizing models. For instance, the non-discrimination principle represents a radical rejection of protectionism of the sort found in the first model. For another instance, the WTO, through its dispute settlement system, does in fact engage in the allocation of regulatory powers between an integrative institution (the WTO) and Member States. In any case, these two models cannot be applied immediately and directly to the WTO in understanding its constitutional function due mainly to its own path-dependent characteristics as well as to the particular degree of federalization in the WTO or the global trading community as a whole. *See* Robert Howse & Kalypso Nicolaidis, *Legitimacy and Global Governance: Why Constitutionalizing the WTO is a Step Too Far*, 2–4 (Conference Paper presented in Harvard Kennedy School of Government on Jun. 1–2, 2000).

handedness,' rather than unduly restricting the choice of domestic regulatory goals.[13]

On the other hand, a significant external reason for convergence can be found in the ever-growing economic interdependence and integration that has come to characterize the global trading system. In particular, the phenomenon of 'synchronized frequency' represents an interesting ambience catalyzing convergence among different trade systems. Generally speaking, every trade system possesses an integrative process that is geared by centripetal (integrative) forces, but at the same time checked by centrifugal (disintegrative) forces. Although the speed, sequence and modalities of integration may vary from system to system, the general pattern of movement is the same.

For instance, the US has experienced a persistent tension or balance between federal and state power throughout its entire constitutional history. The federal dominance achieved in the 1930s thanks to the New Deal spirit has recently been inhibited by the re-emergence of the spirit of the 'Tenth Amendment' under the guise of the 'New Federalism' movement. The EU, once inspired by the 1980s 'Single European Act' *ethos*, has more recently been restrained by the spirit of subsidiarity. Likewise, the WTO system, though launched into tides of globalization and integration, continues to suffer from the disintegrating effects of regionalism. In sum, significant parallels in the experience of the US, the EU, and the WTO suggest that the frequency of integrative operations of all of these trade systems is closely synchronized. In order to account for the close linkage observed among all of these developments, we must look to globalization. Conventional trade barriers have begun to disappear. Investment has already become international.[14] Products as well as producers have become globalized: multinational enterprises (MNEs) make products through global sourcing. Even basic infrastructure such as stock markets tends to be merged.[15] In such an environment, it seems quite natural that great similarity exists in the frequency of integration processes of different trade systems. This synchronized frequency, in turn, tends to facilitate convergence among those systems and eventually enables the creation of a common legal order collectively governing their trade and regulatory operations.

---

13. *Id.*, at 1406.
14. For instance, according to the recent 'World Investment Report' from the UN Conference on Trade and Development (UNCTAD), the total value of international mergers and acquisitions (M&A) reached $720 billion in 1999. Economist.com, *Markets & Data: Cross-Border Mergers (Oct.7 2000)*, *available at* <www.economist.com/markets/PrinterFriendly.cfm?Story_ID + 388043> (last visited on Jan. 31, 2001). Cross-border mergers rose in value from 0.5% in 1987 to over 2% in 1999 in terms of a share of world GDP. *Id.* However, the UNCTAD also shows that 'global investment is being done mainly by the largest corporations in the largest economies.' *UNCTAD: Foreign Direct Investment May Top $1 Trillion—Report*, UN WIRE, Oct. 4 2000, *available at* <http://www.unfoundation.org/unwire/archives/UNWIRE001004.cfm#12> (last visited on Jan. 31, 2001). *See also* ROBERT REICH, THE WORK OF NATIONS 315 (1991) (arguing that 'vanishing is a nationalism founded upon the practical necessities of economic interdependence within borders and security against foreigners outside').
15. *See, e.g.*, London Stock Exchange, *Press & News: The London Stock Exchange's and Deutsche Börse's Plans to Merge Will Create Europe's Largest Stock Exchange - iX -International Exchanges*, 16 August 2000, *available at* <http://www.londonstockexchange.com/press/story.asp?id = 1> (last visited on Apr. 3, 2001); New York Stock Exchange, *Events: NYSE, Tokyo Stock Exchange Agreement*, 15 February 2000, *available at* <http://www.nyse.com/international/international.html> (last visited on Apr. 3, 2001).

5.2 From convergence to a *jus gentium* of international trade on domestic regulation

5.2.1 A *JUS GENTIUM* OF INTERNATIONAL TRADE ON DOMESTIC REGULATION

5.2.1.1 The concept: decontextualization

Thus far, we have observed the emerging phenomenon of convergence among legal disciplines related to the reconciliation of the clash between free markets and state regulation within different trade systems, such as the WTO, the EU and the US. It has also been argued that this convergence is anchored by general principles of law such as consistency, equity, or estoppel. Nevertheless, each of these converging legal disciplines remains 'contextualized.' In other words, the legal disciplines under consideration here are a 'Law of National Treatment' and a 'Law of Exceptions' under the GATT/WTO system, a 'Law of Free Movement of Goods' under the EU system, and a 'Law of the Dormant Commerce Clause' under the US system. All of these Laws are still unique and determined by their own path dependency and institutional structure.

Within the global trading community, however, where different trade systems and different trading nations co-exist and interact among each other in a federalistic and pluralistic fashion, a 'common and general' norm is required to address such a fundamental issue as a clash between free markets and state regulation. In fact, this type of common and general norm is even *necessary* simply for the sake of the stability and solidarity of the system, preventing unnecessary conflict and confusion.[16] In particular, the business community favors predictable and transparent trade rules upon which they may base long-term business plans, as conventional diplomatic intervention has become a burden due to its uncertainty in this sophisticated global marketplace. Therefore, it has become all the more important to businesses that a unified and integrated set of trade rules exists on which they can rely without having to question the trade system that their businesses may be nested in, whether the EU, the WTO, or another system. In sum, the multiplicity of trade systems must not impede global transactions.[17]

---

16. In this context, Friedmann noted that: ... the 'general principles of law recognized by civilized nations' can be used to direct and support the evolution of international law at a time when its social and moral foundations are changing, and when it is rapidly expanding both vertically and horizontally' (emphasis original). Friedmann, *supra* note 179, Chapter II, at 253. *See also id*, at 256 (arguing that 'the differentiation appears to be an essential factor in the approach to the evolution of international law, in a world deeply divided by conflicting ideologies as well as conflicting interests'). *See also* Ralph A. Newman, '*The Principles of Equity as a Source of World Law*,' 1 ISRAEL L. REV. 616, 616 (1966) (emphasizing 'the utilization of the fundamental principles of law which are common to most nations to establish a closer international understanding as a step toward world peace'); GENERAL PRINCIPLES OF LAW, *supra* note 179, Chapter II, at 387 n.3 (introducing various usages of general principles of law under different labels by the Permanent Court of International Justice, including 'principles of jurisprudence accepted by the law of all countries'); Thomas Cottier, *The Impact of New Technologies on Multilateral Trade Regulations and Governance*, 72 CHI.-KENT L. REV. 415, 432 (1996) (arguing that the 'doctrines of justice and equity in international law' should base future trade regulation in the face of the impact of new technologies on international trade).
17. *See Third Party Dispute Settlement*, *supra* note 180, Chapter II, at 65 (arguing that 'growing number of forums may create confusion and contradictory interpretations of international law').

In order to construct a general legal doctrine regarding the interface between trade and regulation one must 'de-contextualize' the converging yet still contextualized legal disciplines examined under the GATT/WTO, EU and US systems. The resulting doctrine may be termed a '*jus gentium* of international trade on domestic regulation.' As a Roman law concept, a '*jus gentium*' is defined as the 'body of law, taken to be common to different peoples, and applied in dealing with the relations between Roman citizens and foreigners.'[18] Yet, as applied to international trade law for the purpose of this book, a *jus gentium* can be redefined as a system of general legal discipline, applicable to all trade systems in addressing the interface of trade and regulation. Reflecting its debt to the original Roman law concept, a *jus gentium* of international trade advocates the development of a common, namely, de-contextualized, perspective out of various trade systems. In this sense, a *jus gentium* of international can be translated into a 'law of trading nations.'[19] In fact, this novel concept has already been envisaged by a few distinguished scholars such as Joseph Weiler. In his pioneering work, Weiler trenchantly identified the emergence of a 'nascent Common Law of International Trade' on the grounds that 'the very same regulatory measure comes simultaneously within the jurisdictional reach of more than one trade regime,' and the fact that 'in the material law of disparate international trade regimes we can see considerable convergence.'[20]

The concept of a *jus gentium* of international trade becomes clearer if one visits the thought-provoking notion of 'distinguo,'[21] developed by Thomas Aquinas. The enterprise of decontextualization for the purpose of constructing a *jus gentium* of international trade to address the interface between trade and regulation involves a transcendent shift from *laws*, plural, to *law*, singular.[22] Whereas the former, which is analogous to *lex, droit, or Gesetz,* represents particular constitutions or trade agreements and their associated jurisprudence, which serve to reconcile the conflict between trade and regulation in a given institutional setting, the latter is analogous to *jus, loi, or Recht*, and represents a common legal precept that is applicable to all trade systems and that is often associated with general principles of law.[23]

In sum, the final objective of this book is to establish, based on the aforementioned phenomenon of convergence, a unified set of norms, or 'legal reference,' which can be employed to reconcile the clash between free markets and state regulation without regard to what trade system is involved. This task basically amounts to a de-contextualization of the converging yet still distinct legal disciplines

---

18. BLACK'S LAW DICTIONARY 865 (7th ed. 1999).
19. The conceptual significance of using *jus gentium* for the purpose of this book lies in its embedded historical dynamism, namely, its gradual ascendancy over *jus civile* to become the Common Law of the Roman Empire. MALCOLM N. SHAW, INTERNATIONAL LAW 15 (4th ed. 1997).
20. Weiler, *Convergence*, *supra* note 3, at 3–4.
21. ROSCOE POUND, A WORLD LEGAL ORDER: LAW AND LAWS IN RELATION TO WORLD LAW 4 (1959) [hereinafter LAW AND LAWS].
22. *A law* represents 'an authoritatively prescribed precept with reference to a defined situation of fact or item of conduct,' while *law* symbolizes 'a body of rationally conceived and organized precepts of social control.' *Id. Cf.* Outi Korhonen, *New International Law: Silence, Defense or Deliverance?*, 7 EUR. J. INT'L L. 1, 12–13 (1996) (discussing *tekhne* as particular knowledge of a certain skill and *phronesis* as holistic understanding of the entire situation); Ronald M. Dworkin, Law's Empire 410 (1986) (urging the conception of 'law as integrity which unites jurisprudence and adjudication').
23. *See* Law and Laws, *supra* note 21, at 4.

of different trade systems for the purpose of transcending their structural particularities.[24] Simply put, the task constitutes a process of discovering a common *jus* from differing *lex*.

5.2.1.2 *Methodology: comparative investigation ('pragmatic attempt')*

From a methodological perspective, a *jus gentium* of international trade on domestic regulation can be developed through a 'comparative' investigation of how different trade regimes such as the WTO, the EU and the US, have addressed the dual crisis of trade and regulatory failure, as discussed above. This comparison is, as Wolfgang Friedmann suggests, a 'pragmatic attempt' to discover common and fundamental legal precepts out of different forms and patterns. According to Friedmann, such a comparison should eventually find that different systems apply substantively the same principles in spite of different forms, which implies a 'modern law of nature.'[25] Inevitably, this comparative approach also merits some caution. After cautioning that it is dangerous to assume that 'intellectual conceptualizations travel with any less difficulty,' Joseph Weiler and Joel Trachtman suggest four traps of comparative analysis: lack of dynamic perspective, difficulty of synchronization, embedded complexity of law as a social phenomenon, and different intellectual prisms for conceptualization.[26] Yet, Weiler and Trachtman also stress that 'it is irresponsible and defeatist to think that no cross-fertilization among legal systems is possible.'[27] It would be fair to say that Friedmann's 'pragmatic attempt' is consistent with such cross-fertilization.[28]

As mentioned above,[29] the judicial organs and the jurisprudence they produce tend to play a pivotal role in providing rich resources for this comparison out of which a meaningful common legal reference can be extracted. In this context, and demonstrating much insight, Maruo Cappelletti and & David Golay submit that:

> Common principles and traditions are clearly not the mechanical sum, but rather the selective choice of the 'best' and 'most suitable' principles and traditions found in the Member States. The search for such principles and traditions clearly requires great discretions, wisdom, and restraint. The nature of the judicial process, we think, peculiarly suits this search and enables the

24. *But cf.* Henry P. Monaghan, *Foreword: Constitutional Common Law*, 88 HARV. L. REV. 1, (1975).
25. Friedmann, *supra* note 179, Chapter II, at 251.
26. Joseph H. H. Weiler & Joel P. Trachtman, *European Constitutionalism and Its Discontents*, 17 NW. J. INT'L L. & BUS. 354, 355 (1996–97). *Cf.* William P. Alford, *On the Limits of 'Grand Theory' in Comparative Law*, 61 WASH. L. REV. 945, 956 (1986) (arguing that we need to assess the Chinese experience 'on its own terms' to better understand it and further comprehend what is 'genuinely universal').
27. Weiler and Trachtman, *supra*, at 26.
28. *Cf.* Joachim Zekoll, *Kant and Comparative Law—Some Reflections on a Reform Effort*, 70 TUL. L. REV. 2719, 2725–32 (1996) (discussing the 'comparative method as a search for the common core and functional equivalents'); David Kennedy, *New Approaches to Comparative Law: Comparativism and International Governance*, 1997 UTAH L. REV. 545, 551 (1997) (proposing to approach comparative law from the perspective of 'internationalists' who address the 'broader international project of public and private governance' as 'legal specialists').
29. *See supra* sub-sec. 5.1.2.

judiciary, perhaps more than the political branches, to discover and articulate common values in a pluralistic society.[30]

5.2.2 TWO SOURCES: *JUS COGENS* OF INTERNATIONAL TRADE AND CUSTOMARY INTERNATIONAL TRADE LAW

5.2.2.1 Overview

After completing the comparative investigation described above, the resulting selection of common legal precepts must be fashioned into an independent legal product, i.e., a *jus gentium* of international trade on domestic regulation. For this purpose certain material 'sources' should be located, such as a '*jus cogens* of international trade' and a 'customary international trade law.' These sources also constitute two different *lenses* through which a *jus gentium* of international trade can be observed and examined, helping us to better grasp its meaning and effects.

A '*jus cogens* of international trade' (JGIT) on domestic regulation can be defined as a peremptory and non-derogable rule that is directly associated with the purpose and objective of the global trading system. In other words, a *jus cogens* of international trade is a legal manifestation of the *telos* of the global trading system, which has been stated variously as 'integration' or 'sustainable development.' Its violation connotes a failure to fulfill the very reason of the existence of the system as a whole. In fact, as discussed above, a comparison of different trade regimes such as the EU and the US reveals that every trade system operates according to a certain 'integrationist' *telos*.[31] For instance, one can identify a *telos* of 'nation-building' and 'community-building' in the US Dormant Commerce Clause, as well as the EU Principles of Free Movement of Goods.[32]

Of course, the *teloi* of all these various trade regimes cannot be identical due to differences in their institutional settings and stages of integration. It is beyond question that the US, as a federal nation, has demonstrated a stronger integrationist *telos* between the federal government and fifty states than the WTO system has shown among 140 Members. Nonetheless, the basic routes that these three trade regimes have followed since their respective creations are similar enough to support a powerful claim about a common *trend*: from a low level of integration to a high level of integration. To state the case in somewhat greater detail, federal regulatory authority consolidated during the Great Depression was a powerful catalyst for integration in the US, ultimately rendering dual federalism a historical artifact. Similarly, European integration was accelerated by the Single European Act initiative in the 1980s, streamlining the decision making process. The WTO system is

---

30. Maruo Cappelletti & David Golay, *The Judicial Branch in the Federal and Transnational Union: Its Impact on Integration*, *in* INTEGRATION THROUGH LAW: EUROPE AND THE AMERICAN FEDERAL EXPERIENCE, METHODS, TOOLS AND INSTITUTIONS (vol. 1), POLITICAL ORGANS, INTEGRATION TECHNIQUES AND JUDICIAL PROCESS 261, 351 (bk. 2, Maruo Cappelletti et al eds., 1985).
31. *See supra* sub-sec. 2, Chapter II.
32. *Id.*

also grounded on a higher level of global market integration than the old GATT system ever dreamed of.

By and large, these three trade regimes tend to envision a common peremptory obligation flowing directly from their integrationist *teloi*: 'anti-unilateralism' or 'duty to cooperate.' This peremptory obligation is simple enough as to warrant no further explanation, yet it is critical to sustaining any trade regime undergoing the process of integration. If Members States in any trade regime were to ignore others' interests and conduct domestic policy-making in a rigidly unilateral manner, serious system failure would eventually result, making the trade regime inoperable. Such a trade regime would be caught in a dual crisis of trade and regulatory failure threatening the very rationale of its existence. To avoid such an outcome, the obligation of 'anti-unilateralism' or 'duty to cooperate' should be respected by Members States on all occasions and without exception. This is what is meant by a '*jus cogens* of international trade' on domestic regulation.

While a JCIT on domestic regulation is defined above in rather philosophical terms, a 'customary international trade law' (CITL) on domestic regulation can be defined on a more 'empirical' basis. A CITL on domestic regulation basically amounts to a crystallization of useful jurisprudence from a comparative investigation of court decisions from different trade regimes seeking to reconcile the clash between free markets and state regulation within their own institutional contexts. Two major parameters of a custom are found in the regularity and consistency of trade tribunals' jurisprudence on a given issue (*practice*), as well as Member States' acceptance of and adherence to such jurisprudence with a normative consciousness (*opinio juris*).

5.2.2.2 Jus cogens of international trade (JCIT) on domestic regulation

The concept of JCIT can be explored in two dimensions: *what* it is ('content') and *where* it is found ('locus'). Firstly, the JCIT doctrine, as was true of traditional *jus cogens* of international law, may be traced back to the *jus naturale* tradition originating with the Roman philosophical jurists who emphasized an *a priori* notion of reason or justice which governs the operation of nature and humanity alike, and which is thus present, to a greater or lesser degree, in any system of positive laws.[33] This quality of a *jus cogens* gives itself a special place as a peremptory rule overarching other statutory laws.[34] However, a JCIT, as defined in a *jus naturale* perspective, cannot but be nebulous and impractical: although the concept itself may be accepted, its content is unlikely to be agreed upon.[35] Therefore, the focus of

33. *See* BLACK LAW DICTIONARY 864, 1049 (7th ed. 1999).
34. This character of *jus cogens* is, as a matter of fact, another expression of the primacy of ethics or justice over the aridity of positive law, betokened as 'legal conscience' (Weil) or the 'ethical minimum' recognized by all the states of the international community' (Verdross). Weil, *supra* note 7, Chapter I, at 422, n. 30; Alfred Verdross, *Forbidden Treaties in International Law*, 31 AM. J. INT'L L. 571, 574 (1937).
35. Juan Antonio Carrillo Salcedo, *Reflections on the Existence of a Hierarchy of Norms in International Law*, 8 EUR. J. INT'L L. 583, 589–91 (1997) (citing AMERICAN LAW INSTITUTE, RESTATEMENT OF THE LAW, THIRD, FOREIGN RELATIONS LAW OF THE UNITED STATES 2 vols. (1987–89)).

discussion on 'what it is' must shift from a philosophical question to a more precise subject-matter question,[36] a shift that inevitably leads to the further task of searching for the *lex lata*,[37] or the positivization of a *jus cogens*.[38] In this connection, basic charters (constitutions or treaties) of trade regimes may be the best source through which to view the content of the JCIT. Such inquiry reveals that the preemptory nature of a *jus cogens* is attributable to its given 'object and purpose.'[39] In other words, the task of constructing a JCIT should be based on a serious quest for the object and purpose, i.e. *telos*, of the global trading community, which is enshrined not only in the treaty text, but also in the *traveau preparatoir* and decisions of trade tribunals.[40]

This leads us to the question of 'where it is found.' The *locus* of a JCIT is a conceptual space in which a *telos* is established and permitted to evolve, namely the 'global trading community' where the half-century history of international economic law has been written.[41] Critically, as the *locus* itself is open to continuing changes, the

---

36. The International Law Commission (ILC) viewed that, 'it is not the form of a general rule of international law but the particular nature of the subject-mater with which it deals that may, in the opinion of the Commission, give it the character of *jus cogens*.' YEARBOOK OF THE INTERNATIONAL LAW COMMISSION (vol.2) 248 (1966); Gennady M. Danilenko, *International Jus Cogens: Issues of Law-Making*, 2 EUR. J. INT'L L. 42, 45 (1991). The ILC later reaffirmed this view by saying that the peremptory nature of *jus cogens* is 'determined by their content, not by the process by which they were created.' YEARBOOK OF THE INTERNATIONAL LAW COMMISSION 85 (vol.2) (1976); Danilenko, *supra*, n.14.
37. Regarding the distinction between *lex lata* ('the law as it is') and *lex ferenda* ('the law as it should be'), *see generally* Anne-Marie Slaughter & Steven R. Ratner, *The Method is the Message*, 93 AM. J. INT'L L. 410, 415–17 (1999).
38. A danger of political misuse of *jus cogens*—for example, to advance self-serving subjective interpretations of fundamental interests of the international community—always exists. In this context, a progressive positivization of *jus cogens* can be understood as an attempt to establish clear criteria of 'higher law.' This attempt at positivization culminates in Article 53 of the Vienna Convention of the Law of Treaties ('... accepted and recognized by the international community of states as a whole.') *See* Danilenko, *supra* note 36, at 49. *But cf.* Shirley V. Scott, *International Law as Ideology: Theorizing the Relationship between International Law and International Politics*, 5 EUR. J. INT'L L. 313, 325 (1994) (arguing that 'a conceptualization of international law as *ideology* has integrated the image of international law as a set of objective rules with its political reality' (emphasis added)).
39. R. St. J. MacDonald, *The Charter of the United Nations and the Development of Fundamental Principles of International Law*, *in* CONTEMPORARY PROBLEMS OF INTERNATIONAL LAW 204 (Bin Cheng and E.D. Brown eds., 1988) [hereinafter *Fundamental Principles*]; H. Mosler, *General Principles of Law*, *in* ENCYCLOPEDIA OF PUBLIC INTERNATIONAL LAW 96 (R. Bernhardt ed. 1984). *Cf.* J.M. Balkin & Sanford Levinson, *The Canons of Constitutional Law*, 111 HARV. L. REV. 963, 970 (1998) (arguing that 'what is regarded as canonical in law depends very much on the audience for whom and the *purposes* for which the canon is constructed' (emphasis added)).
40. In this regard, the idea of the JCIT can be said to reflect the 'intent' of the global trading community as a whole, as expressed in a community-wide forum. *See* Danilenko, *supra* note 36, at 51–2. However, this intent is distinguishable from the 'consent' of the members of trade community in that the intent is not an *instant* one; it materializes progressively over a considerable period of time. Therefore, the JCIT is not a product of a one-time 'consensus,' nor of 'majority voting.'
41. To illustrate the relationship between the global trading community (*locus*), the JCIT and the *telos* of the international trade system on this point, regime theory may be of some help. According to Stephen Krasner, a regime can be defined as 'sets of implicit or explicit principles, norms, rules, and decision-making procedures around which actors' expectations converge in a *given* area of international relations' (emphasis added). *See* Nicholas Onuf, *The Constitution of International Society*, 5 EUR. J. INT'L L. 1, 8–9 (1994) [hereinafter *International Society*]; Stephen Krasner, *Structural Cases and Regime Consequences: Regimes as Intervening Variables*, 36 INT'L ORG. 186 (1982). If we conceive of the international trade system as a regime based on the above definition,

telos also tends to be transformed. In each of the three trade regimes under comparison, the initial *telos* is easily discovered if one pays due attention to the genesis of each regime, whether the GATT/WTO, the EU or the US. These trade regimes were all established against a backdrop dominated by the bitter experience of catastrophic economic balkanization ignited by destructive protectionism: tariff wars under the Articles of the Confederation; trade wars that nurtured and spread the worldwide recession before the Second World War. Therefore, we find that a liberal, anti-protectionist ideology formed a deeply embedded *telos* at the beginning of each of these trade regimes.[42] Hence, at an early stage in the development of the global trading community, a JCIT can be defined as a peremptory obligation of anti-protection, which can be paraphrased as:

> *Thou shall not protect any specific domestic commerce to the detriment of any other trading partner*[43]

However, this JCIT is imperfect because it is incapable of addressing trade failure of the sort that every trade regime is now facing. It fails to cope with 'non-protectionist' yet still 'trade-restrictive' domestic regulations. Every regulation grounded on a legitimate policy objective would be valid under this narrow JCIT no matter what kind of negative trade effects such regulations might involve. These non-tariff barriers (NTBs) are increasing in number as modern regulatory instruments of governments become more complicated and sophisticated. These emerging trade barriers tend to cause market friction or 'market incontestability,'[44] often resulting in serious 'trade failure.' On the other hand, if the reaction to such a trade failure is to seek to uphold trade values at all costs, then social values, such as the protection of the environment or human health, will tend to be sacrificed or at least pushed to the margins of regulatory priority. This would likely be a politically untenable response,

---

cont.
then the *locus* (trade community) can be deemed a place where 'actors' expectations converge in the trade relation' while 'sets of norms and rules' around which such expectations converge can be understood to connote the JCIT.

42. *See e.g.*, Fascal Fontaine, A New Idea for Europe: The Schuman Declaration—1950–2000, *available at* <http://europa.eu.int/comm/dg10/publications/brochures/docu/50ans/txt01_en.html> (last visited on Jan. 19, 2001) ('The solidarity in production thus established will make it plain that any war between France and Germany becomes *not merely unthinkable, but materially impossible*' (emphasis added)); GATT 1947, *supra* note 4, Introduction, pmbl. ('the elimination of discriminatory treatment in international commerce').
43. Within this initial dimension, trade rules may be understood as preventing a variety of 'protectionist' measures that are sometimes manifest as domestic regulations (*e.g.*, taxation or other internal regulations) and sometimes as border measures (*e.g.*, quotas or their equivalents). Although some controversy exists regarding interpretive differences between these two types of measures, the resulting trade barriers can be seen as protectionist in the first place. It would be fair to say that this anti-protectionist discipline is, at least, what the framers of the GATT, the European Community or the US Dormant Commerce Clause had in mind at the beginning.
44. *See generally* OECD, *The International Contestability of Markets—Economic Perspective: Issue Paper*, TD/TC(96)5, Feb. 14, 1996, *available at* <http://www.oecd.org//ech/pub/tc96_5.pdf> (last visited on Mar. 23, 2001). *Cf.* Geza Feketekuty, *The Scope, Implication and Economic Rationale of a Competition-Oriented Approach to Future Multilateral Trade Negotiations* 2–4, OECD, TD/TC(96)9, Feb. 15, 1996; Eleanor M. Fox, *Toward World Antitrust and Market Access*, 91 AM. J. INT'L L. 1, 1–2 (1997) (proposing the 'Agreement on Trade-Related Aspects of Antitrust Measures' (TRAMs) to enhance the global market access).

considering the extent to which (non-trade) social values have gained in prominence in contemporary welfare states. These factors considered, any pro-trade bias is likely to result in 'regulatory failure,' and will almost certainly work to undermine the integrationist *telos* embodied by 'sustainable development.'

Therefore, a new JCIT on domestic regulation should be advanced enough to address this 'dual crisis' of trade and regulatory failure in order to realize a truly integrationist *telos*. This mission for a new JCIT tends to recall the 'new jurisprudence' found in the chapeau test, as well as similar 'process-oriented' disciplines, such as the risk assessment requirement under the SPS Agreement.[45] Tellingly, this new jurisprudence and the various other similar requirements manifest in converging fashion in other trade regimes[46] are capable of dealing with this dual crisis in that they all focus on *how* a domestic regulation is applied or enforced, rather than *what* such a regulation really is. This 'manner-oriented,' rather than 'content-oriented' approach can ensure the free circulation of trade while still safeguarding regulatory autonomy at the local level. In other words, these new legal disciplines help to guarantee that each trade regime or trading nation can trade freely, but in a manner that preserves regulatory diversity, thereby fulfilling the ultimate *telos* of integration.

Consequently, a new JCIT should connote 'manner-oriented' principles such as 'consistency' and 'fairness,' that prohibit arbitrary and unilateral exercise of regulatory power by each trade regime or trading nation. Moreover, this anti-unilateral obligation embedded in the new JCIT eventually leads to a 'duty to cooperate'[47] in the regulatory process by taking into account other trading partners' interests in order to fully realize an integrationist *telos*. In sum, the new JCIT can be paraphrased as follows:

> *Thou shall not unilaterally adopt or apply domestic regulations that affect any other trading partner.*

---

45. *See supra* sub-sec. 1.2.3, Chapter III.
46. *See supra* § 2, Chapter II; § 3, Chapter III.
47. *Cf.* Pierre-Marie Dupuy, *The Place and Role of Unilateralism in Contemporary International Law*, 11 EUR. J. INT'L L. 19, 22–23 (2000). In a post-hegemonic and multi-centered world, cooperation should be in the form of the 'sharing of responsibility.' *See Editorial Note*, 41 THE FEDERALIST 148 (1999). While in the Cold War period, the US-led leadership functioned as the 'capacity to mobilize forces and gather consensus,' we are now witnessing the negative consequence of the absence of such leadership in the form of 'unilateralism' or 'isolationalism.' *Id.*, at 145–46. In the EU context, a meaningful analogy of this 'duty to cooperate' may be found in the 'fidelity' clause of Article 5 EC. Wolf Sauter, *The Economic Constitution of the European Union*, 4 COLUM. J. EUR. L. 27, 44 (1998) (suggesting that 'even where the application of subsidiarity excludes Community action, the fidelity clause of Article 5 EC still binds the Member States'). Even in the eighteenth century, Emmerich de Vattel took the view that 'the first general law of nations requires mutual aid.' *See* Nicholas Greenwood Onuf, *Civitas Maxima: Wolff, Vattel and the Fate of Republicanism*, 88 AM. J. INT'L L. 280, 298 (1994). *Cf. International Relations Theory*, *supra* note 201, Chapter II, at 965 (regarding the constructivists' view that ideas and norms can change the interests and behaviors of nations); *but see id.*, at 963 (pointing out the realists' pessimistic view about cooperation among nations).

5.2.2.3 *Customary international trade law on domestic regulation*

The traditional theory of customary international law involves two elements: state practice and *opinio juris*.[48]

As for the first element, the 'practice' of fleshing out the customary rule can be defined as 'general,' 'consistent' or 'constant and uniform,' but not necessarily 'unanimous.'[49] If we attempt to search for such practices in the area of international trade, the dispute settlement procedure may be one of the best places to look. The old GATT 1947 and the new WTO system alike boast a considerable number of case precedents that have been widely cited in subsequent cases, even in other trade regimes.[50] Such case law is 'general' in that it is regarded as having relevance beyond their own case-specificity with respect to the interpretation of certain important provisions such as National Treatment (GATT Article III). It is also 'consistent' in that they deal with a series of cases involving the same provisions in a like manner and manage to avoid conflicting with each other. Therefore, this case law, collectively, can be said to constitute an essential part of the 'GATT *acquis*'[51] or, 'customary practices followed by the Contracting Parties to GATT 1947.'[52] The WTO Agreement also provides Article XVI (Guidance Clause) to affirm that all GATT 1947 decisions and reports shall guide WTO activities.[53] This 'continuity' of institutional practices and its normative implication as guidance sheds much light on the emergence of 'customs' in the context of international trade law.

The second element, *opinio juris*, which is defined as the 'feeling of conforming to what amounts to a legal obligation,'[54] appears to be more problematic due to the controversy surrounding the question of whether it can be found in the context of

48. *See generally* ANTHONY A. D'AMATO, THE CONCEPT OF CUSTOM IN INTERNATIONAL LAW (1971). *See also* Statute of the International Court of Justice, June 26, 59 Stat. 1055, T.S. No. 993, 3 Bevans 1179, art. 38 ('international custom, as evidence of a general practice accepted as law'); BROWNLIE, *supra* note 5, Chapter IV, at 4–11; Goldsmith and Posner observe that the jurisprudence of customary international law appears to alternate every two hundred years or so between naturalism and positivism. Jack L. Goldsmith & Eric A. Posner, *Understanding the Resemblance between Modern and Traditional Customary International Law*, 40 VA. J. INT'L L. 639, 640 (2000). In a more detailed exploration of different academic perspectives on custom (customary international law), Fidler introduced three representative perspectives : 'dinosaur' (positing that 'customary international law is an outdated relic of a lost age'); 'dynamo' (arguing that 'customary international law remains a vital part of modern international law'); 'dangerous' (asserting that 'customary international law has been abused at the international and national levels'). David P. Fidler, *Challenging the Classical Concept of Custom: Perspectives on the Future of Customary International Law*, 39 GERMAN YEARBOOK OF INT'L L. 198, 199 (1996) [hereafter *Custom*]. Regarding a critical view on customary international law, *see* J. Patrick Kelly, *The Twilight of Customary International Law*, 40 VA. J. INT'L L. 449, 452 (2000) (arguing that 'customary international law should be eliminated as a source of international legal norms and replaced by consensual processes').
49. Weil, *supra* note 7, Chapter I, at 434.
50. *See e.g.*, In the Matter of Lobsters from Canada, USA 89-1807-01, *available at* <http://www.sice.oas.org/DISPUTE/uscanfta/Uc89010e.asp> (last visited on Mar. 23, 2001) [hereinafter *Lobster*].
51. *Japanese Shochu II*, *supra* note 8, Chapter II, E (Status of Adopted Panel Reports).
52. WTO Agreement, *supra* note 1, Introduction, art. XVI:1.
53. John H. Jackson, *Fragmentation or Unification among International Institutions: the World Trade Organization*, 31 N. Y. U. J. INT'L & POL. 823, 828 (1999) [hereinafter *Fragmentation or Unification*].
54. North Sea Continental Shelf (F.R.G. v. Den./Neth.), 1969 I.C.J. 3 (Feb. 20) [hereinafter *North Sea*]; *see also Custom*, *supra* note 48, at 204–08.

case law, such as ECJ decisions or GATT/WTO Panel (or AB) reports. In the case of the ECJ, the *opinio juris* is easily detected since it is one of the essential duties of the Member States to conform to case law.[55] In the case of the GATT/WTO Panel and AB decisions, however, it seems at first glance that they have no formal legal effect since they are not 'binding' *per se*.[56] It is true that these decisions cannot alter or modify legal obligations under the WTO and related agreements; it is only GATT/WTO Members who are given the final say on the interpretation of these provisions.[57] Nonetheless, there can be no doubt that GATT/WTO case law is regarded as 'precedent' which can serve as guides in resolving similar cases, even though they have no formal '*stare decisis*' or '*res judicata*' status.[58] In practice, subsequent panels generally make frequent reference to the decisions of past panels. This referencing practice plays a major role in strengthening the legal arguments presented by the parties in a given dispute as well as the legal reasoning offered by the tribunal. Therefore, one can safely say that GATT/WTO case law possesses a certain degree of normative value sufficient to encourage trading nations to follow them.[59]

It is important to note that the practices and *opinio juris* of different trade regimes are 'cross-jurisdictional.' In other words, the judicial decisions of one trade regime often cite or refer to the case law of another trade regime when addressing similar issues.[60] The end result of such reference, if repeated regularly, is a collective set of jurisprudential customs transcending the particularities of those different trade regimes. This cross-jurisdictional referencing practice, backed by jurisprudential convergence, is a critical element in forming a much broader dimension of 'customary international trade law' beyond GATT/WTO case law. In addition, trade tribunals normally take advantage of opportunities to make such reference in order to legitimize their own decisions by extracting certain normative implications from comparative case law. This tendency presupposes the implicit normative consciousness one thinks of in connection with *opinio juris*. In this regard, the construction of customary international trade law tends to reveal the track record of the global trading community, in which various trade regimes co-exist and interact, in the sense that customary international trade law evolved alongside the development and evolution of the community. In the absence of a central enforcement mechanism, customary international trade law represents a systemic

55. *See* EC TREATY, *supra* note 12, Introduction, art. 10.
56. *See Japanese Shochu II*, *supra* note 8, Chapter II, E (Status of Adopted Panel Reports).
57. *Id.*
58. *See The Great 1994 Sovereignty Debate*, *supra* note 203, Chapter II, at 180. For a more detailed analysis of the international law effects of a GATT dispute panel report, *see* John H. Jackson, *The Legal Meaning of a GATT Dispute Settlement Report: Some Reflections*, *in* TOWARD MORE EFFECTIVE SUPERVISION BY INTERNATIONAL ORGANIZATIONS: ESSAYS IN HONOR OF HENRY SCHERMERS 156–62 (vol. 1, 1994) [hereinafter *Some Reflections*].
59. *Id.*; *Japanese Shochu II*, *supra* note 8, Chapter II, ¶ E.
60. *See e.g.*, In the Matter of Cross-Border Trucking Services, USA-MEX-98-2008-01, The Final Report of NAFTA Arbitral Panel Established Pursuant to Chapter Twenty, Feb. 6, 2001, ¶ 214, *available at* <http://www.nafta-sec-alena.org/english/index.htm> (visited on April 19, 2001) (citing the WTO case law); In a NAFTA Arbitration under the UNCITRAL Arbitration Rules, S.D. Myers Inc. v. Canada, Partial Award, Nov. 13, 2000, para. 244, *available at* <http://www.appletonlaw.com/cases/Myers%20-%20Final%20Merits%20Award.pdf> (visited on April 19, 2001) (citing the WTO case law).

order of stability and predictability within the global trading community.[61] To put it differently, customary international trade law holds such 'durability and importance' that it receives legal support and eventually results in enhanced legal certainty which, in turn, contributes to establishing and maintaining coherence in the global trading community.[62]

Given that the foregoing two elements—'practice' and '*opinio juris*'—can be found in case law developed by international trade tribunals, we can construct customary international trade law on their basis.[63] In terms of an import ban, the GATT/WTO textually favors *de facto* discrimination over *de jure* discrimination via the interpretive note (Ad *Article III*).[64] This interpretive note plays a transmuting function.[65] Without it, all import bans would have fallen under Article XI, which is stricter and more canonical than Article III.[66] Yet, due to this note, an import ban,

---

61. *Cf.* Georg Schwarzenberger, '*International Jus Cogens?*,' 43 TEX. L. REV. 455, 476–477 (1965).
62. *Cf. International Society, supra* note 41, at 9–13. According to a 'Rational Choice' approach, the legal effect and support associated with 'compliance' derive from 'long-term self interest.' Goldsmith and Posner, *supra* note 48, at 658. Goldsmith and Posner conclude that customary international law is 'mostly aspirational' and that states regularly violate customary international law in the face of any pressing reason. *Id.*, at 672.
63. One important question remains concerning the legitimacy of cross-referencing between the customary international trade law developed in different institutional frameworks. For instance, it may be controversial whether customary international trade law developed in the GATT/WTO context is relevant to or can be applied in the context of the intra-Community trade, or *vice versa.* In the former case, it is still debatable whether the GATT/WTO treaties (and panels and the Appellate Body decisions) should have a *direct effect* in the EU legal system. However, as a Member of the WTO, the European Communities, like any other Member, is *de facto* forced to respect customary international trade law (case law) developed under the auspice of the GATT/WTO since the EC itself frequently invokes such case laws in cases in which it is a party concerned. In the latter case, although direct and express citations by the ECJ from the GATT/WTO jurisprudence are difficult to find, considering the long history of cross-fertilization between European and non-European trade specialists (officials and academics alike) it can be said that the ECJ trade jurisprudence has received a certain degree of influence from the GATT/WTO jurisprudence. This may explain why the convergence phenomenon is taking place between the *intra*-Europe trade regime and the GATT/WTO regime.
64. GATT 1994, *supra* note 2, Chapter II, Ad *Article III* ('Any internal tax or other internal charge, or any law, regulation or requirement of the kind referred to in paragraph 1 which applies to an imported product and to the like domestic product and is collected or enforced in the case of the imported product at the time or point of importation, is nevertheless to be regarded as an internal tax or other internal charge, or a law, regulation or requirement of the kind referred to in paragraph 1, and is accordingly subject to the provisions of Article III.')
65. *Canadian Alcoholic Drinks* (1992), *supra* note 23, Chapter II, ¶ 5.28. The Panel also examined minimum prices maintained for beer in certain provinces of Canada.

    > The Panel first examined whether the minimum prices fell under Article XI:1 or Article III:4. The Panel noted that according to the Note Ad Article III a regulation is subject to the provisions of Article III if it 'applies to an imported product and to the like domestic product' even if it is 'enforced in case of the imported product at the time or point of importation'. The Panel found that, as the minimum prices were applied to both imported and domestic beer, they fell, according to this Note under Article III.

    Id.
66. *Compare* GATT Article XI:1:

    > No prohibitions or restrictions other than duties, taxes or other charges, whether made effective through quotas, import or export licences or other measures, shall be instituted or maintained by any contracting party on the importation of any product of the territory of any other contracting party or on the exportation or sale for export of any product destined for the territory of any other contracting party

    with GATT Article III:4:

    > The products of the territory of any contracting party imported into the territory of any other

whose ground regulation applies equally to foreign and domestic products, can now fall under Article III, where violations are harder to establish *prima facie* than under Article XI.[67] Similarly, both the US and the EU jurisprudence tend to apply a more demanding threshold for measures that are explicitly or flatly discriminatory, and thus protectionist.[68] Under the ECJ jurisprudence, 'distinctively applicable' measures cannot fall under the *Cassis de Dijon* or *Keck* case law, and may only be justified by ex Article 36 EEC.[69] Likewise, under the US Dormant Commerce Clause jurisprudence, explicitly discriminatory state measures are subject to a '*per se* invalid' rule according to which such measures are quite difficult to justify.[70] In conclusion, based on these converging hermeneutical practices of trade tribunals under the GATT/WTO, the EU and the US system, the 'customs of international trade law' or 'customary international trade law' can be stated as follows:

- In the case of a 'distinctively applicable (de jure discriminatory)' regulation, such measure shall be invalid per se, constituting a strong prima facie case.[71]
- In the case of an 'indistinctively applicable' or 'de jure non-discriminatory' regulation, such measure shall be valid only when its regulatory process is consistent and evenhanded; otherwise, the measure shall be invalid as a de facto discrimination.[72]

5.2.2.4 Relationship

In terms of the relationship between *jus cogens* of international trade and customary international trade law, the latter tends to provide the former with a prototype or clue, while the former tends to be confirmed and evidenced by the latter. First of all, powerful theoretical support for this argument can be found in the doctrinal dimension of public international law: the relationship between *jus cogens* and customary international law. Despite the strong influence of the *jus naturale* concept at its inception, the doctrine of *jus cogens* has long been positivised, searching for the *lex lata* foundation.[73] In other words, the *jus cogens* derives 'not from a particular alien source but from the most common and general

---

cont.

contracting party shall be accorded treatment no less favourable than that accorded to like products of national origin in respect of all laws, regulations and requirements affecting their internal sale, offering for sale, purchase, transportation, distribution or use.

67. *See Japanese Leather* (1984), *supra* note 46, Chapter II, ¶ 44.
68. *See Aim and Effects*, *supra* note 29, Chapter II, at 62.
69. *See supra* sub-sec. 2.2.2, Chapter II.
70. *See supra* sub-sec. 2.2.3, Chapter II.
71. *See e.g.*, *Keck*, *supra* note 268, Chapter II, ¶ 15; *Oregon Waste*, *supra* note 325, Chapter II, at 99. In this situation, a complaining party is merely required to prove that a defending party maintains a distinctively applicable measure, at which point the burden of proof shifts to the defending party, which must in turn justify its measure by reference to legitimate policy objectives or to certain other tests such as proportionality.
72. *See e.g.*, *Keck*, *supra* note 268, Chapter II, ¶ 16; *Pike*, *supra* note 315, Chapter II, at 54.
73. *See* Danilenko, *supra* note 36, at 44–48.

sources of law,' including *custom*.[74] In the same vein, the Vienna Conference on the Law of Treaties reached a consensus that the rules of *jus cogens* could be acquired only from treaty or *custom*,[75] receiving the positivistic authentication through 'acceptance and recognition' by the international community as a whole.[76] This concept of 'acceptance and recognition,' which forms a critical element of *jus cogens*, is surprisingly associated with the *opinio juris* that molds customary international law.

On the other hand, *jus cogens* is configured by a certain legal community's 'object and purpose' (*telos*) and thus tends to be 'content-specific.' [77] *Jus cogens* acquires a specific substance depending upon the relevant subject-matter; this, in turn, determines the nature of each *jus cogens*.[78] It is under such content-specific *telos* that 'state practices' eventually embodying a specific custom tend to develop and evolve. In other words, a custom cannot but be influenced by and patterned after a particular *telos* and consequently, a corresponding *jus cogens*, which is atmospheric in a particular regime.[79] Therefore, it can be contended that *jus cogens* is confirmed and evidenced by subsequently emerging customs.

In sum, the relationship between *jus cogens* of international trade and customary international trade law is *non-hierarchical* and rather *interdependent*.

5.2.3 Manifestations of a *Jus Gentium* of International Trade on Domestic Regulation

A *jus gentium* of international trade on domestic regulation can find applications and manifestations in various dimensions. First of all, in the legislative dimension, we have witnessed in various legal documents from different trade regimes many procedural rules such as notification and reason-giving requirements that govern the interface between free trade and regulatory values.[80] This emerging 'administrative procedural law' aims to preempt any unilateral and arbitrary policy-making in the domestic context by checking, at every stage, the policy-making process by means of communication and feedback at the international level. Importantly, this administrative procedural law in the field of international trade concerns the *manner* in which a domestic regulation is adopted or applied, rather than the *content* of the regulation itself. Also in the EU context, the peremptory rule of anti-unilateralism and duty to cooperate is found in various procedural requirements of 'negotiation and consultation' included in secondary legislation for harmonization.[81] Even in the domestic context, a certain degree of 'incoherence' exists between competing policies, such as economic and social policies, and it is a paramount task of each government

---

74. *See* Nicaragua v. United States, 1986 I.C.J. 14, 100–1.
75. *Fundamental Principles*, *supra* note 39, at 210.
76. *See* Danilenko, *supra* note 36, at 46; Vienna Convention on the Law of Treaties, opened for signature May 23, 1969, 8 I.L.M. 679, art. 53 ('recognized and accepted by the international community as a whole') [hereinafter Vienna Convention].
77. *See supra* sub-sec. 5.2.2.1.
78. *Id.*
79. *See supra* note 41 ('*given* area of international relations') (emphasis added).
80. *See supra* sub-sec. 3.3.2, Chapter III.
81. *The Impact*, *supra* note 134, Chapter II, at 19, n.57.

to effectively reconcile such divergent pressures.[82] Critically, the 'tools of coherence' concern the *process* (*manner*) of policy-making, such as 'informed decision-making,' not the *content* of policies.[83] In sum, this administrative procedural law is a manifestation of the *jus gentium* of international trade on domestic regulation, which prohibits anti-unilateralism and obliges a trading nation to take 'external' interests into account in its 'internal' regulatory process.[84]

Moreover, in the implementational dimension, we have witnessed the recent legalization of types of 'developmental aid,' such as technical and financial assistance, that seek to bridge the 'capacity gap' by assisting needy Members in implementing certain harmonization agreements, such as the SPS and the TBT Agreements, which serve to reconcile the clash between free market and regulatory values. This emerging 'law of assistance' aims to provide 'tailor-made' packages of assistance for developing countries through a survey of their needs and an evaluation of existing international cooperation schemes. In the same vein, the WTO AB reports in *Gasoline* (1996) and *Shrimp-Turtle* (1998) emphasized that a developed country like the US should make every effort toward 'regulatory cooperation,' which would include certain kinds of assistance, in the regulatory interaction with developing countries.[85] This law of assistance—the 'first general law of nations' according to Vattel,[86]—is nothing but an expression of the 'duty to cooperate' embedded in the *jus gentium* of international trade.[87]

At a more practical level, with the idea of a *jus gentium* of international trade on domestic regulation that can be relied upon to reconcile *any* clash between free markets and state regulation, even a European state acquainted with the EU formula for reconciling such clash would be able to fine-tune its trade and regulatory policies in a manner that is more consistent with the WTO and the NAFTA regimes. Furthermore, a *jus gentium* of international trade, if fully developed and utilized, will provide a foreign producer headquartered in the EU with a choice between filing its complaint directly with the European Court of Justice to invalidate a discriminatory regulation by a European state, and persuading its home country to champion the complaint before the WTO panel. Under these circumstances, domestic and international judicial systems need not necessarily diverge, but could, under certain conditions, conceivably converge. Constructively, domestic judges could employ the relevant WTO or NAFTA jurisprudence in adjudicating international trade cases before them. They would not even need to follow this case law strictly, but could merely 'refer to' or even 'cite' it to support or reinforce their own judicial reasoning.

---

82. OECD, Building Policy Coherence, *available at* <www.oecd.org/puma/gvrnance/strat/coherence/htm> (last visited on Oct. 6, 1998).
83. *Id.*
84. *Cf.* Howse, *Democracy*, *supra* note 6, Chapter III, at 2356.
85. *Gasoline* (1996), AB Report, *supra* note 14, Introduction, at 27; *Shrimp-Turtle* (1998), AB Report, *supra* note 15, Introduction, ¶¶ 166–67.
86. *See supra* note 47.
87. *See Shrimp-Turtle* (1998), AB Report, *supra* note 15, Introduction, ¶ 164:

> 164. However, it is not acceptable, in international trade relations, for one WTO Member to use an economic embargo to *require* other Members to adopt essentially the same comprehensive regulatory program, to achieve a certain policy goal, as that in force within that Member's territory, *without* taking into consideration different conditions which may occur in the territories of those other Members. (emphasis original)

Domestic judges could possibly even contact WTO or NAFTA panelists and seek relevant legal advice from them to help to adjudicate their own cases. This rich judicial collaboration would contribute not only to more rational and acceptable domestic court rulings, but also eventually to a more appropriate and coherent implementation of a *jus gentium* of international trade in its judicial aspects.[88]

In conclusion, a *jus gentium* of international trade generates legitimacy in this highly integrative global marketplace in that it transcends narrow and overly contextualized legal doctrines which have, up to now, addressed the clash only in a specific institutional setting; as a consequence, this common legal precept serves to enhance the predictability of the global trading system as a whole. On the other hand, a *jus gentium* of international trade also involves the interpretation of international agreements by national courts. As Martin Rogoff observed, this involvement 'represents the efforts of the states to harmonize their actions and to settle their differences, as well as differences involving their nationals, on the basis of principles rather than politics.'[89] This enlarged 'legal enclave' eventually contributes to a more stable, predictable international trade order.[90]

5.3 Summary

In the broader context of international economic law, the clash between free markets and state regulation is not limited to the WTO system. Similar constitutional phenomena are occurring in other polities or institutions, such as the EU, the US and NAFTA, as well as within the domestic context.[91] While different vectors can be identified in the process of reconciling this clash according to the particular institutional characteristics of these various polities or institutions, such vectors tend to converge thanks to the ever-growing interaction among these entities, as well as to the inherent constitutional nature of the clash itself. Out of such convergence, a common legal precept can be formulated. Not surprisingly, this common legal precept is nothing but an inward-looking imperative crystallizing, on the one hand, general principles of law—namely, good faith or consistency—and reflecting, on the other, the integrative *telos* legitimizing the communitarian duty to cooperate. This common legal precept, which falls under the rubric of a '*jus gentium* of international trade,' consisting of a '*jus cogens* of international trade' and 'customary international trade law,' is not a recipe, but a *reference* for managing the abovementioned clash in the field of international economic law, no matter where such clash takes place geographically.

---

88. *But cf.* Sean C. Monaghan, *European Union Legal Personality Disorder: The Union's Legal Nature through the Prism of the German Federal Constitutional Court's Maastricht Decision*, 12 Emory Int'l L. Rev. 1443, 1444–45 (1998).
89. Rogoff, *supra* note 29, Chapter IV, at 684–85.
90. *Id.*
91. *See* Deborah Z. Cass, *The 'Constitutionalization' of International Trade Law: Judicial Norm-Generation as the Engine of Constitutional Development in International Trade*, 12 Eur. J. Int'l L. 39 (2001), (observing that international trade law 'shares some of the characteristics of national constitutional law').

CHAPTER V

Epilogue

'When one looks at the enormous accumulation of facts in the sciences of today and the extreme specialization on the part of scholars which this calls for, he can well wish for another Aristotle to organize the mass of unrelated information as to the phenomena of nature and reduce knowledge of it to a body of learning within the powers of comprehension of the ordinary man.

When one looks at the mass of detail of legal precept, the bulk of doctrine and commentary, and the overgrown detail or recorded judicial application in the law of today, and notes the cynical attitude toward these things on the part of the generation that is coming forward in the science of law, he can but wish for another Thomas Aquinas to adjust the actual to the ideal with the philosophical power, the juristic insight and the strength of ethical conviction of the Angelical Doctor.'[92]

92. Roscoe Pound, *The Idea of Law*, *in* JUBILEE LAW LECTURES 97 (1939).

Conclusion

Summary of the Thesis

This book seeks to diagnose challenges and to prescribe solutions for reconciling the clash between free markets and state regulation in international economic law. The book begins its analysis in Chapter I by describing a transformation in the *telos* of the global trading system, from the narrow 'anti-protectionist' emphasis of GATT 1947 toward the much broader vision of the WTO, with its focus on 'integration,' 'anti-unilateralism' and 'sustainable development.' Awareness of this critically important transformation informs much of the subsequent discussion, in terms of diagnosis as well as prescription. Chapter II examines the evolution of GATT jurisprudence to reconcile the clash, focusing on the Law of National Treatment (Article III:4), the Law of Market Access (Article XI:1) and the Law of Justification (Article XX). Chapter II identifies a strong 'pro-trade' bias in this line of GATT jurisprudence and problematizes such bias in terms of a 'dual crisis' involving both regulatory and trade failure. As a solution to this crisis, Chapter II then introduces a new line of jurisprudence under the WTO system—principally, the so-called 'chapeau' test highlighting the *manner* in which a domestic regulation is adopted or applied rather than the *substance* of the regulation itself—which offers considerable promise as a means for achieving the dual goals of free trade and regulatory autonomy. Yet, despite the potential benefits of this new jurisprudence, Chapter II points out that the pro-trade bias still remains due to a structural 'dichotomy' between general obligations such as National Treatment, and exceptions under Article XX, to which the chapeau belongs.

To bridge this dichotomy, Chapter III introduces the WTO's harmonization initiative and its derivative jurisprudence. Under this new approach, side agreements such as the SPS and the TBT Agreements become the tools of choice for addressing the dual objective of free markets and regulatory autonomy. In these side agreements, concerns such as protection of human health and safety, which were treated as troublesome exceptions under GATT Article XX, are recognized as legitimate policy objectives and converted into autonomous *rights* of Members. Recognition of these rights is matched by imposition of various 'process-oriented' *obligations*, which mirror the aforementioned chapeau test. In sum, Chapter III demonstrates that the pursuit of the dual ideal of free trade and autonomous state regulation is treated in a more intellectually sophisticated and balanced fashion under the side agreements than under the GATT.

Chapter IV then deals with the 'domestic' issue of compliance and implementation under which the detailed behavioral changes must take place in order to execute those prescriptions to the dual crisis that the GATT/WTO jurisprudence and agreements offer. Chapter IV begins by addressing fairly broad, long-term issues of implementation and nationalization before moving on to consideration of relatively more narrow, short-term issues related to the post-adjudicative acceptance by a losing party of a given panel or AB decision. Finally, Chapter V surveys the phenomenon of convergence between the WTO and other representative polities and institutions, which may be observed to the extent that the management of the interface between free markets and state regulation is sought through treaties, jurisprudence and implementation of rules and regulations. In the context of such convergence, the final Chapter proposes a '*jus gentium* of international trade on domestic regulations' as a common legal precept that is capable of guiding, in a coherent and integrative way, the reconciliation of the clash between free markets and state regulations within the far-reaching field of international economic law, a precept that encompasses not only the WTO, but also other polities and institutions, such as the EU, the US and NAFTA.

Building up infrastructure for a new international economic law

A *jus gentium* of international trade that is discussed in this book can be analogized to computer software. Anyone who has tried to run a 'state of the art' program on an old computer can confirm that, no matter how elegant and sophisticated a piece of software may be, it will only run properly on equally well-functioning hardware. Accordingly, if the global trading community is to enjoy the full functionality of its 'software'—that is, a *jus gentium* of international trade—it must first invest considerable resources, including political capital, in upgrading its 'hardware.' For instance, trade infrastructure such as the WTO Secretariat, is seriously understaffed and underbudgeted. This must be corrected if the 'software' is to operate effectively.

Furthermore, we need more comprehensive educational programs to disperse knowledge and information about international trade law. Most ordinary people continue to believe that international trade law consists of a mass of special codes and jargon only comprehended by a limited group of trade specialists.[1] Even among lawyers and legal scholars, international trade law can seem like an impossibly abstruse and technical subject. To the extent that it retains these arcane and esoteric features, international trade law cannot be informed, understood or used in the intended manner. Additionally, misunderstanding regarding the nature of international trade law ultimately hurts its legitimacy. Therefore, greater efforts should be exerted to introduce and teach international trade law to non-specialists in an accessible yet systematic manner. This task would be greatly facilitated by compilation of a 'Restatement of International Trade Law.' In the same vein, an

1. *Cf.* PETER GOODRICH, LEGAL DISCOURSE: STUDIES IN LINGUISTICS, RHETORIC AND LEGAL ANALYSIS 7 (1987) (arguing that 'legal practice and legal language are structured in such a way as to prevent the acquisition of such knowledge by any other than a highly trained elite of specialists in the various domains of legal study'); BERNARD S. JACKSON, SEMIOTICS AND LEGAL THEORY 286 (1985) (observing that the 'audience, or *groupe sémiotique*' of judicial discourse is relatively restricted).

increase in the number of academic hubs for education in international trade law, based on the models of the European University Institute in Florence or the Hague International Law Academy, will contribute much to the training of more and better-qualified trade lawyers and scholars.[2]

Epilogue: Seattle, New York and beyond

The Seattle Ministerial Meeting in December 1999 was supposed to be another constitutional moment for the global trading community, however, it turned out to be a moment of failure. Bold aspirations of launching what might have been called the 'Clinton Round,' a grand new series of trade negotiation sessions tantamount to the Uruguay Round, came to naught allegedly due to 'inadequate planning and irresolvable political conflict.'[3] Much post-mortem fault-finding has followed this debacle.[4] Yet, the Seattle debacle was not completely devoid of significance for the future development of the global trading system. It did spotlight the *dramatis personae* in the international trade arena as well as the fact that these players, old (developed and developing countries) and new (NGOs), have markedly different agendas. Some developed countries and NGOs found their policy priority in the so-called 'northern' agenda reflecting concerns related to the environment and biodiversity, while many developing countries supported the so-called 'southern' agenda focusing on market access, debt relief and technical assistance.[5] Ultimately, the failure to bridge the gap between these interests led to the fiasco in Seattle, which vividly demonstrated that the global trading community still remains within the clutches of the dual crisis of regulatory and trade failure. We have not yet reached the Promised Land.

However, the global trading community must not be hijacked by this single unfortunate event. Although greater efforts in these and other directions may be required, the persistence of the dual crisis should not be allowed unduly to chip away at all the hard-fought achievements under the WTO system. Therefore, an enhanced level of compliance and implementation, taking into account the existence of a capacity gap among trading partners, is necessary to make the most of those achievements and thus to successfully manage the interface of free markets and state regulation. Yet, in the course of such enhanced efforts, the global trading community

---

2. As a propitious example of such educational hub, *see* Academy of International Trade Law, The Macau Institute of European Studies, *available at* <www.ieem.org.mo/courses/academy2/index.html> (last visited on Nov. 6, 2001).
3. *See* Robert G. Kaiser & John Burgess, *A Seattle Premier: How Not to Hold WTO Talks*, THE WASH. POST, Dec. 12, 1999, at A 40.
4. Many pointed accusing fingers at then-US President Clinton who, it was alleged, used the forum to play *domestic* politics. *See id.* Clinton apparently wished to mollify organized labor while preserving his own political capital for use in the fight over Chinese accession to the WTO. *See* Sylvia Ostry, *Making Sense of It All: A Post-Mortem on the Meaning of Seattle*, *in* SEATTLE, THE WTO, AND THE FUTURE OF THE MULTILATERAL TRADING SYSTEM 81–2 (Roger B. Porter & Pierre Sauvé eds., 2000).
5. WTO, Symposium on Issues Confronting the World Trading System: Summary Reports By the Moderators, Session III: Trade and Environment, *available at* <www.wto.org/English/forums_e/ngo_symp2001_repenvir_e.htm> (visited on July 15, 2001).

must pay special attention to one critical parameter, the ever-growing global interdependence, which has the potential to reshape the contours of trade governance in a form 'appropriate to the world we live in, not the one that we survived.'[6]

This heightened interdependency tends to transform the nature of the 'interface' of free market values and state regulatory intervention. In other words, the conventional approach to this interface has been *negative*, represented by such terms as 'clash' or 'conflict.' This negative perspective on the interface often leads to a 'dialogue of the deaf,'[7] such as 'free trade versus labor standards,' and eventually begets zero-sum reconciliation because trade and regulatory values are likely to end up canceling or offsetting each other under clashing or conflicting situations. In view of the ever-growing interdependency in the contemporary international trade landscape, this zero-sum effect, if it is allowed to become widespread, will add no net value to the global trading system.

Therefore, the global trading community should take the more audacious step of adopting a *positive* perspective on the interface in order to transform international trade into a 'positive-sum' game.[8] As the former WTO Director-General Renato Ruggiero once commented, economic growth geared by international trade tends to favor 'advancing environmental protection, improving social conditions, or sustaining ethical values.'[9] On the other hand, a domestic regulatory reform may boost trade through eliminating unnecessary barriers. This potentially synergistic aspect of the interface of trade and regulation truly embodies the new *telos* of the WTO having 'larger implications' that 'go beyond the parameters of trade.'[10] Only through such an approach will it be possible for the global trading community to 'widen the winner's circle.'[11]

Another phenomenon that the above-mentioned interdependency encourages is the development of a common trade language,[12] i.e., a '*jus gentium* of international

---

6. *Man and Governance*, WALL ST. J., Dec. 31, 1999, at A 10.
7. Renato Ruggiero, A Shared Responsibility: Global Policy Coherence for Our Global Age, Address before the Conference on 'Globalization as a Challenge for German Business: Export Opportunities for Small and Medium-Sized Companies in the Environmental Field (Bonn, Dec. 9, 1997), *available at* <www.wto.org/english/news_e/sprr_e/bonn_e.htm> (last visited on July 20, 2001).
8. *Cf.* United Nation Environmental Program (UNEP), *Global Environment Outlook (GEO) 2000*, *available at* <http://www.grida.no/geo2000/aps-asiapacific/> (last visited on Mar. 19, 2001) (discussing the so-called 'Kuznetz Curve').
9. *Id.*
10. Renato Ruggiero, Beyond the Multilateral Trading System, Address before the 20th Seminar on International Security, Politics and Economics Institut pour les Hautes Etudes Internationales (Geneva, April 12, 1999), *available at* <www.wto.org/english/news_e/sprr_e/ih_e.htm> (last visited on July 20, 2001).
11. Anna Bernasek, *Free Trade's Weak Spot*, FORTUNE, Dec. 20, 1999, at 57 (quoting New York Times columnist Thomas Friedman).
12. This common language is analogous to a 'reference,' rather than a 'recipe.' Since I conceptualize the international trading community in terms of a pluralistic structure, a 'recipe' that requires only a single way of construction or interpretation in every trade regime runs counter to the idea of *jus gentium* of international trade proposed here. I am indebted to Mary-Anne Glendon for this 'reference versus recipe' analogy. She argues that 'cultural relativism' is misdirected since it implies just one way of understanding human rights in spite of the fact that understanding human rights should be 'pluralistic' based on a universal 'reference,' which guarantees richness and variety. Mary-Anne Glendon, *Confucian Contribution to the Universal Declaration of Human Rights*, Speech at East Asian Legal Studies, Harvard Law School, delivered on October 20, 1999.

trade' as a way of addressing the interface between trade and regulation. As Professor John Jackson has pointedly observed, the more globalized and interdependent economy that we now face suggests a 'need to *unify* the *rules* applying to all market participants, where they may be.'[13] Importantly, this *jus gentium* of international trade has the capacity to generate its legitimacy in this highly integrative global marketplace because it transcends narrow and overly contextualized legal doctrines which have, up to now, addressed the interface only in particular institutional settings. As a consequence, this common legal precept may serve to enhance the predictability of the global trading system as a whole. Finally, the most critical contribution of the idea of a *jus gentium* of international trade to the legitimacy of the global trading community derives from its 'inclusive bases of legitimation.'[14] This inclusiveness transcends the hoary and parochial concept of sovereignty, along with its legacy of *jus feciale*,[15] both of which tend to nurture fragmentation or alienation among trading partners, thereby undermining further their own relevance in an ever-interdependent global marketplace.

In closing, it is high time that we looked around where we stand. Even before the scars of Seattle heal, the global trading community has become engulfed by unprecedented turbulence and uncertainty. The current turmoil from which the world is now suffering undoubtedly exceeds a mere dimension of 'trade,' yet at the same time tends to discourage even more and chill all international trade activities. Nonetheless, we must not jettison the critical historical lesson that trade tends to facilitate and sustain peace by interlocking states in businesses, as Emanuel Kant also observed.[16] History verified its own lesson in the US pre-Constitution experience as well as the Europe's Community-building saga. Against the backdrop of this timeless lesson, a *jus gentium* of international trade will guide, protect and even nourish international trade activities in this pessimistic era through its comprehensive, integrationist and thus powerful legal quality. It should not be another hollow Ideatypus unable to fulfill its promise in the face of hard political, social, and economic realities. Instead, it should be not only a philosophical but practical expedient to take us to the best status as closely as possible, though not to perfection.

---

13. *Fragmentation or Unification*, *supra* note 53, Chapter V, at 824. (emphasis added) *See also* Ernst-Ulrich Petersmann, *The Transformation of the World Trading System through the 1994 Agreement Establishing the World Trade Organization*, 6 EUR. J. INT'L L 161, 189 (1995) (arguing that the 1994 WTO Agreement 'completes the original design of the Bretton Woods system' and 'reduces the existing fragmentation of international economic law, by a "global integration law" for international movements of goods, services, persons, investments and payments'). In addition, such common legal language of trade, in turn expedites a 'trans-judicial' communication not only among trade tribunals, but also across national courts that want to benefit from nourishing experiences of cross-fertilization. *See* Anne-Marie Slaughter, *Judicial Globalization*, 40 VA. J. INT'L L. 1103, 1107 (2000).
14. John Gerard Ruggie, *Territoriality and Beyond: Problematizing Modernity in International Relations*, 47 INT. ORG. 139, 151 (1993).
15. *Jus feciale* or *jus fetiale* means the 'law of negotiation and diplomacy,' and embodies the classical notion of international law. BLACK'S LAW DICTIONARY 865 (7th ed. 1999).
16. Immanuel Kant, *Perpetual Peace: A Philosophical Sketch (1795)*, *in* KANT'S POLITICAL WRITINGS 93, 114 (Hans Reiss ed., H.B. Nisbet trans., 2d ed. 1991). *See also* Fernando R. Tesón, *The Kantian Theory of International Law*, 92 COLUM. L. REV. 53, 76–7 (1992) (observing that 'Kant's views have been confirmed by the success of the European Economic Community and even by the global system of international trade regulated by GATT and similar institutions').

The global trading community must move on and embrace a *jus gentium* of international trade because trade promotes *welfare* and thus prevents *warfare*. This is still true, and most critically, that is where our future lies.[17]

17. *Cf.* Jonathan I. Charney, *Universal International Law*, 87 AM. J. INT'L L. 529, 532 (1993) (arguing that 'the international legal system is supported not only by states' interests in promoting individual rules, but also by their interests in preserving and promoting the system as a whole').

Selected Bibliography

ABBOTT, FREDERICK M., LAW AND POLICY OF REGIONAL INTEGRATION: THE NAFTA AND WESTERN HEMISPHERIC INTEGRATION IN THE WORLD TRADE ORGANIZATION SYSTEM (1995).

Abbott, Frederick M., *The Enduring Enigma of TRIPs: A Challenge for the World Economic System*, 1 J. INT'L ECON. L. 497 (1998).

Ackerman, Bruce A., *The Storrs Lectures: Discovering the Constitution*, 93 YALE L. J. 1013, 1071 (1984); Bruce A. Ackerman, *Constitutional Politics / Constitutional Law*, 99 YALE L. J. 453 (1989).

Ackerman, Bruce, *The Rise of World Constitutionalism*, 83 VA. L. REV. 771 (1997).

Alford, William P., *Intellectual Property, Trade and Taiwan: A GATT-Fly's View*, 1992 COLUM. BUS. L. REV. 97 (1992).

Alford, William P., *Introduction: The North American Free Trade Agreement and the Need for Candor*, 34 HARV. INT'L L. J. 293 (1993).

Alford, William P., *Making the World Safer for What?: Intellectual Property Rights, Human Rights and Foreign Economic Policy in the Post-European Cold War World*, 29 N. Y. U. J. INT'L L. & POL. 135 (1996–97).

Alford, William P., *On the Limits of 'Grand Theory' in Comparative Law*, 61 WASH. L. REV. 945 (1986).

ALFORD, WILLIAM P., TO STEAL A BOOK IS AN ELEGANT OFFENSE: INTELLECTUAL PROPERTY LAW IN CHINESE CIVILIZATION (1995).

Allott, Philip, *The Concept of International Law*, 10 EUR. J. INT'L L. 31 (1999).

Alvarez, Jose E., *Why Nations Behave*, 19 MICH. J. INT'L L. 303 (1998).

Aman, Jr., Alfred C., *A Global Perspective on Current Regulatory Reforms: Rejection, Relocation, or Reinvention?*, 2 IND. J. GLOBAL LEGAL STUD. 429 (1995).

Arnull, Anthony, *The European Court and Judicial Objectivity: A Reply to Professor Hartley*, 112 L. Q. REV. 411 (1996).

Aronson, Jonathan D. & Peter F. Cowhey, *Prospects for Post-Uruguay Round Trade Management*, 4 TRANSNAT'L L. & CONTEMP. PROBS. 47 (1994).

Atik, Jeffrey, *Science and International Regulatory Convergence*, 17 NW. J. INT'L L. & BUS. 736 (1996–97).

Bal, Salman, *International Free Trade Agreements and Human Rights: Reinterpreting Article XX of the GATT*, 10 MINN. J. GLOBAL TRADE 62 (2001).

Balkin, J.M. & Sanford Levinson, *The Canons of Constitutional Law*, 111 HARV. L. REV. 963 (1998).

BATRA, RAVI, THE MYTH OF FREE TRADE (1993).

Bello, Judith Hippler, *The WTO Dispute Settlement Understanding: Less Is More*, 90 AM. J. INT'L L. 416 (1996).

BENINGTON, JOHN, LOCAL DEMOCRACY AND THE EUROPEAN UNION: THE IMPACT OF EUROPEANIZATION ON LOCAL GOVERNANCE (1994).

Berkey, Judson O., *The Regulation of Genetically Modified Foods*, ASIL INSIGHT(Oct. 1999), *available at* <http://www.asil.org/insigh37.htm>.

BHAGWATI, JAGDISH, A STREAM OF WINDOWS: UNSETTLING REFLECTIONS ON TRADE, IMMIGRATION AND DEMOCRACY (1998).

Bignami, Francesca E., *The Democratic Deficit in European Community Rulemaking: A Call for Notice and Comment in Comitology*, 40 HARV. INT'L L. J. 451 (1999).

Bilder, Richard B., *International Dispute Settlement and the Role of Adjudication, in* THE INTERNATIONAL COURT OF JUSTICE AT A CROSSROAD (L. F. Damrosch ed., 1987).

Bodansky, Daniel, *The Legitimacy of International Governance: A Coming Challenge for International Environmental Law?*, 93 AM. J. INT'L L. 596 (1999).

Bower, Jennifer K., *Hogs and Their Keepers: Rethinking Local Power on the Iowa Countryside*, 4 GREAT PLAINS NAT. RESOURCES J. 261 (2000).

Brand, Ronald A., *Direct Effect of International Economic Law in the United States and the European Union*, 17 NW. J. INT'L L. & BUS. 556 (1996–97).

Brand, Ronald A., *Semantic Distinctions in an Age of Legal Convergence*, 17 U. PA. J. INT'L ECON. L. 3 (1996).

Braun, Michael & Leigh Parker, *Trade in Culture: Consumable Product or Cherished Articulation of a Nation's Soul?*, 22 DENV. J. INT'L L. & POL'Y 155 (1993).

BROWNLIE, IAN, PRINCIPLES OF PUBLIC INTERNATIONAL LAW (5th ed. 1998).

Burtless, Gary et al eds., GLOBAPHOBIA: CONFRONTING FEARS ABOUT OPEN TRADE (1998).

Cappelletti, Maruo & David Golay, *The Judicial Branch in the Federal and Transnational Union: Its Impact on Integration, in* INTEGRATION THROUGH LAW: EUROPE AND THE AMERICAN FEDERAL EXPERIENCE, METHODS, TOOLS AND INSTITUTIONS (VOL. I), POLITICAL ORGANS, INTEGRATION TECHNIQUES AND JUDICIAL PROCESS (bk. 2, Maruo Cappelletti et al eds., 1985).

Cappelletti, Mauro et al., *Preface, in* POLITICAL ORGANS, INTEGRATION TECHNIQUES AND JUDICIAL PROCESS (BK. 2), METHODS, TOOLS AND INSTITUTIONS (VOL. I), INTEGRATION THROUGH LAW: EUROPEAN AND THE AMERICAN FEDERAL EXPERIENCE, PT. I, VOL. 1 (Mauro Cappelletti et al. eds. 1988).

Cappelletti, Mauro, *Forward to the Florence Integration Project Series in* A POLITICAL, LEGAL AND ECONOMIC OVERVIEW (BOOK I), METHODS, TOOLS AND INSTITUTIONS (VOLUME I), INTEGRATION THROUGH LAW: EUROPEAN AND THE AMERICAN FEDERAL EXPERIENCE (Mauro Cappelletti et al eds. 1985).

Cappelletti, Mauro, *Is the European Court of Justice 'Running Wild'?*, 12 EUR. L. REV. 3 (1987).

Cassese, Antonio & Joseph H. H. Weiler eds., CHANGE AND STABILITY IN INTERNATIONAL LAW-MAKING (1988).

Chang, H. F., *An Economic Analysis of Trade Measures to Protect the Global Environment*, 83 GEO. L. J. 2131 (1995).

Charney, Jonathan I., *Third Party Dispute Settlement and International Law*, 36 COLUM. J. TRANSNAT'L L. 65 (1997).

Charney, Jonathan I., *Universal International Law*, 87 AM. J. INT'L L. 529 (1993).

Charnovitz, Steve, *The Supervision of Health and Biosafety Regulation by World Trade Rules*, 13 TUL. ENVTL. L. J. 271 (2000).

CHAYES, ABRAM & ANTONIA HANDLER CHAYES, THE NEW SOVEREIGNTY: COMPLIANCE WITH INTERNATIONAL REGULATORY AGREEMENTS (1995).

CHENG, BIN, GENERAL PRINCIPLES OF LAW AS APPLIED BY INTERNATIONAL COURTS AND TRIBUNALS (1987).

Cheng, Bin, *The Contribution of Air and Space Law to the Development of International Law*, 34 CURRENT LEGAL PROBS 181 (1981).

Choi, Stephen J. & Andrew T. Guzman, *Portable Reciprocity: Rethinking the International Reach of Securities Regulation*, 71 S. CAL. L. REV. 903 (1998).

Church, John M., *A Market Solution to Green Marketing: Some Lessons from the Economics of Information*, 79 MINN. L. REV. 245 (1994).

Clark, Bradford R., *Federal Common Law: A Structural Reinterpretation*, 144 U. PA. L. REV. 1245 (1996).

Clavin, Patrica, *The Triumph of Regionalism over Globalism: Patterns of Trade in the Interwar Period, in* REGIONAL TRADE BLOCS, MULTILATERALISM, AND THE GATT: COMPLEMENTARY PATHS TO FREE TRADE (Till Geiger & Dennis Kennedy eds., 1996).

Cleveland, Sarah H., *Norm Internalization and US Economic Sanctions*, 26 YALE J. INT'L L. 1 (2001).

Cottier, Thomas & Krista Nadakavukaren Schefer, *The Relationship between World Trade Organization Law, National and Regional Law*, 1 J. INT'L ECON. L. 83, (1998).

Cottier, Thomas, *The Impact of New Technologies on Multilateral Trade Regulations and Governance*, 72 CHI.-KENT L. REV. 415 (1996).

Cottier, Thomas, *The WTO and Environmental Law: Some Issues and Ideas, Trade & Development Center Essay Series, available at* <http://www.itd.org/issues/essay1.htm>.

Cover, Robert M., *Nomos and Narrative in* NARRATIVE, VIOLENCE, AND THE LAW: THE ESSAYS OF ROBERT COVER (Martha Minow et al eds., 1992).

CRAIG, PAUL & GRÁINNE DE BÚRCA, EU LAW: TEXT, CASES AND MATERIALS (2d. 1998).

Croley, Steven P. & John H. Jackson, *WTO Dispute Procedures, Standard of Review, and Deference to National Governments*, 90 AM. J. INT'L L. 193 (1996).

Cullet, Philippe, *Differential Treatment in International Law: Towards a New Paradigm of Inter-State Relations*, 10 EUR. J. INT'L L. 549 (1999).

D'AMATO, ANTHONY A., THE CONCEPT OF CUSTOM IN INTERNATIONAL LAW (1971). DAM, KENNETH W., THE GATT: LAW AND INTERNATIONAL ECONOMIC ORGANIZATION (1970).

Danilenko, Gennady M., *International Jus Cogens: Issues of Law-Making*, 2 EUR. J. INT'L L. 42 (1991).

Davey, William J., *Dispute Settlement in GATT*, 11 FORDHAM INT'L L.J. 51 (1987). DAVID, RENE, ARBITRATION IN INTERNATIONAL TRADE (1985).

Davis, Mark David, *Multilateral and Regional Efforts to Integrate Markets: The Uruguay Round, NAFTA, Asia Pacific Economic Cooperation Initiatives and the European Community*, 87 AM. SOC'Y INT'L L. PROC. 340 (1993).

De Lange, Roel, *General Aspects of the Horizontalization of Law Enforcement in a European Perspective, in* COMPLIANCE AND ENFORCEMENT OF EUROPEAN COMMUNITY LAW (J.A.E. Vervaele et al. eds. 1999).

De Wet, E., *Labor Standards in the Globalized Economy: The Inclusion of a Social Clause in the General Agreement on Tariffs and Trade/World Trade Organization*, 17 HUM. RTS. Q. 443 (1995).

Dehousse, Renaud, *Comparing National and EC Law: The Problem of the Level of Analysis*, 42 AM. J. COMP. L. 761 (1994).

Dehousse, Renaud, *Regulation by Networks in the European Community: The Role of European Agencies*, 4 J. EUR. PUB. POL'Y 246 (1997).

Dittman, Lisa, Overfiling: *Policy Arguments in Support of the Gorilla in the Closet*, 48 UCLA L. REV. 375 (2000).

Donahue, Alexander M., *Equivalence: Not Quite Close Enough for the International Harmonization of Environmental Standards*, 30 ENVTL. L. 363 (2000).

Downs et al., George W., *Is the Good News about Compliance Good News about Ccooperation?*, 50 INT'L ORG. 379 (1996).

DOXEY, MARGARET P., INTERNATIONAL SANCTIONS IN CONTEMPORARY PERSPECTIVE (1987).

Dubinsky, Paul R., *The Essential Function of Federal Courts: The European Union and the United States Compared*, 42 AM. J. COMP. L. 295 (1994).

Dunoff, Jeffrey L., *'Trade And': Recent Developments in Trade Policy and Scholarship—And Their Surprising Political Implications*, 17 NW. J. INT'L L. & BUS. 759 (1996–7).

Dunoff, Jeffrey L., *The Death of the Trade Regime*, 10 EUR. J. INT'L L. 733 (1999).
Dupuy, Pierre-Marie, *The Place and Role of Unilateralism in Contemporary International Law*, 11 EUR. J. INT'L L. 19 (2000).
DWORKIN, RONALD M., LAW'S EMPIRE (1986).
Eeckhout, Piet, *The Domestic Legal Status of the WTO Agreement: Interconnecting Legal Systems*, 34 COMMON MKT. L. REV. 11 (1997).
Egan, Michelle and Dieter Wolf, *Regulation and Comitology: The EC Committee System in Regulatory Perspective*, 4 COLUM. J. EUR. L. 499 (1998).
Esty, Daniel C. & Damien Geradin, *Market Access, Competitiveness, and Harmonization: Environmental Protection in Regional Trade Agreements*, 21 HARV. ENVTL. L. REV. 265 (1997).
Fallon, Jr., Richard H., *Forward: Implementing the Constitution*, 111 HARV. L. REV. 56 (1997).
Fallon, Jr., Richard H.., *As-Applied and Facial Challenges and Third-Party Standing*, 113 HARV. L. REV. 1321 (2000).
Farber, Daniel A. & Robert E. Hudec, *Free Trade and the Regulatory State: A GATT's Eye View of the Dormant Commerce Clause*, 47 VAND. L. REV. 1401 (1994).
Feketekuty, Geza, *The Scope, Implication and Economic Rationale of a Competition-Oriented Approach to Future Multilateral Trade Negotiations* 2–4, OECD, TD/TC(96)9, Feb. 15, 1996.
Fidler, David P., *Challenging the Classical Concept of Custom: Perspectives on the Future of Customary International Law*, 39 GERMAN YEARBOOK OF INT'L L. 198 (1996).
Fidler, David P., *Neither Science Nor Shamans: Globalization of Markets and Health in the Developing World*, 7 IND. J. GLOBAL LEGAL STUD. 191 (1999).
Finlayson, Jock A. & Mark W. Zacher, *The GATT and the Regulation of Trade Barriers: Regime Dynamics and Functions*, 35 INT'L ORG. 273 (1981).
Fisher, Louis, Book Review, 16 J. LEGAL EDUC. 135 (1996) (reviewing MARTIN H. REDISH, THE CONSTITUTION AS POLITICAL STRUCTURE (1995)).
FISHER, ROGER, IMPROVING COMPLIANCE WITH INTERNATIONAL LAW (1981).
Fitzgerald, Brian F., *Trade-Based Constitutionalisms: The Framework for Universalizing Substantive International Law?*, 5 U. MIAMI Y. B. INT'L L. 111 (1996–97).
Fontaine, Fascal, A New Idea for Europe: The Schuman Declaration - 1950–2000, *available at* <http://europa.eu.int/comm/dg10/publications/brochures/docu/50ans/txt01_en.html>.
Fox, Eleanor M., *Toward World Antitrust and Market Access*, 91 AM. J. INT'L L. 1 (1997).
Fox, Sean T., *Responding to Climate Change: The Case for Unilateral Trade Measures to Protect the Global Atmosphere*, 84 GEO. L.J. 2499 (1996).
FRANCK, THOMAS M., THE POWER OF LEGITIMACY AMONG NATIONS (1990).
Friedman, Barry, *Valuing Federalism*, 82 MINN. L. REV. 317 (1997).
FRIEDMANN, WOLFGANG, THE CHANGING STRUCTURE OF INTERNATIONAL LAW (1964).
Friedmann, Wolfgang, *The Uses of 'General Principles' in the Development of International Law*, *in* INTERNATIONAL LAW IN THE TWENTIETH CENTURY (Leo Gross ed. 1969).
Fuller, Lon L., *The Forms and Limits of Adjudication*, 92 HARV. L. REV. 353 (1978).
Fulton, Scott C. & Lawrence I. Sperling, *The Network of Environmental Enforcement and Compliance Cooperation in North America and the Western Hemisphere*, 30 INT'L LAW. 111 (1996).
Gabriel, Russell & Louis B. Sohn, *Equity in International Law*, 82 AM. SOC'Y INT'L L. PROC. 277 (1988).
Garcia, Frank. J., *Trade and Inequality: Economic Justice and the Developing World*, 21 MICH. J. INT'L L. 975 (2000).
Goldsmith, Jack L. & Eric A. Posner, *Understanding the Resemblance between Modern and Traditional Customary International Law*, 40 VA. J. INT'L L. 639 (2000).
Goldsmith, Jack, *Sovereignty, International Relations Theory, and International Law*, 52 STAN. L. REV. 959 (2000) (reviewing STEPHEN D. KRASNER, ORGANIZED HYPOCRISY (1999)).

Goodman, Richard M. & John M. Frost, *International Economic Agreements and the Constitution*, The Institute for International Economics Working Paper (No. 00–2) 2 (2000), *available at* <http://207.238.152.36/CATALOG/WP/2000/00-2.pdf>.

Goodrich, Peter, Legal Discourse: Studies in Linguistics, Rhetoric and Legal Analysis (1987).

Gormley, Laurence W., Prohibiting Restrictions on Trade within the EEC: The Theory and Application of Articles 30–36 of the EEC Treaty (1985).

Gormley, Laurence W., *Two Years After Keck*, 19 Fordham Int'l L.J. 866 (1996).

Griesgraber, Marie & Bernhard G. Gunter eds., World Trade: Toward Fair and Free Trade in the Twenty-First Century (1997).

Haas, Peter, *Introduction: Epistemic Communities and International Policy Coordination*, 46 Int. Org. 1 (1992).

Habermas, Jürgen, Between Facts and Norms (William Rehg trans., MIT Press 1998) (1996).

Hartley, Trevor C., *The European Court, Judicial Objectivity and the Constitution of the European Union*, 112 L. Q. Rev. 95 (1996).

Hay, Peter, Federalism and Supranational Organization: Patterns for New Legal Structures (1966).

Held, David et al. eds., Global Transformation: Politics, Economics and Culture (1999).

Helfer, Laurence R. & Anne-Marie Slaughter, *Toward a Theory of Effective Supranational Adjudication*, 107 Yale L. J. 273 (1997).

Henkin, Louis, How Nations Behave (2d ed. 1979).

H^{3}ritier, Adrienne et al., Ringing the Change in Europe: Regulatory Competition and the Transformation of the State (1996).

Hilf, Meinhard, *The ECJ's Opinion 1/94 on the WTO—No Surprise, but Wise?*, 6 Eur. J. Int'l L 245 (1995).

Hilf, Meinhard, *The Role of National Courts in International Trade Relations*, 18 Mich. J. Int'l L. 321 (1997).

Hines, Colin, Localization: A Global Manifesto (2000).

Howse, Robert & Donald Regan, *The Product/Process Distinction—An Illusionary Basis for Disciplining 'Unilateralism' in Trade Policy*, 11 Eur. J. Int'l L. 249 (2000).

Howse, Robert & Kalypso Nicolaidis, *Legitimacy and Global Governance: Why Constitutionalizing the WTO is a Step Too Far* (Conference Paper presented in Harvard Kennedy School of Government on Jun. 1–2, 2000).

Howse, Robert & Petros C. Mavroidis, *Europe's Evolving Regulatory Strategy for GMOs—The Issue of Consistency with WTO Law: Of Kine and Brine*, 24 Fordham Int'l L. J. 317 (2000).

Howse, Robert, *Adjudicative Legitimacy and Treaty Interpretation in International Trade Law: The Early Years of WTO Jurisprudence*, *in* The EU, the WTO, and the NAFTA: Towards a Common Law of International Trade? 41–42 (Joseph H. H. Weiler ed. 2000).

Howse, Robert, *Democracy, Science, and Free Trade: Risk Regulation on Trial at the World Trade Organization*, 98 Mich. L. Rev. 2329, 2331 (2000).

Howse, Robert, *Managing the Interface between International Trade Law and the Regulatory State: What Lessons Should (and Should Not) Be Drawn from the Jurisprudence of the United States Dormant Commerce Clause*, *in* Regulatory Barriers and the Principle of Non-Discrimination in World Trade Law (Thomas Cottier & Petros C. Mavroidis eds. 2000).

Hudec, Robert E., *GATT Dispute Settlement after the Tokyo Round: An Unfinished Business*, 13 Cornell Int'l L.J. 145 (1980).

Hudec, Robert E., *GATT/WTO Constraints on National Regulation: Requiem for an 'Aim and Effects' Test*, 32 Int'l Law. 619 (1998).

Hudec, Robert E., *Reforming GATT Adjudication Procedures: The Lessons of the DISC Case*, 72 MINN. L. REV. 1443 (1988).

Hudec, Robert E., *The Expedition to Darkest Geneva*, 20 MICH. J. INT'L L. 121 (1999).

HUDEC, ROBERT E., THE GATT LEGAL SYSTEM AND WORLD TRADE DIPLOMACY (2d ed. 1990).

Hudec, Robert E., *The GATT Legal System: A Diplomat's Jurisprudence*, 4 J. WORLD TRADE L. 615 (1970).

Hudec, Robert E., *The Judicialization of GATT Dispute Settlement*, *in* IN WHOSE INTEREST?: DUE PROCESS AND TRANSPARENCY IN INTERNATIONAL TRADE (Michael M. Hart & Debra P. Steger eds. 1990).

Hudec, Robert E., *The New WTO Dispute Settlement Procedure: An Overview of the First Three Years*, 8 MINN. J. GLOBAL TRADE 1 (1999).

Hudec, Robert E., *The Role of Judicial Review in Preserving Liberal Foreign Trade Policies*, *in* NATIONAL CONSTITUTIONS AND INTERNATIONAL ECONOMIC LAW 503 (Meinhard Hilf & Ernst-Ulrich Petersmann eds., 1993).

JACKSON, BERNARD S., SEMIOTICS AND LEGAL THEORY (1985).

Jackson, John H. & Alan O. Sykes eds., IMPLEMENTING THE URUGUAY ROUND (1997).

JACKSON, JOHN H. ET AL., LEGAL PROBLEMS OF INTERNATIONAL ECONOMIC RELATIONS: CASES, MATERIALS AND TEXT ON THE NATIONAL AND INTERNATIONAL REGULATION OF TRANSNATIONAL ECONOMIC RELATIONS (3d ed. 1995).

Jackson, John H., *Appraising the Launch and Functioning of the WTO*, 39 GERMAN Y. B. INT'L L. 20 (1996).

Jackson, John H., *Comments on Shrimp/Turtle and the Product/Process Distinction*, 11 EUR. J. INT'L L. 303 (2000).

JACKSON, JOHN H., ET AL, IMPLEMENTING THE TOKYO ROUND: NATIONAL CONSTITUTIONS AND INTERNATIONAL ECONOMIC RULES (1984).

Jackson, John H., *Fragmentation or Unification among International Institutions: the World Trade Organization*, 31 N. Y. U. J. INT'L & POL. 823 (1999).

Jackson, John H., *Global Economics and International Economic Law*, 1 J. INT'L ECON. L. 1 (1998).

Jackson, John H., *International Economic Law in Times That Are Interesting*, 3 J. INT. ECON. L. 3 (2000).

Jackson, John H., *International Economic Law: Reflections on the 'Boilerroom' of International Relations*, 10 AM. U. J. INT'L L. & POL'Y 595 (1995).

Jackson, John H., *National Constitutions, Transnational Economic Policy and International Economic Law: Some Summary Reflections*, *in* NATIONAL CONSTITUTIONS AND INTERNATIONAL ECONOMIC LAW (M. Hilf & E.U. Petersmann eds., 1993).

Jackson, John H., *National Treatment Obligations and Non-Tariff Barriers*, 10 MICH. J. INT'L L. 207 (1989).

Jackson, John H., *Perspectives on Regionalism in Trade Relations*, 27 LAW & POL'Y INT'L BUS. 873 (1996).

Jackson, John H., *Reflections on International Economic Law*, 17 U. PA. J. INT'L ECON. L. 17 (1996).

Jackson, John H., *Status of Treaties in Domestic Legal Systems: A Policy Analysis*, 86 AM. J. INT'L L. 310 (1992).

Jackson, John H., *The Great 1994 Sovereignty Debate: The United States Acceptance and Implementation of the Uruguay Round Results*, 36 COLUM. J. TRANSNAT'L L. 157 (1997).

Jackson, John H., *The Jurisprudence of International Trade: The DISC Case in GATT*, 72 AM. J. INT'L L. 747 (1978).

Jackson, John H., *The Legal Meaning of a GATT Dispute Settlement Report: Some Reflections*, *in* TOWARD MORE EFFECTIVE SUPERVISION BY INTERNATIONAL ORGANIZATIONS: ESSAYS IN HONOR OF HENRY SCHERMERS (vol. 1, 1994).

JACKSON, JOHN H., THE WORLD TRADE ORGANIZATION: CONSTITUTION AND JURISPRUDENCE (1998).

JACKSON, JOHN H., THE WORLD TRADING SYSTEM (2d ed. 1997).

Jackson, John H., *The WTO Dispute Settlement Understanding—Misunderstandings on the Nature of Legal Obligations*, 91 AM. J. INT'L L. 60 (1997).

JACOBS, SCOTT H., REGULATORY GOVERNANCE: IMPROVING THE INSTITUTIONAL BASIS FOR SECTORAL REGULATION (OECD, 2000), *available at* <http://www.oecd.org//subject/regreform/Products/Sectoral_regulation.pdf>.

Jacobson, Harold K. & Edith Brown Weiss, *Strengthening Compliance with International Environmental Accords: Preliminary Observations from a Collaborative Project*, 1 GLOBAL GOVERNANCE 119 (1995).

Jenks, C.W., *Craftsmanship in International Law*, *in* INTERNATIONAL LAW IN THE TWENTIETH CENTURY 75 (Leo Gross ed., 1969).

JENNINGS, ROBERT Y., THE PROGRESS OF INTERNATIONAL LAW (1960).

Joerges, Christian and Jürgen Neyer, *From Intergovernmental Bargaining to Deliberative Political Processes: The Constitutionalization of Comitology*, 3 EUR. L. J. 273 (1997).

Kant, Immanuel, *Perpetual Peace: A Philosophical Sketch (1795)*, *in* KANT'S POLITICAL WRITINGS (Hans Reiss ed., H.B. Nisbet trans., 2d ed. 1991).

Kelly, J. Patrick, *The Twilight of Customary International Law*, 40 VA. J. INT'L L. 449 (2000).

Kelso, R. Randall, *Considerations of Legislative Fit under Equal Protection, Substantive Due Process, and Free Speech Doctrine: Separating Questions of Advancement, Relationship and Burden*, 28 U. RICH. L. REV. 1279 (1994).

Kennedy, David, *New Approaches to Comparative Law: Comparativism and International Governance*, 1997 UTAH L. REV. 545 (1997).

KENWOOD, A. G. & A. L. LOUGHEED, THE GROWTH OF THE INTERNATIONAL ECONOMY 1820–1970 (3d ed. 1992).

Kim, Yong K., *The Beginnings of the Rule of Law in the International Trade System despite U.S. Constitutional Constraints*, 17 MICH. J. INT'L L. 967 (1996).

Kingsbury, Benedict, *The Concept of Compliance as a Function of Competing Conceptions of International Law*, *in* INTERNATIONAL COMPLIANCE WITH NONBINDING ACCORDS (Edith Brown Weiss ed. 1997).

KIRGIS, JR., FREDERIC L. INTERNATIONAL ORGANIZATION IN THEIR LEGAL SETTING (2d ed. 1993).

Koh, Harold Hongju, *A World Transformed*, 20 YALE J. INT'L L. ix (1995).

Koh, Harold Hongju, *Transnational Legal Process*, 75 NEB. L. REV. 181 (1996).

Kommers, Donald P. & Michel Waelbroeck, *Legal Integration and the Free Movement of Goods: The American and European Experience*, *in* FORCES AND POTENTIAL FOR A EUROPEAN IDENTITY (BOOK 3), METHODS, TOOLS AND INSTITUTIONS (VOLUME 1), INTEGRATION THROUGH LAW: EUROPEAN AND THE AMERICAN FEDERAL EXPERIENCE (Mauro Cappelletti et al eds. 1985).

Korhonen, Outi, *New International Law: Silence, Defense or Deliverance?*, 7 EUR. J. INT'L L. 1 (1996).

Koskenniemi, Martti, *Hierarchy in International Law: A Sketch*, 8 EUR. J. INT'L L. 566 (1997).

Kozyris, Phaedon John, *Lifting the Veils of Equity in Maritime Entitlements: Equidistance with Proportionality Around the Islands*, 26 DENV. J. INT'L L. & POL'Y 319 (1998).

Kramer, Larry D., *Putting the Politics Back into the Political Safeguards of Federalism*, 100 COL. L. REV. 215 (2000).

Krasner, Stephen, *Structural Cases and Regime Consequences: Regimes as Intervening Variables*, 36 INT'L ORG. 186 (1982).

Kuijper, Pieter J., *The Conclusion and Implementation of the Uruguay Round Results by the European Community*, 6 EUR. J. INT'L L 222 (1995).

Laird, Sam, *Multilateral Approaches to Market Access Negotiations*, WTO Staff Working Paper (TPRD-98-02) 3–4 (1998), *available at* <http://www.wto.org/english/res_e/reser_e/ptpr9802.doc>.

Laird, Samuel, *Quantifying Commercial Policies*, WTO Research Paper (TPRD-96-001).

Langille, B.A., *General Reflections on the Relationship of Trade and Labor (Or Fair Trade is Free Trade's Destiny), in* Fair Trade and Harmonization: Prerequisites for Free Trade? (vol. 2, Legal Analysis) (Jagdish Bhagwati & Robert E. Hudec eds., 1996).

Larson, Arthur, Design for Research in International Rule of Law (1961). Larson, Arthur, World Rule of Law (1960).

Lauterpacht, Hersch, The Development of International Law by the International Court (1982).

Lauterpacht, Hersche, Private Law Sources and Analogies of International Law (1970).

Lessig, Lawrence, *Translating Federalism: United States v. Lopez*, 1995 Sup. Ct. Rev. 125 (1995).

Licht, Amir, *Regulatory Arbitrage for Real: International Securities Regulation in a World of Interacting Securities Markets*, 38 Va. J. Int'l L. 563 (1998).

Lindseth, Peter L., *Democratic Legitimacy and the Administrative Character of Supranationalism: The Example of the European Community*, 99 Colum. L. Rev. 628 (1999).

Lipson, Charles, *Why Are Some International Agreements Informal*, 45 Int'l Org. 495 (1991).

Llewellyn, K.N., *The Constitution as an Institution*, 34 Colum. L. Rev. 1 (1934).

Lockhart et al., William B, Constitutional Law (8th ed. 1996).

MacDonald, R. St. J., *The Charter of the United Nations and the Development of Fundamental Principles of International Law, in* Contemporary Problems of International Law (Bin Cheng and E.D. Brown eds., 1988).

MacDonald, R. St. J., *The Margin of Appreciation, in* The European System for the Protection of Human Rights (R. St. J. MacDonald et al. eds, 1993).

MacGibbon, I. C., *Estoppel in International Law*, 7 Int'l & Comp. L. Q. 468 (1958).

Majone, Giadomenico, *The Rise of the Regulatory State in Europe*, 17 W. Eur. Pol. 77 (1994).

Majone, Giandomenico, *Democracy and Constitutionalism in the European Union* 13 ECSA Rev. Forum (2000).

Majone, Giandomenico, Regulating Europe (1996).

Malloy, Michael P., *Bumper Cars: Themes of Convergence in International Regulation*, 60 Fordham L. Rev. sl (1992).

Mancini, G. Federico, *The Making of a Constitution for Europe*, 26 Common Mkt. L. Rev. 595 (1989).

Mattoo, Aaditya, *Discriminatory Consequences of Non-Discriminatory Standards*, WTO, WTO Staff Working Papers, TISD-96-01, Dec. 1997, *available at* <http://www.wto.org/english/res_e/reser_e/wpaps_e.htm>.

Mattoo, Aaditya, *National Treatment in the GATS: Corner-stone or Pandora's Box*, WTO, WTO Staff Working Papers, TISD-96–02, Jan 22, 1997, *available at* <http://www.wto.org/english/res_e/reser_e/wpaps_e.htm>.

Mavroidis, Petros C., *'Like Products': Some Thoughts at the Positive and Normative Level, in* Regulatory Barriers and the Principle of Non-Discrimination in World Trade Law (Thomas Cottier & Petros C. Mavroidis eds. 2000).

McGinnis, John O. & Mark L. Movsesian, *The World Trade Constitution*, 114 Harv. L. Rev. 511 (2000).

McGovern, Edmond, International Trade Regulation (1986).

McGuinness, Michael Joseph, *The Politics of Labor Regulation in North America: A Reconsideration of Labor Law Enforcement in Mexico*, 21 U. Pa. J. Int'l Econ. L. 1, (2000).

McGuire, Julie Elizabeth, *World Trade Organizations Finds U.S. Foreign Sales Corporation Violates EU Trade Agreements*, 2 NO. 7 Lawyers J. 5 (2000).

McNiel, Dale E., *The NAFTA Panel Decision on Canadian Tariff-Rate Quotas: Imaging a Tariffying Bargain*, 22 YALE J. INT'L L. 345 (1997).

McRae, Donald M., *GATT Article XX and the Appellate Body*, *in* NEW DIRECTIONS IN INTERNATIONAL ECONOMIC LAW: ESSAYS IN HONOR OF JOHN H. JACKSON 232 (Marco Bronckers & Reinhard Quick eds. 2000).

McRae, Donald M., *The WTO in International Law: Traditional Continued or New Frontier?*, 3 J. INT'L ECON. L. 27 (2000).

MCWHINNEY, EDWARD, SUPREME COURTS AND JUDICIAL LAW-MAKING: CONSTITUTIONAL TRIBUNALS AND CONSTITUTIONAL REVIEW (1988).

Meier, Mike, *GATT, WTO, and the Environment: To What Extent Do GATT/WTO Rules Permit Member Nations to Protect the Environment When Doing So Adversely Affects Trade?*, 8 COLO. J. INT'L ENVTL. L. & POL'Y 241 (1997).

Meltz, Robert, '*The Commerce Clause as a Limit on Congressional Power to Protect the Environment*,' The Congressional Research Service Issue Brief (March 12, 1999), <http://www.cnie.org/nle/leg-35.html>.

Miner, Roger J., *The Reception of Foreign Law in the U.S. Federal Courts*, 43 AM. J. COMP. L. 581 (1995).

MITCHELL, RONALD B., INTERNATIONAL OIL POLLUTION AT SEA: ENVIRONMENTAL POLICY AND TREATY COMPLIANCE (1994).

Mitchell, Ronald D., *Compliance Theory: An Overview*, *in* IMPROVING COMPLIANCE WITH INTERNATIONAL ENVIRONMENTAL LAW (James Cameron et al. eds., 1993).

Monaghan, Henry P., *Foreword: Constitutional Common Law*, 88 HARV. L. 1, (1975).

Monaghan, Sean C., *European Union Legal Personality Disorder: The Union's Legal Nature through the Prism of the German Federal Constitutional Court's Maastricht Decision*, 12 EMORY INT'L L. REV. 1443 (1998).

MORGENSTERN, F., LEGAL PROBLEMS OF INTERNATIONAL ORGANIZATIONS (1986).

Mortensen, Jens Ladefoged, *The Institutional Requirements of the WTO in an Era of Globalization: Imperfections in the Global Economic Polity*, 6 EUR. L. J. 176 (2000).

Mosler, H., *General Principles of Law*, *in* ENCYCLOPEDIA OF PUBLIC INTERNATIONAL LAW (R. Bernhardt ed. 1984).

Movsesian, Mark L., *Sovereignty, Compliance, and the World Trade Organization: Lessons from the History of Supreme Court Review*, 20 MICH. J. INT'L L. 775 (1999).

Neuling, Bruce, *The Shrimp-Turtle Case: Implications for Article XX of the GATT and the Trade and Environment Debate*, 22 LOY. L.A. INT'L & COMP. L. REV. 1 (1999).

Newman, Ralph A., '*The Principles of Equity as a Source of World Law*,' 1 Israel L. Rev. 616 (1966).

Nichols, Philip M., *GATT Doctrine*, VA. J. INT'L L. 379 (1996).

Nichols, Philip M., *Trade without Values*, 90 NW. U. L. REV. 625 (1996).

O'Connor, Sandra Day, *Federalism of Free Nations*, 28 N.Y.U. J. INT'L L. & POL. 35 (1995–96).

O'Connor, Sandra Day, *Broadening Our Horizons: Why American Lawyers Must Learn About Foreign Law*, 45–SEP FED. LAW. 20 (1998).

OECD, FOOD SAFETY AND QUALITY: TRADE CONSIDERATION (1999).

OECD, PROCESSES AND PRODUCTION METHODS (PPMS): CONCEPTUAL FRAMEWORK AND CONSIDERATIONS ON USE OF PPM-BASED TRADE MEASURES, *available at* <http://www.olis.oecd.org/olis/1997doc.nsf/linkto/ocde-gd(97)137>.

OECD, REDUCING THE RISK OF POLICY FAILURE: CHALLENGES FOR REGULATORY COMPLIANCE (2000), *available at* <http://www.oecd.org/puma/regref/pubs/compliance.pdf>.

Onuf, Nicholas Greenwood, *Civitas Maxima: Wolff, Vattel and the Fate of Republicanism*, 88 AM. J. INT'L L. 280 (1994).

Onuf, Nicholas, *The Constitution of International Society*, 5 EUR. J. INT'L L. 1 (1994).

OPPENHEIMER, L., OPPENHEIMER'S INTERNATIONAL LAW (Robert Jennings & Arthur Watts eds., 9th ed. 1992).

Ostry, Sylvia, *Making Sense of It All: A Post-Mortem on the Meaning of Seattle*, *in* SEATTLE, THE WTO, AND THE FUTURE OF THE MULTILATERAL TRADING SYSTEM (Roger B. Porter & Pierre Sauvé eds., 2000).

Packer, John, *Making International Law Matter in Preventing Ethnic Conflict: A Practitioner's Perspective*, 32 N.Y.U. J. INT'L L. & POL. 715 (2000).

Palmeter, David & Petros Mavroidis, *The WTO Legal System: Sources of Law*, 92 AM. J. INT'L L. 398 (1998).

Paul, Joel R., *Free Trade, Regulatory Competition and the Autonomous Market Fallacy*, 1 COLUM. J. EUR. L. 29 (1995).

Pauwelyn, Joost, *Enforcement and Countermeasures in the WTO: Rules are Rules—Toward a More Collective Approach*, 94 AM. J. INT'L L. 335 (2000).

Pelkmans, Jacques, *Removing Regulatory Access Barriers—The Case of 'Deep' Integration* 10, OECD, TD/TC(96)9, Feb. 15, 1996.

Perez, Antonio F., *WTO and U.N. Law: Institutional Comity in National Security*, 23 YALE J. INT'L L. 301 (1998).

Petersmann, Ernst-Ulrich, *How to Constitutionalize International Law and Foreign Policy for the Benefit of Civil Society?*, 20 MICH. J. INT'L L. 1 (1998).

Petersmann, Ernst-Ulrich, *How to Promote the International Rule of Law?: Contributions by the World Trade Organization Appellate Review System*, 1 J. INT'L ECON. L. 25 (1998).

Petersmann, Ernst-Ulrich, *The Dispute Settlement System of the World Trade Organization and the Evolution of the GATT Dispute Settlement System since 1948*, 31 COMMON MKT. L. REV. 1157 (1994).

Petersmann, Ernst-Ulrich, *The Transformation of the World Trading System through the 1994 Agreement Establishing the World Trade Organization*, 6 EUR. J. INT'L L 161 (1995).

Pollack, Mark A., *Delegation, Agency, and Agenda Setting in the European Community*, 51 INT'L ORG. 99 (1997).

POUND, ROSCOE, A WORLD LEGAL ORDER: LAW AND LAWS IN RELATION TO WORLD LAW (1959).

Pound, Roscoe, *The Idea of Law*, *in* JUBILEE LAW LECTURES (1939).

POUND, ROSCOE, TOWARD A LAW OF THE WORLD (1957).

Pound, Roscoe, *Toward a New Jus Gentium*, *in* IDEOLOGICAL DIFFERENCES AND WORLD ORDER (F.S.C. Northrop ed. 1949).

PREEG, ERNST H., TRADERS AND DIPLOMATS: AN ANALYSIS OF THE KENNEDY ROUND OF NEGOTIATIONS UNDER THE GENERAL AGREEMENT ON TARIFFS AND TRADE (1970).

RASMUSSEN, HJALTE, ON LAW AND POLICY IN THE EUROPEAN COURT OF JUSTICE: A COMPARATIVE STUDY IN JUDICIAL POLICYMAKING (1986).

Regan, Donald H., '*The Supreme Court and State Protectionism: Making Sense of the Dormant Commerce Clause*,' 84 MICH. L. REV. 1091 (1986).

REHBINDER, ECKARD & RICHARD STEWART, ENVIRONMENTAL PROTECTION POLICY (INTEGRATION THROUGH LAW: EUROPE AND THE AMERICAN FEDERAL EXPERIENCE, VOL. 2) (1985).

Reich, Arie, *From Diplomacy to Law: The Juridicization of International Trade Relations*, 17 NW. J. INT'L L. & BUS. 775 (1996–97).

Riles, Annelise, *Wigmore's Treasure Box: Comparative Law in the Era of Information*, 40 HARV. INT'L L. J. 221 (1999).

Rodrik, Dani, *Sense and Nonsense in the Globalization Debate*, 1997 FOREIGN POL'Y, 33 (1997).

Roessler, Frieder, *Domestic Policy Objectives and the Multilateral Trade Order: Lessons from the Past*, 19 U. PA. J. INT'L ECON. L. 513 (1998).

Roessler, Frieder, *Increasing Market Access Under Regulatory Heterogeneity: The Strategies of the World Trade Organization, in* ORGANIZATION FOR ECONOMIC CO-OPERATION AND DEVELOPMENT (OECD), REGULATORY REFORM AND INTERNATIONAL MARKET OPENNESS (1996).

Rogoff, Martin A., *Interpretation of International Agreements by Domestic Courts and the Politics of International Treaty Relations: Reflections on Some Recent Decisions of the United States Supreme Court*, 11 AM. U. J. INT'L L. & POL'Y 559 (1996).

Rubenstein, Kim & Jenny Schultz, *Bringing Law and Order to International Trade: Administrative Law Principles and the GATT/WTO*, 11 ST. JOHN'S J. LEGAL COMMENT. 271 (1996).

Ruggie, John Gerard, *Territoriality and Beyond: Problematizing Modernity in International Relations*, 47 INT'L ORG. 139 (1993).

Ryssdall, Rolv, *Opinion: The Coming Age of the European Convention on Human Rights*, 1 EUR. HUM. RTS. L. REV. 18 (1996).

Salcedo, Juan Antonio Carrillo, *Reflections on the Existence of a Hierarchy of Norms in International Law*, 8 EUR. J. INT'L L. 583 (1997).

Sam, Corinne, *World Trade Organization Caught in the Middle: Are TEDs the Only Way Out?*, 29 ENVTL. L. 185 (1999).

Sands, Philippe, *'Unilateralism,' Values, and International Law*, 11 EUR. J. INT'L L. 291 (2000).

Sauter, Wolf, *The Economic Constitution of the European Union*, 4 COLUM. J. EUR. L. 27 (1998).

Schloemann, Hannes L. & Stefan Ohlhoff, *'Constitutionalization' and Dispute Settlement in the WTO: National Security as an Issue of Competence*, 93 AM. J. INT'L L. 424 (1999).

Schwartz, Warren F. & Alan O. Sykes, *Toward a Positive Theory of the Most Favored Nation Obligation and Its Exception in the WTO/GATT System*, 16 INT'L REV. L. & ECON. 27 (1996).

Schwarzenberger, Georg, '*International Jus Cogens?*,' 43 TEX. L. REV. 455 (1965).

Scott, Shirley V., *International Law as Ideology: Theorizing the Relationship between International Law and International Politics*, 5 EUR. J. INT'L L. 313 (1994).

SEN, AMARTYA, GLOBAL DOUBTS, HARV. MAG. 68 (Sep.–Oct. 2000).

Shaffer, Gregory, *International Decision: United States—Import Prohibition of Certain Shrimp and Shrimp Products*, 93 AM. J. INT'L L. 507 (1999).

Shapiro, Martin, *Codification of Administrative Law: The US and the Union*, 2 EUR. L. J. 26 (1996).

Shapiro, Martin, *The Globalization of Law*, 1 IND. J. GLOBAL LEGAL STUD. 37 (1993).

Shapiro, Michael H., *Regulation as Language: Communicating Values by Altering the Contingencies of Choice*, 55 U. PITT. L. REV. 681 (1994).

SHAW, JO, LAW OF THE EUROPEAN UNION (2d ed. 1996).

Shaw, Malcolm N., INTERNATIONAL LAW (4th ed. 1997).

Shell, G. Richard, *Trade Legalism and International Relations Theory: An Analysis of the World Trade Organization*, 44 DUKE L.J. 829 (1995).

Shetreet, Shimon, *Judging in Society: The Changing Role of Courts, in* THE ROLE OF COURTS IN SOCIETY (Shimon Shetreet ed., 1988).

Slaughter, Anne-Marie & Steven R. Ratner, *The Method is the Message*, 93 AM. J. INT'L L. 410 (1999).

Slaughter, Anne-Marie, *A Typology of Transjudicial Communication*, 29 U. RICH. L. REV. 99 (1994).

Slaughter, Anne-Marie, *Governing the Global Economy through Government Networks, in* THE ROLE OF LAW IN INTERNATIONAL POLITICS: ESSAYS IN INTERNATIONAL RELATIONS AND INTERNATIONAL LAW (Michael Byers ed. 2000).

Slaughter, Anne-Marie, *International Law in a World of Liberal States*, 6 EUR. J. INT'L L. 503 (1995).

Slaughter, Anne-Marie, *Judicial Globalization*, 40 VA. J. INT'L L. 1103 (2000).

Slaughter, Anne-Marie, *Liberal International Relations Theory and International Economic Law*, 10 AM. U. J. INT'L L. & POL'Y 717 (1995).

Slaughter, Anne-Marie, *The Real New World Order*, 76 FOREIGN AFF.183 (1997).

SMITH, ADAM, AN INQUIRY INTO THE NATURE AND CAUSES OF THE WEALTH OF NATIONS, bk. 2, ch. 4, para. 12 (The Library of Economics and Liberty, at <http://www.econlib.org/library/Smith/SmWNContents.html>).

Smith, Michael E., *State Discriminations against Interstate Commerce*, 74 CALIF. L. REV. 1203 (1986).

Spracker, Stanley M. & David C. Lundsgaard, *Dolphins and Tuna: Renewed Attention on the Future of Free Trade and Protection of the Environment*, 18 COLUM. J. ENVTL. L. 385 (1993).

Starke, J.G., *Monism and Dualism in the Theory of International Law*, 17 BRIT. Y.B. INT'L L. 66 (1936).

Steinhardt, Ralph G., *The Role of International Law as a Canon of Domestic Statutory Construction*, 43 VAND. L. REV. 1103 (1990).

Stephan, Paul B., *Accountability and International Lawmaking: Rules, Rents and Legitimacy*, 17 NW. J. INT'L L. & BUS. 726 (1996–97).

Stewart, Terence P. & David S. Johanson, *The SPS Agreement of the World Trade Organization and International Organizations: The Roles of the Codex Alimentarius Commission, the International Plant Protection Convention, and the International Office of Epizootics*, 26 SYRACUSE J. INT'L L. & COM. 27 (1998).

Strauss, David A., *Common Law Constitutional Interpretation*, 63 UNIV. CHI. L. REV. 877 (1996).

SUNSTEIN, CASS R., FREE MARKETS AND SOCIAL JUSTICE (1997).

Sunstein, Cass, *Lochner's Legacy*, 87 COLUM. L. REV. 873(1987).

Swaine, Edward T., *Subsidiarity and Self-Interest: Federalism at the European Court of Justice*, 41 HARV. INT'L L. J. 1, 128 (2000).

Sweet, Alec Stone, *The New GATT: Dispute Resolution and the Judicialization of the Trade Regime in* LAW ABOVE NATIONS: SUPRANATIONAL COURTS AND THE LEGALIZATION OF POLITICS (Mary L. Volcansek ed., 1997).

Sykes, Alan O., *Regulatory Protectionism and the Law of International Trade*, 66 U. CHI. L. REV. 1 (1999).

Sykes, Alan O., *Strategies for Increasing Market Access under Regulatory Heterogeneity* 2–4, OECD, TD/TC(96)8, Feb. 15, 1996.

Tarullo, Daniel K., *Norms and Institutions in Global Competition Policy*, 94 AM. J. INT'L L. 478 (2000).

Tesón, Fernando R., *The Kantian Theory of International Law*, 92 COLUM. L. REV. 53 (1992).

Tomuschat, Christian, *Ethos, Ethics and Morality in International Relations*, *in* ENCYCLOPEDIA OF PUBLIC INTERNATIONAL LAW 120 (1995).

Trachtman, Joel P., *Bananas, Direct Effect and Compliance*, 10 EUR. J. INT'L L. 655 (1999).

Trachtman, Joel P., *The Domain of WTO Dispute Resolution*, 40 HARV. INT'L L. J.333 1999).

Trachtman, Joel P., *Unilateralism, Bilateralism, Regionalism, Multilateralism, and Functionalism: A Comparison with Reference to Securities Regulation*, 4 TRANSNAT'L L. & CONTEMP. PROBS. 69 (1994).

Trebilcock, Michael J, & Robert Howse, *The Fair Trade—Free Trade Debate: Trade, Labor, and the Environment*, 16 INT'L REV. L. & ECON. 61 (1996).

Trebilcock, Michael J. & Robert Howse, *Trade Liberalization and Regulatory Diversity: Reconciling Competitive Markets with Competitive Politics*, 6 EUR. J. L. & ECON. 5 (1998).

TRIBE, LAURENCE H., AMERICAN CONSTITUTIONAL LAW (3d ed., vol. 1, 2000).

Tribe, Laurence H., *The Curvature of Constitutional Space: What Lawyers Can Learn from Modern Physics*, 103 HARV. L. REV. 1 (1989).

Tridmas, Takis, *The Court of Justice and Judicial Activism*, 21 EUR. L. REV. 199 (1996).

Trimble, Philip R., *International Trade and the 'Rule of Law,'* 83 MICH. L. REV. 1016 (1985) (reviewing JOHN H. JACKSON ET AL., IMPLEMENTING THE TOKYO ROUND: NATIONAL CONSTITUTIONS AND INTERNATIONAL ECONOMIC RULES (1984)).

Trimble, Phillip R., *Globalization, International Institutions, and the Erosion of National Sovereignty and Democracy*, 95 MICH. L. REV. 1944 (1997) (reviewing THOMAS M. FRANCK, FAIRNESS IN INTERNATIONAL LAW AND INSTITUTIONS (1995)).

Tsai, Edward S., *'Like' Is a Four-Letter Word—GATT Article III's 'Like Product' Conundrum*, 17 BERKELEY J. INT'L L. 26 (1999).

Tushnet, Mark, *Keeping Your Eye on the Ball: The Significance of the Revival of Constitutional Federalism*, 13 GA. ST. U. L. REV. 1065 (1997).

Tushnet, Mark, *The Possibilities of Comparative Constitutional Law*, 108 YALE L. J. 1225 (1999).

Vázquez, Carlos Manuel, *The Four Doctrines of Self-Executing Treaties*, 89 AM. J. INT'L L. 695 (1995).

Verdross, Alfred, *Forbidden Treaties in International Law*, 31 AM. J. INT'L L. 571 (1937).

Verdross, Alfred, *Jus Dispositivium and Jus Cogens in International Law*, *in* INTERNATIONAL LAW IN THE TWENTIETH CENTURY (Leo Gross ed. 1969).

Vermulst, Edwin & Bart Driessen, *An Overview of the WTO Dispute Settlement System and its Relationship with the Uruguay Round Agreements*, 29 J. WORLD TRADE 131 (1995).

Victor, David G., *The Sanitary and Phytosanitary Agreement of the World Trade Organization: An Assessment After Five Years*, 32 N.Y.U.J. INT'L L. & POL. 865 (2000).

Vinuesa, Raul Emilio, *The New Role of Equity as a Source of International Law*, *in* THESAURUS ACROASIUM OF THE INSTITUTE OF PUBLIC INTERNATIONAL LAW AND INTERNATIONAL RELATIONS OF THESSALONIKI 'PEACE MESSENGER OF THE UN' (A42/487) (Vol. XIX) (1992).

VOGEL, DAVID, TRADING UP: CONSUMER AND ENVIRONMENTAL REGULATION IN A GLOBAL ECONOMY (1995).

WALTZ, KENNETH N., THEORY OF INTERNATIONAL POLITICS (1979).

Ward, Stephen, *From Hierarchy to Networks?: Sub-Central Government and EU Urban Environment Policy*, 35 J. COMM. MKT. STUD. 439 (1997).

Weil, Prosper, *Towards Relative Normativity in International Law?*, 77 AM. J. INT'L L. 413 (1983).

Weiler, Joseph H. H. & Joel P. Trachtman, *European Constitutionalism and Its Discontents*, 17 NW. J. INT'L L. & BUS. 354 (1996–97).

Weiler, Joseph H. H., *A Quiet Revolution: The European Court of Justice and Its Interlocutors*, 26 COMP. POL. STUD. 510 (1994).

Weiler, Joseph H. H., *Cain and Abel—Convergence and Divergence in International Trade Law*, *in* THE EU, THE WTO AND THE NAFTA: TOWARDS A COMMON LAW OF INTERNATIONAL TRADE 1 (Joseph H. H. Weiler ed., 2000).

Weiler, Joseph H. H., *Epilogue: 'Comitology' as Revolution—Infranationalism, Constitutionalism and Democracy*, *in* EU COMMITTEES: SOCIAL REGULATION, LAW AND POLITICS (Christian Joerges & Ellen Vos eds. 1999).

WEILER, JOSEPH H. H., THE CONSTITUTION OF EUROPE: 'DO THE NEW CLOTHES HAVE AN EMPEROR?' AND OTHER ESSAYS ON EUROPEAN INTEGRATION (1999).

Weiler, Joseph H. H., *The Constitution of the Common Market Place: Text and Context in the Evolution of the Free Movement of Goods in* THE EVOLUTION OF EU LAW (Paul Craig and Gràinne de Búrca eds. 1999).

Weiler, Joseph H. H., *The Court of Justice on Trial*, 24 COMMON MKT. L. REV. 555 (1987).

Weiler, Joseph H. H., *The Transformation of Europe*, 100 YALE L.J. 2403 (1991).

Weiss, Edith Brown, *The Rise of the Fall of International Law?*, 69 FORDHAM L. REV. 345 (2000).

WINHAM, GILBERT R., THE EVOLUTION OF INTERNATIONAL TRADE AGREEMENTS (1992).

Wirth, David A., *International Trade Agreements: Vehicles for Regulatory Reform?*, 1997 U. CHI. LEGAL F. 331 (1997).

Wirth, David A., *The Role of Science in the Uruguay Round and NAFTA Trade Disciplines*, 27 CORNELL INT'L L. J. 817 (1994).

WORLD TRADE ORGANIZATION, WTO ANALYTICAL INDEX: GUIDE TO GATT LAW AND PRACTICE (Vol. II) (1995).

Young, Michael K., *Dispute Resolution in the Uruguay Round: Lawyers' Triumph over Diplomats*, 29 INT'L LAW. 389 (1995).

YOUNG, ORAN R., COMPLIANCE AND PUBLIC AUTHORITY: A THEORY WITH INTERNATIONAL APPLICATIONS (1979).

YOUROW, HOWARD CHARLES, THE MARGIN OF APPRECIATION DOCTRINE IN THE DYNAMICS OF EUROPEAN HUMAN RIGHTS JURISPRUDENCE (1996).

Zamora, Stephen, *Is There Customary International Economic Law?*, 32 GERMAN Y. B. INT'L L. 9 (1989).

Zedalis, Rex J., *A Theory of the GATT 'Like' Product Common Language Cases*, 27 VAND. J. TRANSNAT'L L. 33 (1994).

Zekoll, Joachim, *Kant and Comparative Law—Some Reflections on a Reform Effort*, 70 TUL. L. REV. 2719 (1996).

Zolo, Danilo, *Hans Kelsen: International Peace through International Law*, 9 EUR. J. INT'L L. 306 (1999).

Index

www.ingramcontent.com/pod-product-compliance
Lightning Source LLC
LaVergne TN
LVHW021727021026
849161LV00004BA/754
* 9 7 8 9 0 4 1 1 9 8 9 2 1 *